50 Years of Environment

Singapore's Journey Towards Environment Sustainability

World Scientific Series on Singapore's 50 Years of Nation-Building

Published

50 Years of Social Issues in Singapore
  edited by David Chan

Our Lives to Live: Putting a Woman's Face to Change in Singapore
  edited by Kanwaljit Soin and Margaret Thomas

50 Years of Singapore–Europe Relations: Celebrating Singapore's Connections
  with Europe
  edited by Yeo Lay Hwee and Barnard Turner

50 Years of Singapore and the United Nations
  edited by Tommy Koh, Li Lin Chang and Joanna Koh

50 Years of Environment: Singapore's Journey Towards Environmental Sustainability
  edited by Tan Yong Soon

For more information about this series, go to http://www.worldscientific.com/page/sg50

50 YEARS OF
ENVIRONMENT

Singapore's Journey Towards Environmental Sustainability

Editor

Tan Yong Soon

Former Permanent Secretary
Ministry of the Environment and Water Resources, Singapore
&
Former Permanent Secretary
National Climate Change Secretariat in the Prime Minister's Office, Singapore

World Scientific

NEW JERSEY · LONDON · SINGAPORE · BEIJING · SHANGHAI · HONG KONG · TAIPEI · CHENNAI · TOKYO

Published by

World Scientific Publishing Co. Pte. Ltd.

5 Toh Tuck Link, Singapore 596224

USA office: 27 Warren Street, Suite 401-402, Hackensack, NJ 07601

UK office: 57 Shelton Street, Covent Garden, London WC2H 9HE

Library of Congress Cataloging-in-Publication Data
50 years of environment : Singapore's journey towards environmental sustainability / edited by Yong Soon Tan.
    pages cm. -- (World Scientific series on Singapore's 50 years of nation-building)
  Includes bibliographical references.
  ISBN 978-9814696210 -- ISBN 978-9814696227 (pbk)
  1. Environmental policy--Singapore. 2. Sustainable development--Singapore. 3. Water resources
development--Singapore. I. Tan, Yong Soon. II. Title: Fifty years of environment, Singapore's journey
towards environmental sustainability.
  GE190.S55A2 2015
  333.72095957--dc23

                                                                                        2015018720

British Library Cataloguing-in-Publication Data
A catalogue record for this book is available from the British Library.

Cover image: Zhanrui Ye / Shutterstock.com

In-house Editor: Li Hongyan

Typeset by Stallion Press
Email: enquiries@stallionpress.com

ENDORSEMENTS

"Singapore's transformation from an impoverished and polluted island to the world's beacon of environmental progress has been nothing short of miraculous. Miracles, however, are hard to repeat elsewhere, therefore, we are very fortunate that Singapore's environmental transformation was not at all a miracle. Instead, it happened thanks to clever and consistent strategies and brilliant execution. Over the last 30 years, as I got to gradually know the Singapore miracle workers and their methods, I often prayed that other jurisdictions would learn the steps involved. This book about the Singapore miracle provides an opportunity for environmental leaders everywhere to extract the policies and procedures they need to bring about progress in their own jurisdiction."

Dr. Andrew Benedek
Founder, Chairman and CEO of ZENON Environmental Inc. and Anaergia Inc.
Winner of the inaugural Lee Kuan Yew Water Prize in 2008

"For a seriously resource-constrained nation, Singapore has come a long way since its independence in 1965. Very few people, if any, 50 years ago would have predicted that this city-state would become the envy of the world by 2015. While everyone knows and admires the remarkable progress of the past half century, not many people are familiar with the achievements in the field of environment and the enabling conditions that made this possible. One of the very few serious studies that is available is Tan Yong Soon's earlier book *Clean, Green and Blue: Singapore's Journey Towards Environmental and Water Sustainability*. The present text is a worthy complement that adds to the in-depth analysis of this important journey. The book is strongly recommended."

Professor Asit K. Biswas
Distinguished Visiting Professor
Lee Kuan Yew School of Public Policy, Singapore
and Co-founder, Third World Centre for Water Management, Mexico

"This book charts a 50-year visionary journey that began on the right foot, with recognition that sustainable economic growth and a clean environment are mutually reinforcing goals. Over these decades, Singapore has moved from cleaning up the land and rivers, through controlling pollution and meeting water needs, to the current use of cutting-edge research and technology to build clean and renewable energy for the future. With the city-state now ranking near the top of the world in terms of environmental standards, the book offers many lessons for other countries looking for ways to meet the growing demand for water and energy while preserving a health-promoting environment."

Dr. Margaret Chan
Director-General, World Health Organization

"Singapore celebrates its 50th anniversary of nationhood in a milestone year as countries of the world come together to agree a climate-safe path to sustainable development. Since its establishment, Singapore has sought to leverage sound environmental stewardship and social engagement into prosperity and growth. Singapore has been remarkably successful. The *50 Years of Environment* publication demonstrates how progressive policy such as ecologically sound natural resource management, incentives to innovate and emphasis on clean development are at the heart of this vibrant modern economy. This is a welcome addition to the global dialogue on development as a powerful case study for what is possible. As governments move towards a set of Sustainable Development Goals and a new, universal climate change agreement in Paris this year, the knowledge and experiences in this book showcase real world policy success and inspire the world."

Ms. Christiana Figueres
Executive Secretary, UN Framework Convention on Climate Change

"Singapore's success in becoming a developed country and, at the sametime, taking good care of its environment, is a vindication of what we were trying to achieve at the 1992 Earth Summit. This important book explains how Singapore did it and outlines present and future challenges as Singapore continues its journey into environmental sustainability and sustainable development."

Professor Tommy Koh
Chairman, Preparatory Committee and Chairman, Main Committee
UN Conference on Environment and Development
2006 Champion of the Earth, awarded by UNEP
2006 President's Award for the Environment, Singapore

"Singapore is well known globally for its brilliant economic success story. It deserves to be equally wellknown for its environmental success story. It is truly remarkable that unlike other successful economies, Singapore did not sacrifice its environment in pursuit of economic growth. This is why this book edited by Tan Yong Soon could not be more timely. The world can learn a lot of lessons from this volume."

Professor Kishore Mahbubani
Dean, LKY School of Public Policy, National University of Singapore, and
author of *The Great Convergence: Asia, the West, and the Logic of One World*

"With a population density of around 7,500 people to the square kilometre, Singapore is one of the most densely populated countries on Earth. This book of essays by some of those most closely involved shows how the country evolved through half a century of commitment and foresight into one of the world's most liveable cities with green spaces and fresh water and how it is addressing present environmental challenges to develop sustainable strategies and solutions. Others take notice and follow!"

Lord Ronald Oxburgh
Former Rector of Imperial College of Science, Technology and Medicine (1993–2000)
Former Chairman of the UK House of Lords Select Committee
on Science and Technology (2000–2004)
Honorary President of the Carbon Capture and Storage Association

PREFACE

In celebrating Singapore's 50 years of nationhood, it is useful to remember that achieving a clean environment is an important part of Singapore's remarkable development story. In the early years of independence, Singapore leaders had the vision to accord high priority to the environment and not merely focus on economic and social development. Today, Singapore enjoys a high standard of environment. The 2014 report of the Environment Performance Index (developed by Yale University [Yale Center for Environmental Law and Policy] and Columbia University [Center for International Earth Science Information Network] in collaboration with the World Economic Forum and the Joint Research Centre of the European Commission) ranked Singapore 4th out of 178 countries.[1]

A high standard of environment has contributed to Singapore's economic dynamism and vibrancy and its liveability. Singapore's environmental journey and how it has controlled pollution to achieve a clean environment and how it closed its water loop to ensure long-term water sustainability, as well as the strategies and approaches it applied to Singapore's environmental and water policies have been well documented in the book, *Clean, Green and Blue: Singapore's Journey Towards Environmental and Water Sustainability* by Tan Yong Soon with Lee Tung Jean and Karen Tan (2009). But the journey is a never-ending one. This book comprises a collection of contributions from various authors who are well established in different arenas dealing with environmental issues. It seeks to provide a glimpse of the journey to the present, as well as to discuss present and future challenges and how we can continue to enjoy a clean environment and develop sustainably. Each essay can be read as a standalone and the reader need not read all of them in chronological order, but read together as a whole, they will provide a good general overview of the historical developments which have brought us to where we are today, but also give us a sense of where we are heading in the future.

This book is divided into three parts.

Part One outlines the Journey to the Present. It reproduces with permission three chapters from the book *Clean, Green and Blue* by Tan Yong Soon, then Permanent Secretary, Ministry of the Environment and Water Resources, with Lee Tung Jean and Karen Tan, then Director and Deputy Director respectively in the Ministry.

---

[1] Environmental Performance Index. (2014). Global Metrics for the Environment. Retrieved 11 March 2015 from http://epi.yale.edu.

Reflections on Singapore's Environmental Journey (Chapter 1 of *Clean, Green and Blue*) discusses the fundamental principles and success factors that have guided environmental policymaking in Singapore from the onset: Clear Vision; Long-term Planning; Constant Innovation; and a Practical and Effective Approach.

Cleaning the Land and the Rivers (Chapter 3 of *Clean, Green and Blue*) details Singapore's experience in cleaning up the land and rivers, explaining the motivations behind this clean-up programme — to improve the standard of public health and quality of living for Singaporeans — and how cleanliness was elevated to a national and nationwide priority as the government understood that success could not be achieved without the understanding and participation of all residents. The chapter also explains how achieving clean land and rivers requires a long-term perspective and long-term programmes based on practical solutions which are implemented effectively.

Applying Economic Principles to Environmental Policy (Chapter 9 of *Clean, Green and Blue*) highlights the role economics plays in guiding environmental policies, decisions and legislation. The full environmental cost of a certain initiative should be factored into the decision-making process in order to help one decide on the best course of action. While we value the environment, government decisions must also be made on the basis of stringent analysis as the government has to prioritise competing demands in the face of limited resources. Economics is a useful tool to help one arrive at the best decision in the interest of the public. However, applying economic principles alone may not provide all the answers, and it is also very important to understand and appreciate their limitations. In the final analysis, economics is only a tool. It can support and complement, but not replace, a clear vision and strategic priorities.

Readers who are interested to learn more about Singapore's historical and ongoing journey towards environmental and water sustainability may wish to read the book *Clean, Green and Blue*. However, the chapters included here provide a good starting point in understanding the basic motivations, strategies and long-term vision that formed the foundations for the initial push towards cleaning up the environment.

Part One also reproduces **a speech** by Lee Ek Tieng, the first Permanent Secretary of Environment and former Chairman of PUB, the National Water Agency, which was delivered at the 18th Professor Chin Fung Kee Memorial Lecture on 18 October 2008 which examines how Singapore has overcome its physical limitations to develop new water resources. It outlines the historical context in which Singapore was compelled to find new sources of water, leading to creative solutions like water catchment areas, water reclamation, desalination, and the development of NEWater.

Lee Ek Tieng was in charge of many projects that improve Singapore's environment, including the cleaning up of the Singapore River. Singapore's founding Prime

Minister Lee Kuan Yew wrote in his memoir *From Third World to First, The Singapore Story: 1965–2000* that "There would have been no clean and green Singapore without Lee Ek Tieng. I could spell out broad conceptual objectives, but he had to work out the engineering solutions. He later became head of the civil service."

It also includes a chapter on integrated and long-term land-use planning, **Environmental Planning For Sustainable Development**, by Tan Yong Soon, which outlines the importance of incorporating environmental considerations in urban planning, particularly in land-use zoning and provision of critical environmental infrastructure. It goes on to discuss the critical factors for success in this process, which would be largely dependent on the government, public and private sectors, and the grassroots level, of individuals and the community, all working closely together to maintain and improve upon the high standards of environment Singapore has attained.

Part Two covers Present Challenges, foremost among which, apart from good policymaking, planning and implementation, are technology, industry development, community engagement and regional and international cooperation.

Singapore must continue to innovate and find more efficient and cost effective solutions to deal with new environmental challenges. Useful research and development and its effective commercialisation are important. Researchers from the National University of Singapore (NUS) and the Nanyang Technological University (NTU), both ranked among world's top ten universities for engineering and technology,[2] have contributed two excellent chapters on technology's role in addressing emerging environmental challenges. Prof. Ong Choon Nam, Director of NUS Environmental Research Institute (NERI), and Lee Lai Yoke, Manager for Research at NERI, write on **Frontier Research in Environment and Water**, outlining the frontier research conducted at NUS and how the university works with government agencies and industries to conduct integrated, multidisciplinary research for sustainable solutions. In their essay **Energy Transitions — Energy Efficiency and Renewable Energy Challenges in the Tropics,** Prof. Subodh Mhaisalkar, Executive Director, Energy Research Institute @ NTU (ERI@N), Prof. Hans B. (Teddy) Püttgen, Senior Director of ERI@N, and Nilesh Y. Jadhav, Programme Director at ERI@N explain how Singapore is engaging in cutting-edge research into technology focussed on energy transition, moving towards greater sustainability through increasing energy efficiency and clean energy. The research seeks to give rise to innovative solutions that will help position Singapore as a leader in developing solutions suitable for the tropical region. Such research done at NERI, ERI@N and other similar research institutes are

---

[2] According to the QS World University Rankings by Faculty 2014/15. Retrieved 11 March 2015 from http://www.topuniversities.com/university-rankings/world-university-rankings/2014.

conducted in the universities in collaboration with government agencies and industries, and the technologies are being test-bedded, developed and then commercialised, and there are many potential environmental, economic, and social benefits that could emerge as a result of such research.

Technology development goes hand in hand with the development of a vibrant industry. With changing weather patterns, depleting natural resources, and ever-growing cities, it has become increasingly important for countries to pay more attention to addressing the challenges of climate change and urbanisation and to come up with sustainable solutions. Singapore, as a city-state, is acutely aware of these issues and that drives it to find solutions to reduce carbon emissions in the face of climate change and urbanisation. It is actively promoting sustainable development, integrating policies with research and development and test-bedding new technology. For such solutions to be sustainable, they must ultimately be financially viable. A vibrant sustainable energy industry ecosystem is therefore imperative. The Sustainable Energy Association of Singapore (SEAS) represents the interests and provides a common platform for Singapore-based companies in Renewable Energy, Energy Efficiency, Carbon Development and Trading, and Financial Institutions to meet, discuss, collaborate and undertake viable projects together. The Association extends its focus to include Capacity Building, Technology Strengthening and Market Intelligence, assisting its members in achieving Sustainable Growth locally and regionally via enterprise development, market development, training and learning platforms. **Developing a Vibrant Sustainable Energy Industry** is contributed by Edwin Khew, Chairman of the Sustainable Energy Association of Singapore together with fellow SEAS Council members, Christophe Inglin, Sanjay Kuttan and Low Kian Beng. It examines these issues examines these issues and the growth of the clean technology (cleantech) sector. First it takes a look at the current energy landscape in Singapore, as well as the vast variety of renewable energy technologies that have emerged as a response to present-day issues, and also contemplates potential future challenges and opportunities that are faced by the energy industry, both in Singapore and in the world. Singapore is a living lab and a hub, and the solutions that it comes up with would prove to be useful and successful solutions to the contemporary challenges that not only Singapore faces, but also the region.

Right from the earliest stages of nation building, we already recognised that community engagement is pivotal in improving environmental standards and contributing to a sustainable urban environment. This is an ongoing challenge tackled by the Ministry of the Environment and later by its Statutory Board, the National Environment Agency (NEA). NEA adapts itself to meet the call for greater community involvement and building a more inclusive society, encouraging ground-up, community-led activities and movement. Its programmes also focus on inculcating values and building positive social norms. There is greater support for localised engagements and leveraging touch-points, both through traditional and social media, to reach out to a more diverse populace. Environmental ownership is important and community engagement to promote environmental ownership is also about building relationships and trust with the people. This story is explained in the chapter **Community Engagement to Promote Environmental Ownership and Secure Our Future** by Chew Gek Khim, Chairman of the National Environment Agency from 2008 to 2015.

Finally, environment is not confined to national borders. Achieving a good environment is a global challenge requiring regional and international cooperation. Simon Tay, Chairman of the Singapore Institute of International Affairs and his colleague, Assistant Director Cheong Poh Kwan, explain this in the chapter **Island in the World: Singapore's Environment and the International Dimensions**. It takes a look at how Singapore, the region, and the world are affected by trans-boundary haze, a major environmental issue that comes to the fore annually, as well as climate change, and how we all need to address these issues. It is important that all of us — Singaporeans, our neighbours in Southeast Asia, and the entire international community — are aware of the environmental issues that we all face, and come together to protect our environment.

As we deal with contemporary issues, it is crucial to keep in mind what lies ahead and consider future challenges. In **Part Three**, Tan Yong Soon and Kwek Leng Joo, with their combined experience in working towards improving the environment in the public, private and people sectors, co-authored a chapter on **Environmental Sustainability and Sustainable Development.** They emphasised the continual need for visionary political leadership, effective government-ware, an active private sector role and individual responsibility towards the environment. Resource conservation, research and innovation, as well as global partnerships were also other key issues discussed in the chapter.

Conclusion

To continue to enjoy a high standard of environment, it is important that Singapore continues to have a political leadership that has a clear vision to keep the environment a priority, a strong commitment to implement policies to achieve a good environment, and the communication skills to help the people understand government policies on the environment and the powers of persuasion to gain their support. It is necessary that the public service is able to anticipate the future and plan for the long term, adopt a practical and effective approach in environment management, including infrastructural investment and operations, policy implementation and enforcement, and public education and engagement. Singapore must innovate constantly, both in policy and technology, supporting and harnessing university research, and a vibrant

Singapore-based environment (and water) and energy industry to develop innovative, effective and efficient solutions and working with the international community to protect our environment. Finally, the people must be made aware of the importance of a good environment and have the desire to strive for a better environment, and be willing to take ownership and responsibility for their personal behaviour and consider its impact on the environment.

It has often been said that, "We do not inherit the earth from our ancestors; we borrow it from our children." Protecting the environment helps safeguard the future of our children. Singaporeans must be willing to establish consensus on an environmentally sustainable future in order for that aim to be realised in the long term.

Tan Yong Soon
June 2015

CONTENTS

About the Editor

Tan Yong Soon was the Permanent Secretary in the Ministry of the Environment and Water Resources from January 2004 to June 2010, during which he oversaw many major programmes, such as the opening of Singapore's first desalination plant in 2005, the development of NEWater plants and the completion of the Marina Barrage in 2008. He also played an important role in enhancing Singapore's living environment, growing the water and environment industry and raising Singapore's international profile in the environmental arena. He co-chaired the Executive Committee for Environment and Water Technology, and the Exco supporting the Inter-Ministerial Committee on Sustainable Development that produced the first Sustainable Singapore Blueprint in 2009.

In 2010, he was appointed the first Permanent Secretary in the newly established National Climate Change Secretariat in the Prime Minister's Office, where he built new capabilities to understand and address the challenges posed by climate change and was instrumental in developing Singapore's national climate change strategy and capabilities. He retired from the Public Service in October 2012.

He has also served as Principal Private Secretary to the Prime Minister, Deputy Secretary (Policy) in the Ministry of Defence, Deputy Secretary (Revenue) and Deputy Secretary (Policy) in the Ministry of Finance, and the Chief Executive Officer of the Urban Redevelopment Authority.

He holds a BA (Hons) and MA in Engineering from Cambridge University, an MBA from the National University of Singapore and an MPA from Harvard University. He also attended the Advanced Management Programme at Harvard Business School.

He is the author of *Living the Singapore Dream*, a reflection on his life experiences and those of his childhood friends, which expounds the values that made Singapore — and these individuals — successful, and co-author of *Clean, Green and Blue: Singapore's Journey Towards Environmental and Water Sustainability*.

About the Contributors

Cheong Poh Kwan

Ms. Cheong Poh Kwan is Assistant Director at the Singapore Institute of International Affairs (SIIA). She coordinates the institute's Sustainability Programme, which covers engagement with governments, corporations, NGOs, academics, the media and the public. She also conducts research and writes on the topics of transboundary haze and climate change, among others. Poh Kwan is formerly a journalist at The Straits Times, covering local news for its online video site RazorTV and foreign news for its print edition. She is the winner of the Ministry of Finance Budget 2007 Essay Competition, and the Singapore Tertiary Chinese Literature Awards in 2007. She graduated with a major in Communications Research from the Wee Kim Wee School of Communication and Information, Nanyang Technological University.

Chew Gek Khim

Ms. Chew Gek Khim is the Executive Chairman of The Straits Trading Company Limited. She is also Executive Chairman of Tecity Group, Deputy Chairman of ARA Asset Management Limited, Chairman of ARA Trust Management (Suntec) Limited, and sits on the board of Singapore Exchange Limited.

Ms. Chew is also Deputy Chairman of The Tan Chin Tuan Foundation in Singapore and Chairman of The Tan Sri Tan Foundation in Malaysia. She chairs the board of the National Environment Agency of Singapore (2008–2015) and is a Member of the Securities Industry Council of Singapore, the Council of the Singapore Symphony Orchestra (SSO) and Board of Governors of S. Rajaratnam School of International Studies.

Ms. Chew is a lawyer by training and graduated from the National University of Singapore in 1984.

Christophe Inglin

Mr. Christophe Inglin is a veteran of the solar photovoltaics (PV) industry, with 16 years of experience throughout the value chain from silicon ingots to turnkey solar power plants.

He is currently Managing Director of Phoenix Solar Pte Ltd, which he co-founded in December 2006 as a joint venture with local partners and the German company Phoenix Solar AG, an international photovoltaic (PV) solar systems integrator.

From December 1996 until June 2006 he was Managing Director of Shell Solar Pte Ltd (formerly Siemens Showa Solar), responsible for Asia Pacific business.

Christophe also chairs the Clean Energy Committee at the Sustainable Energy Association of Singapore (SEAS). He is the invited trainer for PV technology courses held regularly at the Building and Construction Authority (BCA).

Before moving to Singapore, Christophe worked for Siemens Semiconductors and Siemens Management Consulting in Munich, California and Zurich.

Christophe is a Singapore Permanent Resident, with Swiss and British nationalities. He has a BSc in Electronic and Electrical Engineering, and an MBA from INSEAD.

Nilesh Y. Jadhav

Mr. Nilesh Y. Jadhav is a Senior Scientist and Programme Director of the EcoCampus initiative at the Nanyang Technological University (NTU), Singapore. He led the research group on Sustainable Building Technologies at the Energy Research Institute @ NTU and his research interests span over building energy efficiency, renewable energy, smart grids and electromobility. Prior to joining NTU in 2011, Nilesh has over 12 years of diverse work experience in management and technical roles in manufacturing, supply-logistics and research functions with an oil and petrochemical MNC. He received his Bachelor's degree from the University (of Mumbai) Institute of Chemical Technology (UICT) and Master's degree from the Delft University of Technology (TU Delft).

Edwin Khew

Er. Edwin T. F. Khew is the Managing Director, Anaergia Pte Ltd, a global leader in offering sustainable solutions for the generation of renewable energy and the conversion of waste to resources with its global headquarters in Canada. He is also a former Nominated Member of Parliament (NMP) and currently the Chairman of the Sustainable Energy Association of Singapore (SEAS), the Vice President of The Institution of Engineers, Singapore (IES), a Council Member of the Singapore Business Federation (SBF), an Advisory Board Member of Solar Energy Research Institute of Singapore (SERIS) and Chairman of the Singapore Standards Council. Er. Khew represents SEAS on the Asian Development Bank (ADB) lead Energy for All Partnership's (E4ALL) Steering Committee as its Co-Chair and Chairman of its Enterprise Development Working Group. Er. Khew has an Executive MBA from the National University of Singapore, a Bachelor's Degree in Chemical Engineering from the University of Queensland, Australia, is a Fellow of the Institute of Engineers, Singapore, a Fellow of the Institute of Chemical Engineers (UK), and a professional engineer of the Professional Engineers Board, Singapore.

Sanjay Kuttan

Dr. Sanjay Kuttan has held various positions across his career since 1994 both in private and public sector. In the private sector he worked in various positions at ExxonMobil Asia Pacific and as a Petroleum Practice Expert/Engagement Manager at McKinsey & Company. In the public sector, he was the Director of Industry Development at the Energy Market Authority, a Statutory Board under the Ministry of Trade and Industry. He played pivotal roles in the Intelligent Energy System Pilot, the Electric Vehicle Test-bed, Pulau Ubin Renewable Energy Project, the Energy Efficiency Programme Office, and the Clean Energy Programme Office. He currently is a council member of the Sustainable Energy Association of Singapore and Singapore Business Council for Sustainable Development, advisory committee member to the School of Electrical and Electronic Engineering at the Ngee Ann Polytechnic and Stamford Primary School.

Kwek Leng Joo

Mr. Kwek Leng Joo is Deputy Chairman of City Developments Limited (CDL), Singapore's property pioneer since 1963. Today, CDL operates in 25 countries and is one of Singapore's largest companies by market capitalisation. With over 30 years of track record in property development, Kwek has played an important role in championing responsible business practices for long-term sustainability in the industry.

For over two decades, Kwek's vision to "Conserve as we Construct" has led CDL to be recognised both locally and globally as a leader in green buildings, sustainable development and Corporate Social Responsibility (CSR). As President of the Singapore Compact for CSR and Chairman of the Board of Trustees of the National Youth Achievement Award Council, Kwek has played an active role in advocating CSR and youth development in Singapore.

Outside of work, Kwek is a philanthropist, dedicated volunteer and an avid photographer. He has raised over S$2 million through sales of his photo works and art books for various charitable and environmental causes.

Lee Ek Tieng

Mr. Lee Ek Tieng was the first Permanent Secretary in the Ministry of the Environment and has served as Chairman of the Public Utilities Board, Permanent Secretary in the Revenue Division of the Ministry of Finance, Chairman of Temasek Holdings (Pte) Ltd, Managing Director of the Monetary Authority of Singapore, and Group Managing Director of the Government of Singapore Investment Corporation. Prior to his retirement in 1999, he served as Head of Civil Service and Permanent Secretary (Special Duties) in the Prime Minister's Office, Singapore.

He was Fellow of The Institution of Civil Engineers and Institution of Water and Environment Management, UK; and Member of The Institution of Engineers, Malaysia. He is Hon. Fellow of The Institution of Engineers and Fellow of The Academy of Engineers, Singapore. He holds a Bachelor's Degree in Engineering from University of Malaya (Singapore) and has a Diploma in Public Health Engineering from the University of Newcastle-Upon-Tyne (UK).

Lee Lai Yoke

Dr. Lee Lai Yoke is the Manager (Research Affairs) at NUS Environmental Research Institute (NERI), National University of Singapore (NUS). She received her MSc and PhD in Environmental Engineering from NUS in 1997 and 2003, respectively. She has more than 15 years of research experience in water and wastewater treatment and reclamation, water resource management, water quality assessment, resource and nutrient recovery, and water safety plan development and implementation. She has thought various postgraduate and undergraduate environmental modules; and mentored researchers in their projects. She was the recipient of the Outstanding Mentor Award for Ministry of Education (MOE)-Science Mentorship Programme in 2009. Dr. Lee is also actively involved in professional organisations, including the Environmental Engineering Society of Singapore, International Water Association and Water Environment Federation.

Lee Tung Jean

Dr. Lee Tung Jean co-authored the book *Clean, Green and Blue* when she was Director of Water Studies at the Ministry of the Environment and Water Resources, Singapore, where she was involved in the formulation and implementation of policies relating to the management of water resources and enhancement of Singapore's living environment. She was concurrently the Deputy Executive Director of the Environment and Water Industry Development Council.

She is currently the Chief Executive Officer of the Early Childhood Development Agency, Singapore.

She holds a BA (Hons) from Harvard University, an MA in Economics from Yale University and a DPhil in Economics from Oxford University that she pursued on a Rhodes Scholarship.

Low Kian Beng

Mr. Low Kian Beng is the Group Deputy Chief Executive Officer and Executive Director of ecoWise Holdings Limited, a Singapore SGX Limited environmental company.

Mr. Low is responsible for the overall management of the operation of the Group's companies, corporate planning and charting and implementing the business strategies of the Group.

He was the Managing Director and CEO of SP Corporation, a SGX listed company, from 2000 to 2006 and was the Managing Director and CEO of Envipure Pte Ltd from 2006 till 2010. Mr. Low has more than 20 years of senior management experience, covering various functions, in the environmental, tyre and rubber, petrochemicals, energy and engineering services industries, across the Asia Region.

Mr. Low holds a Master of Business Administration Degree (with distinction) from Oklahoma City University, Texas (US) and a BSc Degree (with honours) in Engineering from Imperial College of Science and Technology, London (UK).

Subodh Mhaisalkar

Prof. Subodh Mhaisalkar is the Tan Chin Tuan Centennial Professor in the School of Materials Science & Engineering at the Nanyang Technological University (NTU), Singapore. Subodh is also the Executive Director of the Energy Research Institute @ NTU (ERI@N), a pan-University multidisciplinary research institute for innovative energy solutions. Prior to joining NTU in 2001, Subodh has over 10 years of research and engineering experience in the microelectronics industry and his areas of expertise and research interests include semiconductor technology, perovskite solar cells, printed electronics, and energy storage. Subodh received his Bachelor's degree from IIT-Bombay and his MS/PhD degrees from The Ohio State University.

Ong Choon Nam

Prof. Ong Choon Nam is the Director of the NUS Environmental Research Institute and a Professor at the Saw Swee Hock School of Public Health, National University of Singapore. He received his BSc Hons from Nanyang University in 1973, MSc from University of London in 1974, and PhD from Manchester University in 1977. His research interest is Environmental Health Sciences and has published over 300 papers in peer-reviewed journals with more than 15,000 citations. He has served as a consultant to the World Health Organization (WHO) on many occasions and is an editorial board member of several international journals. He chaired the International Expert Panel which advised the Ministry of the Environment and Water Resources on the NEWater study. He is also an advisor to the US National Water Research Institute and has been consulted often by international and local agencies on issues related to environmental health, water quality and toxicology.

Hans B. (Teddy) Püttgen

Prof. Hans B. (Teddy) Püttgen joined NTU late 2013 as Professor and Senior Director, Energy Research Institute @ NTU (ERI@N), where he leads the Renewable Energy Integration Demonstrator in Singapore, REIDS, initiative. Before joining NTU, he was Energy Systems Management chair at École polytechnique fédérale de Lausanne (EPFL), Switzerland, and its inaugural Director of the Energy Center, a university-wide organisation coordinating major energy projects in collaboration with European R&D institutions. Before joining EPFL, Professor Püttgen was Georgia Power Distinguished Professor at Georgia Tech where he launched the National Electric Energy Test, Research Application Center, NEETRAC. Teddy Püttgen is Ingénieur Diplômé Electricien from EPFL. His PhD is from the University of Florida. Teddy Püttgen is a Fellow of IEEE.

Karen Tan

Ms. Karen Tan E-Ling co-authored the book *Clean, Green and Blue* when she was Deputy Director for Strategic Policy at the Ministry of the Environment and Water Resources, Singapore. Her portfolio covered the formulation and implementation of policies to ensure Singapore's environmental sustainability, including air pollution control.

She is currently Director of the Energy Division in the Ministry of Trade and Industry, Singapore.

She holds a BA (Hons) in Politics, Philosophy and Economics from Oxford University and an MA in Political Science from Columbia University.

Simon S. C. Tay

A/P Simon Tay is Chairman of the Singapore Institute of International Affairs (SIIA). He is concurrently Associate Professor, teaching international law at the National University of Singapore, and author of the well-received book on Asian regionalism and the role of America, *Asia Alone* (2010). Professor Tay is also Senior Consultant at WongPartnership, a leading Asian law firm. He serves on the Global Advisory Board for MUFG, and the boards of Hyflux and Far East Organisation. He has also served as Chairman of the National Environment Agency, and taught as a visiting professor at Yale University, the Fletcher School and Harvard Law School.

He graduated in law from the National University of Singapore (1986) and Harvard Law School (1993), where he won the Laylin prize for the best thesis in international law.

APPRECIATION

My appreciation goes to

- Mr. Lee Kuan Yew, founding Prime Minister of Singapore, whose vision and leadership have made Singapore clean, green and blue.
- the extraordinary team of dedicated officers, past and present, in the Ministry of the Environment and Water Resources (and the Ministry of the Environment since its formation in 1972), the National Environment Agency and PUB, the National Water Agency, for their good work and in conjunction with stakeholders in the public, private and people sectors in working hard and achieving the high standard of environment in Singapore.

I would like to thank all the contributors of this volume for their valuable and insightful contributions. In particular, Mr. Lee Ek Tieng, Ms. Chew Gek Khim, Mr. Edwin Khew, Mr. Kwek Leng Joo, Prof. Subodh Mhaisalkar, Prof. Ong Choon Nam and Prof. Simon Tay who readily and unhesitatingly agreed to participate from the start. Without their strong support, this book would not have been possible.

I would also like to thank Dr. Andrew Benedek, Prof. Asit Biswas, Dr. Margaret Chan, Ms. Christiana Figueres, Prof. Tommy Koh, Prof. Kishore Mahbubani and Lord Ronald Oxburgh for taking the time to review the book and provide their reactions and endorsements.

I acknowledge with thanks the Ministry of the Environment and Water Resources, copyright holder of *Clean, Green and Blue: Singapore's Journey Towards Environmental and Water Sustainability* which I co-authored with Lee Tung Jean and Karen Tan, for granting permission to reproduce Chapters 1, 3 and 9 in this book.

Finally, I would like to thank Prof. K. K. Phua, Chairman and Editor-in-Chief of World Scientific Publishing Co. Pte Ltd, for inviting me to edit this volume as part of the series of books celebrating Singapore's 50 years of nation building, and Ms. Li Hongyan, Senior Editor at World Scientific Publishing, for helping to put this book together. Hongyan's tight editing has made this book more readable.

PART 1

Journey to the Present

CHAPTER 1

Reflections on Singapore's Environmental Journey

Tan Yong Soon, Lee Tung Jean and Karen Tan

We have built, we have progressed. But no other hallmark of success will be more distinctive than that of achieving our position as the cleanest and greenest city in South Asia. For, only a people with high social and educational standards can maintain a clean and green city. It requires organisation to keep the community cleaned and trimmed particularly when the population has a density of 8,500 persons per square mile. And it requires a people conscious of their responsibilities, not just to their own families, but also to their neighbours and all others in the community who will be affected by their thoughtless anti-social behaviour. Only a people proud of their community performance, feeling for the well-being of their fellow citizens, can keep up high personal and public standards of hygiene.

Prime Minister Lee Kuan Yew at the launch of the
inaugural Keep Singapore Clean campaign in 1968

Residents in Singapore breathe in clean air, drink clean water direct from the tap, live on clean land, and enjoy good public hygiene. However, Singapore is not a green utopia with zero carbon emissions, large-scale renewable energy sources, or cutting edge zero-energy buildings. What it does have is a practical, cost-effective, and efficient approach towards sustaining its environment, which contributes to the high quality of life in Singapore.

In a world where rapid industrialisation and urbanisation have led to tremendous pressures on environment and water resources, visitors to Singapore often ask: how is it possible that a small city state sitting on barely 700 square kilometres of land, housing close to 5 million people, and bustling with a world class airport, the world's busiest port and many other industries, can remain clean, green, and environmentally

Permission was granted by the Ministry of the Environment and Water Resources (MEWR) to reproduce Chapter 1 from the book *Clean, Green and Blue: Singapore's Journey Towards Environmental and Water Sustainability.*

sustainable? They want to understand how Singapore has achieved this and hear about Singapore's experience.

Clear Vision

The answer is that it starts with a clear vision from the very top that a clean and good quality living environment is important, and a strong commitment to implement that vision. Poverty, economic uncertainty, and a living environment defined by night soil buckets, polluted rivers, water rationing, unhygienic street hawkers, and smoke-emitting/effluent-discharging industries may seem like a distant memory today, but they were a reality faced by many Singaporeans as late as the 1960s and 1970s. The transformation of Singapore from a poor, developing nation to a vibrant and prosperous city state has taken place over a relatively short period of three to four decades.

Singapore is a small country with no natural resources. In the 1960s, it had a small, but rapidly growing population of 1.6 million. The economy was highly dependent on entrepôt trade and the provision of services to British military bases in Singapore. The country had only a small manufacturing base, with little industrial know-how and domestic capital. When Singapore gained independence in 1965, its per capita gross domestic product was barely US$1,525 (S$4,700). As a fledgling nation, it faced problems such as ensuring national security and defence, mass unemployment at rates of 10 to 12%, housing shortages, and a low standard of living. It also had to grapple with the lack of resources and land. This was further compounded by the challenges posed by the planned withdrawal of the British troops from the late 1960s.[1]

To survive, economic development was paramount as it held the key to providing resources to improve Singapore and better the lives of the people. Singapore invested heavily to promote economic growth, embarking on an aggressive strategy of export-oriented industrialisation and attracting foreign investment, backed by government incentives and tax holidays. Education was also viewed as a critical factor, with many schools built in the early post-independence years. Through these efforts, Singapore's per capita gross domestic product in 2005 reached nearly US$27,000 (S$45,000).

However, what is perhaps even more noteworthy is that despite its unrelenting industrialisation, breakneck growth, and rapid urbanisation over its relatively short forty-year history, Singapore has managed to turn itself into a clean and green city with a high-quality living environment.

---

[1] Ministry of Trade and Industry Website, Singapore's Economic History. Retrieved from http://app.mti.gov. sg/default. asp?id=545.

Building Up the Environmental Infrastructure

The government recognised the importance of a good environment, and hence the need to balance economic development with a good environment, very early in Singapore's development. It has always believed that a clean and green environment is necessary to provide a good quality of life, not just for the present generation, but for generations to come. The government also realised that a clean and green environment helps to attract investments and retain talents, supporting further growth. A poor environment and a lack of water will cause health and other serious problems. If the environment and water resources are managed well, quality of life and even economic competitiveness will be greatly enhanced.

The government, therefore, invested in critical environmental infrastructure from the early days, despite competing demands for funding. S$2 billion was spent on drainage development projects over the past thirty years; S$1.8 billion on sewerage and used water treatment infrastructure in the 1970s and 1980s, and another S$3.65 billion on the construction of the Deep Tunnel Sewerage System (DTSS); over S$300 million on cleaning up the Singapore River from 1977 to 1987; S$270 million on constructing the Marina Barrage; S$100 million on Singapore's first incineration plant in 1973, a further S$1.6 billion on its other incineration plants, and S$600 million on an offshore landfill island. The heavy investment in the environment was all the more visionary as the new nation did not have enough money, especially in the early years. The benefits were long term while the costs were immediate, but Singapore was prepared to borrow from the World Bank to develop its environmental infrastructure, where necessary. For Singapore, it was never a case of pursuing growth at all costs and cleaning up afterwards. Investing in the environment continues to be of high priority today, to upgrade Singapore's environmental infrastructure and improve its efficiency.

Communicating the Vision

The Singapore Government has always made clear to the public the national priority placed on the environment so that its vision for the environment can be shared and supported by everyone. The first yearly "Keep Singapore Clean" campaign was launched in October 1968, by then Prime Minister Lee Kuan Yew to educate all Singaporeans on the importance of keeping shared public spaces clean. This annual campaign took on an additional dimension in 1971 with the launch of Tree Planting Day. Far from being just one day in a year, Tree Planting Day symbolised the government's vision for Singapore to be transformed into a tropical garden city — both clean and green — and became a tradition spanning the next twenty years. In 1990, the first Clean and Green Week was launched, incorporating both the Keep Singapore Clean campaign and tree-planting activities. In addition, Clean and Green Week also aimed to increase community awareness of global environmental concerns and encourage community participation in caring for the environment. In 2007, Clean and Green Week was rebranded Clean and Green Singapore, in order to send a clear message that environmentally-friendly lifestyles and habits should be practised all year round. Each successive prime minister, from Lee Kuan Yew to Goh Chok Tong to Lee Hsien Loong, has strongly signalled the importance attached to keeping Singapore clean by personally launching the campaign nearly every year for the past forty years. On the few occasions when the prime minister could not do this, it was the deputy prime minister who officiated at the event.

Building Capabilities

The importance that Singapore has long placed on the environment is underscored by the fact that the Anti-Pollution Unit (APU) formed in 1970 to combat air pollution was placed under the Prime Minister's Office (PMO) at the outset. Not long afterwards, in September 1972, the Ministry of the Environment (ENV) was established. This was immediately after the United Nations Conference on the Human Environment in Stockholm in June 1972. The Stockholm Conference was the first international forum aimed at addressing global environmental challenges, and Singapore was one of the first countries to form a Ministry dedicated to creating and sustaining a good environment for its people.

Prior to the formation of ENV, there were, of course, other organisations responsible for public health and environment-related services in Singapore. Two local authorities, the Rural Board and the City Council, together with the Government Health Department provided both personal and environmental health services in the 1950s. These included water supply, sanitation and sewage disposal, cleansing services, as well as vector and disease control and food hygiene. Drainage was overseen by the Public Works Department (PWD).

Local government was abolished when Singapore gained self-government in 1959. Administrative changes were made to integrate the City Council and the Rural Board with the various ministries. The PWD came under the new Ministry of National Development (MND). The City Engineers Department from the City Council was merged with the PWD. The City Health Department and the Rural Health Department were integrated into the Ministry of Health (MOH).[2]

When the City Council was dissolved, the Public Utilities Board (PUB) was set up as a Statutory Board[3] under the Ministry of Trade and Industry (MTI) on 1 May 1963

---

[2] *Singapore: My Clean and Green Home* (Singapore: Ministry of Environment, 1997).

[3] Statutory Boards are organisations that have been given autonomy to perform an operational function. They report to one specific Ministry and specialise in carrying out the plans and policies of the Ministries. In law, a Statutory Board is an autonomous government agency established by an Act of Parliament that specifies the purpose, rights, and powers of the body. Its overall activities are overseen by a Cabinet Minister. In addition, it has its own Chairman and Board of Directors.

to succeed the City Council in coordinating the supply of electricity, piped gas, and water for Singapore. Specifically in relation to water, the PUB was handed the mission of ensuring that Singapore's industrial and economic development and its population's well-being would be sustained by the provision of an adequate and dependable supply of water. It was entrusted with improving and extending the existing water distribution systems, planning and implementing new water schemes to meet projected water needs, and spearheading public campaigns to conserve water.[4] As a result of these changes, the MOH was in charge of public health services, except for sewerage and drainage, which were carried out by the MND. PUB was responsible for water supply.

When ENV was formed in 1972, the departments under the MOH and MND which dealt with pollution control, sewerage, drainage, and environmental health, were absorbed into the new Ministry. The APU was also subsequently transferred from the PMO to the Ministry in 1983. In 2001, recognising that Singapore's water catchment and supply systems, drainage systems, water reclamation plants, and sewerage systems are part of a comprehensive water cycle, the PUB was reconstituted to become Singapore's national water authority, overseeing the entire water loop. The sewerage and drainage departments from the Ministry were transferred to PUB. PUB itself was transferred from the MTI to the Environment Ministry. The regulation of the electricity and gas industries, formerly undertaken by the PUB, was transferred to a new Statutory Board, the Energy Market Authority (EMA), under MTI.

In 2002, a new Statutory Board, the National Environment Agency (NEA) was formed under the Environment Ministry through integrating the Environmental Public Health and Environmental Policy and Management Divisions of the Ministry with the Meteorological Services Department (MSD), formerly under the Ministry of Transport (MOT). The aim was to create a leaner, more policy-focussed Ministry and a more streamlined, operations-focussed Statutory Board. The division of responsibility between policy formulation and operational implementation would allow the Ministry to focus on setting strategic policy directions and addressing key policy concerns. NEA on the other hand would direct its efforts towards the effective implementation of policies.

Environment and water as well as public health issues in Singapore today are, therefore, comprehensively overseen by the Ministry of the Environment (renamed in 2004 as the Ministry of the Environment and Water Resources) and its two Statutory Boards, NEA and PUB.

Long-term Planning

To turn its vision for the environment into reality, Singapore relies on long-term and integrated planning. This is critical since the environment is a long-term issue. Moreover, while the effects of poor planning may not be immediately observable, they

---

[4] *Water: Precious Resource for Singapore* (Singapore: Public Utilities Board, 2002).

can have longer term repercussions. Policies and measures to protect and improve the environment may oft-times result in short-term costs. Without a clear vision and the adoption of a long-term perspective, it would be difficult for any city to take actions which incur short-term costs in order to achieve long-term environmental gain. For example, requiring industries to satisfy good air emission standards can increase the cost of doing business and may thus turn away some investments, with the resultant loss of jobs. Restricting vehicular usage and setting high emission standards may be unpopular, especially when coupled with an increasingly affluent population's desire to own cars. Providing proper sanitation and sufficient water incurs heavy infrastructural expenditure. Such environmental policies and developments will often have pay-offs only decades later.

That said, having borne the short-term costs in support of its vision, Singapore is enjoying the benefits of many of its past policies and actions today. For instance, the Marina Barrage, which was completed in 2008 to form a reservoir in the heart of the city, is the outcome of cleaning up the Singapore River, which started way back in 1977. Ranked as the most liveable city in Asia[5] and Asia's most competitive economy,[6] Singapore is an example of a bustling city that can be both environmentally "liveable" and economically vibrant.

Integrated Planning and Development Control Process

The formation of the Environment Ministry did not mean that the Ministry and its Statutory Boards operated in isolation to meet and safeguard their own interests. On the contrary, an integrated approach has been adopted in formulating and implementing environmental policies. This is a structured framework in which all government agencies work together to identify a clear vision and shared outcomes, and coordinate the efforts required by agencies to achieve these goals. Such an approach also allows trade-offs to be objectively discussed and deliberated on, with decisions made in light of overall national interest.

Perhaps the best illustration is Singapore's integrated planning and development control process. With limited land, land-use planning is of utmost importance in ensuring that the best possible use is made of Singapore's land without compromising its development needs.

At the macro level, Singapore's development is guided by the Concept Plan, which was introduced in 1971 and updated every ten years. Through the Concept Plan process spearheaded by the MND and the Urban Redevelopment Authority (URA), representatives from all the relevant government agencies come together to

---

[5] Mercer HR Consulting's Quality of Living Survey 2007 and 2008.
[6] World Economic Forum's Global Competitiveness Report 2007–2008.

map out the land-use vision for Singapore over the next forty to fifty years. It ensures that land resources are used well so that quality of life improves even as Singapore continues to develop and its population to grow. One level down, the Master Plan translates the broad, long-term strategies of the Concept Plan into detailed plans, even to the extent of specifying the permissible land use and density for each parcel of land. It guides Singapore's development in the medium term, over a period spanning ten to fifteen years, and is reviewed every five years. Similar to the Concept Plan, the Master Plan is a collaborative effort, taking inputs from a whole gamut of ministries, which together with their Statutory Boards, oversee the various key areas, from national development, to the environment, to trade and industry, and to defence.

Land adequacy aside, proper land-use planning also plays a major role in protecting the environment. First, land is set aside for critical environmental infrastructure such as sewerage as well as waste disposal and incineration facilities. Projections of future land requirements for such infrastructure are also factored into the Concept Plan so that adequate land is safeguarded for these needs. Selected areas that are ecologically rich are also safeguarded.

Second, with limited land space, it is not possible to provide a large buffer between incompatible developments such as industrial centres and residential areas. Environmental controls are, therefore, factored into land-use planning to ensure that developments are properly sited. Thus, major pollutive land-users are grouped together and located as far away as possible from residential areas and population centres. Through the process of development control and planning approval, a project has to satisfy the planners and technical agencies of its limited environmental impact and compatibility with the surrounding land use. Where necessary, environmental pollution control requirements have to be incorporated into the design of the development, particularly with regard to environmental health, drainage, sewerage, and pollution control. Highly pollutive industries and major developments that are likely to be detrimental to the environment are required to carry out pollution control studies covering all possible adverse environmental impacts, as well as the measures recommended to eliminate or mitigate these impacts.

These practices have their roots from the days of the APU that was established by then Prime Minister Lee Kuan Yew who was very concerned about the impact of industrialisation on Singapore's environment. Soon after its inception in 1970, one of the top priorities of APU was to study how industries contributed to air pollution. One industry of particular concern to APU was petrochemicals as it involved many complex processes, each of which had the potential to emit smoke and various gases that could cause severe air pollution if not contained or burnt off properly. Hence APU, with advice from overseas consultants, proposed measures to control pollution from such factories.

One example was the flare system.[7] Elevated flares (where the waste gas is combusted at the tip of a tall stack) are most commonly used in refineries and chemical plants. However, they can give rise to glaring flames at the stack tip or prolonged emissions of dark smoke and soot if the combustion at the flare is incomplete. Hence, in addition to the elevated flares, APU required petrochemical factories to install a ground flare system. This consists of a supplementary set of enclosed furnaces at ground level, allowing for more complete combustion and reducing the need for excess gases to be flared at the stack. However, putting such a measure in place could be very costly. So it was not surprising that APU often met with resistance from the Economic Development Board (EDB), which was responsible for attracting multinational corporations (MNC) to invest in Singapore.

Lee Ek Tieng, the first head of APU (and subsequently Permanent Secretary (ENV) and Head of Civil Service), recalled an early incident involving a big MNC which was planning to build a petrochemical facility here. It was a major investment, very important to Singapore's economic development. The MNC was not prepared to incur the expenditure for a ground furnace (assessed at that time to cost S$5 million), and hence garnered EDB's support to appeal against APU's decision. Nevertheless, APU reported directly to the Prime Minister and he understood that putting in place such preventive measures was better than cleaning up after industries retroactively. Hence, the appeal was rejected and the company had to install the ground furnace. This set the stage for subsequent pollution control measures that the APU introduced, so that all industries had to obtain APU's approval first before they could get the go-ahead to build their factories. The same applies today — a project will only be given the green light to proceed if environmental authorities have been satisfied that its location would not affect the environment adversely, its emissions are within the required standards, and wastes generated are safely managed and properly disposed.

Third, land-use planning also factors in the need to protect Singapore's water catchments. For instance, the Water Catchment Policy was put in place in 1983 to control developments within the unprotected catchment areas.[8] The overall urbanisation cap[9] was set at 34.1% and a population density limit of 198 dwelling units

---

[7] In petrochemical plants, flare systems are installed to provide a safe means of disposal for the gas streams from its facilities by burning them under controlled conditions such that adjacent personnel and equipment as well as the environment are not exposed to hazards.

[8] These are water catchments that are not within the Protected Catchment Areas. Apart from MacRitchie, Upper and Lower Peirce, and Upper Seletar, the rest are unprotected catchments. In the book, however, we have made a further distinction between unprotected catchments in general, and urban catchments, the latter referring to schemes such as Bedok and Marina Reservoirs.

[9] This refers to the total land area that can be developed within water catchments.

per hectare was imposed on anticipated developments up to 2005. Less intensive development, coupled with stringent pollution control measures, enabled Singapore to ensure the good quality of water collected even from these unprotected water catchments. Subsequently, PUB could adopt advanced water treatment technology to upgrade treatment plants to cater for water from increasingly urbanised and unprotected areas. Hence, in 1999, the urbanisation cap and population density limit were lifted, subject to the continuation of stringent water pollution control measures.

The 1983 Water Catchment Policy demonstrates how planners and engineers worked alongside one another to review and improve a policy as technology advanced and pollution management practices evolved. Adopting an integrated approach thus ensures that each agency understands the considerations and constraints of its partner agencies, and where possible, reviews and tweaks its own plans to the net gain of Singapore.

Singapore River Clean-up

This integrated and inter-agency approach spans not just planning, but also extends to the efficient and effective execution of environmental policies and plans. Perhaps the most notable example of inter-agency cooperation is the Singapore River clean-up which took place from 1977 to 1987. The Singapore River is located in the heart of the city. It was here that Stamford Raffles landed in 1819 and established a British trading settlement. Since the early days, the river has been the lifeblood and centre of commercial activities of Singapore, around which the central business district grew. Together with its Kallang Basin catchments, the river covers about one-fifth of the total land area of Singapore, and by the 1960s had become very polluted. As can be imagined, the clean-up programme was an enormous undertaking, involving the development of infrastructure such as housing, industrial workshops, and sewage systems; massive resettlement of squatters, backyard trades, industries and farmers (including pig and duck farms); resiting of street hawkers to food centres; and phasing out of pollutive activities along or close to the river banks by offering them development incentives.[10]

Implementing this action plan required the joint efforts of the Environment Ministry together with the URA, PWD, Housing and Development Board (HDB), Port of Singapore Authority (PSA), Jurong Town Corporation (JTC), and the Primary Production Department (PPD). In 1987, the results of these inter-agency efforts could be seen and enjoyed by everyone. The river was flowing freely. Its banks, once

---

[10] Land was re-zoned to land use of higher value so as to encourage the redevelopment of sites.

cluttered with boatyards, backyard trades, and squatter premises, were transformed into riverside walkways and landscaped parks. Fish returned to the river, and people could engage in activities such as boat races and river cruises. Today, outdoor eateries, entertainment outlets, and waterfront housing line the riverbanks, creating a vibrant buzz. The river mouth has also been dammed with a barrage to create a unique reservoir in an urban environment.

Constant Innovation

Cleaning up a country's environment and sustaining it goes beyond a clear vision and long-term, integrated planning and implementation. Another essential ingredient is continuous improvement and constant innovation on both the policy and technology fronts. To remain ahead of emerging environmental challenges, Singapore has continually searched for innovative solutions and leveraged technology to tackle such challenges. It is prepared to learn from the good practices of other countries where they exist, or innovate if there is no existing model. Two examples of innovations that have served Singapore well are NEWater and its offshore landfill, Semakau Landfill.

NEWater

Produced using advanced membrane technologies, NEWater allows each drop of water to be used more than once, and so multiplies Singapore's effective supply of water. It is a key pillar of the Environment Ministry's efforts to ensure a secure and sustainable supply of water for the long term.

Where other countries have faced resistance in the use of recycled water, public acceptance of NEWater in Singapore is high. One contributory factor was the intensive publicity programme that accompanied the launch of NEWater in 2002. It culminated in the toast with NEWater by 60,000 Singaporeans and foreigners led by then Prime Minister Goh Chok Tong and the entire Cabinet at the National Day Parade on 9 August 2002. The strong support by Singaporeans can also be attributed to their understanding of the safe technology behind NEWater. Demand for NEWater has increased several fold since its launch, especially from industries such as wafer fabrication plants who value NEWater for its ultra pure properties.

Singapore's investment in R&D and the conscious efforts to involve the private sector in the production of NEWater have also led to the development of a vibrant water industry in Singapore. More importantly, it is now able to share the solutions it has developed with other cities, as many will, otherwise, face water shortages in future. It also hopes to build on this good start to develop Singapore as a global hydrohub, with the inaugural Singapore International Water Week (SIWW) in 2008 as a platform to advocate best practices in water management and the successful application of water technologies.

Semakau Landfill — The "Garbage of Eden"

Singapore's limited land area has made it necessary for the Environment Ministry to find innovative solutions to meet the country's waste disposal needs. All incinerable waste in Singapore is incinerated since this reduces waste volumes by 90%. Despite having four waste-to-energy incineration plants, Singapore still requires landfill space for the disposal of the remaining waste volumes as well as non-incinerable waste. To avoid using up space on mainland Singapore, the idea of an offshore landfill was conceived. This gave rise to Semakau Landfill, which is the world's first offshore landfill created entirely from sea space.

The care put into the design and operational work at the landfill, as well as the environmental protection and conservation measures taken by the NEA, have ensured that Semakau Landfill is not only clean and free from smell, but is also a green natural environment thriving with rich biodiversity. It is open to members of the public for recreational activities such as birdwatching, sport fishing, and intertidal walks to allow everyone to enjoy the biodiversity of the island. The April 2007 issue of the *New Scientist* featured Semakau Landfill, dubbing it the "Garbage of Eden".

Practical and Effective Approach

The government's firm belief in the importance of constant innovation also means that policy solutions and approaches evolve over the years in response to changing needs, demands, and attitudes so that the vision for the environment can be realised in a pragmatic and cost-effective manner. In Singapore, practical standards are legislated and enforced. Sound economic analysis is applied and economic pricing are adopted to allocate scarce environment resources. Use of the private sector and market players to bring costs down is encouraged wherever it makes sense.

The right policies will not produce the right results without the awareness, understanding, and support of the people. The public sector must, therefore, forge common goals with the people and private sectors. Only through working together, known as the 3P[11] approach, can sustainable results be achieved.

As we go forward, the pressures of economic and population growth on our environment will become more acute. Major challenges such as tackling climate change and grappling with sustainable development are now key concerns of governments and peoples around the world. Singapore is no different. Recognising the

---

[11] 3P refers to Public Sector, Private Sector, and People Sector.

scale of the challenges, the government has set up two Ministerial Committees to drive efforts to deal with climate change and ensure sustainable development for Singapore.

While the challenges may be new, the fundamental beliefs and principles which have served Singapore well remain unchanged. The country stands firm in the belief of the importance of the environment as a key contributor to ensuring a good quality of life in Singapore. Thinking and planning will continue to be carried out in a long-term and integrated manner, backed up by effective, inter-agency implementation. The private and people sectors will be involved in the government's plans in order to tap their knowledge and expertise. Through these strategies and actions, Singapore will not only be in a better position to overcome the challenges of climate change and sustainable development, but will also be able to create opportunities from necessity.

Sharing the Singapore Environment Experience

The Singapore environment is far from perfect. There are still challenges to be overcome, higher standards to be achieved, as well as greater awareness and better behaviour to be fostered among its residents. But it is an example of the kind of clean environment that can be achieved by any city, and it is a model that can be scalable and replicated in many cities. This is especially pertinent since the United Nations estimates that by 2008, more than half of the world's population live in cities; and between now and 2030, 90% of global population growth will take place in cities. This population explosion in the urban context will put a huge strain on the environment. Nevertheless, if it is properly managed, people living in cities throughout the world should be able to enjoy a good living environment and have access to clean air, sufficient drinking water, and proper sanitation.

The Singapore experience is also useful as Singapore has not always been clean. It was not too long ago when Singapore roads were dirty and its rivers stank, just like in many parts of some developing countries and even some more developed cities. Singapore has shown that a clean, green and blue environment can be achieved within a generation.

CHAPTER 2

Cleaning the Land and Rivers

Tan Yong Soon, Lee Tung Jean and Karen Tan

> *We can make Singapore cleaner by placing community before self. Showing concern for the well-being and cleanliness of the environment is the mark of a mature, refined society. In short, the environment is everybody's responsibility. Everyone has a stake in it. In a society like Switzerland, those who litter are deeply frowned upon. There is great social pressure to conform to good environmental habits. I think there should be more such peer pressure in Singapore. Many litterbugs still do not feel the shame for what they do.*

> Prime Minister Goh Chok Tong, at the Model Environmental
> Workers Award Ceremony, 9 November 1997

The warm and humid equatorial climate in Singapore is highly conducive to the rapid decomposition of refuse and the breeding of vectors or disease-bearing insects such as mosquitoes and flies. In the 1960s, against the backdrop of a high population density of more than 3,000 persons per sq. kilometre (rising to about 15,000 per sq. kilometre in the urban areas), improper disposal of refuse and indiscriminate littering would inevitably create health hazards to the population, and could result in rapid infectious disease transmission.

Keeping Singapore clean was thus one of the foremost challenges that the government had to tackle after the island state gained independence in 1965. It was a challenge born out of necessity.[1] Moreover, during the early days of nationhood, a clean living environment was seen as a boost to the national morale and civic pride of a nascent state, helping to motivate the people to strive for higher standards of performance.

Removing litter is expensive as it involves the labour-intensive task of sweeping roads and drains, as well as subsequently collecting and disposing the litter. With the

---

Permission was granted by the Ministry of the Environment and Water Resources (MEWR) to reproduce Chapter 3 from the book *Clean, Green and Blue: Singapore's Journey Towards Environmental and Water Sustainability*.

[1] This introductory section draws heavily from *Singapore Success Story: Towards a Clean and Healthy Environment* (Singapore: Ministry of Environment, 1973).

cost of litter removal many times that of domestic refuse removal, cost considerations alone would underscore the need to stop or minimise littering.

The government also recognised that improving public cleanliness was a crucial step towards achieving a good standard of public health, which in turn would contribute to a higher quality of life for Singaporeans. In addition to providing a more comfortable living environment for residents, a clean and litter-free Singapore also presents a significant competitive advantage in terms of attracting tourists to visit, foreign talents to work, and businessmen and industrialists to invest in Singapore.

Cleaning the Land

With these motivations, an ambitious plan of action was worked out to transform Singapore into one of the cleanest cities in the world. The formula that has proven to work for Singapore has four components — providing good and reliable public cleansing services and collecting refuse daily; educating the public on the need to keep the environment clean; strict law enforcement; and investing in infrastructural improvements.

Providing Good and Reliable Public Cleansing Services

Since 1961, the Environmental Health Branch, which was then under the Ministry of Health, has been tasked with the responsibility of cleansing the streets. While it may sound straightforward, cleansing the streets was an enormous and highly laborious task in those days. The street cleaners had to make do with primitive and cumbersome methods and tools, pushing large and bulky wooden handcarts to bring their sweepings to the bin points. This was not helped by the prevalence of spitting, indiscriminate littering, and rampant illegal dumping. Although refuse bins were placed in designated open areas in the backlanes and vacant lands, these areas more often than not ended up as public dump sites due to the bad habits of the people. This made the cleansing work all the more difficult.[2]

The street cleaners, also referred to as the "broom brigade", were daily-rated employees (DREs) and were paid a wage for each day of work performed. To this day, every DRE is assigned a "beat", or a length of street that could range from two to five kilometres, and is responsible for ensuring that his assigned beat is free of public health nuisances. Thus, apart from sweeping the streets, he also goes into drains to clear chokages.

---

[2]This subsection draws heavily from *Singapore: My Clean and Green Home* (Singapore: Ministry of Environment, 1997).

Wanting to put in place a reliable system with no lapses in cleansing work, the government amended the labour laws to allow cleaners who worked on a Sunday or public holiday to be given a day off on any other day, in lieu of additional pay. This paved the way for the introduction of a daily public cleansing regime by 1968. Henceforth, the streets were swept and refuse removed every day of the week including Sundays and public holidays. Following the formation of the Ministry of the Environment (ENV), the Environmental Health Branch was transferred to a newly created Environmental Public Health Division (EPHD) in the new Ministry.

Even after the daily cleansing regime was introduced, the government continued to pursue innovative ways to achieve greater operational efficiency. One measure was to decentralise the management of public cleansing services to the district offices under the Environmental Health Department, through integrating the supervision of public cleansing work into the duties of the public health inspectors based in these offices. Because the inspectors were familiar with every nook and cranny of the areas under their charge, they were able to schedule the cleaning work to achieve a high level of performance.

Despite decentralising the management of public cleansing services, a more fundamental problem remained — the difficulty in recruiting DREs as cleaners. The abundance of employment opportunities in the rapidly growing economy meant that many people shunned a cleaner's job, which was seen as a low-grade, menial occupation. As a result, it became necessary to turn to mechanical sweepers.

First brought into Singapore in 1972, mechanical sweepers quickly proved to be an effective substitute for manual labour. Each sweeper is able to take on the work ordinarily performed by thirty to forty workmen. As a result, more of such vehicles were progressively deployed to clean the roads, while ENV continued to source for other labour-saving tools that were lighter and better designed to perform specific tasks such as litter picking.

Although the introduction of mechanical sweepers went a long way towards easing the labour crunch, the ageing DRE workforce soon emerged as a new challenge. By the end of the 1990s, some of the longest serving DREs had worked for more than half a century. The prospect of finding younger workers to replace the retiring DREs was a daunting one. Certainly, judging from the retiring DREs who were still cleaning the same streets decades after their initial employment, the career prospects for their replacements were not rosy.

With this consideration, as well as with the aim of improving operational efficiency, ENV found that it was necessary to deploy mechanical road and pavement sweepers to carry out the cleansing work, as far as the physical conditions of the roads and pavements allowed these machines to be used. This reduced further the number of workmen who had to be recruited. However, the route to mechanisation was not plain sailing. Street fixtures such as lamp posts, signs, and benches obstructed the movement of the mechanical vehicles, particularly the pavement sweepers, such that these areas ended up having to be cleansed manually. To overcome this problem, the relevant government agencies were roped in to ensure that street fixtures and furniture were sited in a way that would minimise obstruction. This facilitated the wider deployment of pavement sweepers. An unexpected positive spin-off engendered by this exercise was that the pavements were also made more user-friendly for the elderly and handicapped on wheelchairs.

The government also decided to outsource the provision of public cleansing services to private contractors to allow private sector involvement and reap the efficiency gains from competition. Today, public cleansing services in two-thirds of the island are provided by private contractors, and there are plans to outsource progressively the remaining part over time.

Educating the Public on the Need to Keep the Environment Clean

In spite of the efficient public cleansing service that has been put in place over the last three decades, the government recognised from the early days that public cleansing alone would not be sufficient to keep the streets clean. While public cooperation and participation are critical to controlling the littering problem, these were also the most difficult to achieve as they required the public to develop a sense of civic consciousness, social responsibility, and discipline. Hence, a two-pronged approach was adopted to cultivate civic consciousness — national public education and law enforcement.[3]

The first national public education effort was a month-long "Keep Singapore Clean" campaign that was launched in October 1968. The campaign sought to educate each individual on the importance of not littering the streets, drains, and public places. This campaign was planned and run by an intersectoral committee headed by the then Minister for Health. The committee comprised representatives from organisations with a broad mass base or those that provided specialised services. These included the chambers of commerce, employers' and trade unions, government ministries (Education, Interior and Defence, and Culture), the Police and the Public Works Department, as well as statutory boards such as the Housing and Development Board, the Public Utilities Board, the Tourist Promotion Board, and the Jurong Town Corporation. It was probably one of the earliest examples of inter-agency collaboration within the government.

The national campaign was a month-long intensive programme of activities, with sustained and extensive coverage by the mass media since this was the most effective channel in reaching out to individuals. Jingles, newsreels, documentaries, filmlets, and slides were broadcast daily over TV and radio, while a roving exhibition was held

---

[3]This subsection draws heavily from *Singapore Success Story.*

to reach out to the rural population. Social pressure was subtly used in the campaign, with "candid camera" style films and photographs of places and establishments found in a bad state of cleanliness, and errant members of the public caught littering the streets.

Children in schools were a key target audience. As they were at an impressionable age, it was hoped that they would internalise the message and form desired habits. Poster design and essay competitions exclusively for school children were organised. Special talks on cleanliness by health officers, inspectors of schools, and principals were made at least twice in each school during the campaign month. Teachers also gave daily reminders against littering and the importance of keeping the premises clean.

To promote mass participation, public and private entities were encouraged to organise their own Keep Singapore Clean activities over and above those at the national level. The most significant were competitions held to select the cleanest offices, shops, restaurants, markets, factories, government buildings, schools, and public vehicles, in which the judges not only picked the ten cleanest premises, but also the ten dirtiest premises. The political leadership provided much support for the campaign. Members of Parliament, together with community leaders, organised activities at the constituency level to get as many of their constituents involved as possible.

While the national public education campaign received resounding responses from all sectors of society, its momentum would be lost unless it was followed up with some concrete action after the campaign. This follow-up action had to be the strict enforcement of the anti-litter laws. However, to provide time for the public to become accustomed to the enforcement, those who were caught littering and indiscriminately disposing refuse during the campaign month were not penalised, but were warned of the possible penalties. The intent was that when the enforcement kicked in after the campaign, there should be no complaints that no adequate warning had been given.

While the majority of the public became aware of the need not to litter and also supported enforcement against litterbugs, there was inevitably a minority who persisted in their bad habits, and on whom the law had to be brought to bear. The government took the unpopular decision to prosecute recalcitrant adult offenders strictly and even published their names in the media. School children offenders were reported to their school principals, who would then discipline them by making them sweep their classrooms or school compounds.

The national public education campaign successfully imprinted indiscriminate littering and dumping in the minds of the public as anti-social acts that would not be condoned.

Riding on this initial success, annual campaigns in the ensuing years were conducted along similar lines, with each focussing on a specific theme in addition to the underlying one of keeping Singapore clean. The theme in 1969, for instance, was "Keep Singapore Clean and Mosquito-Free" to generate public interest and participation in the prevention and control of mosquito breeding so as to contain the mosquito population at a low level.

The "Keep Singapore Clean" campaign took on an additional dimension in 1971 with the launch of the "Tree Planting Day" by then Deputy Prime Minister Dr Goh Keng Swee on Sunday, 7 November at the summit of Mount Faber. It marked the beginning of a tradition that spanned the next two decades, during which Tree Planting Days were held on the first Sunday of each November. The Tree Planting Day was a hallmark event supporting the tropical garden city initiative, which aimed to transform Singapore into a clean as well as green city. In his book, *From Third World to First*, the first Prime Minister Lee Kuan Yew wrote about the drive to make Singapore a tropical garden city. He said that greenery not only raised morale and made people proud, but also demonstrated the efforts put into maintenance. The Tree Planting Day was deliberately set at the beginning of the rainy season in November to minimise watering.

The annual campaigns were significant in many ways. First and foremost, they made Singaporeans aware of the need to be socially responsible and disciplined, and provided an excellent platform to address a number of important public health issues, ranging from communicable diseases and poor food hygiene to mosquito control and pollution. Through the campaigns, the public was informed of public health issues to look out for and changes that were taking place, such as the commencement of daily refuse collection, and the availability of public cleansing services. The campaigns also created avenues of communication between the people and the authorities, and served as a gauge for the public's response to new services and regulations that were introduced.

By the 1980s, the series of annual campaigns had enabled the government to make significant advances in several other aspects of environmental health such as managing the mosquito problem, raising standards of personal hygiene, and controlling air and water pollution. With increasing urbanisation that also improved the physical environment, the focus of the national public education campaign accordingly shifted from broad-based issues to more targeted ones, such as proper disposal of refuse in plastic bags, cleanliness of public toilets, and anti-spitting.

In 1990, the Ministry of the Environment launched the first Clean and Green Week (CGW) as a new approach to environmental education. The CGW incorporated the Tree Planting Day, with tree planting activities still held in every Clean and Green Week.

The CGW was a week-long campaign that occurred in November each year. Apart from continuing to promote an appreciation for a clean and green environment in Singapore, it also sought to increase community awareness for global environmental concerns, as well as encourage their participation in caring for the environment. Consequently, themes such as "Commitment and Responsibility", "Awareness and Action", and "A Better Living Environment" were adopted in different years to make Singaporeans realise that caring for the environment was one aspect of social responsibility.[4]

One particular CGW programme is the Cleanest Estate Competition, which ran from 1995 to 2002. The competition pitted HDB estates against one another in a race to clinch the title of the cleanest estate, thereby encouraging their residents to stop littering and do their part in keeping their surroundings clean. The assessment covered both the physical appearance of the estate, such as the presence of litter in common areas, as well as the social behaviour demonstrated by the residents. Points were deducted for irresponsible acts such as killer litter,[5] vandalism to common property, and the illegal dumping of bulky refuse and other obstructions in common areas.

While the competition was largely successful in the beginning, it became increasingly seen as a battle between town councils managing the estates (including their cleaners) rather than as a healthy competition among the residents. Instead of encouraging the residents to take ownership of keeping their living environment clean, the competition led to town councils competing on the strength of their cleaners. In 2007, the Islandwide Cleanest Estate Competition (ICEC) was introduced, with an emphasis on raising community awareness and promoting social responsibility in keeping the living environment clean, and promoting the residents' sense of ownership over the common areas in the estates. The judging criteria of the ICEC give greater weight to community efforts in promoting social responsibility among residents than to efforts by the cleaners.

Strict Law Enforcement

Although public education has played a significant part in helping Singapore achieve its reputation as a clean and green city, it would be too simplistic to conclude that education alone has had such a transforming effect. No matter how successful public education initiatives may be, there will invariably be a small group of individuals who remain recalcitrant.

Prior to 1968, health officials had been working with legislation that was formulated for a colonial era. However, this would not be adequate in addressing future public health problems since past legislation focussed mainly on preventing the spread of infectious diseases and the control of epidemics, while other challenges such as the

---

[4] *Singapore: My Clean and Green Home*, p. 67.
[5] A term which describes any litter thrown from a high-rise flat that may pose a danger to lives.

cleanliness of the environment were not sufficiently covered. Therefore, a thorough and complete revision of all principal and subsidiary legislation governing matters of public health was necessary.[6]

The revision took into account the prevailing political and social conditions as well as the behaviour and attitudes of the population. It also included a reappraisal of what constituted acceptable health standards or requirements. This culminated in the birth of a new piece of legislation in 1968 that equipped the then Ministry of Health to carry out its battle against litterbugs — the Environmental Public Health Act (EPHA). The EPHA replaced Part IV of the Local Government Integration Ordinance, 1963, which had previously governed the maintenance of public health.

The Act in its fourteen parts covers all fields of environmental health. In particular, Part III (Public Cleansing) deals with the cleansing of streets, the collection and removal of refuse, and the cleanliness of "public places". Comprehensive provisions against littering and the disposal of refuse in public places were introduced. Under the Act, it is an offence to throw or leave behind bottles, paper, food containers, food, and cigarette butts. The spilling of noxious and offensive matter and the dropping or spilling of earth in public is also considered an offence.

The Act further requires the owners and/or developers of flats and industrial complexes to provide at their own expense proper facilities for refuse collection and disposal. Bin centres are now a requirement for building complexes as they provide a convenient point from which refuse can be removed by refuse collection vehicles. Compactors have also been introduced to maximise the storage space in bin centres, as well as improve on the efficiency of transporting the refuse to the incineration plants.

Among the new provisions introduced was a fairly controversial presumption clause, which provided that any litter or refuse found on the frontages of premises would be presumed to be deposited by the occupiers of the premises until proven otherwise. As the burden of proof is on the individuals committing the act, it provided a form of deterrence, and is likely to have also resulted in social pressure against littering.

Most of the offences under the Act carried a fine not exceeding S$500 for the first conviction, and a fine not exceeding S$2,000 for the second and subsequent convictions, which was a hefty sum in the 1960s and 1970s. A more severe penalty was imposed on builders, developers, and contractors who, during the course of their work, left building materials in public places, or failed to take reasonable precautions to prevent people in public places from being injured by falling dust or building fragments.

To achieve the desired outcome of improving public cleanliness, strict legislative provisions had to be accompanied by equally serious enforcement. Much thought was

---

[6]This subsection draws heavily from *Singapore Success Story.*

put into how the legislation should be enforced. The first consideration was that the public should be provided with sufficient means and opportunity to comply with the law, without being overly inconvenienced in their daily routine. For instance, provisions were made for people to have adequate and conveniently sited bins that were emptied and cleaned regularly, to throw their litter.

Second, the new laws were publicised and explained to raise awareness and gain the public's acceptance of the changes in behaviour that were expected of them.

Third, great care was taken to ensure that the legislation was properly spelt out so that the implementation would be uniform and not subject to bargaining. Enforcement officers were expected to be firm, but fair, in enforcing the laws. For instance, if a person unconsciously drops litter and regrets his action, he would be given an opportunity to pick the litter up for proper disposal. However, if the act was deliberate, the person would be penalised. Also, while the maximum penalty or fine for each offence may seem harsh, they are only applied to recalcitrant offenders. For others, lighter penalties, such as the offer of composition, would apply.

Finally, swift action must be taken against recalcitrant offenders who fail to abide by the laws. This is important as environmental offences are often viewed as being negligible when compared with statutory offences. The offender is given an immediate punishment after committing the offence so the deterrent effects of punishment are not lost.

To this end, enforcement procedures for certain offences under the EPHA are designed to be dealt with expeditiously, with minimal paper work. Under this procedure, a littering offender is served a ticket on the spot requiring him to attend a designated Court on a prescribed day. The offender is dealt with summarily if he pleads guilty; the offence is compounded by levying a fine not exceeding S$500. If the fine is paid, no further action will be taken. If the offender claims trial, a date will be fixed for the hearing. Any offender who fails to turn up in court will be arrested on a warrant.

Over the years, the combination of anti-littering laws with fines as penalties and the series of annual "Keep Singapore Clean" campaigns, have helped reduce the littering problem to a large extent. Nonetheless, litter has never been totally eradicated due to the thoughtlessness of litterbugs, especially the "diehards". A Littering Behaviour Survey conducted by the National Environment Agency (NEA) in 2006 found that about 14% of the people interviewed felt that it was acceptable to litter.

The Corrective Work Order (CWO) introduced in 1992, in place of a hefty fine, sets the offender to work in cleaning up the community for periods of up to three hours, subject to a total of twelve hours. This applies to those who are above sixteen years old, are repeat offenders, and/or have committed serious littering offences. The first CWO was performed in 1993 in public places such as parks and beaches, and was subsequently extended to housing estates. Other than being punitive, the CWO regime also had a reparative element as cleaning up housing estates was a means to increase the offenders' awareness of the impact of littering, and to experience the difficulties faced by the cleaners.

Not surprisingly, the CWO regime attracted its fair share of controversy, with many seeing it as a shaming tool. While the majority accepted the CWO as an additional punitive option, there were some who felt that the initiative was introduced ahead of its time, with the public in Singapore still relatively unreceptive to the idea of performing work in lieu of a financial penalty, unlike in developed countries where such punishment was more common. Notwithstanding this, the government stood its ground.

This was not an altogether easy decision. However, to realise the vision of a clean Singapore, the government was prepared to make the unpopular choice by adhering to strict enforcement against littering. This would be borne out in the longer term, when there are clean streets and public places for all to enjoy.

Investing in Infrastructural Improvements — Re-settling Hawkers

Investing in infrastructural improvements has gone a long way in helping Singapore to address a major public health challenge — the unsanitary and hygiene problems posed by itinerant hawkers.

In the post-World War II period, unemployment was a widespread problem. Many unemployed people took to the streets, literally. Street hawking became a thriving trade because the entry barrier was low. The good income attracted many poorly educated individuals with little capital and skills.

The number of street hawkers soon grew, with many congregating in convenient open areas within housing estates, and along major traffic routes. Although they were unsightly, the government then adopted a liberal attitude towards street hawking as it not only encouraged entrepreneurship, but was also a means for the unemployed to earn an honest living.

By the late 1960s, rapid industrial and economic development followed Singapore's independence. The abundance of employment opportunities saw more family members going to work and taking their meals outside. The demand for cheap and convenient hawker food grew, and consequently, many more people were drawn to the lucrative hawking trade. It was estimated that at one stage, hawkers numbered close to 25,000, or nearly one in 100 of Singapore's population.

The rapid proliferation of street hawkers soon posed a major public health problem. Street hawkers lacked proper equipment and amenities (such as refrigeration and clean tap water) and many did not observe good personal and food hygiene. The food was mainly prepared in makeshift stalls, with no direct access to clean water for cooking and washing of utensils. Consuming hawker food was often associated with food-borne disease outbreaks such as cholera and typhoid. Those peddling perishable food items such as cut fruits, cold drinks, and ice cream were particularly culpable, as they often used contaminated water and ice.

Without a refuse management system in place, food waste generated from street hawkers was indiscriminately dumped onto streets, or thrown into drains and waterways, giving rise to severe chokages and water pollution. The market produce hawkers were also a problem, as they left behind vegetable waste, poultry droppings, fish cuttings, and other litter on the roads. These invariably found their way into the waterways and streams.

The accumulation of waste gave rise to the proliferation of vectors such as rats, flies, and mosquitoes. Street cleansing works were practically impossible to carry out because roads and drains were obstructed by the makeshift structures of the vendors and their paraphernalia. The noise generated by hawkers hawking their fare was also a distraction to nearby schools and public institutions.

It did not take long before the appearance of the city deteriorated. The presence of hawkers in almost every street, footway, and backlane was a blight to the cityscape. The dilapidated makeshift structures put up by the hawkers caused many parts of the city to resemble slums. The negative externalities went beyond just public health, with many able-bodied adults preferring street hawking, which was perceived to be a lucrative trade, to joining the workforce to serve in more economically efficient sectors.

It soon became imperative that effective policies and measures be put in place to curb the uncontrolled proliferation of street hawking. As a step towards achieving this, an island-wide census of street hawkers was carried out between December 1968 and February 1969. The government then decided on two courses of action — a short-term and a long-term solution.

The short-term solution involved the licensing of street hawkers and relocating them to temporary sites. This effectively limited the number of street hawkers so that their activities could be properly circumscribed. As this move was not popular with street hawkers, the licensing exercise was carried out in close consultation with the Citizens Consultative Committee members. Because of the political repercussions, a committee was set up to decide on the policies governing licences and to consider complaints and appeals.

A total of 24,000 hawkers were licensed in the exercise. Of these, 6,000 were operating in markets while the remaining 18,000 were operating on the streets. These hawkers were issued with temporary street-hawking licences and resited to side streets, back lanes, side lanes, and car parks, where washing areas connected to the sewers were provided wherever possible. New licences were issued only to those who were genuinely suffering financial hardship. The Environmental Public Health (Hawkers) Regulation and relevant sections of the Environmental Health Act regulating the activities of the hawkers were strictly enforced to ensure that stall sites and their surroundings were kept clean at all times.

The licensing exercise was to pave the way for identifying *bona fide* hawkers who would ultimately be relocated into permanent premises. This represented the long-term solution — to house all street hawkers in purpose-built buildings within five years. This was kickstarted with an initial provision of S$5 million to the Housing and Development Board in 1971 for the construction of permanent hawker centres and markets, which served the dual objectives of resiting street hawkers and providing amenities for residents of new towns.

Each market cum hawker centre comprised a market section and a cooked food section. The centres were provided with essential amenities such as proper sewage connections, piped water and electricity, and bulk bin centres for the disposal of refuse. The cooked food stalls were also compartmentalised, and lined with glazed tiles. Fixed tables and stools for customers became a common feature in all hawker centres. Ceiling fans and toilet facilities were also available for the comfort and convenience of the patrons.

Riding on the initial success, the government embarked on a massive programme to build markets and hawker centres outside the new towns. To accelerate the pace of building such centres, a policy was introduced in which the permission for land redevelopment use was granted to a developer, on the condition that a hawker centre was built to house the street hawkers affected by the redevelopment.

The resettlement of the street hawkers was not without its problems. First, all hawkers along the same street would need to be resettled *en masse* to a nearby location, while ensuring that no new unlicensed hawkers reoccupy the vacated street. This necessitated working closely with the Police. In spite of the better environment, many street hawkers were reluctant to move into the centres as business was deemed to be better on the main streets where there was more human traffic. To encourage street hawkers to relocate into the newly built centres, the rent for stalls was deliberately kept at the same level as that levied on street hawkers. At that time, the need to recover the costs of building and maintaining these hawker centres from the hawkers was the least of the government's considerations when deciding on the rental to be levied. The hawkers also had to be convinced of the benefits of operating in a hawker centre, such as the availability of utilities, and not being subjected to the vagaries of the weather.

To clear the entire nation of street hawkers, the government worked closely with Members of Parliament, grassroots leaders, and the hawkers themselves. In many cases, Members of Parliament themselves presided over the balloting of stalls, to ensure that this was perceived as a fair and transparent way of stall allocation. The entire resiting programme was successfully completed after about fifteen years in 1985. Today, there are 111 government markets cum hawker centres, housing about 15,000 stalls.

The earlier generations of markets and hawker centres were constructed with the main purpose of providing a permanent site for the resettlement of street hawkers.

Practicality was the key consideration, with little attention paid to their façade. By the late 1990s, most of these centres were at least twenty years old. Many of them were in poor physical condition, which made maintenance a big challenge. Visually, these centres had also not kept up with the rejuvenation that had been taking place in the housing estates where they were located.

In 2001, the Environment Ministry, therefore, decided to embark on the Hawker Centres Upgrading Programme (HUP), committing more than S$420 million over ten years. The upgrading works range from complete demolition and rebuilding of the centre to retrofitting such as re-tiling, installation of new tables and stools, widening of passageways, replacement of utility infrastructure such as sewer pipes, rewiring, improvement to the ventilation, bin centres, and toilets, provision of improved lighting, and optimising the space utilisation with better layout.

The newly upgraded centres boast features such as better ventilation and lighting, open courtyards, and outdoor dining areas. They also have a more visually pleasant building façade and finishings, as well as flexible seating arrangements. The toilets have been refurbished, not only to improve them, but to make maintenance easier. The upgrading has not only benefited the stallholders, but the patrons as well, who now have a more pleasant and congenial ambience to enjoy their meals. As of 2008, 63 out of a total of 110 eligible centres have been upgraded under the programme.

Hawker centres may have been born out of necessity. But today, many say they provide the best eating experience in Singapore. In fact, dining in a hawker centre has achieved international acclaim, and was featured in Patricia Schultz's book in 2003 — *1,000 Places to See before You Die.*[7]

The Singapore River and Kallang Basin Clean-up

Much of what pollutes the land will eventually pollute the rivers. Any rubbish on the road, if not cleared, will be washed by rain into the drains, and from there to the culverts, then on to the canals, and eventually into the rivers. The cleaning up of the Singapore River and Kallang Basin serves to highlight the importance of keeping the land clean. By doing so, the high-quality living environment on land can extend to the waters as well.

The Singapore River, the disembarkation point for many early settlers and the birthplace of Singapore's commercial hub, has been associated with the traditional trading and business activities of Singapore for more than a century. Over the years, the Singapore River, together with the Kallang River, which are both waterways with

---

[7] Patricia Schultz, *1,000 Places to See Before You Die* (Kindle Edition, 2003), pp. 495–96.

urban catchments, became highly polluted due to population growth, urbanisation, industrial expansion, and the uncontrolled discharge of all forms of waste and pollution.

From the early 1800s, as more and more settlers arrived on Singapore's shores, many of them found accommodation along the quays and riverbanks. Some of their activities, such as dumping garbage into the water and using the rivers for sewage disposal, probably marked the beginnings of a river that was soon to become extremely polluted. Early industries that were sited along the banks of the Singapore River, such as processing of gambier, sago, and seaweed, also contributed to the pollution.[8]

By the second half of the century, the importance of these industries had diminished, but the escalating problems of pollution did not end. Port-related activities along the Singapore and Kallang Rivers, including warehouses and bumboats that carried goods from the large ships in the harbour, flourished. Ship building and repairs were also carried out at the Kallang Basin. The by-products of these activities, namely oil, sullage water, and solid waste, were either disposed of directly into the rivers, or eventually found their way to the rivers via the drains.[9]

Markets sprang up in the riverside community, where perishables were sold. As they were adjacent to the river, any leftovers were conveniently discarded into the water. Street hawkers also set up shop right by the river, often dumping used water and food into the drains or even directly into the river. Squatters set up homes along the river without sewage facilities. Some had overhanging latrines that would discharge waste directly into streams. Backyard trades and cottage industries in these unsewered premises aggravated the problem. Their trade effluent was also discharged into drains. Pig and duck farms proliferated, adding animal waste to the cocktail of pollution in the rivers.[10]

These rivers were essentially open sewers and became extremely polluted by the 1960s. With office towers and hotels being built along a newly created central business district, there was a pressing need to clean up the rivers.

At the same time, water reserves grew insufficient. The few reservoirs could not hold sufficient water to serve the needs of the expanding population which had reached one million by the 1950s. Water supply for the island had to be imported mainly from the Tebrau River in Johor, as local water sources were inadequate. A drought in 1963 demonstrated the severity of the situation, with local reservoirs

---

[8] Joan Hon, *Tidal Fortunes: A Story of Change: The Singapore River and Kallang Basin* (Singapore: Landmark Books, 1990), p. 27.

[9] COBSEA Workshop on Cleaning up of Urban Rivers, Ministry of the Environment, Singapore & UNEP, 1986.

[10] *Clean Rivers: The Cleaning up of Singapore River and Kallang Basin* (Singapore: Ministry of the Environment, 1987), pp. 16–22.

drying up and the volume of water in the Tebrau River dropping dramatically. Water rationing had to be imposed on the people in Singapore. With high density housing projects springing up to accommodate an exploding population, efforts to ensure the provision of a good water supply and maintain cleanliness were strained to the limit. Hence, a programme to build more local reservoirs and maintain the cleanliness of the water supply at all costs became a matter of utmost importance for the future of Singapore.[11]

It was apt that in declaring the Upper Peirce Reservoir open on 27 February 1977, then Prime Minister Lee Kuan Yew said, "It should be a way of life to keep the water clean, to keep every stream, every culvert, every rivulet free from unnecessary pollution. In ten years, let us have fishing in the Singapore River and fishing in the Kallang River. It can be done."[12]

What was involved was no less than unclogging the way Singapore worked. Engineering solutions to remove pollution could not adequately address the pollution. Rather, the very causes and sources of pollution needed to be tackled. The river was a workplace and a home for the many hawkers and squatters lining its banks. It was not enough simply to prevent them from dirtying the river. They had to be given an alternative way of life where possible.[13]

Since livelihoods were at stake, cleaning up the river meant giving people a different lifeline to the future. Squatters and farmers had to be resettled. Backyard trades and industries had to be relocated. Street hawkers had to be resited. These meant building houses, industrial workshops, and food centres, in addition to developing proper sewage infrastructure. To free the river from pollution meant, in many ways, constructing a new Singapore through which a rescued river could flow. The physical task was gigantic, but it was only one aspect of a larger human drama.[14]

A Master Plan for the cleaning up of the Singapore River and Kallang Basin was drawn up for the purpose. The draft plan indicated that the Singapore River and Kallang Basin were the two most badly polluted catchments in the city. The Kallang Basin was drained by the Kallang River, Bukit Timah-Rochor Canal, Whampoa River, Geylang River and Pelton Canal. The plan also noted the scope of the challenge:

> In general, the pollution problem is three-fold. In areas where pollution control facil-
> ities have been provided, we have to ensure that these facilities are used and efficiently
> operated. In some areas where such facilities have not been provided, but are possible

---

[11] Hon, *Tidal Fortunes*, p. 37.

[12] *Clean Rivers*, p. 8.

[13] *Singapore: My Clean and Green Home*, p. 30.

[14] Ibid., p. 31.

with redevelopment, we need to know what plans there are for redevelopment and if need be, to spur them on and set targets. In the remaining areas where it is either impossible or economically not feasible to provide such facilities (e.g. for roadside hawkers, boat colonies, etc.), we need to have a plan of action to control, minimise or eliminate these sources. The main objective is to restore the Kallang Basin and Singapore River to the extent that marine life can thrive in the water. Organic and inorganic pollution in the form of solid and liquid waste should be prevented or minimised.[15]

As the catchments made up some 30 per cent of Singapore's area, it was a challenge for the planners, who had to piece together an overview of the entire range of pollutive activities in the catchments. These included pig and duck farms, squatter huts, backyard industries, and hawkers, some of which were actually located quite a distance from the rivers.[16]

The draft plan revealed the enormity of the task, the undertaking of which would not be restricted to the departments under the Ministry of the Environment, such as environmental health, sewerage, drainage, and hawkers, but also involved departments and agencies under the Ministry of National Development (MND), Ministry of Trade and Industry (MTI), Ministry of Communications & Information (MICA) and Ministry of Law (MinLaw). These agencies included the Housing and Development Board (HDB), Urban Redevelopment Authority (URA), Jurong Town Corporation (JTC), Primary Production Department (PPD), Port of Singapore Authority (PSA), Public Works Department (PWD) and Parks and Recreation Department.[17]

Approximately 46,000 unsewered squatters were affected by the clean-up exercise. The Kallang Basin was very heavily squattered with about 42,000 squatters in its five catchments, while the Singapore River Catchment had about 4,000 squatters. This included about 26,000 residential families, 610 pig farmers, and 2,800 backyard trades and industries.[18]

The squatters were resettled under a Resettlement Policy, which was introduced in the 1960s. Under the policy, all persons and business establishments affected by resettlement were to be offered rehousing and compensation. However, the benefits only applied to Singaporeans. Some of the squatters were not Singaporeans and hence were not entitled to resettlement benefits. If they were forcibly evicted, they could become destitute vagabonds sleeping on the sidewalks. These were sensitive issues which had to be resolved in a way that would not make the government appear uncaring and callous. Whenever possible, non-Singaporean squatters were allowed

---

[15] Hon, *Tidal Fortunes*, p. 42.

[16] Ibid., p. 43.

[17] *Clean Rivers*, p. 24.

[18] COBSEA Workshop on Cleaning up of Urban Rivers.

to rent flats. Another problem arising from the resettlement process was the question of whether the squatters were on private land or State Land. If they were on State Land, the government could readily resettle them and then spruce up the vacant land. However, if they were on private land, the government had to acquire it, which was not a popular move. The resettlement of squatters was thus a slow process.[19]

The 610 pig farms, as well as 500 duck farms located within the Kallang Basin, were initially relocated to Punggol. However, by the mid-1980s, to eradicate such pollutive and unhygienic activities, as well as conserve Singapore's limited land and water resources for housing and industry, the decision was made to phase these activities out completely.[20]

In 1971, for reasons of hygiene, the hawker resettlement programme was introduced, in which street hawkers were moved to purpose-built hawker centres and markets. The river clean-up project accelerated the programme. Close to 5,000 street hawkers within the catchments were relocated to markets and hawker centres, such as those at Boat Quay, Empress Place, and Chinatown. So that the hawkers would not lose their clientele, the new food centres were built very near the streets where the hawkers were operating. Vegetable wholesalers who had been traditionally operating on the five-foot ways, streets, and vacant land without proper facilities were also relocated to the Pasir Panjang Wholesale Market.[21]

To prevent human waste, sullage water, and other forms of waste from being discharged into the rivers by bumboat operators and their families staying on board the vessels, cargo handling, storage, and mooring facilities were established at Pasir Panjang for the purpose of relocating the lighters there. By 1983, the lighters were completely relocated. The decision to do so was carefully weighed, given its potential impact on Singapore's entrepôt trade. The conclusion was that the phasing out of lighter transport was not undesirable as it would mean moving from a two-transfer system to a one-transfer system where vessels worked alongside wharves, simplifying the process. Initially, there were many complaints about the lighter anchorage at Pasir Panjang, with claims that the waves were stronger there than in the sheltered water of the rivers, and that it was too far away, as most lighter operators lived in the Chinatown area. To make the move less painful, a breakwater was built to buffer the lighters from the waves, and a canteen set up to provide food. The canteen also served to reduce the practice of cooking on the boats and throwing the resulting waste into the water. Four years later, the lightermen were quite happy to be in Pasir Panjang despite their initial complaints.[22]

---

[19] Hon, *Tidal Fortunes*, p. 73.

[20] Regional Workshop on Area-Wide Integration of Crop-Livestock Activities, FAO Regional Office, Bangkok, Thailand, 1998.

[21] Hon, *Tidal Fortunes*, p. 93.

[22] Ibid., p. 91, and COBSEA Workshop on Cleaning up of Urban Rivers.

There were also some sixty-six boatbuilders and repairers in the Kallang Basin catchment. To remove them in one fell swoop would have been too harsh. To let them vanish through attrition would have taken too long. Thus, a compromise was struck. The larger boatyards were required to upgrade their operations to comply with anti-pollution requirements. Where possible, neighbouring boatyards were also advised to join these larger yards so that pollution control facilities could be provided in a more economical and technically feasible manner. Small boatyards, which were unable to upgrade their operations and comply with pollution control requirements but were otherwise viable, were offered alternative sites in Jurong.[23]

Rubbish and flotsam that had accumulated in the rivers and along their banks were dredged and removed after these primary sources of pollution had been addressed. During the month-long removal operation, more than 260 tonnes of rubbish were collected and disposed of. In 1986, the PWD improved and tiled the riverside walkway along the Singapore River, while the Parks and Recreation Department carried out landscaping along the riverbanks. In the same year, the Environment Ministry commenced physical improvement works at the Kallang Basin. The river bed was dredged to remove the mud at the bottom and one metre of sand was put in. Certain sections of the Kallang Basin were also covered with sand to create aesthetically pleasing sandy banks.[24]

The clean-up cost the government nearly S$300 million, excluding resettlement compensation. In addition to addressing the sources of pollution, engineering measures were also used to prevent the entry of further pollution into the river. For instance, drains in litter-prone areas were covered with slabs, vertical gratings were installed at selected outlet drains leading to main canals and rivers, and float booms were installed across rivers and canals to trap inorganic litter, such as plastic bags and bottles.[25]

The entire nation rejoiced when the programme was completed in September 1987. The river could flow freely. Its banks, once cluttered with boatyards, backyard trades and squatters, were transformed, almost unbelievably, into attractive riverside walkways and landscaped parks. Fish and other forms of aquatic life returned to the river. So did the people, to relax along the shores or play in the waters of a riverine stretch that Singapore had reclaimed as its own.[26]

The team behind the clean-up was led by the Permanent Secretary of Environment, Lee Ek Tieng, who would go on to become Head of the Civil Service.

---

[23] Hon, *Tidal Fortunes,* p. 82, and COBSEA Workshop on Cleaning up of Urban Rivers.

[24] *Clean Rivers,* p. 28.

[25] Naidu Ratnala Thulaja, "Clean Rivers Education Programme and Clean Rivers Commemoration" (2004). Retrieved from http://infopedia.nl.sg/articles/SIP_398_2004-12-23.html.

[26] *Singapore: My Clean and Green Home,* p. 32.

He and nine others were each awarded a gold medal by the Prime Minister for their efforts in cleaning up the Singapore River.[27]

On completion of the clean-up in 1987, the Environment Ministry launched the Clean Rivers Education Programme to educate the public on the massive efforts taken to clean up Singapore's waterways, and urge them to act responsibly and do their part in contributing to this effort.[28]

In a television interview shortly after the clean-up, then Prime Minister Lee Kuan Yew said:

> In 20 years, it is possible that there could be breakthroughs in technology, both anti-pollution and filtration, and then we dam up or put a barrage at the mouth of the Marina — the neck that joins the sea — and we will have a huge freshwater lake. The advantages are obvious. One: a large strategic reserve of water — fresh water — for use in emergency: a drought, or some such period. Second, it will help flood control because at high tides — exceptional high tides — which happens about two periods a year, if they coincide with heavy rain, the three rivers and canals will flood parts of the city. Now with the barrage, we can control the flooding. And with the barrage, the water level can be held steady. We need never [sic] have low tides. So the recreational use and scenic effect would be greatly improved. And it is possible in another 20 years, and therefore, we should keep on improving the quality of the water.[29]

The clean-up of the Singapore River and the rivers in the Kallang Basin had become a model for other rivers and set in motion a process to realise the vision of creating a reservoir in the city. Today, that vision has become reality. With the construction of the Marina Barrage, Singapore will have a new source of freshwater, an ability to alleviate flooding in the city, as well as a new venue for recreation and revitalisation. As it was said, "It can be done."

---

[27] *Recipients*   *Appointment in 1987*
Lee Ek Tieng   Permanent Secretary, Ministry of the Environment (ENV)
Tan Gee Paw   Director of Environmental Engineering Division, ENV
Daniel Wang Nan Chee Commissioner of Public Health Division, ENV
Loh Ah Tuan   Deputy Commissioner of Public Health Division, ENV
Chiang Kok Meng   Head of Pollution Control Department, ENV
T. K. Pillai   Head of Drainage Department, ENV
Tan Teng Huat   Head of Sewerage Department, ENV
Wong Keng Mun   Head of Hawkers Department, ENV
George Yeo   Deputy Head of Environmental Health Department, ENV
Chen Hung   Former Director of Environmental Engineering Division, ENV
[28] Thulaja, "Clean Rivers Education Programme and Clean Rivers Commemoration".
[29] Hon, *Tidal Fortunes*, p. 104.

Conserving Singapore's Natural Heritage[30]

Keeping the land and rivers clean not only has benefits for public health and results in a higher quality living environment, but also supports efforts to conserve Singapore's natural heritage through preventing its natural ecosystems from being polluted.

Singapore's conservation model is one that enables environmental sustainability in a small urban setting, balancing growth with conservation. Areas which are representative of key indigenous ecosystems are legally protected by the government as gazetted nature reserves. There are four nature reserves in Singapore, namely the Bukit Timah Nature Reserve and the Central Catchment Nature Reserve which is made up of primary and mature secondary forests and a fresh water swamp; the Sungei Buloh Wetland Reserve which conserves a mangrove forest and is also a bird sanctuary; and the Labrador Nature Reserve which comprises coastal secondary vegetation and a rocky shore. Together, these cover more than 3,000 hectares or about 4.5% of Singapore's land area. Outside of the nature reserves, Singapore's network of green spaces, park connectors, and water bodies cover a further 4.5% of its land area. Through careful management, these areas are also optimised to enhance urban biodiversity. Even Singapore's offshore landfill, Pulau Semakau, defying the common stereotype of a landfill as a dirty, unpleasant dump, is a green natural environment thriving with rich biodiversity. The island is home to over 13 hectares of mangroves, which shelter a thriving community of flora and fauna. A coral nursery has also been established off Semakau to maximise the survival of naturally occurring corals, in which coral fragments are grown for transplanting to existing coral reef habitats.

Through these conservation efforts, Singapore can count itself a city which is rich in biodiversity despite being a small, island city state. For instance, Singapore has some 360 species of birds, which is slightly more than 60% of the 568 species in the United Kingdom. It has eleven out of twenty-three seagrass species found in the Indo-Pacific region. Singapore also has over 250 species of reef-forming hard corals that account for about 30% of the world's hard coral species — there are more coral species per hectare of reef in Singapore waters than there are in the Great Barrier Reef.

Vector-borne Diseases

The systems and processes that the government had put in place in cleaning up the land and waterways also greatly benefited Singapore's environmental public health, particularly in the control of infectious disease transmission. First, the resettlement of street hawkers into purpose-built food centres has minimised the likelihood of

---

[30] Information from NParks.

food being prepared in unsanitary conditions, thus contributing to a low incidence of food-borne diseases and food poisoning. Second, the rodent population has been kept under control with improvements in refuse management practices that deprived these vectors of food sources. This has helped to keep the incidence of rodent-borne diseases low all these years.

Perhaps the most significant impact that a high standard of public cleanliness has made is in helping Singapore tackle the threat of mosquito-borne diseases, since mosquito breeding is often closely associated with poor sanitary conditions. Malaria, in particular, was the most threatening vector-borne disease in Singapore before World War I, and again during and soon after World War II. Fortunately, the rapid urbanisation that took place in the 1970s saw the progressive displacement of hilly and swampy areas that were once conducive to the breeding of the *Anopheles* mosquitoes, the vectors for malaria.

While this had, to a large extent, reduced the availability of breeding sources for the vector, it would not have been possible to bring the disease well under control if not for the intensified integrated disease control programme. This was backed by a well-established epidemiological surveillance regime that was capable of detecting and eliminating the focus of transmission quickly, thus preventing the re-establishment of endemicity. Through these relentless efforts, Singapore's malaria control programme finally achieved success on 22 November 1982, when the name of "Singapore" was entered in the World Health Organization (WHO) Official Register of areas where malaria has been eradicated.[31]

This "malaria-free" status has remained till this very day, even though Singapore is situated in a region that is still endemic for the disease. Today, although Singapore has continued to maintain a low incidence rate for malaria, with a majority of the cases imported, the government still maintains a close vigilance on the disease and the vectors that are present in some poorly-drained areas so as to ensure that the disease has no chance of staging a comeback.

The threats from mosquito-borne diseases were, however, far from over. After indigenous malaria was eradicated, Singapore was soon confronted by a different mosquito-borne disease — dengue, whose vectors, the *Aedes* mosquitoes, are highly adaptable and habituated to an urbanised, domestic environment. They commonly breed in stagnant water found in places such as roof gutters, ornamental flower pot plates, and domestic water containers in houses. The close proximity of their breeding habitats to human hosts and the presence of the virus in the country and the region

---

[31] K. L. Chan, *Singapore's Dengue Haemorrhagic Fever Control Programme: A Case Study on the Successful Control of Aedes Aegypti and Aedes Albopictus Using Mainly Environmental Measures as a Part of Integrated Vector Control* (Southeast Asian Medical Information Center, 1985).

also means that people are always at risk of becoming infected. Since the *Aedes* mosquitoes breed in relatively clean water, dengue will continue to be around in the foreseeable future.

Being located in dengue-endemic Southeast Asia, Singapore is not spared from this public health threat. By the mid-1960s, dengue had replaced malaria as the most menacing mosquito-borne disease in Singapore. A Vector Control Unit (VCU) was set up in 1966 under the then Ministry of Health to develop a comprehensive system of dengue control, with source reduction as the mainstay of control. The government also realised that to maintain adequate control after the initial reduction, it was necessary to involve the people and this could only be achieved through public education supported by law enforcement.[32]

Thus, in 1968, the DDBIA (Destruction of Disease Bearing Insects Act) was introduced to replace the outmoded Mosquito Ordinance that was enacted during the rule of the British colonial government. The DDBIA gave the government more teeth for tighter and more effective control over persons who intentionally or unintentionally propagated disease-bearing insects. Following its enactment, the DDBIA was enforced on a limited scale against persons who bred mosquitoes. In the following year, a countrywide, month-long "Keep Singapore Clean and Mosquito Free" Campaign was launched to educate the public and elicit the widest possible community participation in mosquito control. For the first time, the public was made aware of the seriousness of vector-borne diseases, and that they had a responsibility to act in order to curb its propagation. With the implementation of an integrated system of *Aedes* mosquito control encompassing public education, law enforcement, and source reduction, Singapore was able to achieve long-term suppression of the mosquito vector population, with a concomitant improvement in the disease situation from the mid-1970s.[33]

In 1998, the DDBIA was replaced by the Control of Vectors and Pesticides Act, which strengthened the powers of the government in the destruction of vectors and the control of vector-borne diseases. The Act also provided for the control of the sale and use of pesticides and vector repellents, as well as the registration, licensing, and certification of persons engaged in vector control work, to raise the professional standards of these personnel.

Since the start of the 1990s, Singapore, like many countries worldwide, has been experiencing a resurgence of dengue. In the local context, the interplay of the following factors could have fuelled this trend. First, rapid urbanisation taking place in the country and region has favoured the breeding and propagation of the mosquito

---

[32] K. T. Goh, ed., *Dengue in Singapore* (Singapore: Institute of Environmental Epidemiology, Ministry of the Environment, 1998).

[33] Ibid.

vectors, contributing to a global resurgence of dengue. Next, increased global travel has greatly accelerated the rate of importation of dengue virus. Furthermore, while the decades of intensive vector control operations had successfully suppressed the mosquito population, it has paradoxically also resulted in a lower immunity among the local population. This means that the population has become more susceptible to infection, and transmission can be easily sustained, despite a relatively low *Aedes* mosquito population here. The problem is further compounded by the presence of four different dengue virus serotypes.

Although the odds were clearly stacked against Singapore, NEA pressed on relentlessly with the integrated approach to dengue control. Source reduction continued to be the primary focus of NEA's mosquito control strategy as it is only through removing the source of breeding in outbreaks and, more importantly, during the inter-epidemic months (through the intensive source reduction exercises) that there is a better chance of breaking and preventing disease transmission, given that a dengue vaccine was unlikely to be available any time soon.

Dengue surveillance in Singapore evolved into an integrated approach that includes both passive and active case surveillance from the medical community, entomological surveillance in the field, and virological surveillance in the laboratory. First, accurate and timely "ground intelligence" is gathered. While some 500 field officers collect field entomological data, perform source reduction, and enforce against mosquito breeding in premises to reduce the incidence of *Aedes* breedings, the Environmental Health Institute (EHI) provides virological surveillance and identification of mosquito species collected. This information is fed into a Geographical Information System (GIS) that tracks the spatial and temporal distribution of reported dengue cases obtained from the Ministry of Health. The GIS promptly detects any unusual clustering of cases, which then triggers off epidemiological investigation to determine the source of infection, and concurrently, the ramping up of intensive search-and-destroy operations to eliminate these sources, thus abating disease transmission.

Second, proactive surveillance and source reduction is practised. Source reduction is no longer confined to just the locality or period with a clustering of reported cases. A pre-emptive approach is adopted instead, utilising information about the spatial and temporal distribution of the mosquito population, the geographical distribution of the predominant dengue virus serotype that is circulating in the local population, as well as the ambient temperature and the susceptibility of the population in a particular locality. This allows for the stratification of different localities based on their potential for outbreak into focus areas thereby allowing prioritisation in the deployment of manpower to carry out pre-emptive source reduction, according to the assessed risk level. Such proactive surveillance allows the problem to be nipped in the bud before it has a chance to escalate into an outbreak situation.

Third, NEA focuses on improving operational effectiveness. NEA's environmental health officers, having operated on the ground for years, are highly attuned to seeking out mosquito breeding habitats. In fact, many of them have also acquired the knack for picking out unusual breeding habitats, and this has continuously allowed transmission to be interrupted quickly in most clusters. Last, but not least, NEA adopts a system of continuous follow-up and assessment. Following the successful abatement of transmission in each cluster, NEA continues to survey the cluster area for mosquito activity for up to two weeks, to ensure that the sources of infection are completely eliminated and transmission has abated.

Recognising that tackling the mosquito problem cannot be accomplished by the government alone, NEA has actively continued to encourage the participation of the community and other stakeholders through a combination of intensive public education and community outreach campaigns. Over the years, NEA has built a network of grassroots volunteers who help to disseminate dengue prevention messages to residents in the locality of an outbreak, so as to ensure that transmission is curbed in the shortest possible time. Through the Inter-Agency Dengue Taskforce, the other government land agencies come together to strengthen and intensify mosquito control efforts.

Despite being held up by WHO[34] as having one of the most successful dengue control programmes in the world, it is not possible to eradicate completely the mosquitoes that transmit dengue. Moreover, because Singapore has succeeded in keeping the mosquito vector population low, more intensive vector control efforts are likely to yield only marginal improvements in the disease situation. Consequently, new approaches that are based on scientific understanding of both the vectors and the viruses are needed to achieve a further breakthrough.

Leveraging Scientific Research to Control Diseases

The VCU that was set up in 1966 had functioned as an advisory and research body, providing laboratory support services for Singapore's vector control operations. The Unit was later renamed the Vector Control and Research Department (VCRD), and in February 1992, took over vector control operations to streamline the coordination and lines of commands between planning, research, and operations. However, scientific research on vector-borne diseases was mostly carried out

---

[34] Besides the risk of death, dengue causes ill health and serious adverse social and economic losses. The disease is often times a prominent news. The currently available tools in prevention and control of dengue even though not perfect have known to be effective for more than two decades. Dengue control efforts work if it becomes everyone's concern. Several countries have succeeded in controlling the growing menace of emergence of dengue. Examples are Singapore and Cuba. However, the present dengue control programmes in some countries are inadequately resourced. WHO South East Asian Regional Office, Press Release, 14 February 2007.

on an *"ad hoc* need-to" basis, with studies commissioned from research institutions, universities as well as hospital laboratories. Apart from these studies, some laboratory studies on vector biology and behaviour were conducted in an in-house laboratory under the VCRD. Other than this, research on vector-borne diseases in Singapore was relatively unstructured, as it was felt that outsourcing such research to the private sector was more cost-effective than building up in-house research capability.

The highly competitive biomedical research landscape meant that individual research institutions had their own research focusses and priorities. These were often not aligned with the research priorities of the government agencies concerned with public health. Yet, from the government's perspective, building up capabilities in public health research was necessary to fulfil a national need. Having such capability would enable the government to be better prepared to react to and handle outbreaks as well as the emergence of new viruses, and more importantly, to detect the introduction of these diseases into Singapore, without relying on laboratories overseas.

The development of this capability was made possible with the establishment of the Environmental Health Institute (EHI) in April 2002 as a department under the Environmental Public Health Division of NEA. The mandate for EHI was clear — to support the division's role as the national authority responsible for vector control, through carrying out research on vectors, vector-borne pathogens, and their control. The Institute carries the mission of ensuring that Singapore's environmental public health standards are not compromised in the face of a growing population, increased urbanisation, and emerging infectious diseases of environmental health concern.

The vision is for EHI to leverage scientific research and the latest biomedical technologies to understand better the vectors and the diseases they transmit, with a special focus on the *Aedes* mosquitoes and dengue. The Institute also conducts risk assessments of the vulnerability of the local population to vector-borne diseases, and applied research to develop new, innovative, and cost-effective disease prevention strategies.

Attracting the right talent to join the Institute was an important first step. With the rapidly growing biomedical industry, there was no lack of employment opportunities for biomedical researchers. However, it was critical to attract talented individuals who were interested in carving out a career in public health research and prepared to cast their lot with a nascent set-up that had no track record, and hence no efforts were spared in recruitment. From a humble beginning of fewer than twenty employees, the Institute has grown to a staff strength of forty in 2008, with nine researchers holding postgraduate qualifications, and twenty-five with tertiary qualifications.

Over time, research at the Institute has also shifted from an initial focus on vector-borne diseases, centring on dengue fever and Japanese encephalitis, to becoming organised into five programmes, namely Surveillance, Vector Research, Epidemiology, Diagnostics, and Pathogenicity, as well as Indoor Air Quality, each staffed by specialists trained in the relevant disciplines. Far from being just a speciation of research programmes, this move signified the adoption of an integrated approach to environmental public health research that amalgamates clinical and laboratory surveillance with field vector control operation.

EHI and the SARS Outbreak in 2003

Although the EHI was set up primarily to carry out research work on vector-borne diseases, it contributed its expertise readily during the SARS outbreak of 2003 by agreeing to cultivate the live SARS virus in its laboratory. The live virus was required for the study of the SARS coronavirus and the development of diagnostic kits.

Unfortunately, a student contracted SARS while working in the laboratory. The government took prompt remedial action. All activities within the Institute were suspended and a Review Panel, comprising international and local experts, was invited to audit the laboratory's biosafety procedures and recommend measures to strengthen the work processes at the Institute. Through interviews and laboratory investigations of samples from the laboratory, the panel found that the infection was caused by inappropriate laboratory practices and cross-contamination of West Nile Virus samples with the SARS coronavirus. The Biosafety Level 3 (BSL-3) laboratory was disinfected and downgraded to Biosafety Level 2 (BSL-2).

It was an eye-opening lesson for EHI and Singapore as it highlighted the need to manage inherent risks associated with the operation of a high-containment laboratory, and the need for a robust biosafety framework to govern the conduct of research activities. Since then, biosafety procedures have been put in place, and research staff given refresher training on biosafety.

In 2005, EHI began a new lease of life when it moved into a new facility at Biopolis, the hub of Life Sciences research in Singapore. Apart from the High Containment Laboratory at BSL-3, the facility is also equipped with an Arthropod Containment Laboratory (ACL) Level 3, that allowed the Institute to expand its scope of research to address more vector-borne diseases of public health importance. More importantly, the various biosafety procedures that the Institute has put in place allows it to comply with the requirements prescribed by the Biological Agents and Toxins Act, a legislation which was enacted in 2006 to, among other things, provide for safe practices in the handling of such biological agents and toxins at BSL-3.

The BSL-3 laboratory provides an appropriate setting for surveillance and research of high risk vector-borne viruses, including West Nile virus, Japanese encephalitis virus, Chikungunya virus, and Hanta viruses, while the ACL allows research on infected mosquitoes to be conducted. Until then, most of the research was centred on the vectors that spread the disease. The complexity of vector-borne diseases due to the interplay of many factors, however, means that a holistic understanding of the role played by the viruses, host, and environmental factors in disease transmission is necessary. To this end, the Institute, with the availability of the new facilities, has become better positioned to study the viruses directly responsible for the diseases in order to obtain a fuller picture of the problems, as well as possible solutions.

Contributing to Dengue Prevention Efforts

EHI's capability was put to the test during the dengue resurgence in 2005. The Institute had at the time just completed the development of a PCR (polymerase chain reaction)-based diagnostic assay that could accurately detect the dengue virus and its serotype in an infected blood sample, as early as the first day of disease onset. The new capability shortened the diagnostic and serotyping time from weeks, using the current gold standard of virus isolation, to less than an hour.

Accurate and rapid diagnosis is essential in the fight against dengue. It is needed for patient management and directing vector control response to minimise further transmission and spread of the disease. In the dengue epidemic of 2005, the test contributed to an improvement in the rate of the clinicians' diagnosis. Riding on this success, the EHI went on to develop a test kit that is able to detect anti-dengue antibodies in the saliva. This non-invasive approach holds the potential for early post-infection detection of the disease and is currently undergoing field trial.

Apart from improving the diagnostic capability for dengue, the EHI has also enhanced its surveillance system for early detection of the emergence of any new predominant serotype circulating in the population. The system leverages a close network of medical practitioners who collect blood samples from patients displaying symptoms of dengue, and send them for laboratory diagnosis by the Institute. The early detection of a switch from Dengue 1 to Dengue 2 in 2007 enabled the vector control response to be initiated more promptly to mitigate the effects of an ensuing outbreak. The detection of an emergence of the uncommon Dengue 3 serotype in 2005 and 2007 (in several areas in Tampines) also triggered an enhanced effort in these areas to prevent the spread of the serotype to other parts of Singapore. Since 2006, the Institute has further extended this surveillance system to include the Chikungunya virus, West Nile virus, and Hanta virus.

EHI's research has also contributed to a better understanding of mosquito vector biology. In a study of the dispersal range for dengue vector mosquitoes, *Aedes aegypti* and *Aedes albopictus*, the Institute has found that the mosquitoes could disperse easily and quickly throughout areas of radius 320 metres in search of egg-laying sites. This contrasts with the general belief that the *Aedes* mosquito seldom flies more than 50 metres in its lifetime. In the same study, it was also found that with releases on the twelfth storey of a twenty-one-storey apartment block, the mosquitoes showed a similarly easy and rapid dispersal to the top and bottom of the block. The work, published in an international journal in 2004, won the Royal Entomological Society Award for best publication in Medical and Veterinary Entomology during 2004–2005. These findings provided a firm scientific basis to refine existing vector control practices such as expanding the geographical range of source reduction to ensure better effectiveness.

The research at EHI has also shaped the way mosquito vectors are controlled. For instance, trials conducted by the Institute have found the use of *Bacillus thuringiensis* strain *israelensis* (Bti) to be effective in controlling mosquito breeding at construction sites. *Bti,* a biological vector control agent, eliminates mosquito larvae through degradation of their digestive tract, but is environmentally friendly since it is non-toxic to human and other animals, compared with chemical pesticides. The finding has led to the successful and widespread usage of *Bti* as a mosquito control method, particularly in Singapore's many construction sites. The Institute also conducts other trials, including the use of residual spray, traditionally used for malaria control, for dengue control.

With EHI's research capability gaining better recognition, the Institute has gradually moved beyond the role of supporting the national vector-borne disease control programme, to collaborating with, and supporting other aspects of public health research in Singapore also. EHI's team of researchers has collaborated with various local and international academic bodies, research institutes, and organisations, constantly identifying working partners with relevant expertise for mutual exchange of knowledge and expertise. As a member of the Dengue Consortium and the Malaria Consortium, EHI has worked closely with other major research institutions in Singapore on projects, including the surveillance of rodent-borne diseases. EHI also supports local and overseas pharmaceutical companies in the development of anti-dengue drugs through the provision of supporting services such as viral testing for drug companies that are carrying out trials, as well as sharing of knowledge about the local vector-borne disease situation.

Even though EHI has developed considerable research capability, the Institute is acutely aware of the need to further its understanding of the disease so as to enhance Singapore's own vector-borne disease control efforts. The Institute has, therefore, been actively exchanging notes with other research institutes. In 2007, NEA entered into a Memorandum of Understanding with the Instituto de Medicina Tropical "Pedro Kouri", in Cuba, a country that is also well known for its dengue control programme, to collaborate on various projects in dengue surveillance, control, and research.

Diseases such as dengue or Chikungunya fever do not recognise geographical boundaries or socio-economic status. Singapore cannot fight the battle against dengue alone. To this end, EHI has started to assist in capacity building in less developed countries, through helping to strengthen their disease surveillance capability, and thereby reducing their disease burden. As a way for Singapore to reciprocate the help that international organisations such as WHO rendered it during its early developing years, the Institute has contributed to the WHO WPRO's (Western Pacific Regional Office) efforts in developing research plans on communicable diseases, as well as the Asia-Pacific dengue control strategic plans.

Besides vector and vector-borne viruses research, the EHI's other focus is on gathering scientific evidence to support the formulation of environmental public health policies. This was particularly evident in the assessment of the indoor air quality in entertainment outlets in 2006 in preparation for the introduction of smoking prohibition in these places. Parameters, including the indoor and outdoor levels of respirable suspended particles and carbon monoxide, were measured in these outlets. A comparison of the air quality measurements taken one month before and after the introduction of the smoking prohibition showed a significant reduction in the levels of key indoor air pollutants, thus affirming the value of indoor smoking bans. The Institute has also undertaken surveys to assess the risk of *Legionella* infection in spa pool water as part of the evaluation of the need to regulate spa pool water quality to protect the health of spa users.

Conclusion

Singapore's experience in cleaning up the land and rivers is a unique one. It began with a clear vision by the government, who appreciated that economic development need not progress at the expense of the environment, and more importantly, a high standard of living for the people could not be achieved without a clean and healthy environment.

In translating this vision into reality, the government understood the need to adopt a long-term perspective in planning and executing the various programmes to support the realisation of the vision. For example, to tackle the problem of illegal street hawking permanently, the government was prepared to invest heavily in infrastructure, i.e. purpose-built food centres and markets.

Realising the vision of a clean Singapore could not have been achieved within such a short span of time, if not for the practical and effective implementation of policies and programmes. In solving the pollution problem of the Singapore River, for instance, the government had decided that controlling the sources of pollution was the most practical and effective approach, rather than implementing direct engineering solutions to remove pollution from the river. Other than emphasising practicality, continuous innovation has also been a hallmark of many environmental policies and programmes. The evolution of the "Keep Singapore Clean" campaign in the early years to the "Clean and Green Week" of the 1990s shows how the government explored new approaches of engaging the population to sustain a clean and healthy environment, in response to changing socio-economic trends as well as public expectations.

Today, Singapore can pride itself on being among the few cities in the world where residents can regard a clean environment as a matter of fact. Some may even take this quality living environment for granted, forgetting that not so long ago, the environment in Singapore left much to be desired. Indeed, in spite of the four decades of efforts spent exalting the benefits of a clean living environment, and encouraging all residents to play their part in keeping the country clean, the current state of cleanliness is still far from ideal, and to some extent, still very much dependent on the efforts of the cleaners.

The behaviour and psyche of persistent litterbugs are still poorly understood. This is an area where perhaps socio-psychology experts may provide some insights.

Beyond a better understanding of the motivations of the litterbugs, there is also a need to develop the cleaning industry through raising the professional standards of the workforce, as a skilled and well-trained workforce would be better equipped to meet the rising expectations of the public, and at the same time, address the inferior image that has long been associated with the industry. Moving forward, the government should also be prepared to leverage technological advancements in materials research that could lead to the design of buildings and other structures that facilitate more efficient cleansing.

But most importantly, the people in Singapore must come to the realisation that the cost of keeping the country clean would ultimately be borne by them, in one form or another. Apart from paying directly for the cost of cleaning up public places, the people must recognise that the indirect cost of an environment with poor sanitation would be many times more — the higher likelihood of infectious disease transmission, or tourists and investors staying away.

As the transformation of Singapore's living environment in the last four decades was an achievement made possible only through the dedicated efforts of both the government and the people, this partnership must continue. Sustaining the cleanliness of the land and waterways will need to be a perpetual commitment, one to be carried through to future generations.

Acknowledgements

The following officers helped in the research and writing, or acted as key resource persons, for the original chapter in the book *Clean, Green and Blue* in 2008:

Chan Wai San, Director, Hawkers Department, NEA; Chua Soon Guan, Director, Strategic Policy Division, MEWR; Foong Chee Leong, Director-General Meteorological Services, NEA; Khoo Seow Poh, Director-General Public Health, NEA; Lai Kim Lian, Head, Planning and Development, Hawkers Department, NEA; Andrew Low, Senior Assistant Director, Clean Land, MEWR; Ng Lee Ching, Head, Environmental Health Institute, NEA; Tan Han Kiat, Assistant Director, Public Health, MEWR; S. Satish Appoo, Director, Environmental Health Department, NEA.

CHAPTER 3

Applying Economic Principles to Environmental Policy

Tan Yong Soon, Lee Tung Jean and Karen Tan

The environment has often been neglected in the early stages of growth, leaving air thick with particulates and water contaminated with effluents. We believe this is a mistake, and one that is extremely expensive to fix in the future.

The Growth Report 2008: Strategies for Sustained Growth and
Inclusive Development; Commission on Growth and Development

While it values the environment, the government makes decisions on the basis of stringent analysis as it has to prioritise competing demands in the face of limited resources. The full environmental cost of a certain initiative should be factored into the decision making process in order to arrive at the correct decision. In practice, this is seldom straightforward, due to the inherent complexity of environmental issues, such as quantifying intangibles and externalities, managing subjectivity in the value or cost that different individuals attach to the same outcome, and dealing with long timescales over which future scenarios may be uncertain. However, this does not negate the importance of rigorous analysis. In fact, given the subjectivity, there is a greater need to apply sound economic principles when developing environmental policy, to provide clarity on the choice of economic tools and models, as well as the assumptions and scenarios.

In Singapore, the formulation of environmental policies and legislation has benefited from the judicious use of economic principles. Here, we focus on four key areas in which economics has played a key role in guiding environmental policy: (i) in deciding between which projects or options to implement; (ii) in setting appropriate prices or user fees; (iii) when introducing market competition; and (iv) how market failures should be dealt with. Each of these situations is elaborated in the sections that follow.

Permission was granted by the Ministry of the Environment and Water Resources (MEWR) to reproduce Chapter 9 from the book *Clean, Green and Blue: Singapore's Journey Towards Environmental and Water Sustainability.*

Guiding Decision Making

Long-term Cost Effectiveness

When decisions have to be made on whether to proceed with specific environ-ment projects, a long-term view has to be taken. This means applying econom-ics to evaluate long-term cost effectiveness. While a project might have higher upfront cost, it needs to be balanced against lower lifetime operating cost, poten-tial savings from other related operations, and lower forgone revenue. Low cost projects that are cost-effective in the short term could compromise longer-term cost effectiveness.

Deep Tunnel Sewerage System

This was the basis upon which Singapore decided to embark on the Deep Tunnel Sewerage System (DTSS) project. The growing economy and population in the twenty-first century would impose increasing pressures on the existing used water infrastructure. To cope with the expected increase in used water flow, the options available were to continue expanding the conventional water reclamation plants, or explore a totally novel approach employing new technologies to replace the existing infrastructure. The latter was found to be cost-effective in the long term, albeit more expensive in terms of upfront costs. Hence, despite costing S$7 billion, the option of DTSS was adopted as it would free up scarce land for higher-value economic uses. Moreover, it presented a more sustainable solution that could meet Singapore's needs in the twenty-first century.

Land is a scarce and precious resource in Singapore. The existing sewage treat-ment works, pumping stations, and buffer zones around them occupy a total land area of 880 hectares. By implementing deep tunnel sewers that convey sewage flows by gravity, the existing sewage treatment facilities will be phased out, with only the two large wastewater works at Changi and Tuas occupying a total of 110 hectares remaining. The resulting savings and enhancements in land value were estimated in 1998 at S$1.5 billion.

If the government had decided not to proceed with the DTSS, the existing treat-ment facilities would still have to be replaced when worn out, and expanded to cope with the increasing volume of wastewater. At the ground breaking ceremony for DTSS on 8 July 2000, then Minister for the Environment Lee Yock Suan mentioned that savings from lower capital and operating cost were estimated at S$3.7 billion. The total savings from both land and facilities were thus estimated at S$5.2 billion. While the upfront cost of DTSS is S$7 billion, with these savings, in the long term, the government is effectively paying S$1.8 billion to provide sewerage infrastructure for Singapore's growing needs.

Unaccounted-for-water

The example of DTSS illustrates how lower operating cost and potential land savings have to be balanced against higher upfront cost. In managing the water distribution system, the government also takes into account foregone revenue in its cost computations, as in the case of reducing unaccounted-for-water (UFW). UFW represents water loss due to leaks, illegal draw-offs in the distribution system, meter inaccuracies, and improper accounting. It is usually regarded as a measure of the efficiency of a water supply system. In Singapore, UFW has been reduced by using good pipe materials (such as cement-lined ductile iron, copper, and stainless steel pipes), optimising pipe pressure, replacing old and problematic pipes systematically, and actively detecting underground leaks. UFW leaks result in lost value since water is lost from the system, but undertaking measures to prevent leakages can be quite costly too. Though the key consideration in managing UFW is to ensure service reliability, the cost of reducing UFW leakages still has to be weighed against that of supplying more water by developing new water resources.

In the period from 1990 to 2007 when UFW was reduced from 9.5% to 4.4%, about S$200 million was generated through the sales of water which would otherwise have been unaccounted for and, therefore, forgone. Going forward, the government expects to generate additional revenue of S$24 million each year (based on projected water sales and on maintaining UFW at about 4.4% as opposed to 9.5%). This additional revenue generated would be able to recover more than the costs of the various programmes and measures implemented as part of PUB's network maintenance regime, which cost about S$20 million per year currently. Another significant benefit of reducing UFW is the conservation of a scarce resource of strategic importance.

The Next Best Alternative

As part of the government's decision making process, evaluating long-term cost effectiveness is not only confined to individual projects, but also applies across different types of projects. Comparing the merits of different projects requires questioning what the next best alternative is at the national level, particularly if this cuts across different agencies. If land utilisation for a specific project can be reduced, what is the benefit of the alternative use? How does the government decide whether a piece of land should be used as a disposal site or for residential development? In economics, exploring the next best alternative essentially means including the implicit opportunity cost. Examples of how opportunity cost shapes decisions are those of reducing buffer zones around water reclamation plants and choosing a landfill site.

Buffer zone for water reclamation plants

Water reclamation plants (WRPs) that treat used water were previously located in rural areas. Open tanks were used and, given the tropical climate, odour nuisance was inevitable. Hence, a 1-kilometre buffer zone was imposed on these WRPs, within which only limited development was allowed. As the urban area expanded, demand for more land resulted in higher land prices and greater development opportunities for the vacant buffer land. This led to an examination of how the buffer zone around WRPs could be reduced. While it had previously been expensive to cover up the treatment facilities and install odour control facilities, it now made economic sense to do so, since the resulting reduction in buffer zone allowed land to be freed up for other developments, and the value thus created was more than sufficient to compensate for the cost of upgrading the WRPs.

When the project was initially undertaken, reducing the buffer zones around WRPs was projected to have released a total land area of 1,276 hectares with an enhanced value of about S$3,750 million. In comparison, the total cost of covering up the treatment facilities and installing odour control facilities came up to about S$380 million. Hence, the Environment Ministry proceeded to cover up four of the six WRPs, as well as adopt more compact designs for extensions to WRPs and install special odour control facilities. As a result, the buffer zone for WRPs was reduced from 1 kilometre to 500 metres. Land around the WRP could then be released for higher value developments.

Landfill sites

Projections indicated that existing dumping grounds would be exhausted by the late 1990s. When the Environment Ministry first looked for a new landfill site, the initial intention was to build the next landfill at Punggol. However, with increasing housing demand, HDB had plans to use Punggol for a coastal residential project — this would fetch greater value relative to a landfill due to its waterfront location and its distance away from major industrial developments. Factoring in the opportunity cost of this alternative development, the government took the decision to earmark Punggol as a new housing estate while an alternative site was sourced for the next landfill. After taking into consideration the competing needs for land space on the mainland and the experiences of other countries with similar land scarcity problems, the government conceived the idea of an offshore landfill. This led to the development of Semakau Landfill.

Optimal Timing

In addition to deciding whether to undertake a project, another crucial aspect of the decision making process is determining the best time to initiate the project. In this respect, public sector agencies keep a close eye on global technological developments so that when innovations result in prices becoming economically viable, they are ready to move in. Singapore's NEWater and desalination projects illustrate the need to appreciate the impact of technology on the evaluation of cost effectiveness.

NEWater

Attempts to reclaim water from used water date as far back as the early 1970s. In 1974, the first pilot water reclamation plant was built. However, within a year, the plant was decommissioned, as the 14-month trial concluded that producing potable water from secondary treated effluent was technically achievable, but not cost-effective. Nevertheless, ENV and PUB continued to monitor developments in membrane technology so that when major improvements were made by the late 1990s, they were able to capitalise on this opportunity to reinitiate the water reclamation project. In 1998, a demonstration-scale NEWater plant was commissioned in Singapore, which proved that the cost of water reclamation had indeed come down substantially, making it economically viable to produce NEWater on a large scale. Following a successful trial and extensive testing of water quality, full-scale NEWater factories were progressively rolled out, and NEWater will supply 30% of Singapore's water demand by 2011. The NEWater produced caters primarily to industries demanding ultra pure water such as wafer fabrication, petrochemical plants, and commercial air-conditioning cooling towers.

Desalination

For Singapore, which is an island, desalination is a natural solution to its water needs. Desalination provides a steady source of water, unaffected by variations in rainfall. However, up to the 1990s, desalination technology consisted mainly of evaporating seawater to separate fresh water and dissolved salts, that is, via a distillation process. As this process was highly energy intensive, it was only adopted by oil-rich Middle Eastern countries. Like NEWater, recent technological advancements allowed desalination to be effected using an alternative method — reverse osmosis via membranes, which is estimated to cost about 20% lower than traditional distillation methods. PUB recognised the potential for this new development to bring down the cost of desalination, and decided to call a tender for the private sector to design, build, own, and operate (DBOO) a desalination plant. SingSpring Pte Ltd, a wholly-owned subsidiary of Hyflux, was awarded the contract for the first desalination facility in Singapore. The 30-mgd SingSpring desalination plant at Tuas was successfully delivered and commissioned in September 2005.

Apart from being a lower-cost production method, another major advantage of using membranes for NEWater and desalination is easy scalability. Traditional fractional distillation plants entailed large-scale investments, which locks in a particular technology. In comparison, membrane-based solutions can be implemented in modules and can easily accommodate technological advances.

Setting Appropriate Prices

Cost Recovery

Using economic principles to guide the decision making process helps in determining whether to go ahead with a particular project, following which a decision has to be made on who should pay for the project. Unless market failures exist or public goods are being provided, the user is generally made to pay the full-cost recovery price for the goods or services provided to ensure that market forces work to determine the right allocation of resources. In the next few examples, we highlight sewerage services as a public benefit where the government does not charge full-cost recovery. This is in contrast to the treatment of used water and waste incineration services where charges are set at cost recovery.

As a large infrastructural project, the used water distribution infrastructure required large capital investments. Among these, the sewerage network has been regarded as a public benefit and access to proper sanitation deemed a basic necessity, since the public health benefits that stem from a good sewerage system, such as the control of water-borne diseases, do not diminish with more users, nor is it practical to exclude non-paying users. Therefore, the sewerage network is owned and funded entirely by the government. The same reasoning does not apply to other parts of the used water distribution infrastructure, such as the treatment of used water in water reclamation plants, as consumers have discretion over the amount of used water that they discharge and send to the water reclamation plants for treatment. Hence, the water reclamation plants are owned by PUB, with their capital and operating costs recovered through user fees.

The provision of waste incineration services is costly due to the capital intensive nature of constructing and operating incineration plants. Apart from bearing the financing risk of paying the upfront cost, the government also had to bear the design and operational risk for the first few incineration plants since the concept of incinerating mixed waste in a tropical setting had not been tested on a large scale before. As in the case of the treatment of used water in water reclamation plants, incineration services are not considered a public good since consumers have discretion over the waste disposed. The gate fees at these facilities are reviewed yearly and are set on a cost recovery basis, which includes the recovery of capital cost, to ensure economic sustainability in the waste disposal sector.

Setting Prices to Reflect Other Policy Considerations

Although cost recovery is a primary consideration in setting prices, the government does not always adhere rigidly to this if there are good reasons to deviate from it.

In the previous section, we touched on the provision of public good as a reason for deviation. However, there are also other policy considerations for not setting prices at cost recovery such as promoting conservation of scarce resources, helping consumers adjust, and keeping cost affordable.

Pricing of potable water

In a fundamental review of water pricing conducted in 1997, the price of potable water had two clear components. The water tariff was explicitly set to recover the full cost of production and supply, while the water conservation tax (WCT) was intended to reflect the higher cost of alternative water supply sources. The former ensured that the true cost of supplying water today would be properly accounted for — this was important because experiences in other countries had shown that under-recovery of water charges could lead to deteriorating services and under-investment in future capacity. Neither was it right for PUB to collect more revenue than it required for its operations.

While charging cost recovery rates would cover the cost of meeting water demand today, it would not be an accurate reflection of the marginal cost of supply, since water is a scarce resource. This means that the next available source of water would be more expensive than the current sources, hence pricing at cost recovery alone would result in over-consumption of the scarce resource. To ensure that consumers are conscious of this, they have to pay an additional levy known as the WCT, which is pegged to the cost of the marginal source, which at the time was desalinated water. Unlike the water tariff which is collected by PUB, WCT revenues are channelled directly to the Ministry of Finance, which can then be used to fund other worthy expenditure.

Gate fees at incineration plants

Another instance in which prices deviated from cost recovery rates was in the setting of gate fees at the incineration plants. Before April 1991, gate fees were deliberately priced far below cost recovery levels to discourage illegal dumping. For the same rationale, trucks used to be able to bring one load of refuse a day of less than half a tonne for disposal without having to pay any fees.

However, this was not sustainable. The actual cost of disposing refuse borne by the government was going up as the growing volume of waste from an expanding economy meant that a fourth incineration plant and a larger landfill site (constructed offshore at Semakau due to a lack of alternatives on the mainland) were needed. In tandem with economic growth, land prices were also going up. Furthermore, subsidising refuse disposal inhibited the waste recovery and recycling industry, as waste generators would find it cheaper to dispose of their waste rather than go for recycling.

It was increasingly not feasible to continue subsidising waste disposal in order to discourage illegal dumping. Instead, punitive measures such as fines of S$10,000 and tighter enforcement were put in place to reduce the incidence of illegal dumping.

Even when the government decided to move towards cost recovery, the adjustment process was gradual. It took more than ten years to bring the gate fees on par with costs — from S$15 per tonne in 1991 to S$77 per tonne in 2002. Prices were not adjusted by more than S$10 per tonne each year. Disposal companies were also encouraged to absorb the initial increase. The gradual approach was adopted to ensure that the impact on households would be gradual. For every S$10 increase in incineration gate fees, a typical household in HDB flats would incur an increase of 90 cents a month for refuse collection fees. Apart from adjusting prices, fee exemptions for trucks disposing less than half a tonne of waste were also removed after a nine-month grace period. The grace period was to allow some forty small contractors who had been taking advantage of the exemption to rework their contracts with the waste generators to whom they were providing services.

Differential Pricing

Apart from setting fees and charges at cost recovery, the government also ensures that there is sufficient differentiation and flexibility in the fees and charges, so that price signals can optimise the allocation of scarce resources. Such examples can be found in Singapore's waste management industry.

Solid waste disposal fees

In the incineration industry, Ulu Pandan Incineration Plant (in the central part of Singapore) and Senoko Incineration Plant (in the northern part of Singapore) are sited at more accessible locations. Hence, differential gate fees were used to divert some of the waste to less accessible plants in the west (Tuas and Tuas South), so as to even out the loads arriving at each plant and avoid overcrowding. For this reason, Senoko's gate fee in 2007 was S$81 per tonne while Ulu Pandan's gate fee was S$87 per tonne for peak hours (between 7.30 a.m. to 2 p.m.) and S$81 per tonne for off-peak hours (after 2 p.m.), compared with S$77 per tonne in less accessible plants such as Tuas and Tuas South.

Since about half the waste disposed of in Singapore comes from the industrial and commercial sectors, a framework has been put in place to encourage recycling among the industries. The waste disposal fees for industries are pegged to the volume of waste they produce. Through market forces, industries would be incentivised to recycle if the cost of recycling is lower than waste disposal.

Introducing Market Competition

The previous section discusses how prices are set when the good or service is provided by the government. Increasingly, the government is allowing the market to provide goods and services wherever possible, in line with the economic tenet that free markets are usually more efficient in the allocation of resources. This has been Singapore's experience in introducing market competition in three areas: waste collection, incineration plants, and NEWater.

Waste Collection

In the mid-1980s, there had been many calls to privatise refuse collection services for domestic premises. However, the government decided not to go ahead with privatisation on the following grounds: (i) refuse collection was considered an essential service; (ii) private companies could lock in their collection system and make it difficult and costly to switch; and (iii) service quality could deteriorate as profit maximising companies cut corners.

In the 1990s, the privatisation plan for waste collection was reviewed again and a cautious two-step approach was adopted. First, in 1996, the government waste collection arm was incorporated into a separate entity and given a three-year monopoly. This allowed the government time to monitor and convince itself that service quality and fees were not affected. Subsequently, in 1999, Singapore was divided into nine sectors where domestic waste collection was competitively tendered. Previous concerns over privatisation were addressed through licensing conditions and a transparent fee structure. Efficiency gains have been realised from greater competition. In the second round of tender, the average refuse collection fee fell by approximately 30% for flats and 15% for landed premises, resulting in lower waste collection fees for residents.

Incineration Plants

Following the privatisation of the refuse collection services in 1999, the Environment Ministry decided to liberalise the incineration plant (IP) industry with the objectives of: (i) further increasing efficiency and innovation in the sector by injecting competition; and (ii) developing the environmental engineering industry by transferring environmental engineering expertise residing with the government to the private sector.

In 2001, an open tender was called to develop the fifth IP on a design, build, own, and operate (DBOO) basis under a free market model with the potential developer taking the financial, design, and demand risk. The tender was, however, not well received by the market, with only one non-compliant bid submitted. The primary reason for the poor response was that potential bidders were unable to bear the demand risk associated with uncertain waste growth and a non-guaranteed waste stream, plus the high capital outlay required for IPs.

Learning from the experience, the Environment Ministry then decided to adopt a DBOO scheme under a full take-or-pay approach. In this structure, the government would bear the demand risk of refuse throughput, by giving the DBOO operator full capacity payment regardless of the actual utilisation rate of the IP. In return, the DBOO operator bears the operational risk. This meant that the DBOO operator would receive payments for availability of incineration capacity, the actual amount of refuse incinerated, and for the generation of electricity. In addition, the DBOO operator was required to meet two other performance indicators on quality of the incineration process (measured in terms of ash carbon content) and service quality level to waste collectors (measured in terms of turnaround time). If any of these specified performance levels are not met, the DBOO operator is required to take immediate remedial measures. Financial penalties can also be imposed.

Because of the heavy capital investment involved, a twenty-five-year contract was provided to the DBOO operator. Due to the long-term nature of the contract, payment variations based on changes in the consumer index were built into the fixed and variable components of the payment mechanism to take into account changes in inflation rates. Bidders are required to indicate the variable rates in their bid prices. Payment adjustments and profit sharing were also allowed in cases of changes in law, step change in technologies, refinancing gains, and third-party revenues arising from alternative uses of the plant's assets.

With this approach, a more equitable sharing of risk was achieved, which was well received by the market, with more competitive bids submitted by various companies. The fifth IP DBOO tender was successfully awarded to Keppel Seghers Engineering Pte Ltd in November 2005. This plant is currently being constructed and scheduled to be ready for commercial operation in mid-2009.[1] From the experience gained through this tender and with support from NEA, Keppel managed to secure S$1.7 billion worth of solid waste management contracts in Qatar in 2006. This was followed in 2007 by another contract of a S$1.5 billion wastewater treatment and reuse plant in Qatar. With more private sector involvement in the waste management industry, the government's role is evolving from being a provider of services to being the overall regulator of the industry. This will provide opportunities to tap the private sector's expertise and maximise efficiency.

NEWater Plants

From the two earlier examples on privatisation, one can see that a key success factor is the efficient allocation of risk. Private sector companies, being smaller than

---

[1] The Keppel Seghers Tuas Waste-to-Energy Plant commenced operations in November 2009.

government as a whole, tend to be more risk averse. Therefore, it is important to allocate risk to the party that is in the best position to bear it. In the case of incineration plants, demand risk was a crucial consideration. In the next example on NEWater, not only was there some demand risk, but there was also technology risk in implementing the project, as the NEWater production process was still in its infancy.

Given the risk involved, PUB took the lead in developing Singapore's first NEWater plants at Bedok, Kranji, and Seletar. This helped to facilitate collaboration with global water companies such as General Electric Water & Process Technologies, Veolia Water, and Siemens Water Technologies, together with local companies such as Hyflux, as they worked together to implement various technologies at the NEWater plants. This allowed the private sector to gain confidence in the reliability and effectiveness of the new technologies, and build up its capability in operating a NEWater plant through working with PUB on-site. At this stage, PUB decided to offer private sector companies the opportunity to build and operate a NEWater plant through a DBOO model.

In 2007, about five years after PUB completed its first plant at Bedok, the fourth NEWater plant was commissioned. This plant at Ulu Pandan was built by Keppel Seghers and would supply PUB with 32 mgd of NEWater for twenty years. The payment structure for the Ulu Pandan project was fairly similar to that for the incineration plant. A two-part tariff based on availability and output was used. The availability payment, based on available capacity, covered the fixed cost of capital, overheads, maintenance, and energy. The output payment, which was dependent on the actual quantity of water output, covered the variable part of overheads, maintenance, and energy.

Contractual measures were also structured to ensure that the quantity and quality of water supply meet required standards. To do so, the DBOO agreements included clauses to impose penalties on non-performance such as not maintaining required capacity, or inadequate emergency product water storage. Other measures to mitigate potential impact on service continuity include "step-in" provisions in the event the concession company failed or was in default. For example, PUB could step in to manage the concession company's staff and equipment, or allow private financiers to identify other potential service providers that could take over operations. In addition, a comprehensive monitoring and audit system was put in place for all projects to allow PUB to check regularly on water quality, operation, and maintenance of the plants. This included linking the plant's key online water quality monitoring system to PUB's monitoring systems and having water sampled and analysed regularly at an accredited laboratory.

To meet the growing demand for NEWater, PUB in 2008 further embarked on the construction of a 50 mgd NEWater factory at Changi Water Reclamation Plant under a twenty-five-year DBOO arrangement with Sembcorp Utilities. With economies of scale, productivity gains, and more competitive membrane technologies, PUB was able to bring down the cost of NEWater production over the last few years.

Public-private partnership arrangements through DBOO are not just about reaping efficiency gains. Such arrangements are valuable and highly strategic learning opportunities for private companies to interact with government agencies over an extended period of time, tapping each others' amassed expertise and experience. Keppel had invited PUB to be actively involved in the Ulu Pandan NEWater project from the design and construction phase. In fact, Keppel had attached their plant manager and operators to PUB's Bedok NEWater factory for on-the-job training. PUB also invited Keppel's staff to attend in-house training courses to build up capabilities in construction, commissioning, and the subsequent operation of NEWater factories. Similarly, staff from Keppel Seghers are also receiving training on incineration plant operations at NEA's IPs. Such unusually close collaborations with industry partners help them build up technical expertise and process know-how, The government benefits as it ensures that services outsourced to the private sector will continue to be as reliable and efficient as before.

Dealing with Market Failure

Whilst market solutions are explored wherever possible, free markets generally work well only when there is perfect competition and information. In reality, market failures are common for a variety of reasons. Here, government intervention through grants, price mechanisms, or legislation is required to correct the market failure.

Correcting Externalities

Externalities occur when actions taken by economic agents during a transaction have cost and benefit implications on other parties that are not part of the initial transaction. Common examples of negative externalities include smoking and noise pollution, while positive externalities include good forest management and clean air. Broadly, externalities are dealt with in two ways. One is to get the polluter to face the true cost of the impact imposed on others. The other is through a quota system.

Air pollution

In terms of air pollution, lead concentration levels in Singapore were rising due to strong growth in vehicle population in the first half of the 1980s. Studies have shown that lead can affect the proper functioning of the brain and lungs. Motorists contributing to lead pollution in the air create a negative health externality among pedestrians and those living or working near roads, which motorists themselves do not internalise since most vehicles are air-conditioned.

This market failure was corrected through legislation and by pricing the externality. To control the emission of lead from motor vehicles, lead in petrol was progressively reduced from an uncontrolled level of about 0.84 g/l to 0.15 g/l in 1987. In addition, the use of unleaded petrol was promoted through a differential tax system which made unleaded petrol about 10 cents per litre cheaper than leaded petrol. These measures led to significant improvements in the air quality. The lead level in ambient air dropped to 1.2 μg/Nm^3 in 1990 and then to 0.1 μg/Nm^3 in 2000. Leaded petrol was totally phased out by 1998.

Water pollution

Another common externality is water pollution from industrial plants. Singapore deals with this externality through a combination of legislation and pricing. As rainwater is channelled to the reservoirs and eventually treated to potable quality, catchments need to be protected from pollution resulting from the illegal discharge of trade effluent, which is defined as liquid discharges from any trade, business, manufacturing, or construction site. Regulations have been put in place to control the discharge of trade effluent, both under the Environmental Protection and Management (Trade Effluent) Regulations for the control of trade effluent discharged into watercourses and land, as well as the Sewerage and Drainage (Trade Effluent) Regulations for the control of trade effluent into public sewers. The former is administered by NEA, whilst the latter by PUB.

Under the Environmental Protection and Management Regulations, trade effluent has to be treated before it is discharged into watercourses or land. Any effluent released must not be a hazard to human health or a public nuisance (such as of a foul odour). The party who discharges the effluent is required to install and make available the results from test points, inspection chambers, flow meters, and other recording apparatuses at the point of discharge. First time offenders can be fined up to S$10,000, while subsequent offenders face double the fine.

The Sewerage and Drainage (Trade Effluent) Regulations controls the discharge of used water from domestic, industrial, agricultural, and other premises into the public sewers. The Regulations allow certain industries that produce biodegradable wastewater to discharge their effluent into public sewers, as long as they are in accordance with specified water quality limits. These Regulations ensure that trade effluent collected can be treated by water reclamation plants to levels that comply with discharge standards into the watercourses. The Trade Effluent Tariff Scheme was also introduced to allow applicants to discharge slightly lower quality effluent into the public sewer for a fee. The fee is meant to recover the costs incurred in treating the additional pollution load at water reclamation plants.

Ozone depleting substances

The two above examples tackle externalities through the price mechanism. Another means is through using quotas. A tender and quota allocation system is used to control the amount of ozone depleting substance (ODS) imported for use in Singapore. On 5 January 1989, Singapore became a party to the Montreal Protocol, which is an international treaty to phase out ODS such as chlorofluorocarbons (CFCs) and halon, With an economy highly dependent on the electronics and chemical industries, policies to phase out ODS had to be handled with care.

Singapore's transitional experience was rather unique as it was among the first to regulate the use of ODS with a market-based allocation mechanism. Launched on 5 October 1989, the Tender and Quota Allocation System (TQS) allowed market forces to determine the price that industries had to pay for ODS. The system achieved two desirable outcomes, namely, the distribution of the limited quantity of available ODS to those with the highest replacement costs, and a strong market signal to induce ODS users to look into substitutes, conservation measures, and recycling.

To help companies make the transition, the Singapore Productivity and Standards Board offered technical consultancy and services to firms who wanted to recycle controlled ODS or to switch to substitutes. A sum of S$1.6 million from the Public Sector R&D fund was granted to the Board to initiate the various ODS alternative and conservation programmes. The scheme allowed for the hiring of experts in ODS alternative technologies. Many local SMEs, which generally lacked in-house expertise, benefited from this scheme.

As a result, Singapore successfully phased out the consumption of ODS by January 1996, well ahead of the time frame set for developing countries, which was 2010, For its contributions, Singapore was presented the Outstanding Ozone Unit Award by the United Nations Environment Programme (UNEP) at the 9th Meeting of Parties in Montreal in 1997.

Remedying Information Asymmetries

Another common cause of market failure is information asymmetry, which occurs when economic agents do not have the same amount of information or have imperfect and incomplete information. Information asymmetries are dealt with by passing legislation that facilitates the sharing of more information with those who are making consumption decisions.

One example is the introduction of a water efficiency labelling scheme (WELS), which aims to empower customers by allowing them to make informed choices. WELS was introduced in 2006 on a voluntary basis, covering taps, showerheads, dual-flush low-capacity flushing cisterns (LCFCs), urinals, and clothes washing machines. As WELS was voluntary, most suppliers and manufacturers registered only the more water-efficient models, constituting only 16% of the market. Because of the ineffectiveness of a voluntary approach, the Mandatory Water Efficiency Labelling Scheme (MWELS) will be launched in 2009 for taps, LCFCs, and urinals.

Similarly, NEA mandated energy labelling for two major energy-using devices — air-conditioners and refrigerators — starting in 2008, to make consumers aware of the potential savings of the devices. Informal feedback from retailers suggests that this has spurred increased sales of four-tick (most efficient) air-conditioners, even though these cost more upfront. Labelling endorsed by the government is seen as independent and helps to reduce "search" costs, which is the opportunity cost of the time spent by consumers in finding out about energy and water consumption of the appliances. This also reduces information asymmetry, since manufacturers or retailers can no longer make unsubstantiated claims about their products' resource efficiency.

Public Goods

Public goods are defined as products that are non-rival (consumption of the good by one individual does not reduce the amount available for consumption by another individual) and non-exclusive (difficult to limit consumption to paying individuals). Examples of public goods are beautiful water landscapes and a clean living environment. Since the private sector is unable to recover the cost from those who enjoy a public good, it either does not have any incentive to produce the good or produces an amount that is below the social optimum. Government intervention either through enforcement or direct provision is often needed in the optimal provision of public goods.

Cleanliness, in the form of a pleasant environment and the absence of foul odours and diseases can be considered a public good. One's consumption of cleanliness does not reduce the benefit another person gets from enjoying it. It is also difficult to exclude non-paying individuals from enjoying the benefits of cleanliness. Hence, the government has to help bring about public cleanliness by setting standards and enforcing them. Those caught littering are made to pay a fine or carry out corrective work orders (by cleaning up a public place) as a deterrent. (Details on how the government addresses the issue of public cleanliness are given in Chapter 3.)[2]

Related to public cleanliness is the ABC Waters programme. This programme seeks to transform waterways and waterbodies into beautiful rivers and lakes so that people can enjoy water based activities such as canoeing and sailing, and in so doing, appreciate the value of having clean waters. As the benefits of ABC Waters accrue to the general public, the government has taken the lead in transforming waterways, as this will create a better living environment and improve quality of life in Singapore.

---

[2] Chapter 3 of *Clean, Green and Blue* has been reproduced in Chapter 2 of this volume.

Split Incentives and Bounded Rationality

An emerging form of market failure stems from split incentives and bounded rationality. A good example to illustrate this concept can be drawn from the initiatives to promote energy efficiency in buildings. Developers bear the initial upfront cost of constructing a building, while occupants face the recurrent cost of living or operating in the building. When it comes to the incorporation of energy-efficient features and fixtures, there is a split incentive. Developers tend to build in features and fixtures that minimise the initial upfront cost, even if this means higher recurrent cost imposed on occupants. Compounding this problem, occupants are rationally bounded, that is, they often do not have the time and resources to demand energy-efficient features and fixtures as the benefits are relatively small.

This combination of split incentives and bounded rationality has resulted in a market failure, which calls for government intervention.

The government is beginning to deal with this by setting standards. For instance, in 2007, the Building and Construction Authority (BCA) enhanced current legislation requiring new buildings and existing ones undergoing major retrofitting to meet certain environmental sustainability standards (termed Green Mark) in several areas such as energy efficiency, water efficiency, project management, indoor air quality, and building innovation.

Conclusion

This chapter highlights the role economics plays in guiding environmental policies and legislation in areas such as decision making, setting prices, introducing market competition, and dealing with market failures. When used in setting prices, economics helps allocate limited goods and services to consumers who value them the most as charging helps to reveal what the consumer is prepared to pay. Market competition helps in determining the most efficient and effective means of providing a good or service. With market failure, economics helps correct the failure and enables markets to work better.

Economics is used as a tool to arrive at the best decision in the interest of the public. The rigour of economic analysis ensures that decisions made can stand the test of time and scrutiny. However, there may be occasions when prices have to be calibrated to take into account other policy considerations, such as in meeting social needs. Pricing can be a powerful tool to shape public behaviour and consumption when the correct costs and incentives are in place. To complement the pricing mechanism, targeted help can also be made available to the lower-income groups, for example, in the form of Utilities Save rebates.

Applying economic principles alone may not provide all the answers, and it is important to understand and appreciate their limitations too. Evaluating issues that stem from social or environmental concerns may not be as straightforward as simply carrying out a cost-benefit analysis, since quantifying these concerns would depend on the values and perspectives of different individuals. Nevertheless, economics is a constantly evolving field, and there has been increasing interest in applying economics to the environment, such as in valuing the cost of pollution or the loss of certain habitats. This will offer even more avenues in which economic analysis can be used to guide environmental policy.

In the final analysis, economics is only a tool. It can support and complement, but not replace, a clear vision and strategic priorities.

Acknowledgements

The following officers helped in the research and writing, or acted as key resource persons, for the original chapter in the book *Clean, Green and Blue* in 2008:

Chan Chee Wing, Assistant Director, Clean Land, MEWR; Benedict Chia, Senior Assistant Director, Strategic Issues, MEWR; Chua Soon Guan, Director, Strategic Policy Division, MEWR; Ridzuan Bin Ismail, Deputy Director, Water Studies Division, MEWR; Lin Jing, Policy Executive, Water Studies Division, MEWR; Philip Ong, Director, Climate Change Office, MEWR.

CHAPTER 4

The Search for NEWater: The Singapore Water Story

Lee Ek Tieng, DSO, PJG, BEng, Dipl, PHE, FIES, MIEM

Introduction

Singapore has often been described as a water scarce country. This is not because we lack rainfall, but because in our small island country, there is limited land area to catch and store the rain. Therefore, Singapore's strategy to develop water resources must include both traditional sources, including rain from the sky, and more importantly, unconventional sources, that include salty water from the sea, and used water from industry and households. Today, I would like to share with you the story of how, by closing the water cycle or loop, Singapore has overcome physical limitations to develop new water resources. Figure 1 illustrates the water loop: from rain water to storm water management, collection through drains and rivers and storage in reservoirs. Raw water is treated to potable water for supply to the population and industries. All used water is collected by sewers for treatment and the treated use water is further treated and reclaimed as NEWater and pumped into reservoirs.

Historical Background

Back in 1965, water supply sources on the island comprised solely of reservoirs in the central catchments that were inherited from the British. Even back in those days, when manufacturing and other industries had not taken off in Singapore, the water from the reservoirs was not sufficient to meet demand. We had to depend on Johore for our water supply under two water agreements which were signed in the early '60s. One agreement expired in 2011 and the other agreement in 2061. To meet the

This Chapter is based on a speech given by Lee Ek Tieng at the 18th Professor Chin Fung Kee Memorial Lecture on 18 October 2008.

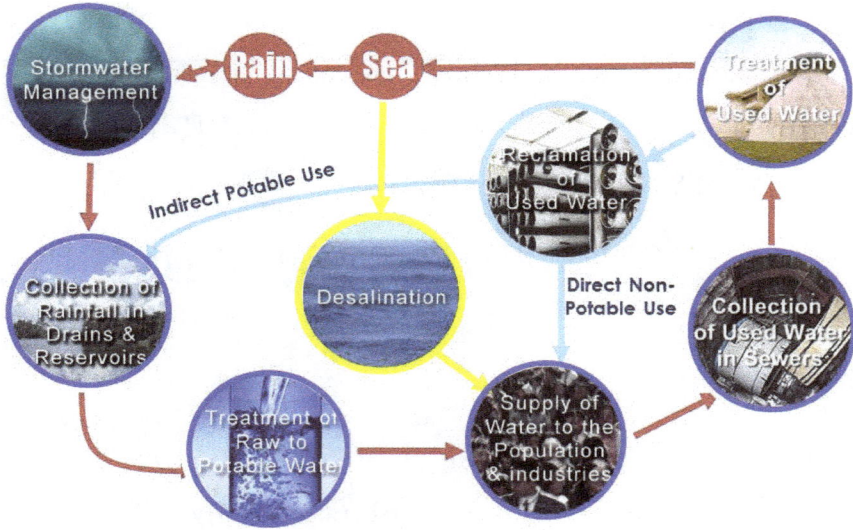

Figure 1.   Closing the water loop.

demands of a growing population and expanding economy, the search for more and new sustainable sources of water became urgent and a national priority.

Finding Solutions

Moving from Protected to Unprotected Catchments

This search began with the central catchments in Singapore. These include the MacRitchie, Seletar and Peirce Reservoirs, located in the central nature reserve area. But these "protected" reservoirs alone, where no development was allowed, could only give us a fraction of our water needs. To balance the competing need of land for development, in the 1970s and 1980s, we began to develop unprotected catchments in the western and northern reaches of Singapore (Figure 2). These catchments were "unprotected" in the sense that some development was allowed. However, this was limited to only mainly residential, light and clean uses. In addition, stringent pollution control measures were also enforced.

Estuarine Reservoirs

From the 1970s, we began to develop what we call "estuarine reservoirs" in the northern and western reaches of Singapore. The whole idea behind the estuarine reservoirs was really to dam all the possible rivers.

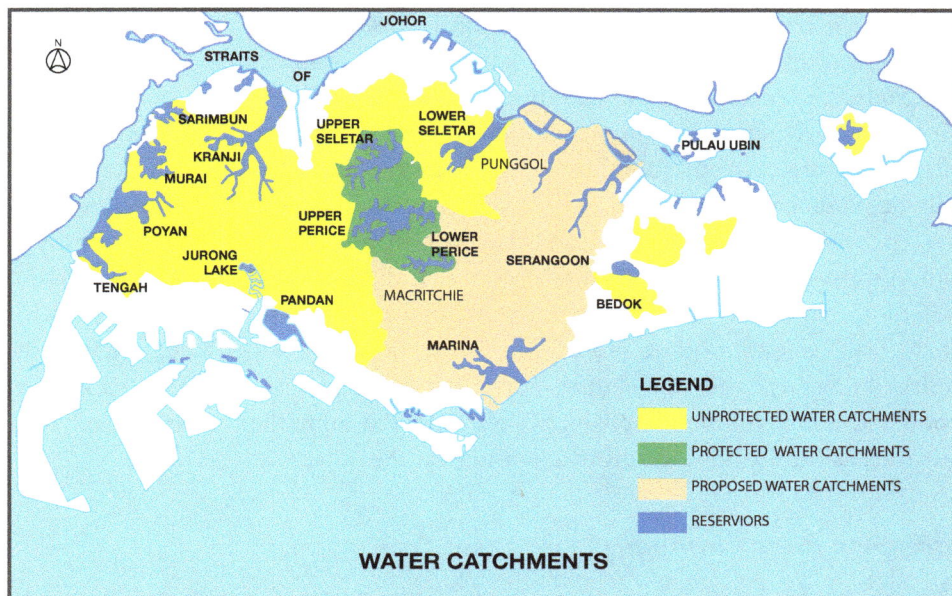

Figure 2.   Reservoirs and water catchments in Singapore (prior to 2008).

Some of these reservoirs were located in the forested western catchment. However, others, such as Kranji Reservoir in northern Singapore, were located in semi-urbanised catchments that contained animal and vegetable farms and squatter settlements, which resulted in polluted surface run-off. This led to the need to institute pollution control measures to ensure clean runoff could be captured and used for our water supply. For example, we had to resite the pollutive pig farms from Kranji in the north, to Punggol in the east. Similar to what Malaysia was doing, we also experimented with centralised pig farms. However, even with these high density farms, a lot of land was required for waste treatment. Then, pigs were an important source of food for Singapore and we wanted to be self-sufficient in our pork supply. But equally important was the need to have enough water, clean water. Thus, given our land constraints, in 1984 we finally decided to phase out all pig farming as it would be in the longer term more economic to import pork instead!

Urban Unprotected Catchments

Even more ambitious than forested and semi-urbanised unprotected water catchments were the urban unprotected water catchments. In other words, instead of traditional water catchments that would collect runoff from undeveloped forested areas, these urban catchments would collect water from townships and buildings. This would almost necessarily mean that the runoff tapped would be less clean.

Thus, we not only had to take measures to ensure that the necessary environmental infrastructure was in place, but equally importantly, that there was also effective enforcement of pollution control measures and adequate water treatment. The development of urbanised catchments also involved some interesting engineering. For example, under the Sungei Seletar-Bedok Water Supply Scheme, storm water collection systems were designed to ensure that only the cleaner part of the storm water is extracted and pumped into the reservoir. The system is designed such that the "first flush", the immediate runoff that is usually the most polluted, bypasses the collection facility, while the cleaner part of the storm water is diverted to a holding pond and pumped into a reservoir. We also adopted some then-advanced technologies such as the use of ozone disinfection to treat the water.

Singapore River Clean-up

Alongside the development of these schemes, we embarked on a big clean up of the Singapore River and its catchments in 1977. The river clean-up was a massive exercise, which involved a cross-section of government ministries, departments and statutory boards, to collect used water from all premises, build new towns and flats to relocate squatters, develop new markets and hawker centres to house the street hawkers, relocate pollutive motor workshops and construct new piers and facilities to relocate the boat operations and shipyards out of the rivers. These facilities were provided with water, gas, solid waste and sewerage systems. Finally, with the dredging of the river bed and beautifying of the banks, the river water turned clean and fishes returned. The clean-up took 10 years and was completed in 1987 and the Singapore River received a new lease of life — there was a new promenade running alongside the river; new restaurants lined the banks, transforming the Singapore river area into a popular spot for night life.

The effort to further clean up the river water led to continuous renewal and improvements to our environmental infrastructure. At the turn of the millennium, we decided to build a barrage across the Marina Channel where the five rivers which run through our city centre, including the Singapore River, meet before emptying into the sea. The reservoir would also serve as a flood control for low lying areas of the city with crest gates and high capacity axial pumps to regulate the reservoir level and flood water. Dubbed the 3-in-1 reservoir, Marina Reservoir would also be a venue for recreation in the heart of the city. The barrage was completed in 2008 and a large fresh water reservoir right in the middle of our city was formed once we started the flushing process in 2009. The water would then be tapped as an additional source of water *supply*.

In addition to the Marina Reservoir, we are also building our 16th and 17th reservoirs formed by damming the mouths of the Punggol and Serangoon Rivers in the north-eastern part of Singapore. Together, two-thirds of our land surface would be turned into catchment area for large scale rainwater harvesting.

Water Reclamation

Supplying Industrial Water

This began as early as 1966 when Singapore commissioned its first water recycling plant. This plant, the Jurong Industrial Water Works, uses conventional water treatment technology — coagulation, flocculation, clarification, sand filtration and aeration — to polish up secondary treated effluent to supply low grade industrial water for refineries, shipyards, paper and textile factories and other industries. This water was targeted at industries that used large amounts of water for say, cooling and washing. Other industries also further treated industrial water, for use in their manufacturing processes.

Trial with Water Reclamation in 1974

While industrial water was already being implemented in the late 1960s, the first trial with reclaiming water for drinking began in 1974 when a pilot water reclamation plant was set-up. Back then, secondary treated effluent similarly underwent the reverse osmosis process and other advanced treatment processes of ion exchange, electro-dialysis and ammonia stripping to produce water of drinking standard. The water even met the World Health Organisation (WHO) guidelines for drinking water! However, membranes were expensive, making the water reclamation process not cost-effective. On top of that, membrane technology was unreliable as fouling of the membrane was a significant issue then and frequent cleaning was required. Thus, the advanced water reclamation demo plant was shut down in December 1976 following a continuous run of 14 months.

NEWater

The Development of NEWater (Figs. 3 and 4)

Today, with the advancement in membrane technology, water of drinking standards can be reclaimed from secondary-treated effluent both more cheaply, and more reliably. In 1998, Singapore revisited the idea of water reclamation. This time, however, the technology was different. Major breakthroughs in materials used have enabled new microfiltration membranes used in pre-treatment and reverse osmosis mem-

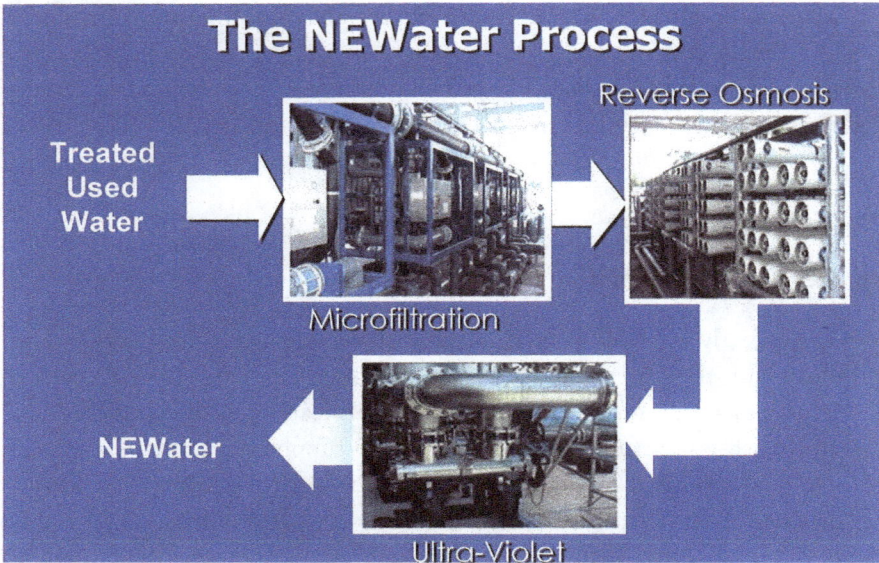

Figure 3.   The NEWater process.

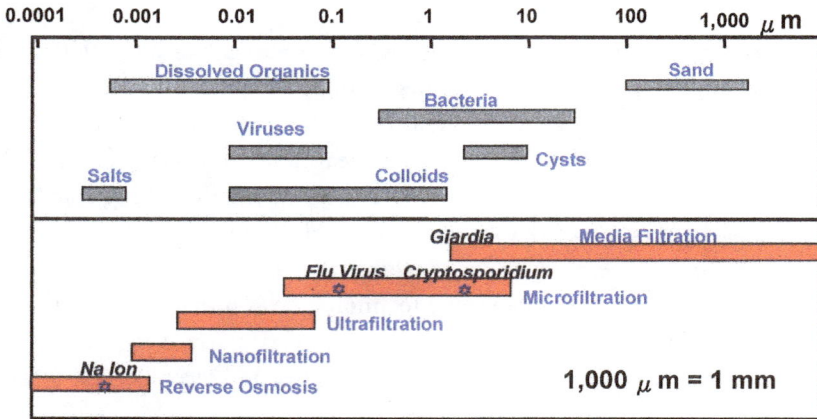

Figure 4.   Contaminant removal by membrane treatment processes.

branes to be more resistant to fouling, operate at low pressure and be manufactured cheaply. Today, we make use of a multiple safety barrier water reclamation process that comprises the conventional used water treatment process, microfiltration or ultrafiltration, reverse osmosis and ultraviolet disinfection to produce water of drinking standards which is now registered and branded as NEWater.

First, used water is treated through the conventional biological treatment process to produce consistently good quality secondary treated effluent. It is then followed by the Microfiltration or Ultrafiltration process with a membrane pore size of 0.2 microns to filter out all suspended solids, colloidal particles, bacteria, some viruses and protozoan cysts. Next, we make use of reverse osmosis (RO), which is essentially a semi-permeable membrane with a pore size of 0.0001 microns that effectively removes all dissolved salts and organic contaminants while allowing water to go through. Thus, total dissolved solids that used to be of concern in the 1970s are no longer a problem as they can be easily removed by the RO process. The final stage is an added safety step of high intensity ultraviolet disinfection to ensure integrity of the system in the event of an unlikely breach of the RO process.

These membrane technologies have been extensively tested with the construction and operation of a 2.2 mgd (10,000 m^3/day) demonstration scale plant in 2000. The water quality of NEWater has also been independently verified and confirmed by an Expert Panel comprising both foreign renowned water experts and local experts from our academia. Overall, more than 20,000 tests were carried out for some 190 water quality parameters and the results showed that the reclaimed water's quality was well within the United States Environmental Protection Agency (USEPA) and WHO drinking water standards and guidelines. Today, the plant continues to consistently and reliably produce NEWater that is audited regularly by an External Audit Panel of local and international water experts.

Desalination

Since September 2005, we have been desalting seawater for supply as drinking water. The same RO technology is used. But with much greater salt content in seawater (50–100 times that of treated effluent), the operating pressure for desalination can be as high as 70 bars, some 7 to 8 times higher than that used for NEWater production. Thus, power consumption and costs are much higher for desalination than NEWater production. However, when we integrate both sources, desalted seawater forms "new" water input which not only adds to our water inventory but can multiply our water resources by being reused many times as NEWater. The salts rejected by the RO processes are discharged as brine into the sea and therefore, there is no solid build-up in the water supply system.

NEWater — Public Education

Quality wise, reclaimed water is nearly as good as distilled water and safe for drinking, but the problem was really psychological due to its source and lack of minerals. Even if the process was scientifically sound, the question was: How can we overcome the psychological barrier and convince Singaporeans that this reclaimed water is good enough for drinking?

Thus, we needed a branding and marketing plan for this high quality reclaimed water. We wanted the name to give the impression of something innovative. We did not want the name to describe water quality either — it would sound too scientific and would not appeal to the masses. Thus, we rejected names such as "Pure Water", "High Quality Water", and finally decided to name it NEWater, a name that speaks for itself. NEWater not only reflects the "rebirth" of used water, but also implies cleanliness and purity without explicitly touching on water quality. With the NEWater brand now finalised, what we needed was a marketing plan.

In Singapore, we believe in a multi-stakeholder approach involving the community, the government and the private sector. Thus, we brought the media on study trips to the United States to learn about water reuse in practice; we worked with community leaders to brief Singaporeans and educate them on the sophisticated technology used; we also rolled out a publicity programme involving news coverage through newspapers, television and even a specially commissioned documentary to launch NEWater to the public.

But other than just disseminating messages through the media, we also bottled NEWater for the public to sample, so that they could taste for themselves how pure and fresh the water is.

For sustained public education, we also launched the NEWater Visitor Centre that combines fun with learning through interactive games and vivid and engaging displays. Visitors can even see the NEWater factory in operation while on a walk through of the visitors' centre!

You will have noticed that we have used the term "used water" in place of "waste water". This is not just a matter of semantics; it is a belief that water is a resource to be used and reused over and over again, something which has been a practice all over the world where downstream communities take their water source from the same rivers that receive used water discharged from upstream communities. Hence, it is not a wastewater stream that should be discarded.

With the successful introduction of NEWater, we have closed the water loop by using membranes to produce ultra-clean water. NEWater can even be used by the sensitive wafer fabrication industry which requires water much purer than tap water.

Since its launch in 2003, the demand for NEWater has increased very rapidly, driven in part by huge water users such as wafer fabrication plants, refineries and petrochemical companies, which welcomed NEWater as a high quality substitute for potable water. Other customers include power stations, electronics companies and commercial premises. Currently, we are supplying NEWater to about 300 customers.

To meet the growth in demand, we have increased NEWater supply. From the initial three NEWater factories at Bedok, Kranji and Seletar, a fourth NEWater factory at Ulu Pandan was completed in 2007, through public-private partnership based on the Design-Build-Own-Operate scheme. Together, the four NEWater factories are capable of supplying some 15% of Singapore's water demand. Earlier in 2008, a tender was awarded to another private company to construct the fifth and largest plant, the Changi NEWater Factory, also under a Design-Build-Own-Operate scheme. When this was completed in 2010, our NEWater factories would have a combined capacity to meet up to 30% of Singapore's water needs.

Water Recycling — An Urban Water Solution

For densely populated Singapore, water reuse has some obvious and some not so obvious benefits. First and foremost, recycling water effectively multiplies our water resources. Instead of linear single use, with NEWater, the same amount of water can be planned for reuse indefinitely. For an example, if I can recycle 50% of the water used, the water supply will theoretically double. You start with one litre of water, you recycle it, and get 0.5 litre; you recycle this 0.5 litre again and you get 0.25 litre, then 0.125 litre and so on. Theoretically, we are able to extract $0.5 + 0.25 + 0.125 + \cdots = 1$ litre from recycling the first litre, thereby multiplying the first litre. This way, for the mathematically inclined, with recycling, the augmented water supply is really a simple summation of a geometric series $\sum_{n=0}^{\infty} ar^n$, where the first term, a, equals to the first litre, and the common ratio, r, equals the recycling rate. This summation is equal to $a/1-r$ and gives us the total amount of water we can get by recycling!

Secondly, for a small island nation, land is a highly valuable commodity. In recycling, the source water is continually available as we use the water. We do not need large land space to create reservoirs to store water in between rains. Modern water reclamation technology makes use of modular membranes that can be stacked upwards, reducing the plant's footprint. Thus, water reclamation technology is not only capable of recycling water to a very high standard, but is also land efficient and is highly suitable for Singapore's growth, or for that matter, growth of any urban setting. In fact, the NEWater Factory which is constructed at Changi, in the eastern reaches of Singapore, is being built on the rooftop of the Reclamation Plant that feeds it treated effluent, thus maximising the use of land.

The fact that NEWater has become one of our main water sources is made possible only because of our efforts over the past 40 years, which had ensured all used water is collected through a comprehensive network of more than 3,000 km of sewers which cover almost the entire Singapore and treated to meet international standards before discharge. With NEWater, every litre of water supplied becomes a resource after it is used. Thus, water recycling is a perfect complement for an urban, fully-sewered city.

Thirdly, water reclamation is a controlled process that is not subject to the vagaries of weather. Rather than wait for rain, and then collect it in reservoirs, by making use of treated effluent for water reclamation, we can plan in advance to get the quantity and quality of water we require.

Cost of NEWater

Lastly, energy-wise, water reclamation is much less energy intensive compared to desalination. With current technology, desalination requires about 4 times as much energy as water reclamation to produce clean drinking water. The cost of producing NEWater, as evidenced by the bid price for the latest Changi NEWater Factory, is about S$0.30 per cu m while water desalination cost is more than double that of NEWater. This compares favourably with conventional sources of water from water catchments.

Conclusion — New Water Management Strategy

The Singapore Water Story offers a new water management strategy for a sustainable water supply system. With limited land area, there is only so much water we can collect, store and treat in the conventional way i.e. through collection in pristine reservoirs, treatment with flocculation, sedimentation and sand filtration. We have embarked on a new water management strategy that involves harvesting water from unconventional sources. This new strategy must take a hard and soft approach. By making use of proven technology, and more importantly, by removing psychological barriers, water reuse can be made mainstream and a viable source of water for the future. That is why NEWater is key in the water supply strategy for Singapore.

Acknowledgement

The author would like to thank PUB, Singapore's national water agency, for all the assistance in preparing this paper and for providing the figures used therein.

CHAPTER 5

Environmental Planning for Sustainable Development

Tan Yong Soon

A clean and green environment offers a high quality of life for a country's residents as well as enhances economic growth. Singapore, a tiny island state with very limited land and resources, has been able to achieve a good balance between economic growth and environmental protection. This requires clear visions, long-term environmental planning and effective implementation.

Land Use

Long-term and integrated land-use planning plays a major role in protecting the environment. At the macro level, Singapore's development is guided by the Concept Plan, a strategic, long-term land-use plan that maps the land-use vision for Singapore over the next 40 to 50 years, and is reviewed every 10 years. This process is spearheaded by the Ministry of National Development and Urban Redevelopment Authority, but is really a collaborative effort involving all relevant agencies, especially environment and economic agencies, working together to ensure that the environment is protected in tandem with development. Consequently, land resources are used optimally so that quality of life improves even as Singapore continues to develop and its population grows. One level down, the Master Plan translates the broad, long-term strategies of the Concept Plan into detailed plans, even to the extent of specifying the permissible land use and density of development for every parcel of land.

Environmental controls are factored into land-use planning to ensure the developments are properly sited. Major land users with potential to cause extensive pollution are grouped together and located as far away as possible from residential areas and town centres. Through the process of developmental control and building plan approval, a developer of a project has to satisfy the planners and environment agencies of its environmental pollution controls to limit its impact on the environment and ensure the compatibility with the surrounding land use.

Environmental pollution control requirements have to be incorporated into the design of the development, particularly with regard to environmental health, drainage, sewerage, and pollution control. Industries with the potential to cause extensive pollution and major developments that are likely to have major impacts on the environment are required to carry out pollution control studies covering all possible adverse environmental impacts, as well as the measures recommended to eliminate or mitigate these impacts.

Pollution control for industries goes beyond the planning and development phase. Even after approval is given, pollution levels are closely monitored. Pollution standards are reviewed over time and adjusted with improvements in technology.

As many green spaces as possible are set aside for recreation and the protection of the environment and biodiversity. Some nature areas, designated as national parks or nature reserves, are protected by legislation enacted by the Parliament. These nature areas are limited in land-scarce Singapore. Where areas rich in biodiversity are not protected by legislation, they are kept from development for as long as possible. Chek Jawa, a 100-hectare wetlands with different ecosystems and biodiversity located on the southeastern tip of Pulau Ubin, an island off the northeastern coast of the main island of Singapore is such an example. Most land parcels are, however, open for multiple use. To enhance green areas, where appropriate, the drainage reserves along roads and canals are turned into green corridors and park connectors. The offshore Semakau Landfill, Singapore's only remaining landfill, has been designed and operated to conserve the biodiversity of the surrounding areas and protect and preserve the marine ecosystem. It is also an idyllic and scenic attraction, open for activities such as educational tours, guided intertidal walks, bird watching, sport fishing or overnight stargazing. As a result of such careful planning, Singapore's green cover has grown from 35.7% to 46.5% between 1986 and 2007.

Land will always be a scarce and precious resource in Singapore. Going forward, Singapore will have to continue putting in significant effort to explore innovation in land and space optimisation. Aiming to take advantage of R&D to develop groundbreaking and pioneering technological solutions to increase Singapore's land capacity for its long-term development needs and to create alternatives for future generations, the National Research Foundation has allocated S$135 million from 2013 to 2018 for a land and liveability national innovation challenge that would "create new space cost-effectively and optimise the use of space to sustain Singapore's long-term growth and resilience".[1]

---

[1] National Research Foundation, Singapore (NRF) (2014), National Innovation Challenges. Retrieved 10 January 2015 from http://www.nrf.gov.sg/about-nrf/programmes/national-innovation-challenges?

Critical Environmental Infrastructure

Land also has to be set aside for critical environmental infrastructure such as drainage, sewerage, water supply as well as waste disposal facilities. Projections of future land requirements for such infrastructure are also factored into the Concept Plan so that adequate land is safeguarded for these needs. Selected areas that are ecologically rich will also be safeguarded. Having a good infrastructure in place is important.

Drainage

Singapore is located in the equatorial belt with abundant rainfall. Regular and severe flooding will occur if the storm water drainage infrastructure is not adequate. Managing flooding from heavy monsoon rains is important as floods cause not only great inconvenience and disruption to people's lives but also potentially tremendous damage to properties. In some flood incidents, lives might even be lost. Adequate storm water drainage infrastructure requires setting aside extensive land parcels to build the drainage system. Hence the environment and water agencies, in consultation with URA, HDB, JTC and other development agencies, prepared and put into action a comprehensive Drainage Master Plan, taking into consideration current and future land use as well as intensities of developments. The Drainage Master Plan also sets aside land for widening existing storm water drains and canals as well as for building future drains, canals and detention facilities to minimise future flooding in tandem with developments. New policies are also introduced, such as requiring higher platform levels for developments, and getting new developments to implement on-site detention measures to reduce peak runoff discharged from their sites during intense rainfall. As a result, flood-prone areas have been reduced to 36 hectares at the end of 2013, from about 3,200 hectares in the 1970s.

Sanitation

Sanitation is another critical infrastructure, as diseases would otherwise spread. A Sewerage Master Plan was developed drawing from the apportionment of proposed land uses under the Concept Plan. The Sewerage Master Plan served as a detailed guide for the development of sewerage facilities, specifying corresponding projected sewage flows based on pre-determined zoning, and even micro-level design considerations of sewers and the layout of the sewerage facilities. Under the Sewerage Master Plan, Singapore was divided into a number of sewerage catchment zones, based on the contours of the island. A centralised sewage treatment plant served each zone, where the sewage was treated to international standards before the treated effluent was discharged into the sea. Pumping stations were installed to transfer sewage flows to the plants.

The design of Singapore's sewerage management system requires a clear separation of storm water and sewage streams and systems. Ensuring sewage goes into a central sewerage system and is kept separate from storm water has been critical in keeping waters in and around Singapore clean. This separate sewerage system is a more effective and economical approach in the long run as it ensures that the inland waterways, reservoirs, and the sea surrounding Singapore are not polluted by the discharge of untreated or semi-treated sewage and industrial effluent; and ensure all wastewater is collected for treatment before discharge into the sea or further processing to produce industrial or potable water. The separation of the systems also prevents storm water from entering the sewerage systems and causing overflows during heavy storms, as may happen in the case of combined sewers.

All premises are required to connect to public sewers. Developers of housing and industrial estates have to incorporate a sewer network to collect and convey sewage and industrial wastewater effectively into the public sewerage system. Proposals for development are scrutinised to ensure that they do not encroach on the public sewerage system (i.e. sewers, pumping, mains, etc.). This helps to avert any potential damage to the public sewerage system and, in turn, prevents pollution resulting from overflow or leakage of sewage. In addition, stringent sewer pipe laying and sanitary work requirements are also imposed through legislation.

With the development of NEWater (potable water reclaimed from treated wastewater, but is mostly used by industries as high purity water), sewage and industrial wastewater becomes used water, a resource that can be reclaimed for reuse. A deep tunnel sewerage system was built to consolidate the collection of used water into a central water reclamation plant for treatment and conversion to NEWater, freeing for redevelopment a number of parcels of land previously used for sewage treatment plants and pumping stations.

Water Supply

Achieving water sustainability is a strategic goal. Inland streams were dammed to form reservoirs, which were expanded. Estuarine rivers were also dammed up, the salty water flushed out to create large bodies of freshwater. The water catchment areas had to be protected to ensure storm water collected meets raw potable water quality. Where developments were necessary, such development was limited to residential estates and industries with clean and light uses. In addition to land-use planning, stringent pollution control was also required. Yet land scarcity does not allow us to have all water catchment areas to be protected. In fact, two-thirds of the island's land mass are water catchments areas, most of which are unprotected. Proper sanitation and strict regulation of sewage and industrial wastewater allow development in these unprotected water catchment areas.

NEWater or reclaimed water, the purification of used water to drinking water standards, and desalinated water combined can now meet up to 40% of Singapore's water demand.

Waste Disposal

Land must also be set aside for an effective solid waste management infrastructure to ensure no potential threats to public health. Initially refuse were disposed of at sanitary landfills located on the main island, in areas that were not suitable for development without intensive preparation such as swampy areas, and far away from heavily populated areas. As land became increasingly scarce and with ever increasing solid wastes, Singapore introduced incineration in the late 1970s to reduce the refuse to be dumped into landfills to about 10% of its original volume. The closed landfills could be cleaned up and re-zoned for other uses. Heat from refuse incineration is recovered as electricity. However, land has to be allocated for refuse incineration plants and ash from refuse incineration is still required to be disposed of at a landfill, although the landfill requirement is much reduced. With no more swampy land available on the main island, an offshore landfill at Pulau Semakau was built for disposal of incineration ash and solid wastes that could not be incinerated.

Critical Success Factors: The 4 Ps

While the physical planning aspects — land-use planning and critical environment infrastructure — are important, a good environment can only be achieved through the critical success factors of the 4Ps — political leadership, public sector efficiency and effectiveness, private sector competitiveness and social responsibility and people participation and ownership.

Political Leadership

Political leadership is key to achieving a good balance between economic growth and environmental sustainability because there must be a clear vision from the very top that a clean and good quality living environment is important; a strong commitment to implement such a vision; and the ability to communicate that vision so that it can be shared and supported by everyone.

In the first 50 years, Singapore had political leaders who possessed the foresight to see beyond economic development — that preserving the environment and growing the economy are not only not mutually exclusive, but complementary. Our leaders had the resourcefulness and mettle to take the long view and build capabilities, and also the skills to communicate the vision and persuade the people and businesses to suspend some of their immediate needs that the foregone economic development could have met.

Public Sector Effectiveness and Efficiency

In addition to sound political leadership, an effective and efficient public sector is critical to achieving success. The political leadership must be ably supported by a public sector that helps to design good policies and implement them effectively. It has to organise and work as an effective integrated government, develop and manage infrastructure projects well, innovate, continually set high environmental standards and regulate judiciously. The public sector would also have to introduce the right mix of market mechanisms to deter polluters and to encourage the development of a vibrant private sector which can produce environmental goods and services efficiently.

Private Sector Competitiveness and Social Responsibility

The private sector is certainly in the position to contribute to new environmental goods, as business is often good at innovating and searching for opportunities. Thus the desalination plants and the latest NEWater plants and incinerator plant are all privately owned and operated on a Public-Private Partnership arrangement with the relevant government agencies. In fact, Singapore-based companies such as Keppel, SembCorp and Hyflux have also made successful forays overseas, for example, into China and the Middle East, to help deliver environmental and water services and supplies competitively.

The private sector must also be socially responsible. Companies have to abide by the environmental standards set up by the government. Businesses are encouraged to provide feedback to proposed new regulations and standards so that they can be introduced effectively, and in a reasonable timeframe.

People Participation and Ownership

People must want a better environment for themselves and their children. Public participation and ownership are critical to a better environment. The first national public education effort was a month-long "Keep Singapore Clean" campaign in 1968. It took many years of public education to enable the public to develop a sense of civic consciousness, social responsibility and discipline. Such government-led platforms have now been replaced largely with mass participation, sharing of long-term plans and bottom-up initiatives by a healthy civil society.

Initially people may be more attuned to their immediate needs and need to be persuaded of the benefits of a clean environment. But once people have reaped the benefits of a clean environment, they would be inclined to desire it and may even be a few steps ahead of the government, if the government is slow in delivering a clean environment.

People have started to desire a clean environment, but they also have to organise and educate themselves, and to be motivated to assume the role of stewards of the environment for their children, to modify their behaviour, to help and not rely solely on the government to deliver a clean environment.

New Environment Challenges

Singapore has done well to protect its environment through effective environmental policy, planning and implementation. As a result of the good environment and concomitant economic progress, Singaporeans are better educated, widely travelled and hence, more environmentally sophisticated and demanding. We must continue to upgrade our environmental infrastructure and raise our standards to give our people a better quality of life. This is particularly important when climate change will pose tremendous dangers and unpredictable risks. We will need to take the necessary measures to mitigate and adapt to climate change.

We must move from the mindset of environmental protection to one of environmental sustainability. Sustainable development, as defined in the 1987 UN World Commission on Environment and Development report Our Common Future, is "development that meets the needs of the present without compromising the ability of future generations to meet their own needs".[2] Singapore has already embarked on an environmental sustainability programme. It is an ongoing journey. The top-down approach to protecting the environment is still necessary but increasingly insufficient. An effective bottom-up approach is even more important now.

A Higher Quality of Environment

As Singapore progresses, Singaporeans will come to better understand the linkages between the environment and our health and social well-being, and that the quality of the environment is an important contribution to our quality of life. Good basic public hygiene and human health will no longer be sufficient. Our environmental infrastructure and standards must constantly be upgraded to truly meet first world standards. The challenge is to introduce and incorporate innovative environmental

---

[2] UN World Commission on Environment and Development (WCED) (1987), Chapter 2: Towards Sustainable Development, in *Our Common Future: Report of the World Commission on Environment and Development*. Switzerland: WCED. Retrieved 8 December 2014 from http://www.un-documents.net/ocf-02.htm.

infrastructure/measures and make such facilities efficient and convenient for residents to practise environment-friendly programmes like waste recycling and energy conservation.

New forms of pollution threats and causes of environmental degradation need to be tackled effectively. The public deserves and will demand a higher quality of the environment.

Climate Change

Climate change, with the resultant rising sea level, extreme weather with very intense rainfalls and energy requirements, poses new challenges, not just infrastructural and economic, but also has tremendous important environmental, social and health impacts. We need to be able to address these issues and keep in mind the impacts in the future. More and more, we need long-term planning and policy and technological innovation to find effective and efficient solutions for both climate change mitigation and adaptation.

Environmental Sustainability

Singaporeans must want to live sustainably — environmentally, socially and economically. While many Singaporeans want a better quality of the environment, they must also be willing to pay, either in improving behaviour and habits so as to keep public places clean and reduce energy consumption, or footing the higher immediate economic costs required to safeguard the environment for future generations. Strong political leadership and committed public ownership will be needed to persuade and bring along the public to support a good environment. There will be a cost to improving the environment, but there is a greater cost to inaction.

Environment: Singapore's Competitive Advantage

Singapore has placed so much importance on the environment from our early days. Because of our unique circumstance as a city-state with no natural resources and hinterland, taking good care of our environment and making the most efficient use of our resources, is a necessity for us and not a choice.

Singapore environment agencies from the Anti-Pollution Unit (set up in 1970) to the Ministry of the Environment (set up in 1972 and later renamed as the Ministry of the Environment and Water Resources in 2004), and its agencies, PUB, the national water agency, and the National Environment Agency, have always planned for the long term, innovated constantly and implemented effectively and pragmatically to help Singapore to develop in a sustainable way.

Land-use planning has always and will continue to be important to ensure that environmental considerations are incorporated in urban planning in Singapore. Environment agencies have and will continue to work with the urban planning authority to ensure integrated land-use planning. Critical environmental infrastructure must also be planned and implemented.

Our clean and green environment is our competitive advantage in ensuring a good quality of life for our residents as well as for attracting investments. As Singapore develops and grows into a first world country, it is even more important that we move successfully from the mindset of environmental protection to one of environmental sustainability. The political leadership's vision, the public sector's ability to help facilitate the execution of that environmental vision, the vibrancy of the private sector and the people's support for a good environment and taking personal responsibility and ownership, these are all factors which have brought us where we are today and are sources of great strength that will continue to propel Singapore forward.

Acknowledgements

The author, a former Permanent Secretary of the Ministry of the Environment and Water Resources (MEWR), and a former Chief Executive Officer of the Urban Redevelopment Authority (URA), wishes to thank his former colleagues in both MEWR and URA for their good work in environmental planning for a sustainable development. The author would also like to thank Loh Ah Tuan, former Deputy CEO and Director General of Environment Protection, National Environment Agency (NEA), Foong Chee Leong, former Director General Meteorological Services and Director Pollution Control, NEA, and Yap Kheng Guan, former Director Drainage and Director 3P (Public, Private and People sectors) Network, PUB, for their comments and suggestions on the draft of this chapter.

PART 2

Present Challenges

CHAPTER 6

Frontier Research in Environment and Water: Integrated Research Approach for Sustainable Solutions

Lee Lai Yoke and Ong Choon Nam
NUS Environmental Research Institute

Abstract

NUS through coordinated research at NUS Environmental Research Institute (NERI) has been leading frontier research in environment and water. The approach is based on integrated multi-disciplinary environmental research for sustainable solutions. Since Singapore's early exploration for potable water from unconventional supply, NUS researchers have contributed actively to the Health Effects Studies on toxicological assessment of reclaimed water. Today, NUS continues to lead research in sustaining supply of quality water with innovative ideas for environmental surveillance in water catchments and advanced treatment technologies. Challenges of emerging contaminants, such as small particulate matters, nanomaterials and persistent organic pollutants in air and water that may affect Asian cities are also key research programmes currently being pursued by NERI researchers together with local agencies and international institutions. Climate Change research at NUS contributes to further understanding of potential vulnerability, creating a sustainable climate change adaptation and mitigation measures for Singapore and the region. NUS multi-disciplinary research on water-food-air is generating new knowledge and breakthrough findings related to safety, health and environment effects for the rapidly growing Singapore and regional countries. NERI serves as NUS Point-of-Contact for government agencies, industries, and institutions for environmental and water research. These collaborations are the key emphasis at NERI to bring innovative research ideas and outcomes to commercialisation.

The Beginning — Sourcing the Unconventional Supply

Singapore has been known to be a water source-scarce country, and this has driven the country to look into innovative technologies to achieve water self-sufficiency at national scale more than three decades ago. As the membrane technology matures, the scale of economy and reliance of the treatment gave rise to NEWater plants in Singapore today. The technology lies in the multi-barrier membranes, microfiltration (MF) followed by reverse osmosis (RO), and lastly ultraviolet (UV) disinfection to produce NEWater from secondary treated domestic wastewater effluent. In Singapore, NEWater serves as the 3rd National Tap. NEWater supplies raw water for direct non-potable industry use, while indirect potable reuse is being practiced by blending a portion of NEWater with raw water from reservoir, which is then further treated at water treatment facilities before supplying for household use. The latter is essential to sustain potable water supply especially during the dry months. Currently, NEWater supplies up to 30% of Singapore's water need and this will increase by twofold by 2060 (PUB, 2014a).

Research is one of the major cornerstones to the success of NEWater implementation in Singapore. A team of multidisciplinary researchers from National University of Singapore (NUS) and their collaborators were involved in the Health Effects Studies on the toxicological assessment of reclaimed water (later known as "NEWater" in Singapore). Mice and fish were used as models to evaluate the short and long-term toxicity and carcinogenicity effects of NEWater. This health effect studies were carried out to complement the comprehensive sampling and monitoring programme (comprising 293 water quality parameters; more than the 100 specified by the US Environmental Protection Agency (USEPA) and 122 specified by the World Health Organisation (WHO)). Fish, the Japanese Medaka (*Oryzias latipes*), were also assessed on the estrogenic effects of the NEWater from the Bedok NEWater Pilot plant, which had a capacity of 10,000 m³/d, as compared with Public Utilities Board, Singapore (PUB) traditional water source from Bedok Reservoir (PUB, 2002).

The modified and improved fish testing was set-up and evaluated for one year at the pilot plant facility, while the mice testing using the B6C3F1 strain were carried out by feeding the mice up to 2 years with 150x and 500x NEWater and reservoir water concentrates at the Animal Holding Unit in NUS (Rodriguez *et al.*, 2009).

To further explore the possibility of similar technology using aquarium fish for water quality health monitoring, transgenic fish including medaka and zebrafish (*Danio rerio*) were developed by the NUS team to fluoresce in response to the presence of environmental toxins (Gong *et al.*, 2001) (similar to Figure 1, left). The first line of transgenic fish was inserted with gene encoding green fluorescent protein (GFP), isolated from a jellyfish that could naturally fluoresce in bright green (Gong *et al.*, 2003). This gene was integrated into the fish genome through the embryos. Other colours such as red and yellow or orange fluorescent transgenic fish were also developed by adding genes from sea corals and variants of GFP (Gong *et al.*, 2003). These living colour proteins provide a unique feature that fluorescent colours on the fish can be visualised directly under the natural white light and ultraviolet light (Gong *et al.*, 2001). A patent was spun off as part of the research outcome in creating a constant

Figure 1. Fluorescent transgenic zebrafish (Left) and automatic zebrafish culture system (Right). The left picture shows currently commercialised GloFish, which are produced based on the patent of NUS (courtesy of Yorktown Technologies). The right picture shows a researcher working in front of zebrafish tanks with circulating water.

fluorescing fish, which are eagerly welcomed by ornamental fish lovers.[1] A US company, Yorktown Technologies, L.P. has been licensed for worldwide rights to market this transgenic zebrafish under the brand name "GloFish" (Figure 1, left).

Over the past decades, the research capabilities in water assessment and treatment have provided the basis for scientists and researchers in Singapore and around the globe to build upon and further develop advanced technologies for improved and more efficient treatment; rapid, sensitive and online sensing; green technologies for better environment and human health protection. It is becoming even more challenging to ensure that water is of consistently high quality for its intended use.

Research institutions including the NUS Environmental Research Institute (NERI)[2] are continuously exploring frontier science and technologies; and building collaborations with regional and international institutions and industries to bring innovative research ideas and outcomes to commercialisation. This concurs with Singapore's vision to be a global hydrohub and global leader in water management and technology (PUB, 2014b).

Sustainable Supply of Quality Water

Environmental Surveillance

Trace level detection of water pollutants

Water serves as an important resource for economy growth to sustain industrial activities and the population's daily needs. Besides the increasing concern of traditional

---

[1] Patent no.: WO2000049150 "Chimeric Gene Constructs for Generation of Fluorescent Transgenic Ornamental Fish." National University of Singapore.

[2] NERI is an interdisciplinary research institute at the National University of Singapore (NUS). The institute serves as the NUS Point-of-Contact for Singapore and international government agencies, industry and institutions for environment and water research. http://www.nus.edu.sg/neri.

pollutants such as nutrients (nitrogen and phosphorus) and heavy metals, discharge of non-conventional pollutants of emerging concerns into the environment are also drawing attention of water specialists. These include traces of pharmaceutical compounds, nanomaterials from cosmetics and skincare products, pollutants from surface runoff, etc. In addition, with the increase of water reuse practices, it is important to ensure water supplied is able to meet the highest quality.

Assessment of non-conventional pollutants is essential in order to understand their potential impacts on the environment and human health. As most of these pollutants are present in trace micrograms to nanograms levels, it becomes highly challenging for detection using conventional analysis methods; and to some extent, development of new methods is necessary for sensitive and accurate quantification. These need to be complemented with information on the occurrence and general concentrations in the environment that could have impacts on human and environment health, using in vivo or in vitro testings such as representative human cell lines or animal models. The followings are some of the examples on water quality surveillance developed by researchers in NUS.

Green analytical chemistry for environmental pollutants detection

The emerging contaminants in water can be generally classified into two major groups, namely organic compounds and inorganic substances.

Analytical chemistry using gas chromatography (GC) or liquid chromatography (LC) provides a quick assessment of organic compounds found in the environment. As for inorganic pollutants of emerging concerns such as nanomaterials, this can be analysed with Inductively Coupled Plasma Mass Spectrometry (ICPMS) which could be coupled with Ion Exchange for species analysis. Both organic and inorganic compounds analysis in the water matrix require extensive sample preparation, which is the major factor determining accuracy of the assessment. Traditionally, the sample preparation involves use of large volume of hazardous chemicals (solvents or acids) for extraction of pollutant compounds from at least 1 to 10 litres of water samples. New research developments in the analysis are being pursued abiding the green analytical principles. This involves minimal use of hazardous chemicals, i.e. solvent or even into solventless sample pretreatment. This would eliminate concerns with the use and disposal of hazardous substances in the extraction steps prior to analysis using GC and LC for organic compounds, and ICPMS for inorganic matters.

Liquid-phase microextraction (LPME) is a sample preparation procedure that requires low microlitre amounts of solvent for extraction from water samples, while solventless extraction is achieved through the solid-phase microextraction (SPME). Various implementations of LPME have been developed over the past years by the NUS team at Department of Chemistry. These include the use of polymer-coated

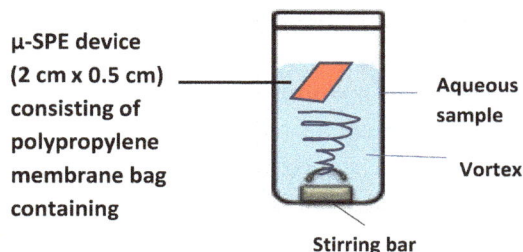

μ-SPE device (2 cm x 0.5 cm) consisting of polypropylene membrane bag containing

Aqueous sample

Vortex

Stirring bar

Figure 2.   Schematic of micro-solid-phase extraction (μ-SPE, or "tea-bag extraction") (Courtesy of Prof. Lee Hian Kee).

hollow fibre LPME, solvent-bar microextraction, continuous flow microextraction (CFME) and micro-solid phase extraction (μ-SPE) or commonly known as "tea-bag extraction" (Figure 2). These methods are simple, environmentally friendly and can be conveniently applied.

The μ-SPE method had been applied for determination of pharmaceutical compounds in water. Liquid–liquid microextraction combined with micro-solid phase extraction, and liquid chromatography had shown to yield promising results with high recovery and consistency. Various solid-phase had been used as sorbent. These include zeolite imidazolate framework-4 (ZIF-4), polar sorbents with surface-displayed amino groups (APS) and non-nucleophilic urea-groups (UPS) (Ge and Lee, 2013; Lim *et al.*, 2013). The method generally uses a few hundred microlitres of organic solvent with less than 10 ml of samples. The whole extraction procedure could be completed within minutes. The desorbed solvent containing the extracted targeted compound is then injected into the LC for further quantification. The micro-scale methods provide the convenience for sample preparation to be carried out on-site. This enables better sample storage and ease of transport; or analysis could even be carried out on-site to avoid sample disintegration. Thus far, good analytical results have been demonstrated by many research teams using the micro-scale methods (Matheson, 2008).

Engineered nanomaterials (ENM) of significant health and environmental concern — it is one of the major groups of inorganic emerging pollutants which are challenging the research community due to the difficulty in differentiating between the anthropogenic and natural occurring nanomaterials, in addition to their presence in low nanograms in natural environment. Silver and titanium (IV) are among the ENMs that are important components utilised in personal care and other consumer products. These materials would find their paths to the environment following increased use of these materials in the industries. These ENMs are predicted to be present in nanogram levels in surface water and sewage treatment plant effluent.

The detection method using microscopic, spectroscopic and separation techniques are mainly limited to assessing the toxicity and bioavailability. Besides this, research focus of ENMs has been mainly on synthesis and purification. Therefore, developing quantitative assay methods of ENMs found in the environment would fill in the knowledge gap on available concentrations of these materials in the environment and to provide better environmental assessment.

The ENMs quantitative assay methods include pretreatment using various steps of extraction and preconcentration such as cloud point extraction (CPE) with Triton X-114 for thermo-irreversible separation of various nanoparticles (Hinze and Pramauro, 1993; Watanabe and Tanaka, 1978), which can then be analysed using microscopy (such as transmission electron microscopy (TEM), scanning electron microscopy (SEM)) combined with energy-dispersive X-ray spectroscopy (EDS), and UV-visible spectroscopy, and determined using inductively coupled plasma mass spectrometry (ICPMS) after microwave digestion. The criteria in these methods are good reproducibility, high extraction efficiency and low detection limit. The NUS team was the first to apply the orthogonal array design (OAD), an efficient statistical method to optimise pertinent CPE conditions and two-variable interaction parameters and to evaluate their simultaneous influence on the extraction efficiency and speciation analysis of zinc oxide nanoparticles (ZnO NPs) in water samples. This chemometric method results in time and chemicals savings. Together with ANOVA (analysis of variance), the variables including surfactant concentration and pH were found to have the most significant effects on the extraction and can be further optimised (Majedi et al., 2012). Research is ongoing in NUS and other national agencies such as PUB and the National Environment Agency (NEA) to further develop and improve on quantification and speciation of ENMs, especially those commonly found in the environment.

Biomonitoring using aquarium species

Biological assessment of emerging pollutants provides the detailed information on health and environmental impacts with respect to the exposure concentrations.

As mentioned earlier, the Singapore team is among the pioneers to use transgenic medaka fish for online water quality monitoring, a competency developed since the early testing on NEWater. NERI research team further developed this competency to use zebrafish (*Danio rerio*) for monitoring environmental pollution. They have developed several GFP transgenic lines using different inducible promoters of florescent transgenic fishes which can induce GPF expression specifically in response to several classes of environmental pollutants, including estrogenic compounds, polycyclic aromatic hydrocarbons and heavy metals (Lam et al., 2008; Wu et al., 2008).

The zebrafish model had also been demonstrated to respond biologically to the mentioned environmental pollutants in a similar manner as mammals (Lam et al.,

2008; Parng *et al.*, 2002). In addition, the zebrafish embryo, up to the free feeding stage, about 4 to 5 days of post-fertilisation (dpf), can be applied as an alternative to animal experiments under the European legislation (Belanger, 2010; EU, 2010). Thus far, the zebrafish model has been widely used for teratogenicity, cardiotoxicity and nervous-sensory organ toxicity screening as well as omics application over the past decade (Sukardi *et al.*, 2011).

The zebrafish model also offers many advantages over the animal models for environmental toxicants screenings. The development stage of zebrafish takes only about 5 days from the single cell stage, through embryonic, post-embryonic and free-feeding larvae with fully functioning organ-systems, and eventually reaches sexual maturity within 3 to 4 months. High-throughput toxicity screening can be achieved using zebrafish embryos/larvae in a microtitre plate with up to 96 wells by dosing different concentrations, low volume of pollutants of concern. This enables rapid screening of various types of toxicants' effects on the targeted organ-systems during developmental stages as well as teratogenicity (multigeneration and reproductive toxicity) evaluations. Thus far, the toxicology assessment has been assessed on conditions related to nervous, cardiac, liver, immune, musculoskeletal, vasculature and kidney, as well as evaluation in the late embryonic and early larval stages of the zebrafish. The transparent nature of zebrafish during the development stage also allows easy visual assessment of internal organs. To further facilitate this, the introduction of fluorescent (e.g. GFP) reporter genes under a tissue specific promoter allows real-time monitoring and high resolution qualitative and quantitative assessments of specific organ-tissue toxicity (Yang *et al.*, 2009a).

The NUS researchers are currently working on identifying specific biomarker genes for determination of environmental contaminants. The research goal is to develop practical polymerase chain reaction (PCR) arrays using biomarker genes for zebrafish.

Recently, "omics" technology which involves extraction of biomolecules (such as mRNA transcripts, proteins and metabolites) from the fish for global profiling, complements the phenotype assessment after compound exposure to provide additional predictive and mechanistic insights of toxicity (Lam *et al.*, 2008). The team studied on transcriptional and proteomics changes during different stages of embryogenesis of zebrafish. GC-MS and LC-MS were used to detect the metabolite levels followed by multivariate analysis (OPLS-DA) for metabolites identification that are responsible for differentially regulating the embryogenesis process (Huang *et al.*, 2013). These data would provide the reference for future toxicological or developmental studies.

Among some of the emerging pollutants tested, NUS researchers have developed screening protocols for bisphenol-A, which possesses endocrine disrupting activities that originates from polycarbonate plastic and epoxy resin manufacturing, on early stage development using zebrafish embryo/larvae as a toxicogenomic model (Lam *et al.*, 2011); and hepatotoxicity of 4-nitrophenol using transcriptomic analysis of genes from adult male zebrafish (Lam *et al.*, 2013).

Thus far, both the medaka and zebrafish models have been successfully applied for water pollutant-related health and environmental research. New screening protocols using these models are constantly being pursued for new classes of emerging pollutants. Research efforts are also ongoing to further develop methods to better understand the responses using metabolomic techniques, which would help to shed more light on the biological response to exposure to emerging pollutants.

Innovation in sensor development

Research into sensor development for an environmental purpose aims to provide better water and environmental monitoring and management. The main criteria for sensor development are sensitivity, accuracy, minimal or maintenance-free, and ability for online sensing with wireless data transmission to a central control station would be highly desired.

The demand for online sensing has been increasing due to many advantages including savings of manpower and analysis costs that involved the handling of samples by specialised personnel and use of sophisticated equipment. In addition, online sensing allows simultaneous monitoring at different locations and comprehensive data points can be obtained for prompt data analysis and decision-making.

Online sensors ranging from simple physical parameters such as pH, dissolved oxygen, temperature to more sophisticated chemical sensors such as the ion-selective electrodes for the detection of ammonia, nitrate, nitrite, chloride and various types of heavy metals are readily available. In addition, sensors for chlorophyll-a and blue-green algae are also available for monitoring of surface water and prediction of potential algae bloom. In the past two decades, incidents of algae bloom in various parts of the world had led to taste and odour problems in drinking water, and for extreme cases, toxic algae proliferation had caused fish-kill incidents and making treated water not fit for potable use.

A major parameter, which is also the limiting nutrient in algae bloom, is phosphates. Generally, phosphates are present in trace concentrations in surface water. Hence, this makes accurate detection highly challenging. Total phosphorus and orthophosphate (which is the bio-available phosphorus form) would need to be below 0.5 mg/l and 0.05 mg/l, respectively, for long-term eutrophication prevention, while algae blooms can be triggered if orthophosphate level is above 0.08 mg/l (Dunne and Leopold, 1978).

Due to the low concentration present in surface water, the traditional sample collection, transport and measurement in laboratory require extensive steps in apparatus pre-treatment to remove interfering contaminants and the use of expensive equipment for the trace phosphate analysis. The NUS team, together with Shanghai Jiao Tong University researchers under the Energy and Environmental Sustainability Solutions for Megacities (E2S2) Programme, has developed a relatively low-cost portable system, based on the diffusive gradients in thin films (DGT) technique, for dissolved phosphate monitoring in freshwater. The device comprises two parts: (i) the DGT device which functions as a pre-concentrator, containing a polydiallydimethylammonium chloride (PDA) aqueous solution as a binding phase and a dialysis membrane as a diffusive layer in the DGT; and (ii) a detection chamber. The amount of phosphates pre-concentrated in the DGT device was further measured by ultraviolet-visible spectroscopy (UV) in the detection chamber to determine the phosphate concentrations in the water sample (Figure 3). The sensitivity of this newly developed phosphate sensor is comparable to the existing laboratory methods and to a certain extent, more sensitive and estimated to cost only a small fraction as compared with laboratory-based analytical equipment. This new sensor had been applied to measure phosphates in synthetic and natural river water. The results have shown good agreement with the theoretical values and comparable with the standard method (Li *et al.*, 2014a). The research teams are also exploring the use of this DGT device concept for sensing heavy metals and other water pollutants of interest.

Novel detection sensors have also been developed using molecular technique, known as molecular beacon (MB) sensor for heavy metal ions detection in environmental samples. One of the widely applied heavy metals sensing is for mercury ion (Hg^{2+}) (Freeman *et al.*, 2009; Ono and Tagashi, 2004; Teh *et al.*, 2014). This method is based on functional nucleic acids, i.e. using the "turn-on" reaction of a hairpin

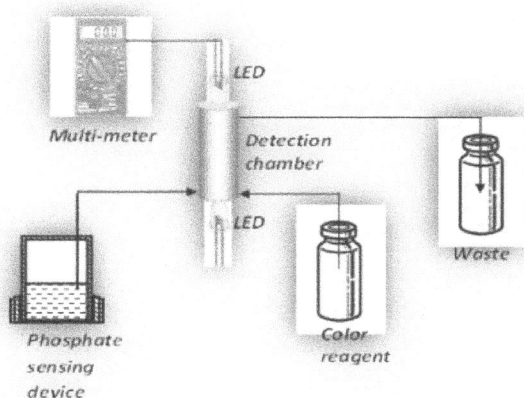

Figure 3. Using advanced technology for water quality assurance; In Situ Pre-concentration and On-Site Analysis for Phosphate Monitoring. US Provisional Application No. 61/945,919. 2014 (Courtesy of Dr. Li Weijia).

DNA probe upon binding with mismatched target and Hg^{2+} ions through the formation of $T-Hg^{2+}-T$ coordination. The conformational change of the MB caused a significant increase in fluorescence intensity, which could be used for Hg^{2+} sensing. This method of detection is highly sensitive and selective even in the presence of other metal ions with short response time, and possible achieving real-time applications. The MB sensor had shown to be in good agreement with Hg^{2+} spiked value, with recovery above 95% and variation below 5% in lake water samples (Teh *et al.*, 2014).

The NUS team had also ventured into developing the microbial fuel cell (MFC) as a sensor along the wastewater stream prior to the wastewater treatment plant. The MFC is a device whereby the chemical energy from bacteria activities is converted to electricity. Much research has been focussed on optimising MFC design to harvest the microbial energy generated through converting the organic matters in the wastewater to electrical energy. This green energy harvesting technology is still in the infancy stage of research. However, the NUS team has found a new application for MFC as an early warning toxicity sensor in wastewater stream before the wastewater enters the treatment plant. The concept used in this application is based on microbial activities inhibition effects in the presence of toxicants found in wastewater, and thus, reduced the electrical energy generated. The MFC device is able to provide real-time biomonitoring toxicity sensing. Shen *et al.* (2012) demonstrated the MFC toxicity sensing feasibility by simulating toxic incident with addition of hydrochloric acid (HCl) in the wastewater to alter the pH. The response showed an immediate decrease in the voltage, followed by subsequent recovery. The MFC design was optimised in this study and had demonstrated to show high sensitivity and prompt recovery following an acidic toxic event. The sensitivity of MFC as a toxicity sensor was found to be dependent on the hydraulic retention time of the wastewater stream flow, and the toxicity level would influence the extent of inhibition.

The multidisciplinary approach to the sensor development, which is the main emphasis at NERI, builds up the synergisms in creating new dimensions for better and more efficient water and environment management.

NUSwan: New Smart Water Assessment Network

Freshwater quality monitoring is highly challenging, especially when water serves as raw water source for treatment to potable use. Adding to this, Singapore's Active, Beautiful and Clean (ABC) programme is promoting active recreational use of water bodies to enhance urban liveability in this densely populated country. Hence, constant monitoring is essential to ensure the freshwater meets the quality of its diverse use at all times. One of the many research focusses led by NUS and PUB is the research on alternative microbial indicators as markers for potential pathogenicity assessment and this could be applied for source-tracking in surface waters from tropical urban watershed (PUB, 2014c). An important factor in the water quality monitoring programme planning is often the cost. It includes major labour and laboratory testing costs which limit the boundaries for extensive assessment of the water bodies. The criteria for better water quality management are to obtain a denser dataset in time and space at an affordable cost, and it is also highly desirable for real-time data.

NERI, together with the Tropical Marine Science Institute (TMSI)[3] worked to transform the technology of STARFISH, a torpedo-shaped autonomous underwater vehicle (Koay *et al.*, 2011), to a low-cost robot that is able to autonomously collect spatial data based on the global positioning system (GPS) for continuous data collection and transmission. Thus, NUSwan, an abbreviation for "New Smart Water Assessment Network", was developed as a whole new concept into spatial-temporal water quality monitoring, to provide an increased resilience assessment solution to maximise use of resources and cost effectiveness (Figure 4). This creates simultaneous multi-node, high speed sensing capability that opens up the possibility of observing concentration gradients, to better characterise the field and detect time-varying hotspots. The initial prototype of this platform monitoring technology takes the physical shape of a swan, which builds upon the aesthetic and recreational qualities of the natural reservoirs or lakes, and enhances the essence of clean surface water. This physical shape functions as a housing and vehicle to carry the monitoring sensors, electronics for mission control and data transmission. This physical shape is highly flexible and can take on other shapes to blend into the local surroundings.

A fleet of NUSwans deployed to different locations would be able to provide simultaneous water quality measurements and drive models to guide the NUSwans to locations where data could be most valuable, such as in the pollutant source tracking mission. NUSwans are programmed to return to specified sites for power recharge depending on the extent of power source (EConnect, 2014). The use of NUSwan enhances capability of manual monitoring and commercial monitoring systems by complementing spatial-temporal dimensions of existing stations.

NUSwan has attracted many local and overseas government agencies and commercial sectors, who are interested in technology transfer and looking into customisation of this platform technology for overseas environments. This is in view that NUSwan has great potential to provide extensive cost savings and the high spatial-temporal dimension of data collection would enhance and improve water quality monitoring.

---

[3]TMSI is a NUS centre for research, development and consultancy in tropical marine science as well as environmental science. These include projects relevant to Physical Oceanography, Acoustics, Marine Biology, Marine Mammals, Biofuels, Water Resources and Climate Change. http://www.tmsi.nus.edu.sg.

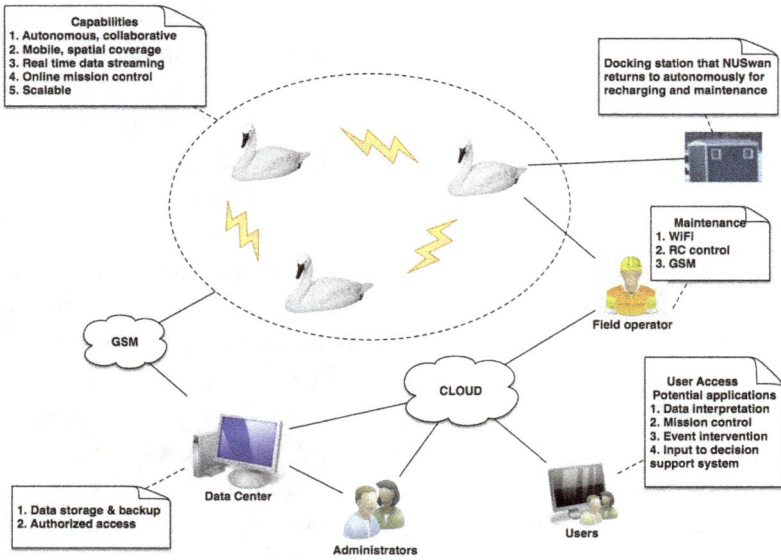

Figure 4. NUSwan prototype tested for water quality monitoring and mission control software (Courtesy of Mr. Koay Teong Beng) (Photo taken at Pandan Reservoir, courtesy of PUB, Singapore's national water agency).

Innovations in Treatment from Catchment to Plant

Pollutant removal in surface runoff using bioretention systems

As part of the PUB's ABC programme, bioretention basins (commonly known as "rain gardens") and bioretention swales are being implemented in residential, commercial and public areas to intercept and treat surface runoff using vegetation with engineered soil before it enters the drains and subsequently reservoirs (PUB, 2014d). Besides offering pollutants removal, both the rain gardens and swales provide aesthetical and ecological functions. The Balam rain garden was the first pilot rain garden in Singapore, which collects surface runoff from roads and the carpark of a public housing estate for treatment before discharging to a nearby canal (Ong *et al.*, 2012). Since then, many bioretention systems have been implemented island-wide to enhance Singapore's landscape as a City of Gardens and Water.

The bioretention systems concept for treating surface runoff has been widely applied in many countries such as Europe, US and Australia. It is gradually attracting interest in Asian countries. Besides Singapore, China and Taiwan have also invested in research and have applied to full-scale implementations.

Many of the biorentention systems' applications are established based on climatic conditions, plant species and construction materials native to overseas conditions. Hence, there is limited information on bioretention systems designs for tropical climates, especially that of Singapore and the countries in the region.

Design criteria based on the local rainfall events and intensity is important to avoid over- or under-sizing of the bioretention system to optimise the treatment efficiency. In addition, construction materials to be used should be widely available locally and cost effective. Sandy loam, the typical soil type recommended for rain garden use in the US and Australian design guidelines, is not a common soil type in Singapore. Therefore, engineered soil containing an optimised proportion of different materials will be needed to provide the desired hydraulic conductivity, maintain a consistent pollutants treatment efficiency and ability to sustain plant growth. Selecting the suitable plants for bioretention systems could enhance treatment efficiency through nutrient uptakes. Selected plants could also enhance the removal of heavy metals. Besides this, the root systems create a micro-environment to sustain a healthy diverse microbial community for pollutant removal, as well as to maintain the soil hydraulic conductivity of the bioretention systems. The latter is essential to avoid soil compaction which would lead to undesirable effects of prolonged ponding in the bioretention systems.

With the support from PUB, NUS has incorporated a multidisciplinary team of engineers and scientists specialising in environmental, geotechnical engineering, hydraulics and plant physiology from the Departments of Civil and Environmental Engineering, Biological Science and Geography to establish the design and criteria for bioretention systems optimisation for tropical conditions. Together with the PUB's engineers, the team had experimented on laboratory, pilot and full-scale testing of the jointly developed engineered soils, screened and selected suitable native and non-native plants, established the design criteria and maintenance requirement that could provide consistently high treatment efficiency of runoff to meet the ABC design guidelines.

The engineered soil developed by the NUS team, which contains small portions of recycled materials including residuals from the local waterworks (commonly known as "water treatment residuals") and compost or coconut fibre, could provide more than 90% removal of total suspended solids (TSS), total nitrogen (TN) and total phosphorus (TP) in the runoff (Guo *et al.*, 2014). Through the extensive research by applying varying material compositions and the search on different recyclable materials, the research team eventually developed a patented engineered soil[4] with 30–60% of the engineered soil, made up of topsoil from the excavation site, with remaining portion composed of sand and small amount of waste materials. The reuse of topsoil reduced the cost of materials significantly especially the requirement for sand which is an expensive construction commodity in Singapore.

The team also screened and tested plants, scrubs and tree species for their ability in maintaining hydraulic conductivity, through studying the roots development; ability to uptake nutrients; and plant health under the bioretention system conditions (Chang *et al.*, 2013; Chen *et al.*, 2013). To avoid adding additional pollutants to the water, fertilisers and pesticides are not used in the bioretention systems. Thus, the selected plants for the bioretention systems must be able to adapt and survive under low nutrient conditions. The team also designed the planting scheme, which listed the suitable plants used with the lowest depression or the "wet zone" in the system, and the dry zone (Chen *et al.*, 2013). The plants list includes flowering and non-flowering, native and non-native species which could enhance the flora and fauna of the bioretention systems.

The NUS team together with PUB also collaborated in developing the newly designed "soaked-away" rain garden that offers a simple design with only one layer of filter media. This design does not require subsoil drainage pipes such as those in typical rain garden designs. This provides the advantage for the new rain garden to be implemented even at sites which are limited by the availability of deep drainage to connect the subsoil pipe from typical rain gardens. In addition, the simple soaked-away rain garden design does not require extensive engineering expertise and could promote its island-wide adoption in Singapore (PUB, 2014d). Thus far, four

---

[4] Singapore Patent Application No: 201308272-2. An engineered soil composition and a method of preparing the same. Hu J. Y., Ong S. L., Chiew S. H., Tan C. Y., Guo H. L., Lee L. Y., Lim F. Y., Ong B. L., Chen X. T., Chang T. H., Lim H. S., National University of Singapore.

test-bedding soaked-away rain gardens had been implemented in four local schools. Teachers and students were involved in designing the educational signage, samples collection and maintenance. The pilot bioretention systems would be eventually adopted as part of the schools' and institutions' educational activities.

Training workshops had been conducted by the project team, to share and disseminate the knowledge and research findings to engineers and designers, landscape contractors and schools. The project had attracted interest from schools and tertiary institutions. The project team also mentored research teams from schools in their rain garden projects under the Science Mentorship Programmes and other similar programmes. These activities helped to provide the community with better knowledge of rain garden and its contributing role in Singapore's Garden and Water programme.

Control and removal of toxins and off-flavour compounds in water

Singapore is not spared from incidences of algal bloom even though the country does not have major agriculture activities. Being a tropical country, the high temperature and abundant light source provide a suitable environment for the proliferation of algae in lakes and reservoirs. Algal bloom, which is mainly dominated by cyanobacteria species, could lead to production of toxins, with microcystin as the most widespread cyanotoxin capable of damaging liver and nervous systems (USEPA, 2012) and also responsible for the production of off-flavour compounds that could adversely affect the taste and odour of water even after treatment.

Singapore's drinking water quality guidelines for microcystin-LR is regulated following the WHO provisional value for drinking water at 1.0 μg/l microcystin-LR due to its potential adverse health effects (EPH, 2008; WHO, 2003). However, the taste and odour compounds are not regulated even though they can be detected by the human olfactory system at extremely low odour threshold concentrations (10 ng/l for 2-Methylisoborneol (MIB) and 30 ng/l for geosmin, the two main compounds responsible for taste and odour in water) (Persson, 1980). The typical conventional drinking water treatment facility comprising coagulation, sedimentation and filtration is insufficient to remove the taste and odour compounds. More advanced water treatment technologies including advanced oxidation processes such as ozonation, UV, and hydrogen peroxide had produced satisfactory results in taste and odour control. However, applying these methods would increase the cost of drinking water treatment significantly due to the high operating cost (PUB, 2014e).

NUS researchers have taken a holistic approach to control algal bloom from source to tap. A team of biologists and environmental engineers is involved in the source control research. These involved screening of algal species responsible in producing the toxins and off-flavour compounds and understanding the environmental conditions for production and release of these compounds into the water.

In the algal toxins production study, the research team isolated indigenous cyano-bacterial species, namely, *Microcystis*, *Cylindrospermopsis*, *Limnothrix*, *Pseudanabaena*, *Synechococcus*, *Merismopedia* and *Anabaena*, from Singapore reservoirs. Genetic sequences and morphological characteristics were applied to identify these isolates, while polymerase chain reaction (PCR) specific to toxin-producing genes and enzyme linked immunosorbent assay (ELISA), were used to screen the *Microcystis* isolates on hepatotoxin and microcystin production capability. The isolated cultures were cultivated to assess the environmental and/or genetic factors leading to cyanotoxin production under controlled laboratory conditions (Te and Gin, 2011).

In addition, isolates of indigenous cyanophages (viruses that attack cyanobacteria) that are capable of causing cyanobacteria, *Microcyctis* and *Anabaena*, lysis were obtained. Two cyanophage isolation methods, namely the well assay and double layer plaque assay, were established by the team (Yeo and Gin, 2013). The exponential growth phase of the cyanobacteria had been noted to be most susceptible to cyano-phage attack, with rapid and significant lytic effect. The isolated cyanophages can be potentially used as biological control agents to control the harmful cyanobacterial bloom events in the surface water (Yeo and Gin, 2013).

In drinking water treatment, feasible technology for removal of off-flavour com-pounds would need to be efficient to avoid generation of secondary harmful byprod-ucts. Besides this, the technology would have added competitive advantage if it is of low energy consumption and operating cost. A low-energy technology and high-performance alternative to the advanced oxidation process had been developed by NUS together with Harvard University. Unlike conventional membrane technology, this newly developed membrane technology introduces electricity into the filtration process and incorporate a novel graphene-based electrochemical filter. The electro-chemistry could reduce filter fouling rates by in situ foulant destruction and bio-logical inactivation and in turn reduce the frequency of physical and/or chemical cleanings needed to maintain optimal permeability.

Graphene, a 2-D one-atom-thick layer of graphite possesses high specific surface area of up to 2630 m^2/g. Besides this, the high electrical and thermal conductivity, high mechanical strength, and the lower toxicity potential of graphene compared with carbon nanotube (CNT), have positioned graphene as a promising material for envi-ronmental applications (Novoselov *et al.*, 2004; Schipper *et al.*, 2008; Stoller *et al.*, 2008; Yoonessi *et al.*, 2012). The ability for graphene to form highly ordered mem-branes or films at cost-effective mass production has driven its progress for further applications in recent years (Hu *et al.*, 2013; Jeon *et al.*, 2012).

The use of graphene membranes based on the adsorption mechanism was shown to be limited due to the active site saturation. Liu *et al.* (2014a) reported breakthrough occurred within a short filtration time of less than 30 min for 0.1 mmol L^{-1} tetracycline and 0.53 mmol L^{-1} phenol. Building on this information and the characteristics of graphene, namely, high specific surface area and high conductivity, the team ventured further to develop a novel graphene-based electrochemical filter to physically adsorb and electrochemically oxidise chemical contaminants (Liu *et al.*, 2014b).

The team optimised the filter fabrication by adding CNT as a conductive binder to graphene nanoplatelets (GNP) which served as scaffold for pollutants adsorption (Liu *et al.*, 2014b). This method enhances the durability and conductivity of the novel electrochemical filter. Optimum GNP:CNT ratio of 70%:30% was used in developing the filter for further applications. The operating conditions of the filter were optimised using a model target molecule, ferrocyanide ($Fe(CN)_6^{4-}$). This molecule is non-sorptive and undergoes a single electron transfer, which enable oxidation to be easily and quantitatively monitored by spectrophotometry and chronoamperometry. It was shown under the electrochemical filtration mode, the kinetics of up to 15-fold more than the classical batch system was achieved (Liu *et al.*, 2014b). This was due to the convection-enhanced transfer of the target molecule to the electrode surface and reduction of mass transfer overpotential. In addition, the electrochemical filtration system only require low voltage for electrochemical destruction of the target compounds that are physically trapped on the filter, hence membrane fouling can be significantly reduced.

The lab-scale electrochemical CNT filter was shown feasible with removal efficiency more than 90% on two common off-flavour compounds, geosmin and 2-MIB, under optimum operating conditions, even in the presence of interfering natural organic matters (NOM) (Liu *et al.*, 2014a). The conditions for removal required only a short residence time of 1.2 s with an applied voltage of 1 volt and flow rate of 1.5 ml/min. Besides these compounds, the electrochemical GNP-CNT filters had also demonstrated high removal of other organic pollutants (Figures 5a and 5b). These include tetracycline (antibiotic compound commonly found in wastewater), phenol (common organic compound in industrial wastewater), and oxalate (classified as a recalcitrant organic compound in wastewater) removals of more than 85% through a single-pass filtration (Liu *et al.*, 2014b).

The system can be potentially driven with renewable energy such as solar energy. This will enhance portability of the system to remote areas with no electricity supply. Further optimising and retrofitting the lab-scale design for pilot-scale and full-scale applications are being explored by the NUS team to bring the system to commercial and practical application.

New dimension in water recovery — biomimetic membranes

Coastal and marine plants and fishes possess unique survival capabilities to regulate water and ions in environmental stress conditions such as change in salinity to sustain their basic survival needs. Understanding the mechanisms involved in these processes

Working principle of the electrochemical filters

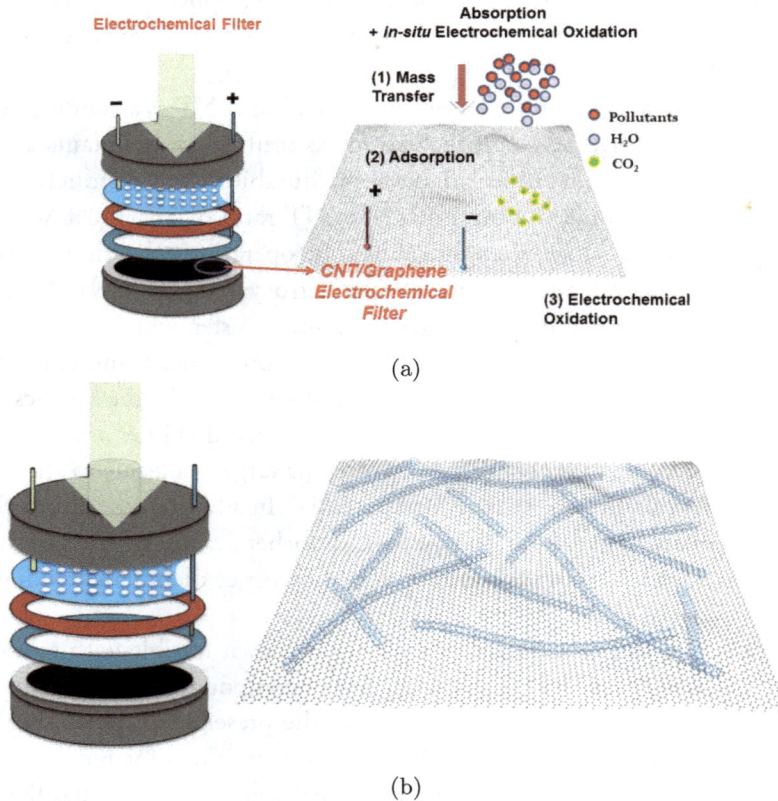

(a)

(b)

Figure 5. (a) Schematic of an electrochemical graphene filter and (b) a graphene/CNT filter for point of use (Courtesy of Dr. Liu Yanbiao).

could provide insights in developing novel, bio-inspired energy efficient water purification devices.

The research teams in the Department of Biological Sciences at NUS have devoted years of research to study how these coastal species, specifically mangroves and euryhaline fishes, cope with salt and environmental stress, and examining the underlying processes that drive the bio-regulatory mechanisms. Together with researchers in the Faculty of Engineering, NUS is making breakthroughs in developing the novel biomimetic (as the term implies, lessons from nature that can be applied to solve human problems) membranes that could desalinate salt water to produce pure water, without the high energy demand in the traditional pressure-driven membranes.

The more common type of mangrove tree found in the coastal areas of Singapore, *Avicennia officinalis* (which is also known by its local name "Api-api Ludat"), had been extensively studied by the team. This mangrove plant is a type of salt secretor which is able to maintain low sodium ion (Na^+) levels in the plant by filtering 85–95% of salt at the roots, and further secretion of excess sodium chloride (NaCl) through the salt glands present on the leaves (Drennan and Pammenter, 1982; Sobrado, 2001).

Salt exclusion at root uptake is a result of a biseriate exodermis, along with an enhanced deposition of hydrophobic barriers in the endodermis. The biseriate exodermis could efficiently block the apoplastic permeability which in turn aids in increasing mangrove resistivity towards high saline conditions. These provided *A. officinalis* the ability to reduce 85–90% salt and reduced the Na^+ loading into the xylem (Krishnamurthy *et al.*, 2014). The remaining salt in the system is secreted through the microscopic salt glands (each gland is approximately 30–40 μm in diameter) on the leaf surfaces of this mangrove species, which further function as a bio-desalination factory to regulate both salt and water (Tan *et al.*, 2013). The excess salt secreted from the salt glands would eventually dry and form salt crystals. This enabled the plant to derive pure water from sea or brackish water to meet its metabolic requirements.

The bio-desalination process of the *Avicennia sp.* salt glands were evidently documented by the NUS research team. Fresh shoots of *A. officinalis* were collected from a mangrove swamp from the southern coast of Singapore and treated with different concentrations of NaCl in the laboratory. Salt secretion was observed on leaf surfaces in less than a day of treatment. More secretions on the leaves were noted when treated with higher concentration of NaCl. X-ray microanalysis of these salt crystals revealed the main compositions were sodium and chloride. This shows that the salt glands function to remove excess ions, which are predominantly, Na and Cl, the major salt in brackish and seawater.

The NUS research team developed a novel epidermal peel technique to extract peels from the *Avicennia sp.* leaves in order to study the secretion pattern and determine the rate of secretion. This technique was able to isolate individual salt glands on the peel for continuous monitoring of dynamic changes in the secretion profiles at short time interval. The research on epidermal peel studies the response to salinity changes was extremely tedious and require high skill set in preparing the peels. The research team needed to produce 60 peels for each salinity treatment, with at least 30 secretions observed for each peel. With the aid of real-time imaging techniques, and the Laser Scanning Confocal Microscope, evidence of the phenomenon of individual salt gland secretion was recorded at 1 s intervals for 8 mins. The recording showed repeated observations of a well-coordinated rhythmic pattern, with positive secretion rates alternating with zero or negative secretion rates. However, the increase in secretion diameter above the glands was non-linear and fluctuated significantly. Thus, the negative secretion suggested some of the water excreted could be reabsorbed to conserve water for the plants. However, researchers are still investigating the reasons for the negative secretion.

The role of aquaporin (or commonly known as "water channel") in the rhythmic secretion rates was evident. The use of aquaporin blocker, Mercury(II) Chloride ($HgCl_2$) led to significant reduction in the secretion rate and it was further noted that the reduction correlates with the dose of $HgCl_2$ used. The blockage was shown to be reversible using a reducing agent, Dithiothreitol (DTT) or Cleland's reagent (Tan *et al.*, 2013). In addition, using molecular techniques by cloning two cDNA corresponding to plasma membrane intrinsic protein (AoPIP) and tonoplast intrinsic protein (AoTIP) from the leaves of *A. officinalis*, these two aquaporin genes which were also found to be highly homologous to various plant aquaporins were rapidly induced and expressed in the salt gland cells. Thus, the role of aquaporins in the salt glands is essential in providing the selective passage that allows only water molecules to pass through, while salts are being retained.

Aquaporin also plays essential roles in the survival of euryhaline fish under extreme environmental-stress conditions. Instead of the known role of aquaporin as a "water channel", researchers at NUS demonstrated the branchial aquaporin 1aa (aqp1aa) from the freshwater climbing perch (*Anabas testudineus*) (a freshwater teleost that is able to survive in seawater, terrestrial exposure and strive in high environmental ammonia concentrations) functions to facilitate ammonia permeation, which had high expression in gills and skin of this fish (Ip *et al.*, 2013). This is in view that this fish would increase its ammonia production by utilising amino acids as energy sources for locomotor activity when on land. During emersion, the increased aqp1aa mRNA expression was considered necessary to facilitate increased ammonia excretion. It was also noted when the fish was exposed to high environmental ammonia, mRNA expression of aqp1aa in the gills and skin was reduced, presumably to reduce the ammonia influx. Thus, the different aquaporin isomers have diverse roles and functionalities including high selectivity in ion transports critical for survival of the biological system.

The Mozambique tilapia, known by the scientific name, *Oreochromis mossambicus*, served as a unique biomimicry model as it possesses the ability to acclimate to changing salinities ranging from freshwater, seawater and even in the hypersaline water condition (up to four-fold the salinity of seawater) (Fiol, 2007; Whitfield, 1979). It has been well documented that tilapia needs to iono-osmoregulate to maintain its body fluid homeostasis by dynamically regulating ion and water balance (Li *et al.*, 2014b). NUS researchers documented the first study to determine the iono-osmoregulate role of gills and different sections of the esophageal-gastrointestinal (EGI) tract, namely, esophagus, stomach, anterior intestine (AI), middle intestine (MI), and posterior intestine (PI) of tilapia when acclimated to three different environmental salinities conditions — fresh, sea and hypersalinity.

State of the art techniques involving gene expression and immunohistochemical staining were used to provide evident insights of the functional roles. The team successfully cloned and used gene expression to quantify seven major ion transporters critical for Na^+ and Cl^- ion regulation (nkcc1a, nkcc1b, nkcc2, ncc, cftr, and nka-a1, and nka-a3) in the gill and EGI tract of tilapia acclimated in freshwater, seawater and hypersaline water (double the salinity of seawater), while immunohistochemical localisation of the encoded proteins in the anterior and posterior intestine was performed for the first time to confirm the roles of the studied sections for Na^+ and Cl^- ion regulation.

The abovementioned techniques had provided new insights and evidently demonstrated the expression and functional sections responsible for iono-osmoregulation when the fish was exposed to different salinities. The study added to the knowledge gap that the gill and posterior intestine section of tilapia are the most responsive to salinity change, while the other sections of the EGI provided a lower response. In a freshwater environment, the highly expressed genes at the gills indicated its function to reduce and replace salt loss by actively sequestering ions, while the EGI tract absorbed from ingested food to sustain the salt level in the body. On the other hand, in seawater and hypersaline water, the fish replaced water loss by imbibing salt water and absorbed the salt and water via the EGI tract. Water is retained in the body and excess salt is extruded through the gills.

This study also generated novel findings that the EGI tract in tilapia plays an essential role in iono-osmoregulation especially for its survival in hypersaline conditions, and the expressions of selected genes used in this study can served as biomarkers to understand the osmoregulatory roles of different EGI tract segments in future studies.

Besides the freshwater climbing perch and tilapia, the NUS research team is also studying other fish species, namely, marble goby (*Oxyeleotris marmorata*) and lungfish (*Protopterus annectens*), which are capable of acclimating to fluctuating salinity and water-stress conditions, respectively. The research on different fish species could offer the possibility of different sources for channels and transporters of small molecules, and hence, providing more options of potential components to be used in biomimetic membranes. Further research is ongoing to evaluate the genetic blueprint, protein structure and functions using the omics technology of the selected channels and transporter in the euryhaline fishes (S.H. Lam, personal communication, 2 September 2014).

Thus, the research findings from scientists in NUS and the international community showed that different aquaporin isoforms in biological systems play essential roles in osmo- and iono-regulation, offering passive water/ion channels with high permeability and selectivity. The knowledge of the relationships of structure-function in biological systems weave together the multidisciplinary research ties between biologists and engineers, which enable the design of breakthrough novel biomimetic membranes.

There has been extensive research and development on aquaporin biomimetic membranes in the recent years, which mainly focussed on the synthesis method of the membrane to enhance robustness and water permeability rate. Most of the biomimetic membrane research uses bacterial aquaporin, known as Aquaporin Z (AqpZ) which can be produced through the laboratory fermentation of *E.coli* and harvested in high purification. The AqpZ is the smallest member of aquaporin with only 32 kDA molecular and permeated only by water, which made it a preferred choice for application in freshwater production (de Groot and Grubmuller, 2005).

The scientific community in NUS has also contributed to some of the new techniques in the design and synthesis methods. These include vesicles suspended over membrane pores (Wang *et al.*, 2011); coupling vesicles to support substrate in a layer of material substantially impermeable to water to form the membrane (Xie *et al.*, 2013);[5] and subsequent improvement through immobilisation of aquaporin embedded vesicles on the membrane support via covalent binding (*Sun et al.*, 2013) or stabilising through a layer-by-layer polydopamine-histidine coating process (Wang *et al.*, 2013) had increased the robustness of aquaporin biomimetic membranes. The biomimetic membrane designed and synthesised by Wang *et al.* (2013) was able to achieve water flux of an order-of-magnitude higher than the commercial forward osmosis membrane, while attaining high salt retention (more than 90%) using 6000 ppm NaCl as feed and 0.8 M sucrose as draw solute.

Recent research in NUS has also been focussed on improving the membrane performance especially for long-term application, and the scale up fabrication technology to produce large pieces of high performance biomimetic membranes and to design the modules for housing the membrane for industrial application (Wang *et al.*, 2013). In addition, suitability of aquaporin isomers from other sources such as mangrove plants and euryhaline fishes could provide alternative options and functionalities to AqpZ, to potentially develop different biomimetic membrane applications or even possible multifunctional membranes. Thus, the basic scientific research in aquaporin offers the key to revolutionise water purification technology, for the next novel, bio-inspired model for future water purification.

Climate Change, Air Quality and Environmental Impacts

As Singapore, is in the Intertropical Convergence Zone (ITCZ), its air composition and climate are heavily influenced by the winds that bring clouds and air from the northern and southern hemispheres, and natural and anthropogenic activities within

---

[5] Patent no.: WO2013180659. "Method of making a membrane and a membrane for water filtration". W. Xie, Y. W. Tong, H. Wang, B. Wang, F. He, K. Jeyaseelan, A. Armugam, National University of Singapore.

the region. Regional anthropogenic activities such as land-use change and the related activities in peatlands would contribute to Singapore's air quality through transboundary transport, in addition to local emission sources. In addition, Singapore's topography is relatively flat, with most land less than 15 m above sea level. Thus, this low-lying, densely populated country is highly vulnerable to climate change effects (NEA, 2010). In 2007, the Singapore government, through the NEA, commissioned a Climate Change Study, led by TMSI at NUS, and comprising both local and foreign experts, to look into Singapore's vulnerability to climate change, providing a projection of climate change effects such as changes in temperature, sea level and rainfall patterns in Singapore in the next century, and the impacts of such effects, including increased flooding and impacts on water resources (NCCS, 2011). The findings from the study aimed to facilitate identification of new adaptation measures as well as to review the existing adaptation measures to enhance Singapore's readiness to curb the effects of climate change. Some of the climate change concerns and impact on Singapore highlighted by NUS experts (H. F. Cheong, personal communication, 24 September 2014) include: (i) urban drainage especially in the low-lying areas — the increase in high-intensity and short-duration rainfall would drive the need for larger storm water storage capacity for short periods; (ii) water resources planning — contingency plans for worst case scenarios, especially during long periods of little or no rain; and (iii) the economic impact of higher mean temperatures and heat island effect — temperature can be lowered by around 2°C with vegetation shading, while physical shading is less effective due to heat absorption and release properties.

The land-air-climate relationship research focusses by Centre for Climate Change Studies (C3S) established at NERI, NUS, complements the study on climate change effects on Singapore. C3S's approach focusses on regional activities that could impact Singapore, such as land-use change, impact of transboundary air pollutants, and regional and global radiative forcing and the impacts on climate change. These add on to the knowledge gap to further the understanding of potential vulnerability, creating more holistic and sustainable climate change adaptation and mitigation measures for Singapore and the region. These multidisciplinary research projects involved NUS researchers from NERI, the Centre for Remote Imaging, Sensing and Processing (CRISP)[6], TMSI, and the Faculties of Engineering and Science. The areas of research pursued included impacts of land-use change in the biogeochemical basis of peat oxidation using modern life sciences and computational approaches; identification of fingerprints of peatland emissions, in particular smoke during biomass burning, to apportion the impacts of transboundary aerosols on the Singapore urban environment; estimation

---

[6] CRISP is a research centre of NUS with the mission to develop an advanced capability in remote sensing to meet the scientific, operational and business requirements of Singapore and the region. http://www.crisp.nus.edu.sg.

of impacts of aerosols on the atmosphere over the Southeast Asian region, including Singapore; computation modelling of regional and global radiative forcing, atmospheric burden imposed by these emissions, and effective impacts on associated global climate response; and estimation of how carbon credits (particularly greenhouse gases such as carbon dioxide (CO_2) and nitrous oxide (N_2O)) can be harvested, as well as how actual climate impacts (next generation carbon credits) can be harvested from mitigating peatland emissions.

Coastal Protection and Management

Seawater rise is one of the major concerns for Singapore, since it is an island country with low-lying coastal areas. The adverse effects are far more than just land loss and coastal erosion but it is also a threat to Singapore's water supply. The freshwater supply from Singapore's coastal reservoirs would be highly vulnerable to seawater intrusion should the seawater level rise.

According to the Intergovernmental Panel on Climate Change (IPCC) Fourth Assessment Report (AR4) (IPCC, 2007), by the end of the 21st century, the sea level rise was projected to be 59 cm in the worst case scenario. There were several measures that Singapore had undertaken to overcome this, namely, in 1991, new reclamation projects were required to be built to a level 125 cm above the highest recorded tide level and this was further revised to 225 cm in 2011; development and improvement of drainage infrastructure in Singapore, the completion of the unique 3-in-1 Marina Barrage, as well as other flood alleviation projects; and a policy to raise low-lying areas was enacted in conjunction with redevelopment proposals (NEA, 2010). In 2010, Singapore's Building and Construction Authority (BCA) had also started risk-mapping to identify coastal areas at risk of erosion or flooding, and the possible related damages, taking account of the potential loss of biodiversity.

NUS researchers at TMSI had applied different techniques encompassing the use of the GIS system to integrate and analyse field datasets — the short-and long-term coastline change data to develop erosion hazard and risk map (Raju *et al.*, 2010). This was illustrated using Singapore's East Coast Park. The findings would aid in better coastline and land use management, as well as for developing effective strategies for erosion control measures. The study was limited by the lack of information on coastline change and sand volume used for beach nourishment. Nonetheless, the erosion hazard and risk map produced from the study provided a first approximation and would need to be further refined once more field monitoring data becomes available. The study highlighted frequent reviews and updates of the erosion hazard and risk map would be needed due to the dynamic changes in erosion rate and pattern.

Sustainable Land-use Management — Peatlands Research

Climate change due to terrestrial processes poses a major concern in Southeast Asia. Peatlands occupy 12% of the total land area in Southeast Asia, and are the major store of soil carbon, accounting for approximately 69 Gt of carbon and freshwater (Page *et al.*, 2011). The rich carbon content in the peatlands was formed over hundreds of years via accumulation of partially decayed vegetation matter under waterlogged conditions. In recent decades, peatland activities through land-use change and recurrent burning have caused severe degradation of peatlands, and are rapidly converting the peatlands from a carbon sink to a significant global greenhouse gas emitter. It was estimated that carbon dioxide (CO_2) emission from peatland drainage in Southeast Asia contributed to 1.3–3.1% of global CO_2 emission from fossil fuel (Hooijer *et al.*, 2010). These values could have been underestimated as it had not accounted for CO_2 emissions due to other peatland-related activities. Even so, these emission values are alarming and pose serious impacts on air dynamic and climate system over Singapore and regional countries. The transboundary transport of biogenic gases and smoke plumes from terrestrial processes had resulted in significant changes in atmospheric particles and generated climate altering substances. The impact of this source of CO_2 emissions will be even more severe in years ahead with more peatland development and if sustainable management practice is not implemented.

From an ecology sustainability consideration, changes in land-use activities would also lead to the shift in microbial diversity (Putten, 2012). NUS scientists realised there is a huge knowledge gap and lack of scientific evidence of microbiological and metabolic processes involved related to the peatland activities. This critical knowledge would aid in developing scientific methods to manage the rapid change in land use from pristine conditions of peatlands and monitor the progress as well as effectiveness of ecosystem restoration interventions. NUS led this task in close collaborations with national, regional and international partners, including the Singapore Centre on Environmental Life Sciences Engineering (SCELSE), the Indonesian Institute of Sciences (LIPI), University of Jambi; and Deltares (Figure 6). The team used two approaches, namely molecular profiling to capture shifts in community structure, and metabolic profiling to reflect the functional outcome of metabolic activities of microbes, plant roots and their exudates, respectively, to determine the effects of water table depth, oxygen availability, land use patterns, age of drainage and peat thickness on bacteria diversity in degraded peatlands of Indonesia (Mishra *et al.*, 2014). This is in view that microbial communities play critical roles in biogeochemical cascades in the functioning of peatlands, thus microbial and metabolic profiles were used as surrogates of community structure and functions, respectively.

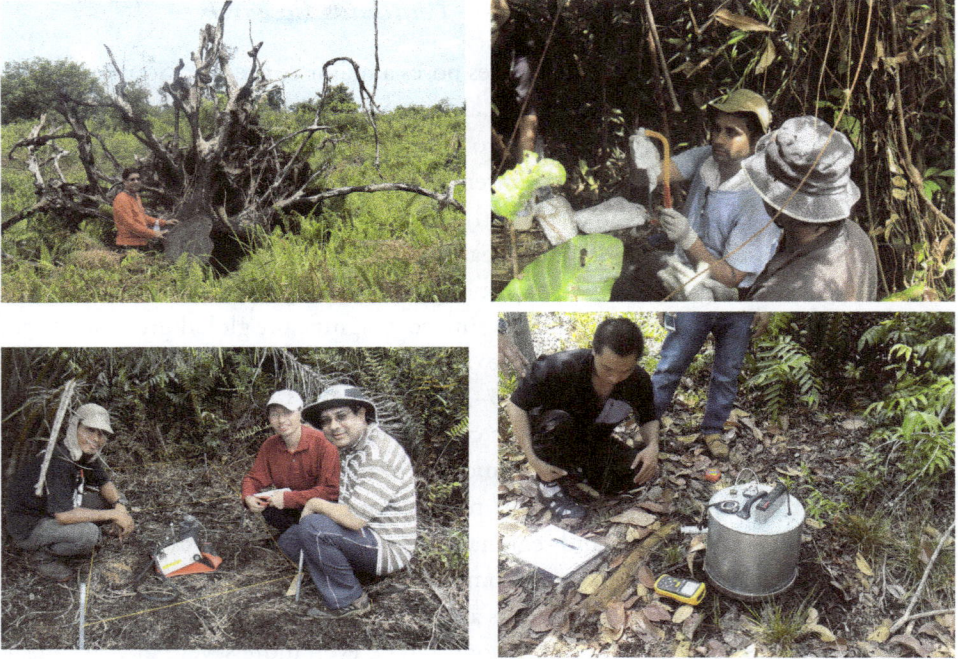

Figure 6.   Peatland in Sumatra. Measurements of greenhouse gas emission (Courtesy of Associate Professor Sanjay Swarup and Mr. S. Mishra, NUS).

Soil samples from five different land-use patterns, covering degraded forest, degraded land, oil palm plantation, mixed crop plantation and settlements, were collected from a 48 km^2 contiguous study site in Indonesia, including samples collected from above and below the water table. The work was carried out in collaboration with University of Jambi, who assisted in the field samples collection. The soil samples yielded 230 bacterial 16 S rDNA fragments and 145 metabolic markers. The study showed variations in groundwater table and land-use patterns had the highest influence on the bacterial profiles, followed by age of drainage and peat thickness. Soil samples from mixed crop plantations also had the most diverse bacterial and metabolic profiles, giving the "rhizosphere (root region) effect" (Mishra *et al.*, 2014). The high microbial and metabolites diversity found at the roots could be due to the root exudates from the diverse plants found on the peat surface. The team is also working on identifying the enzymes found in the root region that sustain the microbial diversity and community structure. More importantly, this research provides an understanding on nature's work in retaining minimal peat loss rate in these mixed crop plantations. Thus, the practice of mixed crop plantations could provide the solutions in managing plantations and reducing greenhouse gas emissions from peat.

Results from the study are useful to formulate recommendations that will help in the classification, improve management and sustainability of tropical peatlands. In the long term, the information will be useful for environmental mitigation, conversion, and sustainable development of regional resources.

Air Quality in Urban Environment

The air quality in Singapore is highly influenced by urban sources generated from vehicular — land, air and shipping, and the dynamic industrial sources — chemical, electronic and metallurgic industries, petroleum refinery, power plants, etc; waste incinerators, and transboundary pollutants from periodic forest fires and land-clearing from neighbouring countries (Velasco and Roth, 2012).

In 2012, NUS researchers in collaboration with the Center for Environmental Sensing and Modeling (CENSAM), Singapore, published a review on Singapore's air quality and greenhouse gas emissions (Velasco and Roth, 2012). Based on the available data, local air quality met all pollutant criteria under the US Environmental Protection Agency (USEPA) and WHO air quality standards and guidelines, respectively. The review commented on the lack of information available on PM2.5 (particles with an aerodynamic diameter ≤ 2.5 micrometers), which was yet to be listed as one of the criteria pollutants in Singapore at the time of the review. It was recommended that PM2.5 should be monitored frequently as it is a major local air pollutant of adverse health-impact concerns. Noting the importance of PM2.5 values, Singapore's NEA had hourly PM2.5 values (averaged from readings in the previous 24 hours) made publicly available since May 2014.

Urban air quality and aerosol sciences have been one of the major research focusses at NUS. Researchers have been studying the characteristics of pollutants from combustion sources including aerosols (Lim *et al.*, 2009), and behaviour of oxygenated organic compounds in atmospheric particulates, in particular, processes of photooxidation and chemical transformation of dicarboxylic acids (Stone *et al.*, 2012; Yang and Yu, 2009; Yang *et al.*, 2009b).

Dicarboxylic acids (DCA) (C_2-C_9) constitute up to 50% of organic aerosol, contribute to hydroscopic and radiative forcing effects. Concentration values of the two DCA species, oxalic acid (C2) and malonic acid (C3) in different atmospheres, urban and suburban, etc., have been reported but highly variable, which could be due to the sampling sites and seasonal effects. The NUS team also found that the varying concentrations were caused by the different analytical approach in quantifying DCAs, specifically, oxalic acid and malonic acid (Yang and Yu, 2009). The team recommended approaches to properly quantify oxalic and malonic acids and the corresponding dicarboxylates in PM2.5, which employed separate water extraction and solvent (using tetrahydrofuran (THF)) extraction and further quantified using IC or

GC-MS (Yang and Yu, 2009). This study also estimated the C2 and C3 DCA concentrations in PM2.5 using concentration ratios of oxalate-to-oxalic acid and malonate-to-malonic acid obtained from atmospheric samples in Singapore. However, the team cautioned that this estimate was only based on two datasets collected during the study period and hence, more field measurements would be needed to quantify the concentration ratios. A comprehensive characterisation of PM2.5 aerosols collected in Singapore from January through December 2000 showed factors contributing to the composition, a soil dust component, a metallurgical industry factor, a factor representing emissions from biomass burning and automobiles, a sea-salt component, and an oil combustion factor (Balasubramanian *et al.*, 2003).

The team also worked with regional partners to enable knowledge sharing and gain a better understanding of urban air pollution in the region. NUS and its regional collaborators are among the first research teams to characterise organosulfates in ambient aerosol in Asia. Urban aerosols were collected from urban and remote locations in Hanimaadhoo, Maldives, Gosan, Korea, Singapore, and Lahore, Pakistan, to determine the molecular formulas and atmospheric abundance. It was determined from this study the observed organosulfates were mainly biogenic secondary organic aerosols from isoprene or monoterpenes (Stone *et al.*, 2012).

Regional fire events from land-clearing activities also lead to periodic "smoke haze" caused by transboundary pollutants. It is known that biomass burning is an important primary source of aerosols, which effect global warming (Simoneit, 2002). This concurred with the findings from earlier studies carried out on Singapore air quality by NUS researchers, which showed reported elevated atmospheric loading of PM2.5 aerosols in Singapore due to biomass burning impacted air masses from Sumatra, Indonesia during the March to May 2000 and June to September 2001 periods (Balasubramanian *et al.*, 2003; See *et al.*, 2006).

NUS researchers are also studying the smoke haze transboundary transport using levoglucosan (1, 6-anhydro-β-D-glucopyranose) as the fingerprint, which provided a basis to further understand the chemical pathway and fate of this pollutants. Levoglucosan accounts for 1–6% of total carbonaceous aerosols and most abundant during biomass burning events. It was found that levoglucosan was completely depleted through photooxidation process in airborne droplets within 2.5 hours. However, levoglucosan serves as a precursor of abundant short chain dicarboxylic acids and monocarboxylic acids in particulates related to burning events, whereby the concentration profiles of these intermediates were identified and characterised in the study (Yang *et al.*, 2009b). Thus, this also explained the higher concentrations of DCAs found in PM2.5 and PM10 of the air samples collected in Singapore concurred with the biomass burning event in September/October 2008. The photooxidation process in the smoke could have enriched the C2-C5 DCA, with oxalate salts exhibiting the highest concentration with malic acid as more prominent (Yang *et al.*, 2013).

Understanding the physical-chemical evolution of peatland fire emission during atmospheric transport could provide better projection of the impacts on Singapore and the regional ambient environment, and the potential effects on public health. More concerted effort is needed to better characterise the peatland burning smoke due to the fast changes in land usage, peatland composition and types of biomass which would have substantially varied over the recent years. Recently, the research teams lead by NERI, in collaboration with Indonesia, have embarked on the research quest to address the missing information in peatland fire emissions. The team is currently working to characterise the peatland fire emission at the source and receptor sites, i.e. Singapore, to determine the possible atmospheric evolution of peatland fire emission during transboundary transport and further assess the transboundary peatland burning smoke effect on the urban environment in Singapore.

NERI, leading a team of experts in urban aerosols and air quality, analytical chemistry and health scientists in NUS, with collaboration and support from the Singapore's Ministry of the Environment and Water Resources (MEWR), had recently initiated a 5-year programme to carry out in-depth research on urban air quality in Singapore. This programme covers detection and characterisation, source apportionment, evolution and removal, and the potential health impacts of urban aerosols and emerging pollutants including ENMs. The overall approach in this programme is through integrating established ground-based monitoring and remote sensing at NUS and CRISP, and advanced laboratory studies and analysis, such as aerosol sampling and analysis, photooxidation kinetics, chemical isolation, chemical speciation, etc., to address the complex questions related to Singapore's air quality. Leveraging on the state-of-the-art instruments available at various laboratories in NUS including NERI, the highly skilled expertise in both hardware and software, together with researchers, scientists and engineers from NUS, MEWR and NEA, and overseas collaborators who have established experiences on atmospheric environment in Singapore or Southeast Asia, the programme would be able to generate insightful results and could efficiently achieve the aims in unveiling the science to sustain good air quality in Singapore and develop capability in air quality surveillance.

Research for Rapid-growing Singapore and the Region

Singapore has progressed over the years to be a water self-reliant country. However, clean air and safe food are another two essential basic elements to sustain the quality of life. Noting that Singapore imports more than 90% of its food supply and is a highly urbanised city-state island country, understanding the potential dietary habit, ensuring that there are minimal contaminants in our food are critical for the present and the future of a rapidly growing Singapore.

Moreover, there are increasing concerns on emerging pollutants and issues of safety assessments especially lifestyle, dietary habits and food contaminants. NUS, through NERI, has created an integrated and versatile platform for systematic investigations involving multidisciplinary teams from Engineering, Science and Medicine. The teams have established ready assessment capabilities and constantly research on novel assessment methods to respond in times of need. The four core research focusses in the water-food-air areas at NERI include: (i) evaluation of biomarkers for diet and disease; (2) detection of food contaminants for safety assessment; (3) effects of air and water pollutants on human health; and (4) safety, health and environmental effects of engineered nanomaterials.

The complexity of chemical compositions of food and human physiological responses to diets offer significant scientific challenges. Scientists at NERI use an integrated epidemiological and laboratory approach to identify and assess useful molecular biomarkers. This approach will facilitate the identification of new targets for disease prevention. The current research focusses on diet and chronic diseases, such as cancer and heart ailments. The team had also studied the underlying metabolic enzyme glycine decarboxylase (GLDC) which is critical for tumour initiating cells (TICs) in non-small cell lung cancer (NSCLC) (Zhang *et al.*, 2012).

Another area of growing concern is the assessment of food safety. Safety assessment of potential food contaminants involves complex chemical and biochemical assays. These assays are pivotal in revealing the possible toxic and carcinogenic reproductive systems. NUS teams from the Department of Chemistry and NERI have successfully employed proton nuclear magnetic resonance (^{1}H NMR) spectroscopy, GC/MS fingerprinting and chemometrics to characterise oils and fats for quality control and hence, enable detection of adulteration (Fang *et al.*, 2013). The team had also optimised the assessment method using coupled microwave-assisted extraction-solid phase extraction for the determination of pesticides in infant milk formula via LC–MS/MS (Fang *et al.*, 2012). The core research laboratory facilities at NERI are well established with advanced analytical equipment for food analysis to identify chemical food contaminants with high sensitivity and accuracy.

Air and water are two basic elements which we are exposed to in our daily lives. Thus, it is inevitable that any pollutants in these elements would have a direct impact on human health. The NUS multidisciplinary research team is interested in the health effects of air pollutants of different particle sizes and chemical compositions in water and air. Researchers at NERI are also studying the underlying disease mechanisms of air pollutants such as inflammation, oxidative stress and biomolecular profile changes that may lead to chronic diseases. These investigations have been extended to examine the environmental and health impacts of climate change on air quality in this region, in particular haze from tropical forest fires.

Building on the capabilities established from the heath effect studies of reclaimed water studies in the late 1990s, more advanced techniques have been established by the NUS research teams to conduct comprehensive studies on emerging water contaminants and their potential health risks on humans. These advanced techniques provide more rapid and high throughputs, such as the use of zebrafish embryo and metabolomics techniques for better understanding of the related impacts on targeted organs and thus enable us to provide more accurate assessment. NUS, among other global researchers, is using the metabolomic platform to enhance the assessment techniques. The metabolomic platform is able to provide comprehensive (qualitative and quantitative) analysis of all metabolites from a single cell to the whole biological system. Thus, metabolomics analysis can potentially provide critical information to help understand the changes occurring in relevant metabolic pathways in response to any emerging pollutants or environmental conditions (Xu *et al.*, 2014).

In the zebrafish studies, the research on transcriptomic analysis to determine the molecular events leading to 4-nonylphenol (4-NP) (an organic compound commonly used in manufacturing industries) induced acute hepatotoxicity in adult male zebrafish (Lam *et al.*, 2013); and metabolomics profiling of developing zebrafish embryos using gas chromatography- and liquid chromatography-mass spectrometry would serve as a basis for future toxicological or developmental studies (Huang *et al.*, 2013). The risk evaluation of these pollutants can help formulate control strategies and protect the water environment. NUS researchers have also successfully applied metabolomic approach to assess urinary metabolic changes in human with long-term environmental cadmium (Cd) exposure (Gao *et al.*, 2014) and accumulation and detoxification of heavy metals in the aquatic food chain, *Chlorella vulgaris* (Zhang *et al.*, 2014). The metabolomics platform offers a novel approach for in-depth understanding of the biological response and could provide critical information for better water and environment management practices.

Engineered nanomaterials, another class of emerging pollutants, have been used in vast amounts in industry and would thus find their way into the environment. Therefore, the assessment of their potential impacts on human health would be useful information for a greener management practice. The exposure impacts of engineered nanomaterials have been studied using both in vitro and in vivo models. Human cell lines provide a promising in vitro model for rapid high throughput screening for toxic effects, while in vivo studies using rodents and the *Caenorhabditis elegans* (*C. elegans*) worm offer insights on mechanistic changes and an opportunity to explore the health implications of nanoparticles in biological systems. Figure 7 shows the potential nanomaterial bioaccumulations in the rodent model through inhalation and intravenous exposure pathways. The NUS team evaluated the biodistribution of gold nanoparticles (AuNPs) in rodents through intravenous exposure (Balasubramanian

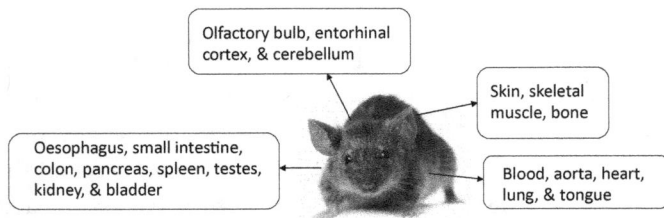

Figure 7. Tissues/organs found with gold nanoparticles after 15 days of inhalation exposure (Courtesy of Professors Yu Liya and Ong Wei Yi, NUS).

et al., 2010). More than 25 organs of the rodents were assessed through a 2-month period after the single intravenous injection. The highest AuNPs bioaccumulation was found in the kidney followed by testis after exposure of a month but was later found to have bioaccumulated in the liver followed by the spleen after 2 months. The finding coincides with the microarray results, showing that the liver and spleen contained gene expressions for detoxification, lipid metabolism, cell cycle, defence response, and circadian rhythm.

As a rodent's response could be easily related to humans, the drawback would be the slow response time and high maintenance cost for the study. Thus, using a complementary model, *C. elegans*, rapid pre-screening of engineered nanomaterials can be achieved prior to advanced evaluation using small animals. *C. elegans* provide unique assessment which include length, movement, swallowing (pharyngeal pumping), lifespan, oxidative stress, gene expression (some are difficult to perform on rodents) (W. Y. Ong, personal communication, 11 March 2014). The targeted cell lines are then used for in vitro studies to determine the mechanistic understanding on the impacts of nanomaterial and accumulation on the affected tissues/organs. This unfolds potential impacts on health and the delivery of nanomedicine. Advanced imaging in cells and tissues provides insights on the characteristics and mechanistic behaviour of nanomaterials inside the cells as well as the cell's response to the presence of nanomaterials. These methods provide rapid and high-throughput assessment on the potential toxicity of engineered nanomaterials. They are also capable of monitoring airborne engineered nanomaterials in situ and in real time. These approaches are used for researches in drug delivery, toxicity screening, risk assessment, imaging and metrology. The research team together with Nanyang Technological University (NTU) researchers further demonstrated that the exposure of endothelial cells to TiO_2 nanomaterials causes endothelial cell leakiness. This effect is caused by the physical interaction between TiO_2 nanomaterials and endothelial cells' adherens junction protein VE-cadherin. They further show that TiO_2 nanomaterials cause leakiness of subcutaneous blood vessels in mice and increase the number of pulmonary metastases (Setyawati *et al.*, 2013). These findings uncover a novel non-receptor-mediated mechanism by which nanomaterials trigger intracellular signalling cascades via specific interaction with VE-cadherin, resulting in nanomaterial-induced endothelial cell leakiness.

In brief, the research capabilities established in the four focussed areas enhance preparedness and provide the capability needs for Singapore and the region in meeting the challenges in sustaining the basic livelihood needs — water, air and food.

Collaborative Regional and International Research on Regional Issues

NERI is the NUS Point-of-Contact for government agencies, industry, and institutions for environment and water research. The Institute plays a pivotal role to engage government agencies, industry and institutions to understand the research needs and bring together researchers and expertise from across the University to develop possible research initiatives and solutions to address these needs.

NERI also hosts distinguished scientists as Visiting Professors under various funding schemes. One of the schemes is the Environmental and Water Technologies (EWT) Visiting Professor Programme (VPP) which aims to develop expertise in strategic research areas to meet the future challenges in Singapore's water industry. Two internationally renowned water experts — Professor Avner Adin from The Hebrew University of Jerusalem and Professor Shane Snyder from the University of Arizona are collaborating with NUS and local industry experts on methods for detection and removal of nanomaterials and impacts of re-mineralised seawater reverse osmosis product on stability of water in distribution pipelines; and development and practical applications of "green" sample preparation procedures, respectively. The programme has been a success for knowledge and experience sharing of international and Singapore water expertise.

NERI has also embarked on two key programmes as initiatives for overseas research and research manpower training outreach collaboration. These are the (1) Singapore-Peking-Oxford Research Enterprise (SPORE) Programme, which is supported by the Singapore National Research Foundation (NRF) through the Environment and Water Industry Programme Office (EWI), the National University of Singapore, The University of Oxford, and Peking University. The Programme focusses on research, education, and commercialisation of technology in water eco-efficiency with the end goal to develop new water technological solutions using less energy and resources; and (2) the Shanghai Jiao Tong University and National University of Singapore Joint Programme on Energy and Environmental Sustainability Solutions for Megacities (E2S2). This Programme is supported by the Singapore National Research Foundation under the Campus for Research Excellence and Technological Enterprise (CREATE) scheme and focusses on the challenges facing megacities. The programme addresses sustainable solutions for coupled problems, covering waste management and energy recovery, and challenges of emerging contaminants on the environment in megacities.

Close collaborations between NERI and Singapore and regional government agencies, institutions and industry have been sealed to promote awareness and develop projects of mutual interest. This collaboration is prominent in the success brought by the Centre for Climate Change Studies, C3S at NUS. The Centre leads multidisciplinary research programme focussing on evaluating vulnerability, adaptation methods, mitigation opinions, plans and solutions to response to climate change. At NUS, NERI works closely with the Department of Civil and Environmental Engineering, TMSI and CRISP on advancing climate change research, and with regional institutions, Indonesian Institute of Sciences (LIPI), Bogor and the University of Jambi, Indonesia on peatland studies. In the biofilms and environmental metabolomics research, NERI is collaborating with Centre of Environmental Life Sciences Engineering (SCELSE), Singapore's fifth Research Centre of Excellence (RCE) to promote the development of infrastructure and capability in the area.

Industry collaborations are also key emphasis at NERI. This helps to understand the industrial trend, keeping pace with industry research needs, and to bring ideas and technologies to commercialisation. NERI has been supporting the Singapore Economic Development Board's mission in attracting multinational companies and organisations to establish research footholds in Singapore. Over the years, NERI has established close relations with key local and international companies. These include water and environment companies, namely GE Singapore Water Technology Centre on research on water treatment, joint seminars, development of student training programmes and joint hosting of visiting scientists; and Wong Fong Engineering on projects related to Waste to Energy; and leaders in water and environment instrumentation: Agilent Technologies on manpower development and training, instrumentation and development of new and novel methodologies for further joint R&D projects; Thermo Fisher Scientific on metabolomics study of urban water systems; Shimadzu (Asia Pacific) Pte Ltd on collaboration for the setting up of the NUS-Shimadzu Advanced Facility for Ecoanalytics (NUSAFE); Lab Science Solution (LSS) Pte Ltd on collaboration in environmental applications in the areas of metabolomics, chemical analysis and emerging contaminants using Bruker mass spectrometers; and Waters Technologies Corporation on a collaborative research framework relating to environmental microbial metabolomics.

A tripartite collaboration among NERI, under the Energy and Environmental Sustainability Solutions for Megacities Programme (E2S2), Shanghai Jiao Tong University (SJTU) and Shanghai National Engineering Research Centre of Urban Water Resources Co. Ltd (NERC) on water quality studies in China, will bring revenue to technology transfer and joint-research collaboration with agencies and industry in China.

The Singapore International Water Week (SIWW) together with the WasteMet Asia and CleanEnviro Summit and World Cities Summit had attracted a huge growing number of worldwide participation since the inaugural SIWW in 2008. These major events in Singapore serves as an effective platform for academia and industry from local and international to network and provide collaboration opportunities in environment and water. The R&D advancement and the growing local and international collaborations established at research institutions provide the technology and product development in making and sustaining Singapore as a Global Hydrohub, and creating sustainable urban living in Singapore and other Asian cities.

Acknowledgements

The NUS Environmental Research Institute (NERI) [http://www.nus.edu.sg/neri/] acknowledges the research funding and support provided by the National Research Foundation (NRF), Ministry of the Environment and Water Resources (MEWR), Environment and Water Industry Programme Office (EWI), PUB, Singapore's national water agency, National Environment Agency (NEA), Economic and Development Board of Singapore (EDB), Singapore's Ministry of Education (MOE), SPORE Programme funding, E2S2 Programme funding, NUS-GE support and partner organisations.

References

Balasubramanian, R., Qian, W. B., Decesari, S., Facchini, M. C., and Fuzzi, S. (2003). Comprehensive characterization of PM2.5 aerosols in Singapore. *Journal of Geophysical Research, 108*, 4523–4533.

Balasubramanian, S. K., Jittiwat, J., Manikandan, J., Ong, C. N., Yu, L .E., and Ong, W. Y. (2010). Biodistribution of gold nanoparticles and gene expression changes in the liver and spleen after intravenous administration in rats. *Biomaterials, 31*, 2034–2042.

Belanger, S. E., Balon, E. K., and Rawlings, J. M. (2010). Saltatory ontogeny of fishes and sensitive early life stages for ecotoxicology tests. *Aquatic Toxicology, 97*, 88–95.

Chang, T. H. A., Chen, X. C., and Ong, B. L. (2013). Plant selection criteria. Presented at the Workshop on Design and Construction of Soak Away Rain Garden, 25 July 2013, National University of Singapore, Singapore.

Chen, X. C., Chang, T. H. A., and Ong, B. L. (2013). Planning of plant layout. Presented at the Workshop on Design and Construction of Soak Away Rain Garden, 25 July 2013, National University of Singapore, Singapore.

Intergovernmental Panel on Climate Change (IPCC). (2007). Contribution of Working Groups I, II and III to the Fourth Assessment Report of the Intergovernmental Panel on Climate Change, Core Writing Team, Pachauri, R. K. and Reisinger, A. (Eds.), IPCC, Geneva, Switzerland. p. 104.

de Groot, B. L., and Grubmuller, H. (2005). The dynamics and energetics of water permeation and proton exclusion in aquaporins. *Current Opinion in Structural Biology, 15*, 176.

Drennan, P., and Pammenter N. W. (1982) Physiology of salt secretion in the mangrove Avicennia marina (Forsk.) Vierh. *The New Phytologist, 91*, 1000–1005.

Dunne, T., and Leopold, L. (1978). *Water in Environmental Planning*. New York, NY: W. H. Freeman and Co.

EConnect. (2014). NUSwan — A tool for persistent monitoring of water bodies. *EConnect, 8*, March 2014.

European Union. (2010). Directive 2010/63/EU of the European Parliament and of the Council of 22 September 2010 on the protection animal used in scientific purposes.

Fang, G., Lau, H. F., Law, W. S., and Li, S. F. Y. (2012). Systematic optimisation of coupled microwave-assisted extraction-solid phase extraction for the determination of pesticides in infant milk formula via LC–MS/MS. *Food Chemistry, 134*, 2473–2480.

Fang, G., Goh, J. Y., Tay, M., Lai, H. F., and Li, S. F. Y. (2013). Characterization of oils and fats by 1H NMR and GC/MS fingerprinting: Classification, prediction and detection of adulteration. *Food Chemistry, 138*, 1461–1469.

Fiol, D. F., and Kultz, D. (2007). Osmotic stress sensing and signaling in fishes. *Federation of European Biochemical Societies (FEBS) Journal., 274*, 5790–5798.

Freeman, R., Finder, T., and Willner, I. (2009). Multiplexed analysis of Hg^{2+} and Ag^+ ions bynucleic acid functionalized CdSe/ZnS quantum dots and their use for logic gateoperations. *Angewandte Chemie International Edition, 48*, 7818–7821.

Gao, Y. H., Lu, Y. H., Huang, S. M., Gao, L., Liang, X. X., Wu, Y. N., Wang, J., Huang, Q., Tang, L. Y., Wang, G. A., Yang, F., Hu, S. G., Chen, Z. H., Wang, P., Jiang, O., Huang, R., Xu, Y. H., Yang, X. F., and Ong, C. N. (2014). Identifying early urinary metabolic changes with long-term environmental exposure to cadmium by mass-spectrometry-based metabolomics. *Environmental Science & Technology, 48*, 6409–6418.

Ge, D., and Lee, H. K. (2013). Ionic liquid based dispersive liquid-liquid microextraction coupled with micro-solid phase extraction of antidepressant drugs from environmental water samples. *Journal of Chromatography A, 1317*, 217–222.

Gong, Z., Ju, B., and Wan, H. (2001). Green fluorescent protein (GFP) transgenic fish and their applications. *Genetica, 111*, 213–225.

Gong, Z., Wan, H., Tay, T. L., Wang, H., Chen, M., and Yan, T. (2003). Development of transgenic fish for ornamental and bioreactor by strong expression of fluorescent proteins in the skeletal muscle. *Biochemical and Biophysical Research Communications, 308*, 58–63.

Guo, H., Lim, F. Y., Zhang, Y., Lee, L. Y., Hu, J. Y., Ong, S. L., Yau, W. K., and Ong, G. S. (2014). Soil column studies on the performance evaluation of engineered soil mixes for bioretention systems. *Desalination and Water Treatment, 1–7,* Paper presented at 5th IWA-ASPIRE Conference, 8-12 September, 2013, Daejon, Korea. Retrieved 17 February 2015 from http://www.tandfonline.com/doi/abs/10.1080/19443994.2014.922284#.VONboPmUfD8.

Hinze, W. L., and Pramauro, E. (1993). A Critical review of surfactant-mediated phase separation (cloud-point extractions): Theory and applications. *Critical Reviews in Analytical Chemistry, 24*, 133–177.

Hooijer, A., Page, S., Canadell, J. G., Silvius, M., Kwadijk, J., Wosten, H., and Jauhiainen, J. (2010). Current and future CO_2 emissions from drained peatlands in Southeast Asia. *Biogeosciences, 7*, 1505–1514.

Hu, K., Gupta, M. K., Kulkarni, D. D., and Tsukruk, V. V. (2013). Ultra-robust graphene oxide-silk fibroin nanocomposite membranes. *Advanced Materials, 25*, 2301–2307.

Huang, S. M., Xu, F., Lam, S. H., Gong, Z., and Ong, C. N. (2013). Metabolomics of developing zebrafish embryos using gas chromatography- and liquid chromatography-mass spectrometry. *Molecular Biosystems, 9*, 1372–1380.

Ip, Y. K., Soh, M. M., Chen, X. L., Ong, J. L., Chng, Y. R., Ching, B., Wong, W. P., Lam S. H., and Chew, S. F. (2013). Molecular characterization of branchial aquaporin 1aa and effects of seawater acclimation, emersion or ammonia exposure on its mRNA expression in the gills, gut, kidney and skin of the freshwater climbing perch, Anabas testudineus. *PLoS One, 8*, e61163.

Jeon, I. Y., Shin, Y. R., Sohn, G. J., Choi, H. J., Bae, S. Y., Mahmood, J., Jung, S. M., Seo, J. M., Kim, M. J., Chang, D. W., Dai, L. M., and Baek J. B. (2012). Edge-carboxylated graphene nanosheets via ball milling. *Proceedings of the National Academy of Sciences of the United States of America, 109*, 5588–5593.

Koay, T. B., Tan, Y. T., Eng, Y. H., Gao, R., Chitre, M., Chew, J. L., Chandhavarkar, N., Khan, R., Taher, T., and Koh, J. (2011). STARFISH — A small team of autonomous robotic fish. *Indian Journal of Geo-Marine Sciences, 40*, 157–167.

Krishnamurthy, P., Jyothi-Prakash, P. A., Qin, L., He, J., Lin, Q., Loh, C.-S., and Kumar, P. P. (2014). Role of root hydrophobic barriers in salt exclusion of a mangrove plant Avicennia officinalis. *Plant, Cell and Environment, 37*, 1656–1671.

Lam, S. H., Hlaing, M. M., Zhang, X. Y., Yan, C., Duan, Z., Zhe, L., Ung, C. Y., Mathavan, S., Ong, C. N., and Gong, Z. (2011). Toxicogenomic and phenotypic analyses of bisphenol-A early-life exposure toxicity in zebrafish. *PLoS One, 6*, e28273.

Lam, S. H., Mathavan, S., Tong, Y., Li, H., Karuturi, R. K. M., Wu, Y., Vega, V. B., Liu, E. T., and Gong, Z. (2008). Zebrafish whole-adult-organism chemogenomics for large-scale predictive and discovery chemical biology. *PLoS Geneics, 4*, e1000121.

Lam, S. H., Ung, C. Y., Hlaing, M. M., Hu, J., Li, Z.-H., Mathavan, S., and Gong, Z. (2013). Molecular insights into 4-nitrophenol-induced hepatotoxicity in zebrafish: Transcriptomic, histological and targeted gene expression analyses. *Biochimica et Biophysica Acta (BBA) — General Subjects, 1830*, 4778–14789.

Li, W. J., Lee, L. Y., Yung, L. Y. L., He, Y., and Ong, C. N. (2014). Combination of in situ preconcentration and on-site analysis for phosphate monitoring in fresh waters. *Analytical Chemistry, 86*, 7658–7665.

Li, Z., Lui, E. Y., Wilson, J. M., Ip, Y. K., Lin, Q., Lam, T. J., and Lam, S. H. (2014b). Expression of key ion transporters in the gill and esophageal-gastrointestinal tract of euryhaline Mozambique Tilapia *Oreochromis mossambicus* acclimated to fresh water, seawater and hypersaline water. *PLOS One, 9*, e87591.

Lim, J., Lim, C., and Yu, L. Y. E. (2009). Composition and size distribution of metals in diesel exhaust particulates. *Journal of Environmental Monitoring, 11*, 1614–1621.

Lim, T. N., Yang, C., He, C., Hu, L., and Lee, H. K. (2013). Membrane assisted micro-solid phase extraction of pharmaceuticals with amino and urea-grafted silica gel. *Journal of Chromatography A, 1316*, 8–14.

Liu, Y., Zhou, Z., Vecitis, C. D., and Ong, C. N. (2014a). Graphene-based electrochemical filters for water purification. A poster presented at Water Convention, Singapore International Water Week (SIWW), 1–5 June 2014, Singapore.

Liu, Y., Lee J. H. D., Xia Q., Ma Y., Yu Y., Yung L. Y. L, Xie J. P., Ong C. N., Vecitis C. D. and Zhou Z., (2014b). Graphene-based electrochemical filters for water purification. *Journal of Materials Chemistry A, 2*, 16554–16562.

Majedi, S. M., Lee, H. K., and Kelly B. C. (2012). Chemometric analytical approach for the cloud point extraction and inductively coupled plasma mass spectrometric determination of zinc oxide nanoparticles in water samples. *Analytical Chemistry, 84*, 6546–6552.

Matheson, A. (2008). Seeing green. *The Column, 4*(4), 30–32.

Mishra, S., Lee, W. A., Hooijer, A., Reuben, S., Sudiana, I. M., Idris, A., and Swarup, S. (2014). Microbial and metabolic profiling reveal strong influence of water table and land-use patterns on classification of degraded tropical peatlands. *Biogeosciences, 11*, 1727–1741.

National Climate Change Secretariat (NCCS), Prime Minister's Office Singapore. (2011). Adaptation measures. http://app.nccs.gov.sg/(X(1)S(i2a31q45urdr35eor0mpyn3m))/page.aspx?pageid=84&AspxAutoDetectCookieSupport=1.

National Environment Agency (NEA). (2010). Chapter 3: Vulnerability and adaptation measures. In *Singapore's Second National Communication*. Retrieved 2 September 2014 from https://www.nccs.gov.sg/sites/nccs/files/SINGAPORE%27S%20SECOND%20NATIONAL%20COMMUNICATIONS%20NOV%202010.pdf.

Novoselov, K. S., Geim, A. K., Morozov, S. V., Jiang, D., Zhang, Y., Dubonos, S. V., Grigorieva, I. V., and Firsov A. A. (2004). Electric field effect in atomically thin carbon films, *Science, 306*, 666–669.

Ong, G. S., Kalyanaraman, G., Wong, K. L., and Wong, T. H. F. (2012). Monitoring Singapore's first bioretention system: Rain garden at balam estate. In *WSUD 2012: Water sensitve urban design; Building the water sensitive community* (pp. 601–608); 7th international conference on water sensitive urban design, 21–23 February 2012, Melbourne Cricket Ground. Barton, A.C.T.: Engineers Australia.

Ono, A., and Togashi, H. (2004). Highly selective oligonucleotide-based sensor for mercury(II) in aqueous solutions. *Angewandte Chemie International Edition, 43*, 4300–4302.

Page, S. E., Rieley, J. O., and Banks, C. J. (2011). Global and regional importance of the tropical peatland carbon pool. *Global Change Biology, 17*, 798–818.

Parng, C., Seng, W. L., Semino, C., and McGrath, P. (2002). Zebrafish: A preclinical model for drug screening. *Assay and Drug Development Technologies, 1*, 41–48.

Persson, P. E. (1980). On the odor of 2-methylisobornol. *Water Research, 32*(7), 2140–2146.

Public Utilities Board, Singapore (PUB). (2002). Singapore Water Reclamation Study, Expert Panel Review and Findings, June 2002.

PUB. (2010). Environmental Public Health (EPH) (Quality of Piped Drinking Water) Regulation 2008 (updated 1 Nov 2010). Retrieved 29 January 2015 from http://www.pub.gov.sg/general/watersupply/Pages/DrinkingWQReport.aspx.

PUB. (2014a). NEWater. Retrieved 29 January 2015 from http://www.pub.gov.sg/about/historyfuture/Pages/NEWater.aspx.

PUB. (2014b). *Innovation in Water, Singapore, 6,* June 2014.

PUB. (2014c). Keeping the waters in Singapore safe for recreational activities. *Innovation in Water, Singapore, 6, 30.*

PUB. (2014d). Active, beautiful and clean waters design guidelines. Retrieved 29 January 2015 from http://www.pub.gov.sg/abcwaters/abcwatersdesignguidelines/Documents/ABC_DG_2014.pdf.

PUB. (2014e). Removing off-flavour compounds in water. *Innovation in Water, Singapore, 6, 31.*

Putten, W. H. V. (2012). Climate change, aboveground-belowground interactions, and species' range shifts, *Annual Review of Ecology, Evolution and Systematics, 43,* 365–383.

Raju, D. K., Santosh, K., Chandrasekar, J. and Teh, T. S. (2010). Coastline change measurement and generating risk map for the coast using geographic information system. *The International Archives of the Photogrammetry, Remote Sensing and Spatial Information Sciences, 38, Part II,* 492–497.

Rodriguez, C., Buynder, P. V., Lugg, R., Blair, P., Devine, B., Cook, A., and Weinstein, P. (2009). Indirect potable reuse: A sustainable water supply alternative. *International Journal of Environmental Research and Public Health, 6,* 1174–1209.

Schipper, M. L., Nakayama-Ratchford, N., Davis, C. R., Kam, N. W., Chu, P., Liu, Z., Sun, X., Dai, H., and Gambhir, S. S. (2008). A pilot toxicology study of single-walled carbon nanotubes in a small sample of mice. *Nature Nanotechnology, 3,* 216–221.

See, S. W., Balasubramanian, R., and Wang, W. (2006). A study of the physical, chemical, and optical properties of ambient aerosol particles in Southeast Asia during hazy and nonhazy days. *Journal of Geophysical Research-Atmospheres, 111*(D10), D10S08, 1–12.

Setyawati, M. I., Tay, C. Y., Chia, S. L., Goh, S. L., Fang, W., Neo, M. J., Chong, H. C., Tan, S. M., Loo, S. C., Ng, K. W., Xie, J. P., Ong, C. N., Tan, N. S., and Leong, D. T. (2013). Titanium dioxide nanomaterials cause endothelial cell leakiness by disrupting the homophilic interaction of VE-cadherin. *Nature Communications., 4:* 1673, 1–12.

Shen, Y. J., Lefebvre, O., Tan, Z. and Ng, H. Y. (2012) Microbial fuel-cell-based toxicity sensor for fast monitoring of acidic toxicity. *Water Science and Technolnology, 65,* 1223–1228.

Simoneit, B. R. T. (2002). Biomass burning: A review of organic tracers for smoke from incomplete combustion. *Applied Geochemistry, 17,* 129–162.

Sobrado, M. A. (2001). Effect of high external NaCl concentration of xylem sap, leaf tissue and leaf glands secretion of the mangrove Avicennia germinans (L.) L. *Flora, 196,* 63–70.

Stoller, M. D., Park, S., Zhu, Y., An, J., and Ruoff, R. S. (2008). Graphene-based ultracapacitors. *Nano Letters, 8,* 3498–3502.

Stone, E. A., Yang, L., Yu, L. E. and Rupakhetic M. (2012). Characterization of organosulfates in atmospheric aerosols at four Asian locations. *Atmospheric Environment, 47,* 323–329.

Sukardi, H., Chng, H. T., Chan, E. C., Gong, Z., and Lam, S. H. (2011). Zebrafish for drug toxicity screening: Bridging the in vitro cell-based models and in vivo mammalian models. *Expert Opinion on Drug Metabolism Toxicology 7,* 579–589.

Sun, G. F., Chung, T. S., Jeyaseelan, K., and Armugam, A. (2013). Stabilization and immobilization of aquaporin reconstituted lipid vesicles for water purification. *Colloids and Surfaces B: Biointerfaces 102*, 466–471.

Tan, W. K., Lin, Q., Lim, T. M., Kumar, P. and Loh, C. S. (2013) Dynamic secretion changes in the salt glands of the mangrove tree species *Avicennia officinalis* in response to a changing saline environment. *Plant Cell Environ, 36*, 1410–1422.

Te, S.H., and Gin, K. Y. H. (2011). The dynamics of cyanobacteria and microcystin production in a tropical reservoir of Singapore. *Harmful Algae, 10*, 319–329.

Teh, H. B., Wu, H., Zuo X., and Li, S. F. Y. (2014). Detection of Hg^{2+} using molecular beacon-based fluorescent sensor with high sensitivity and tunable dynamic range. *Sensors and Actuators, B: Chemical, 195*, 623–629.

United States Environmental Protection Agency (USEPA). (2012). Cyanobacteria and Cyanotoxins: Information for Drinking Water Systems. EPA-810F11001, July, 2012.

Velasco, E., and Roth, M. (2012). Review of Singapore's air quality and greenhouse gas emissions: Current situation and opportunities. *Journal of the Air and Waste Management Association, 62*, 625–641.

Wang, H. L., Chung, T. S., Tong, Y. W., Chen, Z. C., Hong, M. H., Jeyaseelan, K., and Armugam, A. (2011). Preparation and characterization of pore-suspending biomimetic membranes embedded with Aquaporin Z on carboxylated polyethylene glycol polymer brush. *Soft Matter, 7*, 7274–7280.

Wang, H. L., Chung, T. S., Tong, Y. W., Jeyaseelan, K., Armugam, A., Duong, H. H. P., Fu, F. J., Seah, H., Yang, J., and Hong, M. H. (2013). Mechanically robust and highly permeable Aquaporin Z biomimetic membranes. *Journal of Membrane Science, 434*, 130–136.

Watanabe, H., and Tanaka, H. (1978). A non-ionic surfactant as a new solvent for liquid — liquid extraction of zinc(II) with 1-(2-pyridylazo)-2-naphthol. *Talanta, 25*, 585–589.

Whitfield, A. K., and Blaber, S. J. M. (1979). The distribution of the freshwater cichlid *Sarotherodon mossambicus* (Peters) in estuarine systems. *Environmental Biology of Fishes, 4*, 77–81.

World Health Organization (WHO). (2003). Cyanobacterial toxins: Microcystin-LR in Drinking-water: Background document for development of WHO guidelines for drinking-water quality. WHO, WHO/SDE/WSH/03.04/57.

Wu, Y. L., Pan, X., Mudumana, S. P., Wang, H., Kee, P. W., and Gong, Z. (2008). Development of a heat shock inducible gfp transgenic zebrafish line by using the zebrafish hsp27 promoter. *Gene, 408*, 85–94.

Xie, W., He, F., Wang, B., Chung, T. S., Jeyaseelan, K., Armugam, A., and Tong, Y. W. (2013). An aquaporin-based vesicle-embedded polymeric membrane for low energy water filtration. *Journal of Material Chemistry A, 1*, 7592–7600.

Xu, Y. J., Wang, C., Ho, W. E., and Ong, C. N. (2014). Recent developments and applications of metabolomics in microbiological investigations. *TrAC Trends in Analytical Chemistry, 56*, 37–48.

Yang, L., and Yu, L. Y. E. (2009). Measurements of oxalic acid, oxalates, malonic acid, and malonates in atmospheric particulates. *Environmental Science and Technology, 42*, 9268–9275.

Yang, L., Ho, N. Y., Alshut, R., Legradi, J., Weiss, C., Reischl, M., Mikut, R., Liebel, U., Müller, F., and Strähle, U. (2009a). Zebrafish embryos as models for embryotoxic and teratological effects of chemicals. *Reproductive Toxicology, 28,* 245–253.

Yang, L., Nguyen, D. M., and Yu, L. E. (2009b). Photooxidation of levoglucosan in atmospheric aqueous aerosols. *Geochmica et Cosmochimica Acta, 73*(13S), A1477.

Yang, L., Nguyen, D. M., Jia, S., Reid, J. S., and Yu, L. E. (2013). Impacts of biomass burning smoke on the distributions and concentrations of C2-C5 dicarboxylic acids and dicarboxylates in a tropical urban environment. *Atmospheric Environment, 78,* 211–218.

Yeo, B. H., and Gin, K. Y. H. (2013). Cyanophages infecting Anabaena circinalis and Anabaena cylindrica in a tropical reservoir. *Bacteriophage, 3*(3), e25571.

Yoonessi, M., Shi, Y., Scheiman, D. A., Lebron-Colon, M., Tigelaar, D. M., Weiss, R. A., and Meador, M. A. (2012). Graphene polyimide nanocomposites: Thermal, mechanical, and high-temperature shape memory effects. *ACS Nano, 6,* 7644–7655.

Zhang, W. C., Shyh-Chang, N., Yang, H., Rai, A., Umashankar, S., Ma, S. M., Soh, B. S., Sun, L. L., Tai, B. C., Nga, M. E., Bhakoo, K. K., Jayapal, S. R., Nichane, M., Yu, Q., Ahmed, D. A., Tan, C., Sing, W. P., Tam, J., Thirugananam, A., Noghabi, M. S., Pang, Y. H., Ang, H. S., Mitchell, W., Robson, P., Kaldis, P., Soo, R. A., Swarup, S., Hsuen, E. and Lim, B. (2012). Glycine decarboxylase activity drives non-small cell lung cancer tumor-initiating cells and tumorigenesis. *Cell, 148,* 1066–1066.

Zhang W., Tan, N. G., and Li, S. F. (2014). NMR-based metabolomics and LC-MS/MS quantification reveal metal-specific tolerance and redox homeostasis in Chlorella vulgaris. *Molecular Biosystems, 10,* 149–160.

CHAPTER 7

Energy Transitions — Energy Efficiency and Renewable Energy Challenges in the Tropics

Nilesh Y. Jadhav, Subodh Mhaisalkar
and Hans B. (Teddy) Püttgen
Energy Research Institute @ NTU

Abstract

Singapore is strategically positioned as a regional hub in Asia for various economic activities including, energy and carbon intensive operations such as oil refining, manufacturing, port operations and a well-planned urban infrastructure. However, Singapore does not have its own fossil-based energy resources and has only very recently started embarking on renewable energy options with energy security, decarbonisation of electricity and energy conservation as the key strategic objectives. Energy transition comprises a carefully executed country-wide process towards sustainability by means of energy efficiency and by deployment of clean energy. The Energy Research Institute @ NTU, Singapore, spearheads research in these domains and recently launched two flagship programmes with the objective of providing a bold vision and impetus for development of innovative solutions that will have significant impact on Singapore's energy transition and green growth while also putting Singapore in a leadership position in developing solutions relevant to the tropical region.

Introduction

Singapore's Energy Situation

Singapore's strategic location between the Indian and Pacific Oceans and with close access to the Strait of Malacca has enabled its strong development into a major petrochemical and oil refining hub in Asia in addition to its role as a manufacturing, trade, commerce and finance centre. Singapore's world-class harbour and airport sustain this broad palette of economic developments.

By the end of 2013, the population in Singapore had reached 5.47 million over a land area of 718 km^2, resulting in the highest population density in the world, at 7,615 inhabitants/km^2, aside from the territory of Macau and Monaco. The country has no natural fossil energy resources.

The only domestic energy production, which reached 600 ktoe (kilo tonnes oil equivalent) in 2012, i.e. less than 4% of the total final consumption, is from waste incineration at four local power plants. The ashes from the incineration plants are barged to the Semakau Island Landfill.

Singapore's Energy Balances

As per the IEA 2012 energy balances, the most recent publicly available worldwide information [*www.iea.org*], Singapore:

- Imported a total of 49,781 ktoe of crude oil of which 301 ktoe were re-exported resulting in:

  Net Total Primary Energy Supply (TPES) import of crude oil of 49,480 ktoe.

- Imported a total of 98,910 ktoe of oil products (including a small stock reduction) of which:
  - 83,330 ktoe were exported after various transformations
  - 41,100 ktoe went to marine bunkers for the harbour activities
  - 6,850 ktoe went to aviation bunkers for the airport activities

  Net TPES export of oil products of 32,370 ktoe.

- **Net TPES import of 7,330 ktoe of natural gas.**

As a result, the TPES consumption of Singapore in 2012 was 25,000 ktoe

Of these 25,000 ktoe:

- 4,920 ktoe were consumed in the electric power plants.
  - The total TPES consumed by the power plants was 8,960 ktoe of which 75% was natural gas.
  - The total electricity generation was 4,035 ktoe, resulting in an overall efficiency of 45%.
- 3,820 ktoe were consumed by the oil refineries and the energy industry itself.
- 300 ktoe were due to statistical errors and losses.

As a result, the total final consumption in 2012 for Singapore was 16,000 ktoe.

This final consumption was distributed as follows:

- Industry   5,170 ktoe   32.3%
- Transport   2,520 ktoe   15.7% (excluding shipping and aviation which are in the bunkers)
- Commerce and public services   1,620 ktoe   10.1%
- Residential   650 ktoe   4.1%
- Chemical and petro-chemical   5,300 ktoe   33.1%
- Other non-energy   750 ktoe   4.7%

The importance of the manufacturing (industry) and the chemical & petrochemical sectors is confirmed by the 65.4% they represent of the final energy consumption.

Evolution Toward Natural Gas

As mentioned above, other than the incineration of its waste, after careful recycling and triage, Singapore has no natural fossil energy resources. While the country has never relied on coal as an energy source, it has traditionally relied on crude oil of which more than 50% was imported from the United Arab Emirates, Saudi Arabia and Qatar. More recently, the Singapore government is promoting the use of natural gas. Since 2008, Malaysia and Indonesia, by way of pipelines, have provided for over 80% of Singapore's natural gas. Figure 1 illustrates the country's shift from oil to natural gas.

In support of this policy, a Liquefied Natural Gas (LNG) terminal/harbour installation was completed at Jurong which commenced operations in May 2013 and which was officially inaugurated by Prime Minister Lee Hsien Loong in February 2014. The capacities of the LNG facilities are being expanded to make it possible to only rely on LNG imports by 2024 as the pipeline-based contracts expire.

Singapore's Energy Indicators

Table 1 summarises Singapore's key energy indicators for 2012, the most recent statistics publicly available worldwide [*www.iea.org*].

A few salient observations:

- The country's Gross Domestic Product (GDP) has grown at an average annual growth rate of 6.1% between 1990 and 2012.

IEA Energy Statistics

Statistics on the web: http://www.iea.org/statistics/

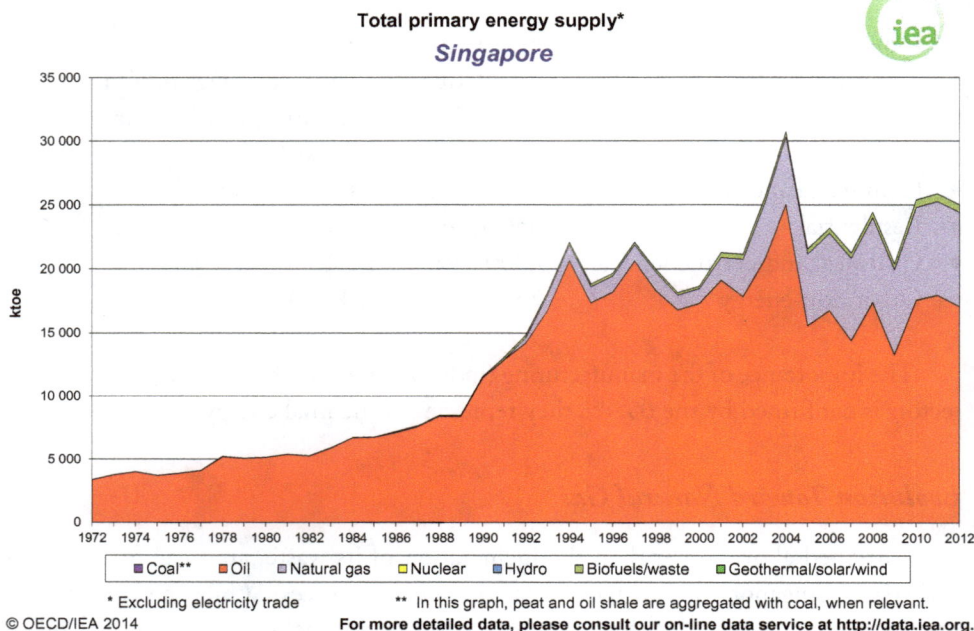

Figure 1.   Singapore's total primary energy supply (1972–2012).

Table 1.   Singapore's key energy indicators (2012).

Singapore key energy statistics		2012	2000	1990
Population	Millions	5.31	4.03	3.05
GDP	Billion 2005 USD	183.37	99.35	49.83
Energy production	Mtoe	0.60	0.20	0.07
Net imports	Mtoe	70.74	40.83	24.52
TPES	Mtoe	25.05	18.67	11.53
TPES/cap	toe/capita	4.72	4.63	3.78
TPES/GDP	toe/thousand 2005 USD	0.14	0.19	0.23
CO_2 emissions	Million tons	49.75	44.40	30.25
CO_2/cap	ton CO_2/capita	9.36	11.02	9.93
CO_2/TPES	ton CO_2/toe	1.99	2.38	2.62
CO_2/GDP	kg CO_2/2005 USD	0.27	0.45	0.61
Elect. cons.	TWh	46.16	30.51	15.18
Elec. cons./Cap	MWh/capita	8.69	7.58	4.98

- While the energy intensity per capita has *increased* from 3.78 toe/capita in 1990 to 4.72 toe/capita, the energy intensity based on the GDP has *decreased* from 0.23 toe/thousand 2005 USD to 0.14 toe/thousand 2005 USD.

  This is a clear confirmation of Singapore's overall commitment to a more rational energy end use.

- While the CO_2 emissions per capita remain high, at 9.36 ton CO_2/capita, the two key indicators of CO_2/TPES, which is indicative of the country's overall energy mix, and CO_2/GDP, which is indicative of the local industry's efforts to decrease its environmental footprint, have *decreased* significantly since 1990.

  These two indicators confirm Singapore's commitment toward an economy which is less carbon intensive.

Electric Energy Sector

Singapore's total electricity consumption increased by 1.6% to 45 TWh in 2013.

The distribution between contestable and non-contestable loads is shown below in Figure 2.

According to the Singapore Energy Management Authority (EMA), as of the end of June 2014, 17 generation licensees in Singapore had a total installed generation

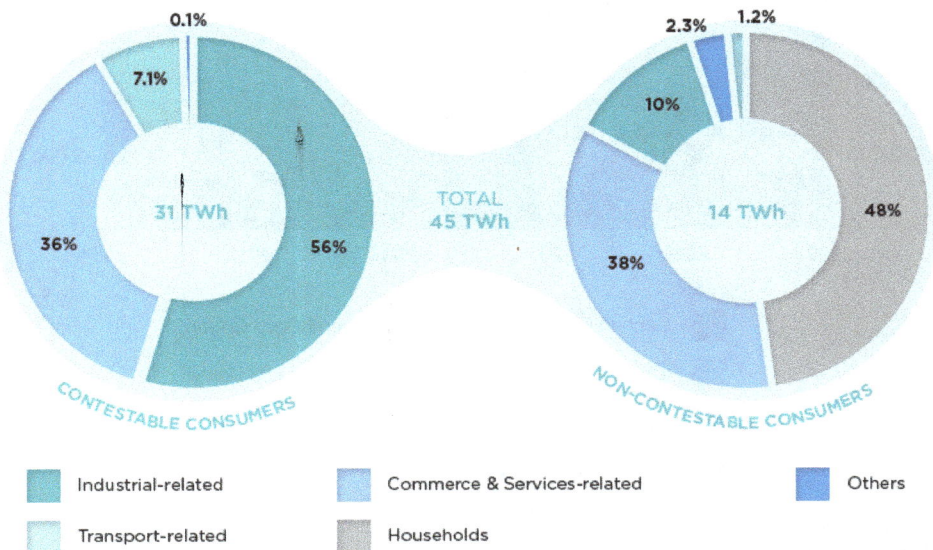

Figure 2.   Electricity consumption by contestability and sector in 2013 (Source: EMA, 2014).

capacity of 12,521 MW and the total electricity generation was 48 TWh in 2013 (EMA, 2014). The overall system capacity factor was 48.6% in 2013, confirming the prudent maintenance of a significant generation margin.

Among the 17 generation licensees, the six largest ones account for 95% of the generation capacity. The growth of generation capacity over past 6 years and the share of generation companies can be seen in Figure 3.

As shown by Figure 4, the contribution of natural gas toward electricity production is growing rapidly to reach 84% in 2012. It has reached as high as 92% in 2013 and 95% by mid-2014 with petroleum products accounting for less than 1% while other energy products (e.g. municipal waste, coal and bio-mass) accounted for the other 4% of the generation share (EMA, 2014).

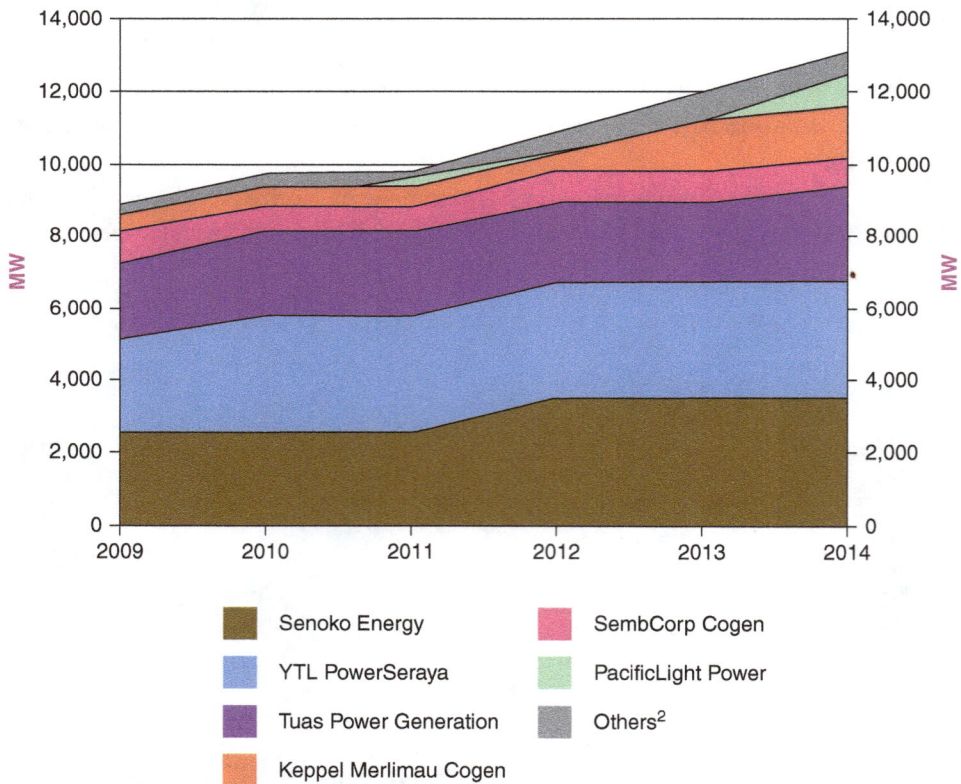

1   Data for 2014 is as of 1H 2014.
2   Others refer to all other electricity generators in 2013 as follows: National Environmental Agency, Keppal Seghers Tuas Waste-To-Energy Plant, Senoko Waste-To-Energy, Shell Eastern Petroleum, ExxonMobil Asia Pacific, Pfizer Asia Pacific, ISK Singapore, Singapore Oxygen Air Liquide, MSD International GmbH, Green Power Asia and GlaxoSmithkline Biologicals.

Figure 3.   Licensed generation capacity by generation companies (Source: EMA, 2014).

IEA Energy Statistics Statistics on the web: http://www.iea.org/statistics/

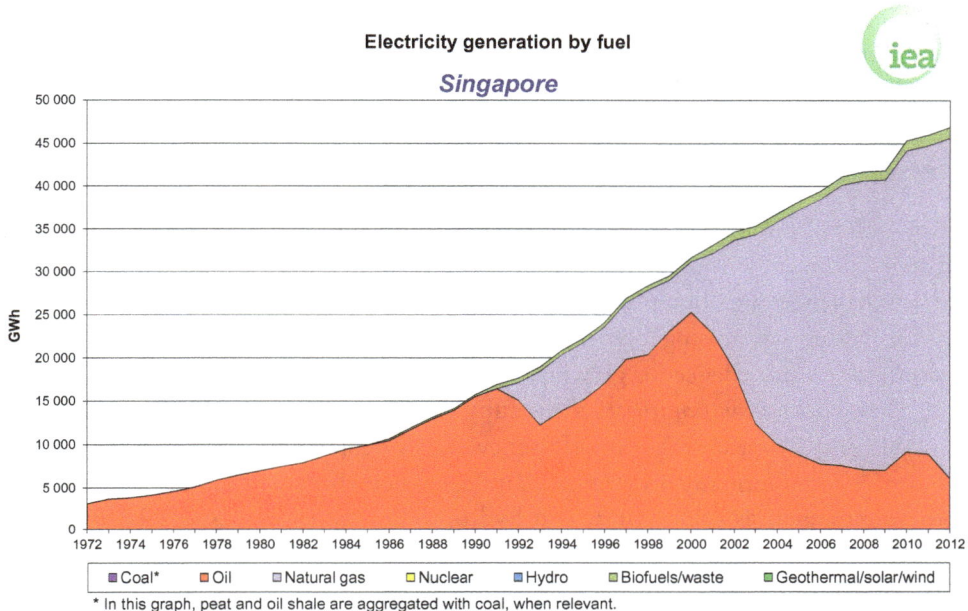

Figure 4. Electricity generation by fuel types in Singapore (1972–2012) (Source: IEA).

Renewable Energy

The grid-connected installed capacity of solar PV systems in Singapore reached 33 MWp (megawatt peak) at the end of 2014, spread over 636 installations across the island. The amount of electricity generated per month from these solar PV systems is sufficient to support the monthly consumption of all households residing in public housing across Novena in the same year. Of these, 410 installations — comprising 93% (30.8 MWp) of the total installed capacity — were operated by non-residential users including town councils and the Housing Development Board. There were 226 households installed with solar PV systems with a combined grid connected capacity of 2.3 MWp (EMA, 2015).

Early 2014, the Singapore government announced a plan to install 350 MWp of additional photovoltaic panels on public buildings. As per the Sustainable Energy Association of Singapore (SEAS), solar power can contribute 4.8% of 2025's forecasted electricity demand in Singapore (SEAS, 2014).

Wind energy

Given measured wind energy resources, it has been determined that wind energy will most probably not play a major role in the country's future electricity supply.

Ocean energy

Studies are recently underway to fully assess the potential of ocean energy around Singapore while focussing on in-stream tidal machines.

Energy Transitions

Rising global population and living standards, urbanisation, concerns over climate change and reliable low-carbon energy supplies have made energy a global priority. These challenges are often perceived as a threat and/or an opportunity by nations and by businesses; galvanising innovative technologies and policies that support *energy transition* and precedence for growing a *green economy*.

Energy transition comprises a carefully executed country-wide process towards sustainability by means of energy efficiency and by deployment of clean energy. While countries like Germany and Switzerland approach this energy transition through renewables such as solar, wind, and hydropower; the United States is leveraging opportunities in shale oil and shale gas to achieve energy independence by 2035.

The National Research Foundation (NRF), Singapore and National Climate Change Secretariat (NCCS), along with other governmental agencies, initiated the Energy National Innovation Challenge (NIC) in February 2011. Allocating a budget of S$300 million for the 2011–2015 period, Energy NIC sets forth to develop cost-competitive energy solutions deployable within a 20-year horizon to improve Singapore's energy efficiency, reduce its carbon emissions and broaden its energy options. Two key strategies in the Singapore energy transition include the increased focus on natural gas including secured LNG supply and deployment of at least 350 MWp of solar energy by 2020. Energy efficiency in residential and industrial complexes, deployment of green data centres, effective waste management, and public transportation centric low-carbon transport solutions are considered to be key to Singapore's sustainability strategy.

Green growth or *green economy* signifies a strategic focus on economic growth and environmental protection; with investments in resource savings as well as sustainable management of natural capital. Countries such as Germany and Denmark have committed to cover up to 35% of their energy from renewables by 2020, and see the green economy also as a significant driver for economic growth through the global export of energy efficiency and renewable energy solutions.

Worldwide, annual new investments in clean technologies have risen five-fold in the last decade, from US$55 billion in 2004 to US$254 billion in 2013, with the Asia-Pacific now contributing to 47% of these investments (Bloomberg New Energy Finance, 2014). To position the cleantech sector as an engine of economic growth, Singapore is adopting a multi-pronged approach along the entire value chain with investment in Research & Development, test-bedding, and demonstration pilots.

Opportunities available for Singapore include a modern urban metropolis that reinvents itself rapidly, socio-economic-cultural diversity to test new ideas and social attitudes, and a rich global talent pool. Unique also to Singapore is to turn around on its two biggest shortcomings namely land scarcity (very high population density) and being disadvantaged in terms of renewables (solar radiance tempered by rain/clouds/urban density; low wind/tidal resource compared with temperate climates).

With these challenges and opportunities in mind, the Energy Research Institute @ NTU (ERI@N), along with its partners in the Economic Development Board (EDB), JTC Corporation, and Building and Construction Authority (BCA) embarked on a substantial challenge to demonstrate reduction in electricity, water and waste resource, and carbon emissions by 35% over a period of 10 years. This EcoCampus project situated on the tropical campus of NTU and on the CleanTech Park led by JTC is intended to be a research and innovation-led effort to set the standard in energy efficiency in a campus environment, results of which provide technologies ready for deployment at scale as well as a blueprint that could be duplicated in other residential precincts or industrial complexes in tropical environments.

Beyond energy efficiency, to support the energy transition in the tropics, the Renewable Energy Integration Demonstrator — Singapore (REIDS) targets to deliver systemic research in integration of renewables in a distributed generation and islanded microgrid setting on the Semakau Island Landfill that is emblematic of Singapore's exemplary waste management ecosystem. The REIDS project, supported by the EDB and National Environmental Agency (NEA) will enable a carbon-free electricity supply for the Semakau Landfill operation, first of its kind in Southeast Asia. The REIDS project will be of particular relevance when Singapore and other countries progress in their specific energy transitions and need to pay attention to high penetration of renewables and on grid stabilisation including the need to integrate energy storage along with renewables.

Both the EcoCampus and REIDS flagship projects provide a bold vision and impetus for development of innovative solutions that will have significant impact on Singapore's energy transition and green growth and will also contribute to similar efforts in the tropical belt ranging from Southern China, Southeast Asia, across the Indian sub-continent to Africa and South America.

EcoCampus: A Framework for Sustainability in the Built Environment

Vision

The vision of the EcoCampus initiative is to be the greenest campus in the world via demonstration of high-impact energy efficiency and sustainability, and accentuating innovation and green growth as cornerstones of sustainable urban development.

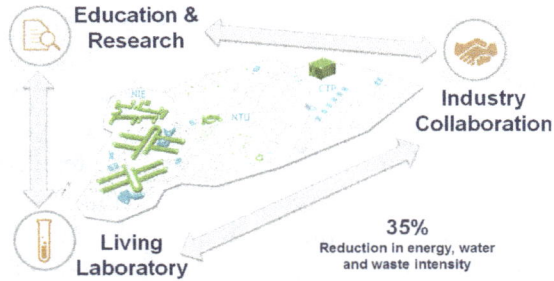

Figure 5.   Schematic representation of the EcoCampus framework.

Objectives

The objective of the EcoCampus initiative is to develop a campus-wide sustainability framework underpinned by research and innovation with a pathway to demonstration and deployment to achieve 35% reduction in energy, carbon, water and waste intensity. The primary mission of the programme is to be a cutting edge "Living-Lab" platform that epitomises research, innovation, and "green growth" by leveraging on technical expertise and industry participation. This will have a multiplier effect on growth in the energy sector that is based on job creation, productivity, capability building and entrepreneurship development. The EcoCampus will be a leading example towards the nation's goal of reducing energy intensity (per dollar GDP) by 35% from 2005 levels by 2030. Figure 5 depicts the sustainability framework of EcoCampus with Education and Research, Living Lab philosophy and Industry Collaboration as three key supporting pillars.

Context

Today, cities represent only 2% of the planet's surface, but house 50% of the world's population and consume 75% of the world's energy. Singapore is one such city, and with its limited land and natural resources, possesses unique challenges and opportunities for sustainable development. With rapid growth in urbanisation, it is predicted that 75% of the global population will live in cities by 2050. There will be a burgeoning energy demand coming up from the developing cities of which, cities in Asia will hold a significant share. It is hence imperative that sustainability in cities be focussed upon with emphasis on energy efficiency and alternative energy integration options for the future. The EcoCampus initiative would help Singapore take a position of leadership in the sustainable development of cities in the region by developing high-impact energy efficiency and sustainability solutions.

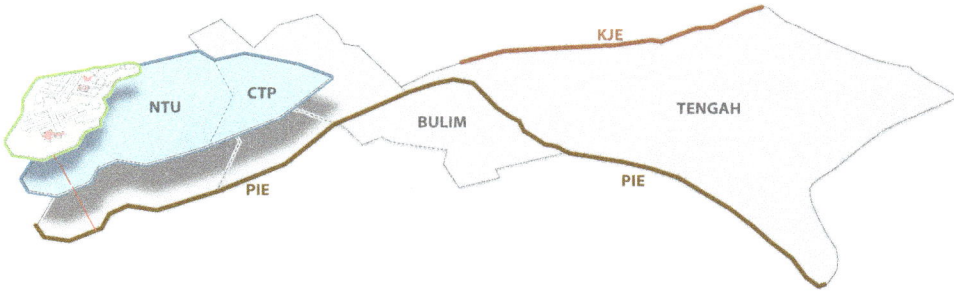

Figure 6.   NTU campus and surrounding developments.

NTU Campus as a Test-Bedding Site (A "Living Laboratory")

The NTU campus has more than 100 buildings with more than 1 million square metres of built-up area. With 10,000 students and 600 staff staying on the campus, it has a large residential campus and that number is set to double as more students would be accommodated on the campus. NTU currently has about 33,000 students and 7,000 staff studying and working on the campus. The various types of buildings, such as offices, laboratories, lecture theatres and residential apartments, make NTU a representative test-bed for a city. NTU is also part of a larger development in the west of Singapore with industrial, commercial and residential mixed-use facilities that upcoming in the neighbourhood such as the Cleantech Park (CTP), which is Singapore's first eco-business park, hosting companies and institutions in the Clean Environment Technology domain. The technologies that are developed and tested on the campus can be applied in the neighbouring new developments (see Figure 6) and also across other campuses and urban environments in the region.

The EcoCampus initiative covers several domains of sustainability including green buildings, transportation, renewable energy and user behaviour management. Here we discuss the various domains, their relevance to Singapore and some of the cutting-edge technologies that are being developed and demonstrated in the EcoCampus initiative research programme.

(a) Green buildings

Energy consumption in the building sector is trending upwards due to increasing population and rapid urbanisation in most parts of the world. In Singapore, non-residential and residential buildings (households) combined consume about 50% of the country's end-use electricity (see Figure 7).

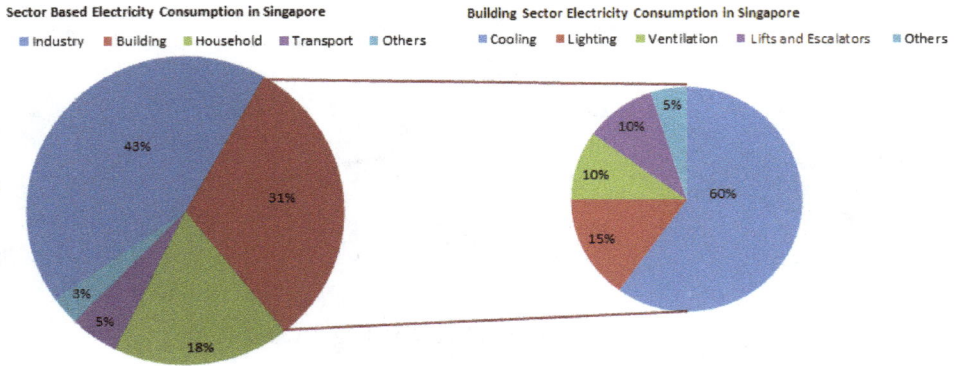

Figure 7.   Typical electricity consumption by end-use in Singapore and in the building sector (Chua *et al.*, 2013).

The 3rd Green Building Master Plan has been formulated and released in September 2014 by the Building Construction Authority with the vision of making Singapore "A global leader in green buildings, with special expertise in the tropics and sub-tropics — enabling sustainable development and quality living."

There has been a lot of technology advancement in Green Buildings and the Sustainable Buildings Technologies Group at the Energy Research Institute at NTU (ERI@N) spearheads technology development in areas such as advanced modelling and simulation tools for building design, advanced façade materials, innovative cooling technologies for tropics, and smart building controls.

With the use of modelling and simulation tools such as Energy-Plus and Computational Fluid Dynamics (CFD), the architects and engineers are well equipped to evaluate the energy performance of a building in the early design stages and make appropriate decisions on energy-saving techniques and tools to be introduced. Right from selecting the right building orientation, form-factor and façade to the cooling systems, the building design can determine its potential for natural ventilation and energy efficient features that can lead to energy savings of 30–50% compared to a code-compliant building. ERI@N was involved in the design of the CleanTech Two building (see picture of the building in Figure 8) via the process of Scientific Planning and Support to be able to achieve a high energy performance of the building from its inherent design. This was done using a scientific and integrative approach to building design with the aid of advanced modelling and simulation tools.

Being near the equator, buildings in Singapore are exposed to a lot of solar heat gain throughout the year. Scientists at ERI@N have been able to devise and develop "cool coating" materials that can reduce the heat gain from building rooftops and façade. In collaboration with industry partners such as AkzoNobel, Sky Cool and

Figure 8. CleanTech Two building in the CleanTech Park which was inherently designed as a green building with a scientific and integrative design process.

Nippon Paints, these coating materials have been developed and tested to be able to achieve substantial reduction in the indoor temperature (up to 20°C in buildings) (Figure 9).

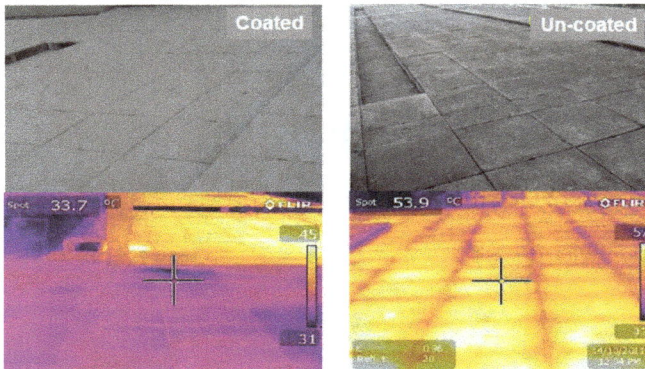

Figure 9. Thermal scan images demonstrating the impact of cool coating materials on actual buildings in Singapore.

As cooling demand constitutes the bulk of the energy consumption in buildings, it is important to focus on energy-efficient cooling systems. A test-bed of a "chilled ceiling" cooling concept, which requires far less air movement on cooling and relies on radiation and natural convection-based cooling, has proven to reduce the energy consumption of a cooling system by about 26%. This test-bed has been successfully implemented in collaboration with SGL Carbon as the industry partner. It has been in operation since November 2012 at the ERI@N office in the CleanTech One building (for an example, see Figure 10).

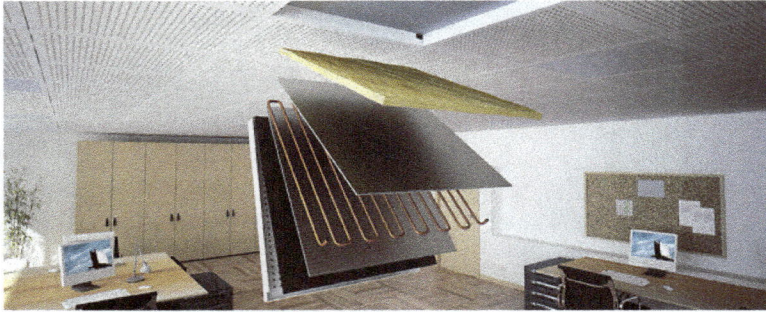

Figure 10.   Chilled ceilings rely on radiation and natural convection to reduce energy demand by 26% compared to conventional air conditioning.

With the tropical humid conditions of Singapore, a significant amount of energy is also used in dehumidifying the air to a comfortable level in air-conditioned spaces. A new technology being developed by ERI@N uses membrane-based system to reduce humidity in air via materials known as liquid desiccants (see Figure 11).

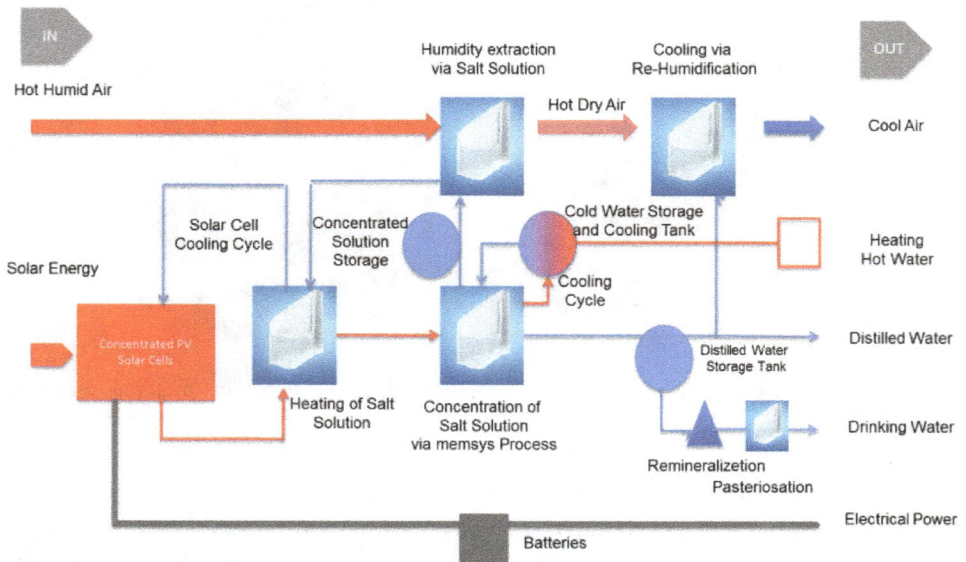

Figure 11.   Schematics of membrane-based liquid desiccant cooling system.

The membrane used in the system ensures that the liquid desiccant is not in direct contact with the air and at the same time allows for modular compact design of such system. This system is currently being developed at ERI@N via funding support from the A-Star and MND (Ministry of National Development) research programme and in collaboration with industry partner, memsys.

Cooling is also the major source of energy consumption in Data Centres, which have the reputation of being "energy guzzlers". Singapore is moving towards becoming a data centre hub of Asian region and hosted 58% of the regional data in year 2012 with massive growth anticipated in this sector over the coming years because of the excellent telecommunication infrastructure in the country. ERI@N has worked with industry partners such as Toshiba to develop and demonstrate high-efficient outdoor-air cooled data centres, which can achieve up to 50% reduction in the energy used (see Figure 12).

Under the EcoCampus programme, there are now experiments ongoing to be able to demonstrate an immersive cooling system for data centres, which can directly cool servers without the need for air-conditioning and hence achieve substantial reduction in cooling energy in data centre operation. This project will be implemented in the High Performance Computing Centre at NTU.

Figure 12.   Outdoor-air cooled data centre test-bed at NTU.

(b) *Energy information management and analytics*

The intelligent or smart energy systems of the future would need to collect, categorise and analyse a large amount of data to be able to effectively control the energy balances. This would require smart sensors and controllers along with data analytics capabilities. Building and facility managers need to have visibility into the energy use and performance of their equipment, creating opportunities for energy and capital expenditure savings.

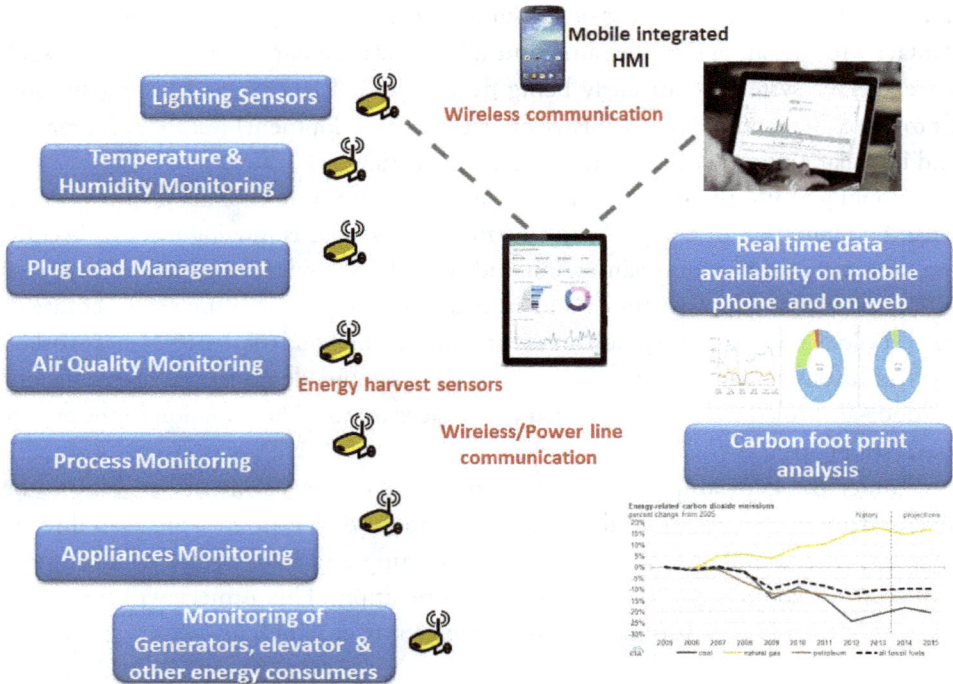

Figure 13.   Framework of a campus-wide monitoring and analysis system (Source: Wifinity).

ERI@N has worked with research partners such as NXP in development of wireless and autonomous sensors and sensor networks to collect data across buildings in a quick and non-intrusive way. Under the EcoCampus programme, a campus-wide smart energy monitoring and control system is being researched and developed with industry research partners (see Figure 13).

(c) *Renewable energy and smart grids*

NTU is installing one of the largest Solar PV systems in Singapore with a capacity of 5 megawatt peak (MWp) by 2015. This installation will be done on rooftops of NTU buildings and the first 3.5 MWp is already installed and commissioned by end of 2014 (Figure 14 shows a picture of a Rooftop Solar PV installation at the NTU campus). As Solar PV is a variable energy generator, depending on the weather conditions, it poses a challenge of grid integration and adaptation. Along with prediction and forecasting tools, energy storage solutions and demand response programmes have to be developed to be able to achieve a high penetration of this renewable energy in cities.

The traditional grid structure in Singapore is quite reliable with an average interruption time of one minute per customer per year. The country has already employed supervisory control and data acquisition that detect the disruptions in the power supply.

Figure 14.   Rooftop Solar PV installation at the NTU Campus.

This makes Singapore an ideal market to implement "Smart Grids" which are seen to be the electricity delivery system of the 21st century. Smart grids combine the electrical grid with information technology and automation to improve energy efficiency, and sustainability of the electricity generation and distribution systems. As part of this initiative and to optimise the energy produced from various renewable energy sources, the Energy Market Authority of Singapore has launched the "Intelligent Energy Systems" pilot project which was implemented in the NTU campus and in Punggol.

The new system will help to enhance the capabilities of the current grid, making it more receptive to load changes, adding sensors/information devices such as smart meters and offer dynamic pricing plans to consumers. The new grid system will also be able to embed new electricity generation from renewable energy and storage sources (EMA, 2010). Smart grids also have the potential of integration with building energy management systems. For instance, as a pilot project, around 400 residents of Marine Parade and West Coast were given the opportunity to monitor the electricity consumption in real time. They can also select a appropriate retailer based on their needs using smart meters.

ERI@N is working with corporate partners such Murata to develop and test Smart Energy Management Systems that allow for improved grid stability and self-sufficiency

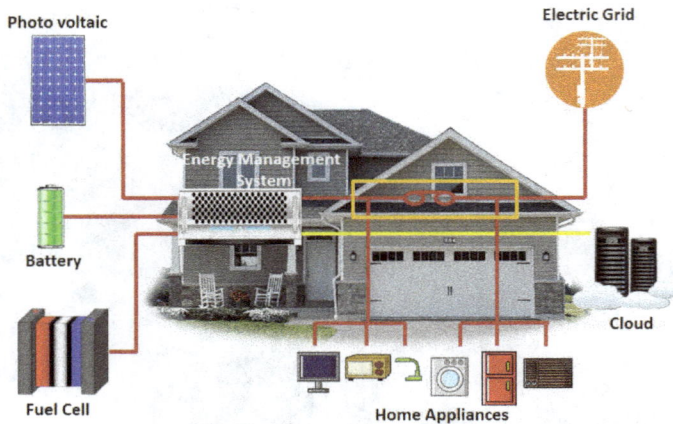

Figure 15.   Integration of renewables via a smart energy management system (Source: Murata).

while incorporating renewable energy sources. It integrates DC renewables (like solar PV and fuel cell), storage battery and grid power into one system, and intelligently manages the distribution of energy in various circumstances (see Figure 15). The system is able to operate autonomously by deciding how to distribute grid power and electricity from solar PV or storage batteries to household appliances, and control energy allocation through bidirectional DC-AC inverters and bidirectional DC-DC converters.

Smart grids around the world primarily focus only on the electricity network. NTU, along with its partners, is embarking on a programme that delivers "Smart multi-energy grids" that will capitalise on the synergies and interactions of the three main energy vectors: electricity, heat, and, gas/fuels to deliver significant gains in energy efficiency and sustainability. Smart multi-energy grid systems represent an effort to combine, integrate and operate different energy sources by means of smart control strategies similar to smart grids.

Smart multi-energy grid systems find its application in the entire energy supply chain that goes from power generation, energy distribution, energy storage to conversion. It is envisioned that the deployment of smart-multi energy grid systems on a large scale (e.g. Singapore campuses, residential precincts, and industrial complexes) will contribute to improved energy efficiency, reduced GHG emissions, and will help Singapore adapt efficiently to the ongoing energy transitions that includes solar energy along with LNG.

(d) *Low carbon urban mobility solutions*

In 2010, the transport sector utilised 15% of Singapore's total energy. More than 90% of this is consumed by internal combustion engines. Greenhouse gas emissions from road transport can be reduced in four ways: (i) improving the fuel efficiency of conventional fossil fuel vehicles, (ii) use of biofuels, (iii) hydrogen and fuel cell vehicles, and (iv) electric vehicles. Given that Singapore does not have an automotive industry, electric vehicles represent the most significant opportunity to reduce energy usage and carbon emissions.

The design, development and deployment of clean and energy efficient transport system technologies are aimed at a broad market inception of environment friendly and high efficiency electric and other vehicles. These technologies bring business competitiveness, creating market value chain, lowering CO_2 emissions, creating a higher quality of life, achieving sustainable smart growth, transitioning to a resource-efficient economy and attractive green campus. The research area focusses on requirements of a typical campus transport and is being developed with industry partnerships to demonstrate innovative solutions for low carbon and sustainable mobility solutions at EcoCampus. Some of the technology developments in this area are mentioned below:

Electric public transportation based on opportunity charging

It is known that applications involving electric buses need to overcome significant obstacles due to the lower battery energy density resulting in extra weight and space constraints and thus the cost. This drawback leads to opt for either limited driving distance or limited passenger capacity.

To address these challenges, alternate methodologies such as Flash/Opportunity Charging are being explored through use of hybrid electric buses. These buses would bridge to transition towards a fully electric solution in future. ERI@N, along with its industry partners, is developing a test-bed project based on the "Charge and Go" strategy using optimised battery pack and a back-up diesel engine, which allows for a 24/7 electric solution with opportunity charging (see Figure 16 below).

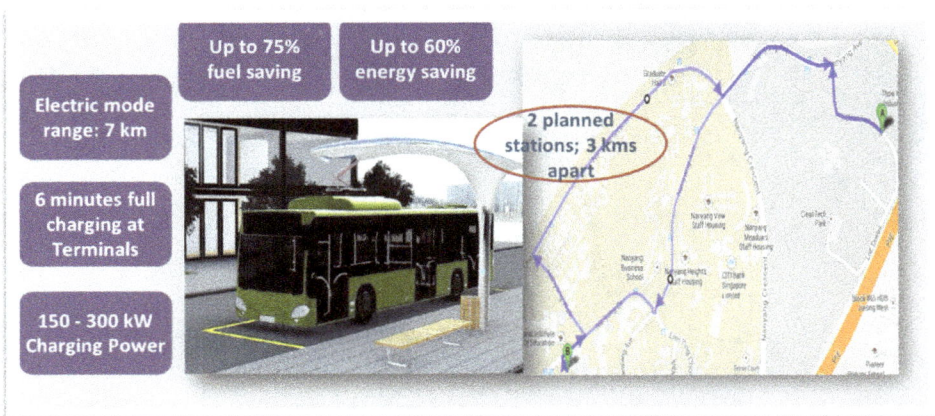

Figure 16. Opportunity charging-based public transport test-bed proposed at the NTU Campus.

Autonomous vehicles with wireless flash charging

Convenient alternative mobility technologies are required to reach a transit service. This requires a different arrangement for bridging the "first mile/last mile" gap through the integration of on-call autonomous shuttles. These vehicles and services, which are customised for shorter distance (<20 km) mobility needs, are deemed promising for shorter commutes and multiple users. This research work is focussed to address these aspects of supplementing the public transport or designing eco-transportation hubs, which are wholly composed of systems that are clean, convenient and cost efficient.

A project developed by ERI@N, along with industry partners Elbit and Navya, aims to develop an Autonomous Transportation Model (ATM) for the first and last mile coverage for people and goods with support for the existing transportation system (see Figure 17 below). To be on the road 24/7, the energy storage concept is based on the Supercapacitor technology which allows a fully electric solution, in which the system is automatically charged in less than 2 minutes with the charging power of 50 kW. The charging system is powered through the solar panels and charges wirelessly to the on-board supercapacitors of an autonomous vehicle.

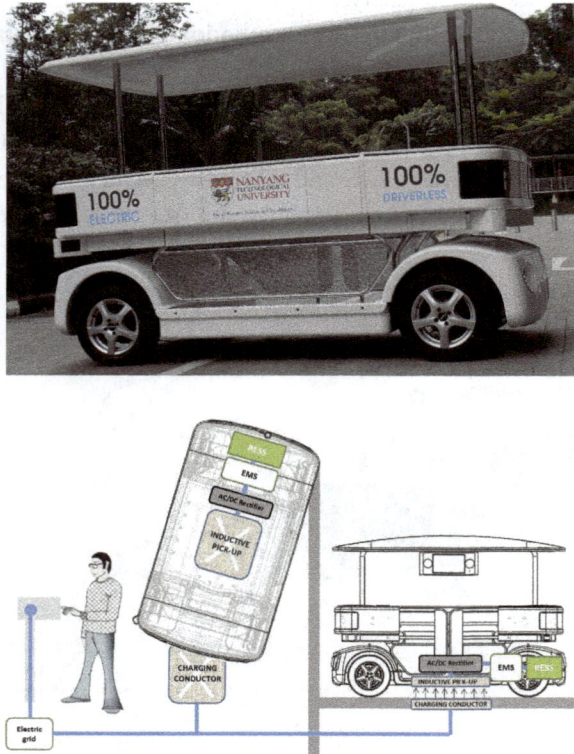

Figure 17.   Advanced Autonomous Shuttle Vehicle test-bed proposed at the NTU Campus.

Personal Light Electric Vehicle (PLEV) based co-modal end to end urban mobility needs

To meet the door-to-door mobility needs of individual users, simple and low-end transport technologies are required to supplement the other modes of transport. This research work in collaboration with industry partner Peugeot is focussed on addressing these aspects of supplementing the mass transport with e-bikes/light electric vehicles that are safe, convenient and cost efficient. The project will focus on design and development of cost-efficient PLEVs suitable for tropical climatic conditions for single-user/personal mobility needs. It includes a centralised smart connectivity and management system that enables users to check the availability and location of sharing vehicles and book them through smartphones.

(e) *User behaviour aspects of energy conservation*

Energy conservation, at the individual, family and work place levels, is strongly linked to user behaviour, awareness and education. In 2013, the Singapore Land Transport Authority (LTA) successfully tested and implemented the "Travel Early-Travel Free" scheme on its Mass Rapid Transit (MRT) trains to influence travel behaviour change, to shift travelling commuters to off-peak periods and avoid congestion. Such behaviour socioeconomic models need to be extended to other areas of sustainability such as energy conservation.

One such project on user-behaviour-based energy savings will be piloted at the NTU Campus along with industry partner GDF-Suez. The project will involve gamification of the energy conservation concepts that will engage students and staff via mobile apps focussed on energy savings (Figure 18).

Figure 18.   Pilot project at NTU to engage users in energy savings via gamification approaches. The video demonstration can be viewed at http://youtu.be/RnFyGkF9riQ.

Figure 19.   Launch of EcoCampus Initiative with supporting industry and agency partners.

Official Launch of EcoCampus Initiative

The EcoCampus initiative was officially launched on 30 April 2014 in the presence of Mr. S. Iswaran, Minister, Prime Minister's Office and Second Minister for Home Affairs and Trade and Industry. In partnership with Singapore's Economic Development Board (EDB) and JTC Corporation, the EcoCampus initiative will transform NTU's 200-hectare campus and the adjoining CleanTech Park into a super test-bed for research projects in cutting-edge green technologies. During the launch of the initiative itself, it gathered interest from more than 10 industry partners including multinational companies such as Siemens, GDF Suez, Murata, 3M and Philips, and local firms such as Joule Air and Alfatech. Minister S. Iswaran noted during the launch that "as a high-impact integrated Living Lab, the EcoCampus will create exciting green-collar jobs, raise our international standing, and inspire Singaporeans to adopt sustainable practices." Figure 19 shows a picture taken during the launch of the EcoCampus initiative with Minister Iswaran, agency partner representatives from EDB and JTC as well as representatives from industry partners who signed the support plaque.

Renewable Energy Integration Demonstrator — Singapore, REIDS

Vision

The vision of the *Renewable Energy Integration Demonstrator — Singapore*, **REIDS**, is to foster technology development and commercialisation efforts in the broad energy market in support of Singapore corporate stakeholders thereby strengthening their position within the rapidly growing renewable energy and microgrid markets and to support Singapore's commitment to a path toward a broader energy mix, including a growing renewable energy portion, and a more rational energy end-use.

Objective

The *REIDS* objective is to test and demonstrate, at a large-scale level, the proper integration of a broad range of renewable energy production — onshore and offshore, energy storage and rational energy end-use technologies to provide for the supply of a wide palette of industrial, commercial and residential loads. The *REIDS* initiative will provide a broad range of private and public sector entities with a unique platform in support of their ongoing R&D efforts, as required for early testing, followed by large-scale demonstration and eventually showcasing all along the usually long energy technology and product development cycle.

Hybrid microgrid technologies will allow for flexible — "plug and play" — interconnectivity between the various sources, storage components and end-uses as required, for example, to provide for the electrification of islands and remote villages as well as to rapidly deploy energy supply and distribution systems during emergency situations.

REIDS aims to be a partnership, structured as a consortium between: (i) Singapore public agencies, (ii) corporations active in the energy arena with a focus on the integration of a broad range of sources, end-uses and storage, and (iii) academia and public R&D institutions. ERI@N, the Energy Research Institute at Nanyang Technological University (NTU), will lead the consortium.

Context

As industrialised countries seek to formulate and implement energy transition strategic plans, they face two main challenges: (i) support more fundamental — "over the horizon" — research to envision and develop the technologies which will lead to major paradigm changes in the energy arena and (ii) support the broad deployment of the many technologies which are already available, or which will soon be, to demonstrate that significant progress towards a more sustainable energy mix is possible in the near future while maintaining the present quality of life and while not hampering that of future generations.

This second challenge can only be met by way of large-scale demonstrators where a broad range of technologies are deployed in a properly coordinated manner to serve the energy needs of actual, real-life situations.

Furthermore, meeting the future energy needs of not yet fully developed regions of the world requires a significantly enhanced access to electricity including in remote villages or islands. These needs could largely be addressed by way of renewable energies integrated by way of microgrids. Microgrids will also be increasingly deployed in emergency situations to rapidly connect locally available supplies with the loads to be serviced under a broad range of circumstances.

While challenging, energy transitions also represent formidable opportunities for export-oriented industries. REIDS will provide Singapore with a platform from which to enhance its position as an energy innovation hub as well as an energy science and technology knowledge hub.

Microgrid Market Overview

The overall energy demand, in general, and the electricity load, in particular, will continue to see rapid growth during at least the next two decades. The bulk of this growth is anticipated to come from India, China and ASEAN countries, with their combined worldwide electrical generation share rising from 27.5% in 2010 to 40.1% in 2030 (33,370 TWh). Following the Fukushima accident and pressure from international communities to address global warming and climate change, alternative renewable energy sources (wind, solar PV, solar thermal, biomass, geothermal and marine) are expected to see their share of the global electricity generation increase from a modest 3.6% in 2010 to a substantial 12.9% in 2030 (Frost and Sullivan, 2012).

The top five regions with largest growing electricity demand and generation are shown in Figure 20.

Traditional High Voltage (HV) transmission system expansion is becoming increasingly difficult in industrialised counties, primarily due to public resistance and the investment costs associated with underground systems. Most renewable energy sources rely on electricity as the energy vector putting further pressure on the ubiquitous access to electric infrastructures, centralised or otherwise. Addressing the growing requirements to provide electricity to remote regions — villages and/or islands — in Africa, Latin America and ASEAN countries will not be economically feasible using large HV transmission systems; this is also true in conjunction with

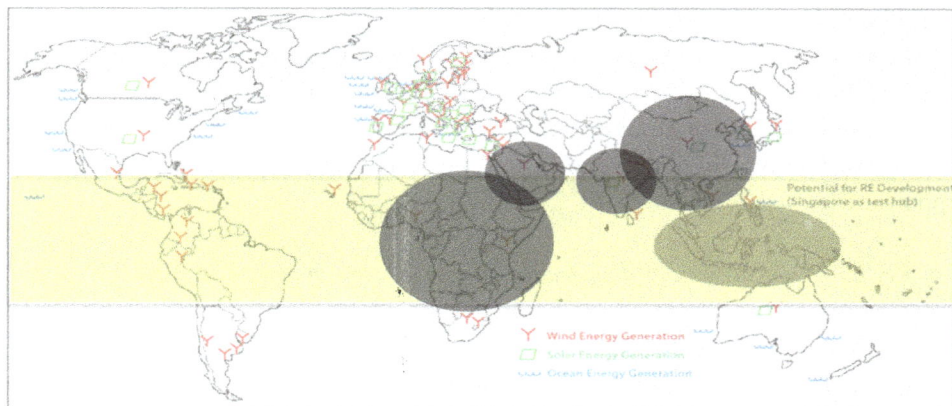

Figure 20.   Top five fastest growing electricity production regions in the world from 2010–2030, majority near tropical belt.

various emergency situations such as the aftermath of natural disasters and in refugee camps during conflicts.

> *While legacy interconnected HV transmission systems will remain the norm in industrialised countries, the development of electric infrastructures in emerging regions will largely happen by way of local microgrids.*

Some alternative renewable energy sources, such as solar PV, inherently produce electricity in DC (Direct Current) while others, such as wind, inherently rely on AC (Alternative Current). In addition, the fast development of electronic technologies in conjunction with an ever broader range of applications inherently encourages the deployment of DC supply systems. This means that future microgrids should be AC/DC hybrid systems capable of interconnecting renewable energy sources, be they inherently AC or DC, with loads which could also best be served using AC or DC supplies.

In 2010, the world market for microgrids (including institutional and campus microgrids) reached US$4.14 billion, up significantly from 2009. At this time, North America has nearly 74% of the total microgrid market share; by 2020, it is expected that the microgrid market will be more evenly distributed among all regions of the world. Remote microgrids, still a small segment of the global microgrid market, reported a 349 MW generation capacity in 2011 and is expected to increase to 1.1 GW coming 2017.

In Asia Pacific, where microgrids are still in a nascent stage, the microgrid market is expected to increase from US$42 million in 2010 to US$438.6 million in 2017, a compound annual growth rate (CAGR) of 39.8%, with the main drivers being the focus on renewable energies, reliable power, quality and power shortages, rural electrification, efficiency improvements and natural disasters in Asia. At this time, only a very limited number of equipment manufacturers feature a significant breadth of microgrid offerings while several other companies are still assessing the market opportunities.

Key microgrid markets and types addressed in the context of REIDS include:

- *Remote islands in the Pacific Southeast*
- *Remote villages in Africa and close to the poles*
- *Emergency refugee camps*
- *Remote mining operations*
- *Temporary military operations*

Selection of the Semakau Island Landfill

The selection of the Semakau Island Landfill for the REIDS implementation is justified by the exemplary role of the site in Singapore's integrated waste management cycle.

As shown in Figure 21 below, the Semakau Island Landfill is situated south of Singapore; it is used as a final disposal ground for burnt waste ashes from the four main waste incineration plants located on the main island.

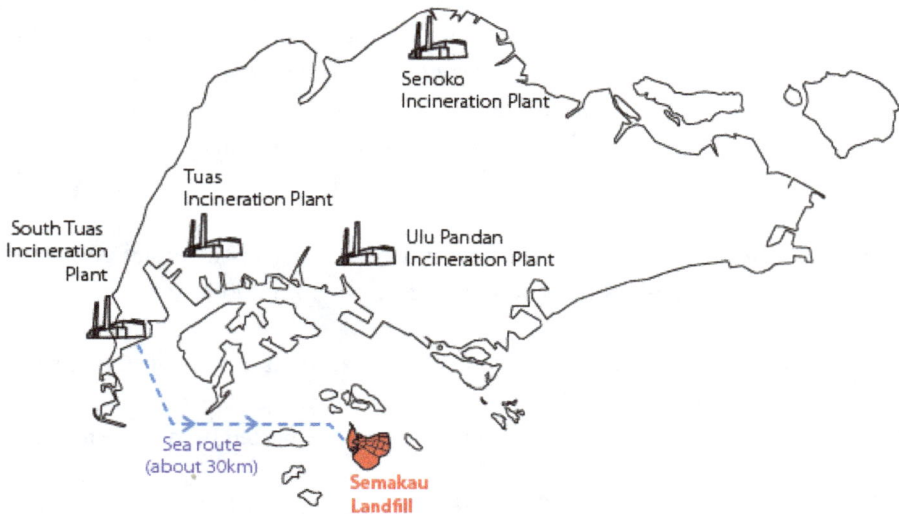

Figure 21.   Semakau Island Landfill integration within the Singapore waste management cycle.

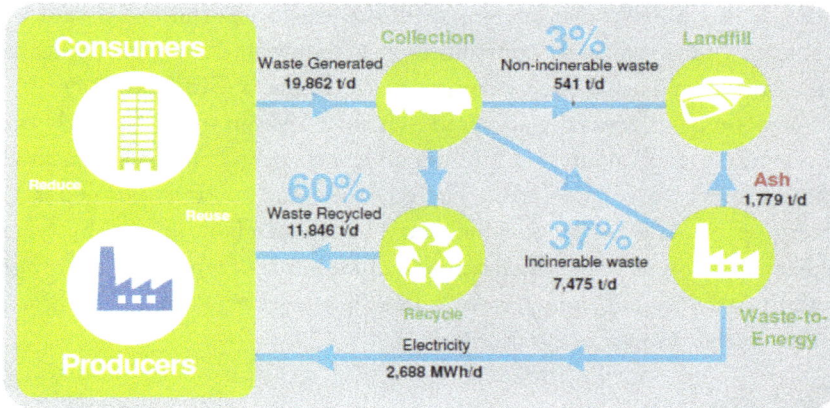

Figure 22.   Combined operations of the four waste incineration plants on Singapore's main island.

The combined operation of the four incineration plants is summarised by Figure 22 where the 2012 daily averages are shown.

The solid inorganic and non-toxic waste ashes are transported from the Tuas Marine Transfer Station via a 30 km sea route to be disposed of at the Semakau Island Landfill where the current solid waste disposal capacity is estimated to last beyond 2030. An administration and operations office is located on the island. The primary source of energy on the island is diesel fuel which is transported from the mainland. Diesel fuel is used for the diesel-electric generators as well as for all the vehicles and heavy machineries on the island.

> *The Semakau Island Landfill constitutes the final stage of Singapore's exemplary waste management programme. As a result, using the landfill to build a large-scale renewable energy test and demonstration platform will have a highly symbolic impact in closing the waste cycle. This symbolic image would be unique to the Semakau Island site, in addition to its many other advantages mentioned above.*

Main Renewable Energy Sources to be Addressed in the Context of REIDS

Solar energy

Solar energy is a natural choice for Singapore, which, thanks to its position close to the equator, has high solar irradiance with minimal seasonal variation. However, the low spatial power density of solar energy along with Singapore's highly urbanised densely populated landscape limits the full potential for solar energy for

Singapore. Nevertheless, solar energy is still the most important renewable energy deployable in Singapore with contributions of between 6 to 14% forecasted by 2050 in a business-as-usual energy consumption scenario (SERIS, 2014).

In Singapore, it is generally accepted that solar PV can only effectively produce energy during an equivalent of 3.5 hours or less in a day, taking cloud cover and other limitations into consideration. The day-time and intermittent generation of solar energy presents a challenge which may be effectively addressed by renewable energy diversification strategy which would include a mix of renewable energy generation options such as wind energy, wave, and tidal energy generation, combined with appropriate energy storage integration.

Wind and marine energy

Although wind and wave energy is also subject to intermittency due to wind speeds, tidal in stream-energy generation is predictable with great accuracy linked directly to combined effects of the gravitational forces of the Moon and the Sun and the rotation of the Earth. The main advantage of a combined solar, wind, tidal, wave energy generation, with backup generation from diesel power is a reliable energy generation profile with great potential for overall CO_2 abatement.

Wind speeds in urban Singapore are between 2 m/s (on the north shore) and 3.5 m/s (Karthikeya *et al.*, 2014a) from 4 measurement sites. However there is a case for wind energy generation on areas near the southern shoreline (e.g. East Coast, Tuas), on offshore islands (e.g. estimated winds speeds on Semakau are 6 m/s at 50 m hub height), and the shallow seas that would not interfere with maritime traffic. A comprehensive wind resource assessment conducted by ERI@N for a period of two years has shown relatively significant potential (~320 MW) for harvesting wind power in the shallow waters within Singapore (see Figure 23). Estimates of wind energy generation potential range from 0.5 to 1.5 TWh of annual energy production are in the range of 1 to 3% of Singapore's needs. To illustrate the possibility further, on Semakau and near the tip of Tuas, the wind potential is strong enough for the installation of 10–15 wind turbines of up 600 kWp–1 MWp in a wind farm configuration which could generate 40 GWh of wind energy on an annual basis (DNV, 2011).

A look at the job distribution in the US wind energy industry reveals that 21% of jobs created are related to manufacturing, 10% related to construction, 5% in operation and maintenance, and other jobs related services, financial consultancy and logistics for which local expertise and employment is necessary (de Oliveira and Fernandes, 2012). According to a recent study by the International Energy Agency, it has been estimated that a net capacity increase of 1,500 MW requires 12,765 full-time employees related to project development, project planning, manufacturing,

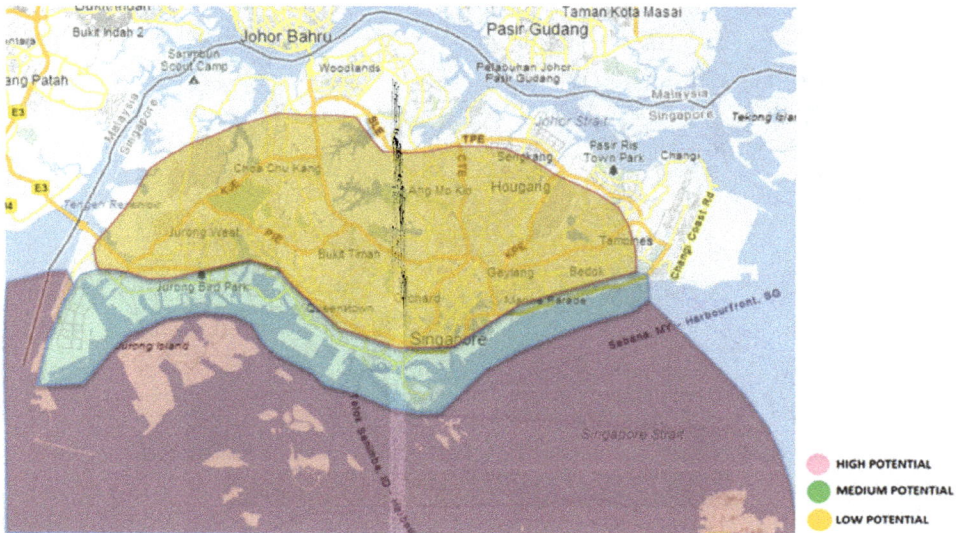

Figure 23. Wind energy potential in Singapore and its offshore (Karthikeya *et al.*, 2014b; Prabal *et al.*, 2013).

construction and installation activities. Operation of an installed wind energy capacity of 10 GW requires 2,000 full-time employees.

Wave energy is correlated with wind energy; however, the diurnal tidal energy current pattern of the Singapore Strait is dominantly bi-directional (ebbing towards the northeast and flooding towards the southwest). ERI@N has done extensive wave energy resources assessment along with the Tropical Marine Sciences Institute (TMSI) and has observed wave heights exist up to 0.5 m at several locations near the coast of Singapore. The wave energy devices developed by ERI@N demonstrate energy generation potential of 300 Wp for 0.3 m wave heights. (Ly *et al.*, 2014)

Tidal in-stream energy (TISE) devices convert the kinetic energy of moving water into electrical energy. As with any tidal in stream resource, the velocity profile varies in magnitude throughout the lunar month; however is highly predictable and thus creates an ideal contributor to any renewable energy mix. The available TISE potential of Singapore is estimated to be about 3 TWh annually; and the key opportunities (excluding areas of interest to shipping) lie in the region between Tuas, Semakau, and the southern islands. Figure 24 shows the tidal energy potential based on the seabed information and tidal flow measurements conducted by the company DHI and Tropical Marine Science Institute (TMSI) (Abundo *et al.*, 2012, 2013).

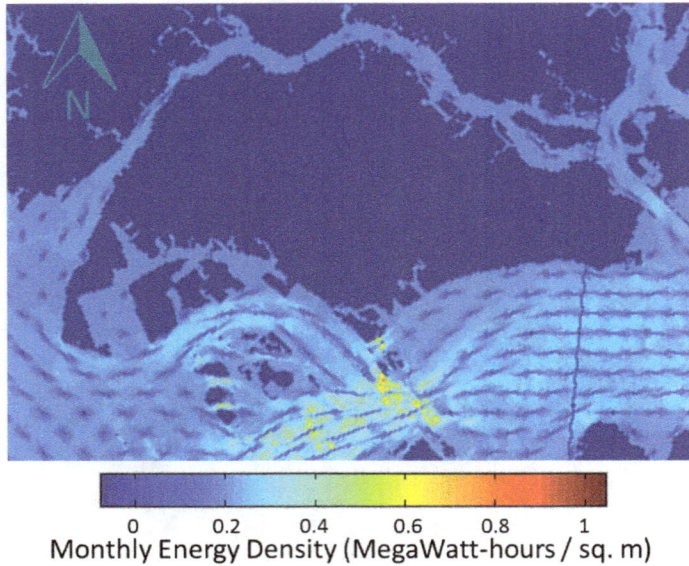

Monthly Energy Density (MegaWatt-hours / sq. m)

Figure 24.   Tidal energy potential in Singapore waters.

The TISE energy generation potential (based on extraction efficiency of turbines) of Singapore is estimated at 0.6 to 1 TWh/yr and represent a similar contribution to Singapore's electricity needs (1 to 3%) compared with wind energy potential. It should be noted that unlike wind energy, the tidal energy generation technology is yet to reach full commercialisation scale in the tropical environments. Active areas being investigated include high efficiency low-flow turbines, near-shore turbine deployment, light-weight materials and corrosion resistant construction, anti bio-fouling solutions, and environmental impact assessment. Presently indigenous tidal turbine designs are being tested by ERI@N at the scaled test site (shown in Figure 25) to study field level performances of pilot designs.

Both wind and marine energy generation may not contribute to Singapore's energy mix to the same scale as solar energy; however, with Singapore's inherent strength in marine engineering (e.g. ship building/repair, oil and gas, rig/FPSO construction) represent a strong opportunities for green growth and to help Singapore establish itself as a cleantech hub. The wind and marine industry is also in its infancy and Singapore could have a significant competitive advantage to position itself as a solution provider in the tropical island communities that span from the Philippines to Indonesia and onward to Sri Lanka and Africa.

NTU installed Singapore's first tidal turbine system at the Sentosa Boardwalk (November 2013) to test the viability of tapping tidal energy. The NTU tidal turbine

Figure 25.   ERI@N's tidal energy scaled test site at Sentosa Boardwalk to test indigenous designs.

system consists of few low-flow turbines mounted on the test-bed, optimised for local conditions. The project aims to demonstrate the feasibility of capturing energy for small-scale devices and infrastructure in low tidal current areas.

The REIDS project will be an ideal test-bed for both wind and marine renewables and will see installations of large wind turbines (e.g. 50–70 m tip height, 300–600 kW), small and medium-sized vertical and horizontal axis turbines on the Semakau Landfill. Installations of TISE devices ranging from 10–20 m would also follow a detailed resource assessment and environmental risk assessment in the areas near Semakau and St. John's Island.

Bioenergy

Singapore has already implemented a very proactive waste management process, including recycling and waste incineration plants. Given the high demand on free land for residential, commercial and industry needs, growing crops strictly for bioenergy purposes on the main island is not realistic. However, using yet undeveloped islands for bioenergy agricultural purposes using crops that are suitable given the local conditions, such as Jatropha, should not be neglected.

Furthermore, a broad range of potential algae bioenergy processes remain largely unexplored and Singapore's geographical location with broad ocean access on the equator provides for significant development possibilities.

In addition, the renewable energy produced locally can be used to power on-site Bio Refineries.

Systems Approach to Renewable Energy Integration

Time variations of solar, wind and tidal in-stream

Renewable energies — solar, wind and ocean — are free of fuel costs.

However, both solar and wind energy are non-dispatchable, i.e. their production scheduling is fully beyond man's control. In-addition, their availability is highly varying from one day to the next while their forecasting is only possible, with a sufficient degree of precision to be useful, a few hours/days in advance.

Ocean tidal in-stream, while predictable with a high degree of precision during a very long period of time — months/years — in advance, is also non-dispatchable.

These daily variations are illustrated below for a solar, wind and tidal in-stream production. The sum of the three sources is also shown. Clearly, both the timing and amplitude of each production source during any one day will change — this is illustrated below for two example situations. From the simple illustration below, Figure 26, three key conclusions can be drawn:

- A proper integration of all three renewable energy sources "dampens" their individual variations.
- For the resulting energy production to be fully useful to serve actual loads, they need to be integrated with one or more energy storage devices.

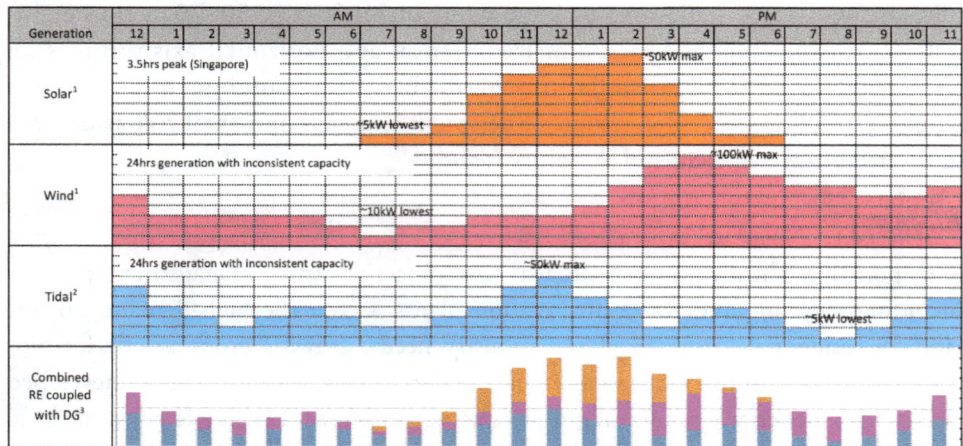

Figure 26. Various renewable energy (RE) sources with their daily generation capacity (preliminary prediction — rapid increase in generation during the day), which could be used for a multiple RE microgrid system.

[1]Solar/wind chart: Based on NEA's Semakau Island weather station wind speed data.

[2]Tidal chart: Based on MPA's tidal speed data near Semakau Island.

[3]Data of Semakau Island's average daily energy consumption provided by NEA.

- The energy storage technologies deployed must be able to store and the restitute high levels of energy over rather short periods of time — they need to have high storage and restitution *power* capacities. They must also be able to store large amounts of *energy* over longer periods.

As a result, the integration of several complementary energy storage technologies may be necessary to fully leverage the various renewable energy sources.

The advantages of a multi-technology renewable energy approach can be summed up as follows:

- 24/7, some combination of available renewable energy sources should be available to provide energy to the local grid.
- This integration of multi-renewable energy sources is also attractive for island grids with access to marine energies.
- A proper integration of multi-renewable energy sources could reduce the capacity of energy storage needed to buffer for the intermittency.

Energy storage and fuel cells

It is now widely recognised that one of the key roadblocks towards the large-scale deployment of solar and wind energy is energy storage. The Renewable Energy Integration Demonstrator Singapore, REIDS, offers unique opportunities to demonstrate the proper integration of small to mid-sized energy storage technologies for Singapore needs:

- Batteries: Li-ion, Redox Flow, Supercapacitor, and/or
- Flywheel, and/or
- Compressed Air.

In the Singapore context, energy storage is important to:

- Integrate large-scale renewables (e.g. Solar PV) into the Singapore energy mix
- Rational energy end-use for reduction of Green House Gas (GHG) emissions
- Economic development — Green Growth

Hydrogen

One of the still open questions to be resolved is the role hydrogen will play in the future as an energy vector. While the long distance transport of hydrogen remains problematic, the production of hydrogen using momentarily available excess electricity from solar and/or wind energy followed by its on-site storage to be subsequently used in various types of fuel cells is quite realistic and should be demonstrated within the REIDS.

Hybrid grids and microgrids

As mentioned above, to be readily deployable in a variety of situations, microgrids should be hybrid AC/DC systems which both connect to a broad range of sources and service an equally broad range of loads. The extensive experience acquired by faculty and researchers at NTU and ERI@N in the field of hybrid electric networks will find an excellent large test and demonstration venue by way of the REIDS. Figure 27 shows a schematic for a hybrid AC/DC microgrid as proposed by NTU and ERI@N researchers.

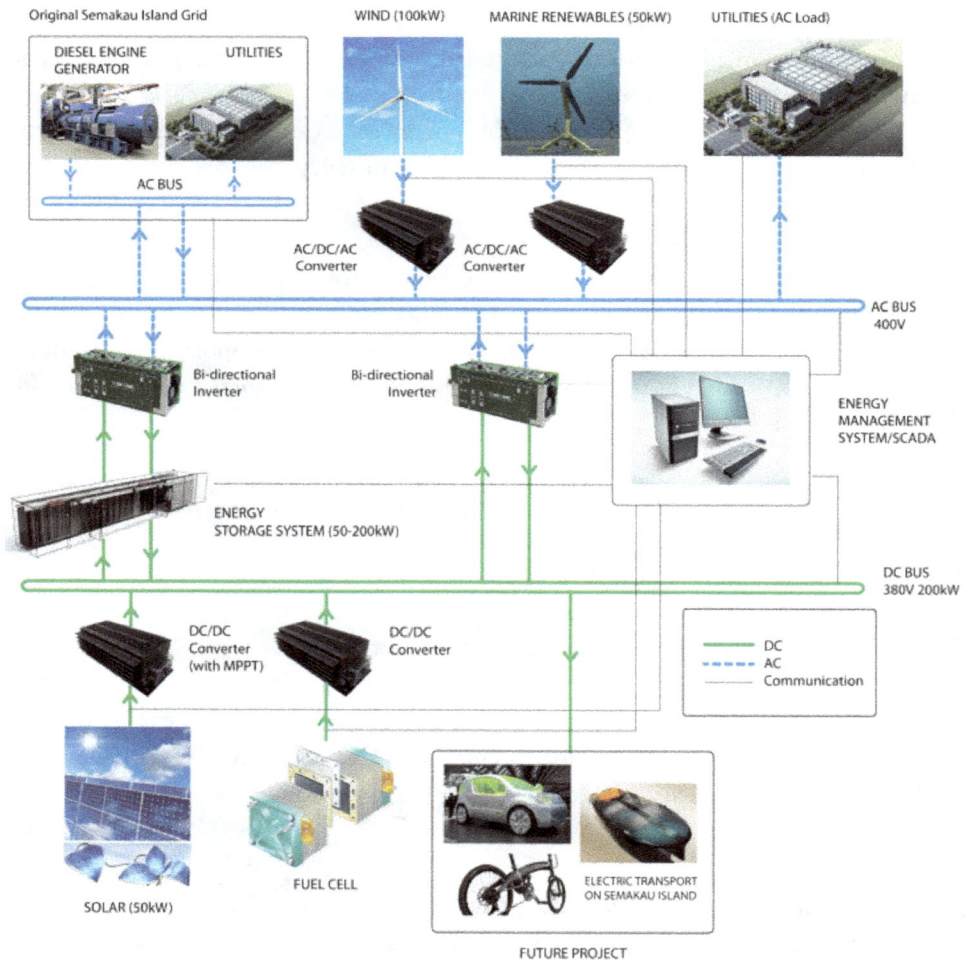

Figure 27.   Overview of hybrid AC/DC microgrid.

Targeted Technologies

The technologies targeted by the REIDS initiative are depicted in Figure 28.

Production

The main production technologies to be demonstrated include:

- Solar — both PV and solar thermal electric as well as combined solar PV and solar thermal. There will be opportunities to test microgrid management and control strategy for high PV penetration in combination with other renewables and large energy storage solutions. The granularity of the typical solar PV modules to be tested and demonstrated will be in the order of 500 kWp–1 MWp.
  Other solar related research and demonstrations include system issues of PV installation in tropical, coastal and island environment with the possibility to extend the testing of sea-based floating PV systems in the near shore of Semakau.

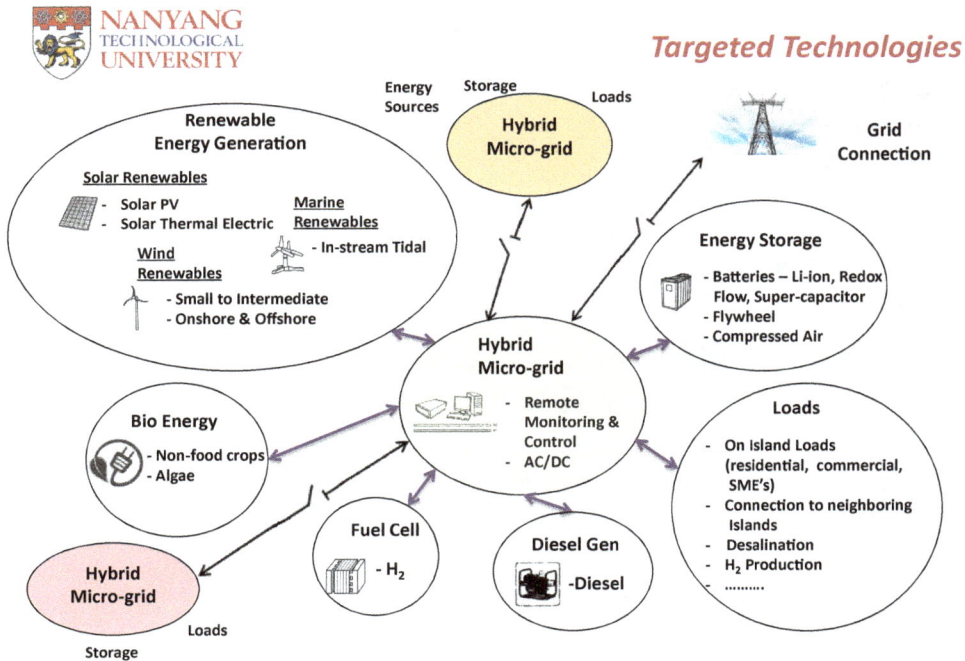

Figure 28.   Integrated demonstration platform and microgrid configuration.

- Wind energy, focussing on small to intermediate capabilities including innovative horizontal and vertical axis machines, i.e. rated below 1 MWp.
- Selected marine/ocean technologies will also be part of the REIDS while conducted as a specific, while fully integrated, set of activities — see Figure 29. The focus will be on in-stream tidal turbines.
  The expected tidal in-stream power from Semakau's Southern tip and around St. John's Island is about 2.5 MWp. The granularity of the typical in-stream tidal turbines to be tested and demonstrated is expected to be below 200 kWp.
- The local tides could also be taken advantage of to install a pumped storage for quadrant hydropower plant capable of both pumping and turbining water at incoming and ebbing tides.
- As the Semakau Island Landfill cells are filled up and the land is readied for further use, the island offers unique opportunities to deploy and test new crops toward biofuel production, using second-generation technologies for non-agricultural crops. REIDS allows for a broad range of bioenergies such as energy crops "Jatropha" and algae. In addition, the renewable energy produced locally can be used to power on-site Bio Refineries.

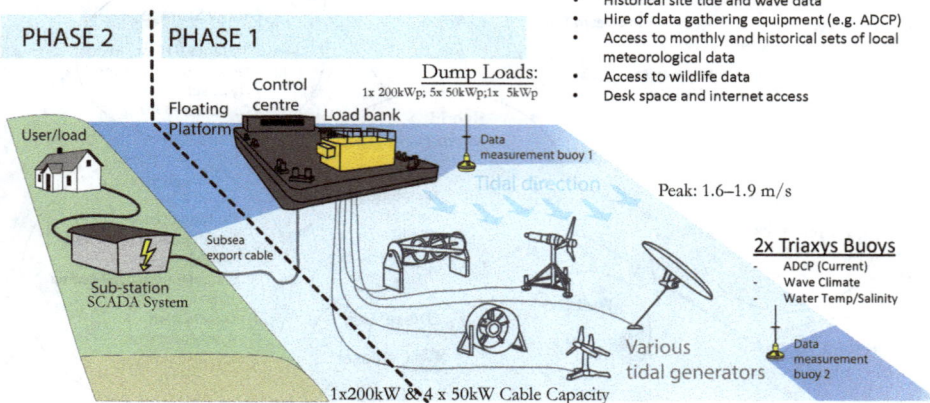

Figure 29. Illustration of installed tidal platforms and generators in offshore test sites.

Loads

As mentioned above, it is critical that the renewable energy production and energy storage technologies to be deployed serve actual, real-life, loads.

On Semakau Island among these loads would be:

- The other electric loads already to be serviced in conjunction with the waste operation handling and disposition operations. (~400 kW day and ~200 kW night)
- The local fish hatchery already on site also presents a unique load demonstration opportunity. At the present time, this load is some 100 kW but could be significantly expanded to satisfy the needs of Singapore fish farms, a development which will become increasingly important as Singapore seeks to implement a more sustainable supply of its seafood.
- As discussed further below, the Semakau Island Landfill provides an excellent opportunity for R&D in biofuels. One potential partner is envisioning installing an algae test-bed there. The associated load could reach 200 kW.
- As more land is made available for test and demonstration purposes, additional renewable energy capacity could be used in conjunction with innovative water desalination and/or the production of hydrogen, either using electrolysis or photoelectrochemistry, which could then be used for electricity production using fuel cells.
- At this time, the waste handling equipment is generally powered by diesel engines. Initially, on a limited scale, one could test biofuel. In addition, local transportation needs could be converted to Electric Vehicle technologies.
- In the context of providing for access to electricity for a cluster of islands, it would be desirable to test and demonstrate low infrastructure cost connections between islands. During Phase 2 of the REIDS the intent is to also test and demonstrate such inter-island connections. One possible inter-island connection would be a medium-voltage cable to the neighbouring island of Bukom — up to 2 MW — to gain access to the refinery residential area and, eventually, gain grid access thus making REIDS a fringe network.

Official Launch of REIDS — 28 October 2014

The Renewable Energy Integration Demonstrator was officially launched on 28 October 2014 during the opening ceremony of the Asia Clean Energy Summit, ACES, in the presence of Mr. S. Iswaran, Minister, Prime Minister's Office and Second Minister for Home Affairs and Trade and Industry.

Ten industrial partners pledged their support of REIDS during the ceremony as seen in Figure 30. During the official launch of REIDS, the graphical rendition shown in Figure 31 was released.

Figure 30. Launch of the Renewable Energy Integration Demonstrator at the Asia Clean Energy Summit (28 October 2014).

Figure 31.   3-D rendering of REIDS.

Conclusion and Future Developments

Singapore is going through its energy transition amidst changing global perspectives on energy sources, advent of alternative energy options and climate change concerns related to carbon-emissions of fossil fuel powered energy economy. Energy efficiency, diversification of energy sources into alternative energy options and decarbonising electricity generation are the key strategic options for Singapore. The combined focus on economic growth and environment protection requires a critical balance to be achieved considering long-term sustainability. Although Singapore is disadvantaged from the point-of-view of natural resources and alternative energy options, it acts as a leading model of sustainability for the region. Notably, Singapore has devoted significant resources to carry out research and development in sustainable energy and at the same time focus on demonstration and deployment of energy efficient systems and renewable energy options. The Energy Research Institute @ NTU (ERI@N), Singapore is formed with the mission to be a centre of excellence for advanced research, development, and demonstration of innovative energy solutions with a global impact.

The EcoCampus initiative led by ERI@N is a bold step towards a demonstration of deep energy efficiency and energy conservation in real life on the NTU Campus and CleanTech Park. Innovation being one of the cornerstones, this "living lab" initiative not only promises a fertile test round for impactful new technologies but also engages industry partners to ensure commercial viability and growth in adoption. The EcoCampus initiative has had a good launch with strong commitments from supporting government agencies as well as industry partners. There has been already progress made in terms of hard energy savings on the NTU campus and development of cutting-edge energy efficiency technologies in the fields of airconditioning, lighting, smart energy management systems, low carbon mobility and user-behaviour-based energy conservation methods.

Over the next two-three years, the EcoCampus programme will continue to work with industry partners to bring innovative technologies to life while taking bold steps in achieving its target of 35% reduction in energy, water and waste intensity. The aim of EcoCampus is also to build common knowledge and guidelines for adoption of these innovative technologies, especially for the tropical region. To this effect, there will be increased focus on documenting the findings, providing access to useful data and engaging students and the community at large in various projects within the programme. The desired impact of the initiative is that other campuses and industrial parks are able to adopt the technologies developed in the programme and companies are able to commercialise innovative and cost-effective energy efficiency/conservation products and services in the region.

The Renewable Energy Integration Demonstration — Singapore, REIDS, initiative seeks to test and demonstrate, at a large-scale level, the proper integration of a broad range of renewable energy production — onshore and offshore, energy storage and rational energy end-use technologies to provide for the supply of a wide palette of industrial, commercial and residential loads. Hybrid microgrid technologies will allow for flexible — "plug and play" — interconnectivity between the various sources, storage components and end-uses such as required, for example, to provide for the electrification of islands and remote villages as well as to rapidly deploy energy supply and distribution systems during emergency situations. A key focus of the REIDS project is the design, construction and subsequent operation of integrated electric distribution systems in an "off-grid" mode, i.e. without access to a utility electric system. While this causes significant and new challenges, the off-grid operation is a requirement in the context of several applications envisioned for the technologies and systems to be tested and demonstrated within the REIDS context.

REIDS is to be structured as partnership between (i) Singapore public agencies, (ii) corporations active in the energy arena with a focus on the integration of a broad range of sources, end-uses and storage, and (iii) academia and public R&D institutions.

While engineering issues are at the core of the REIDS planned projects, socioeconomic considerations will also be integrated within the projects undertaken.

Officially announced on 28 October 2014, REIDS is entering an intensive project implementation planning on the Semakau Island Landfill. While the first projects have been underway since early 2015, construction on the site will last through 2016. As additional industrial partners join REIDS, new technologies and system coordination technologies will be integrated and tested. A deliberate focus on innovative energy storage technologies and their system integration will provide for a wider penetration of variable renewable energy sources such as solar and wind. An important activity will be the dissemination of results by way of workshops, seminars, and publications to ensure that the key outcomes of REIDS are implemented not only in Singapore but also as broadly as possible around the world.

References

Abundo, M. (2012). Assessment of Potential Tidal In-Stream Energy Sites in Singapore. 1st Asian Wave and Tidal Energy Conference, Jeju Island.

Abundo, M. L., Lin, H., Seah, S., Norman, A., Garg, N., and Srikanth, N. (2013). *Ocean Energy Assessment for Singapore, Report to NCCS*. Energy Research Institute @ NTU, August 2013.

Bloomberg New Energy Finance. (2014). Global Trends in Clean Energy Investment-Fast Pack as at Q4 2013, 15 January 2014.

Chua, K. J., Chou, S. K., Yang, W. M., and Yan, J. (2013). Achieving Better Energy-efficient Air Conditioning — A Review of Technologies and Strategies. *Applied Energy, 104*, 87–104.

de Oliveira, W. S., and Fernandes, A. J. (2012). *Global Wind Energy Market, Industry and Economic Impacts*. Energy and Environment Research.

DNV (2011). *Report — Singapore Wind Potential Estimation*. Norway: DNV.

Energy Market Authority (EMA). (2010). Intelligent Energy System Pilot. Retrieved 15 November 2014 from http://www.ema.gov.sg/ies.

Energy Market Authority (EMA). (2015). The Singapore Energy Statistics 2015. Publication by the Research and Statistics Unit of EMA. Retrieved 29 June 2015 from http://www.ema.gov.sg/Singapore_Energy_Statistics.aspx.

Frost & Sullivan. (2012). Annual Global Power Generation Forecasts 2012 — Growth Opportunities to 2030 in the New Age of Gas, August 2012.

Karthikeya, B. R., and Srikanth, N. (2014a), *HDB Wind Measurement Installations — Fourth Biannual Report to HDB*. Energy Research Institute @ NTU, April 2014.

Karthikeya, B. R., Prabal, N., and Srikanth, N. (2014b), Wind Resource Assessment for Urban Renewable Energy Application in Singapore, Renewable Energy.

Ly, D. K., Aboobacker, V. M., Murray, C., Abundo, M., Tkalich, P., and Srikanth, N. (2014, October). *Wave Energy Resource Assessment for Singapore*. ACES 2014 Conference, Singapore.

Prabal, S. N., Garg, N., and Srikanth, N. (2013). *Wind Resource Assessment for Coastal Singapore and Offshore Islands, Report to NCCS*. Energy Research Institute @ NTU, August 2013.

Sustainable Energy Association of Singapore (SEAS). (2014). *White Paper on Accelerating Renewable Energy in Singapore*, January 2014.

SERIS (Solar Energy Research Institute of Singapore). (2014). Solar Photovoltaic (PV) Roadmap for Singapore (A Summary). Published by the National Research Foundation (NRF) and National Climate Change Secretariat (NCCS), 30 July 2014.

CHAPTER 8

Developing a Vibrant Sustainable Energy Industry

Edwin Khew, Christophe Inglin, Sanjay Kuttan and Low Kian Beng
Chairman, Vice-Chairman, and Council Members
Sustainable Energy Association of Singapore (SEAS)

Introduction

As the world begins to address the issues of climate change, depleting natural resources and rapid urbanisation, extreme weather patterns have pushed us to take a closer look at the importance of mitigating climate change. Depleting natural resources and a growing urban population with rising demand for energy and resources are also issues that we need to tackle. Thus cities and companies are increasingly embracing sustainable development and green growth. To capture opportunities arising from this trend, Singapore is looking towards cleantech to boost our economic growth; "By 2015, the cleantech sector is expected to contribute S$3.4 billion to Singapore's gross domestic product (GDP) and employ 18,000" (Contact Singapore, 2014). Singapore is committed to growing the cleantech industry, which comprises the Environment and Water, and Clean Energy sectors. Since 2006, Singapore has allocated more than S$2 billion in public sector R&D funding to grow the cleantech sector.

Given this backdrop, Singapore, a city-state with very limited natural resources and almost wholly dependent on imported oil and gas for its energy needs, has to constantly manage and resolve the challenges of its "energy trilemma", i.e. to "ensure economic competitiveness, energy security and environmental sustainability" (MTI, 2011).

Since Singapore depends a lot on imported natural resources, it is very easily affected by the price changes in global energy markets. Singapore is also an island-state and susceptible to changes in sea levels. Hence, it continues to pursue energy efficiency and carbon mitigation and to develop sustainable solutions which can be applied to other urban cities, as 70% of the world's growing population will reside in cities by 2050. Singapore hopes to be a model for these urban cities now and going into the future. Thus, it has taken steps to develop itself into a Sustainable Energy Hub for Asia.

Singapore emphasises the deployment of clean energy solutions using Singapore's unique position as a living lab where companies can develop, test and commercialise innovative urban solutions in a real-life setting. Many interesting and innovative clean energy projects being developed here with the most recent being a pilot 1 MW floating solar farm on one of our reservoirs, a multi-energy source microgrid on Singapore's only offshore landfill, a 1 MW biomass cogeneration plant to supply the Gardens by the Bay's iconic controlled-environment green houses, and a combined 4.5 MW chicken waste to biogas/power at two of the largest chicken-layer farms in Singapore. These make Singapore a "Living Lab" for innovation in the sustainable energy sphere.

But we are well aware that technology is only part of a bigger picture to provide sustainable long-term solutions for many rapidly growing cities in Asia and the rest of the world. Climate change requires us to reduce carbon emissions. The solutions for this must be sustainable as well, meaning they must be commercially viable without long-term government assistance or subsidies. We thus need governments, companies and industry to not only provide sustainable solutions but also to adopt these solutions for their buildings, manufacturing plants and supply chains as well as customers.

However, such projects only flourish with appropriate financing. Singapore is a thriving financial hub of Asia and thus a great location for financial institutions and funds that actively finance clean energy projects not just in Singapore but also in Asia. A key ingredient for investors and banks to provide capital and funds for such projects and technologies is long-term, stable energy policies that enable project bankability. But in many instances, despite appropriate technology and financing, these solutions cannot be deployed because existing regulations and policies make clean energy unviable or infeasible. A case in point is fossil fuel subsidies that make renewables uncompetitive due to an uneven playing field unless renewables are heavily subsidised, thus unleashing a cycle of subsidies for renewables that are unsustainable in the long run, as experienced by many European countries.

It is also important to establish new policies that make clean energy and distributed generation viable. Most existing government policies were devised for centralised generation, i.e. large power plants that feed a transmission and distribution grid infrastructure. This can be costly and inefficient, losing much energy during transmission. Today we can have solar systems on roofs of buildings, biomass systems in hotels converting wastes into renewable energy and many such distributed solutions. Policies need to be adjusted to accommodate such a distributed mode of energy production alongside the traditional generation. Once these government policies are in place, and if they are stable and viable, investors will be willing to invest in clean energy projects because they have confidence that these projects are bankable, ensuring manageable risks. They will provide banks and investors with viable returns on their investments.

Singapore, because of its open market policies, has been careful not to provide subsidies or incentives for either conventional or renewable energy, such as the feed-in-tariffs (FIT) for renewable energy that many other countries initiated. Thanks to the sharp decline in solar system costs in recent years, solar energy is now truly cost competitive in Singapore without any market-distorting subsidies. This has led to a viable utility model of solar power purchase agreements (PPA) where consumers pay competitive prices for solar electricity with no upfront cost for installation of the systems. This and many other viable models for renewable and energy efficiency technology systems are in the pipeline and will be discussed below.

Current Energy Landscape in Singapore

Electricity Generation and Consumption in Singapore

Stable and reliable electricity supply has been one of the fundamental factors behind Singapore's economic success. Without a constant and reliable 24/7 electricity supply, Singapore would not have attracted so many foreign as well as local investments into its high technology manufacturing and services base, providing one of the highest living standards in the world today. Singapore's electricity demand has grown 4.5 times from 1986 to 2012.

Under Singapore's current centralised generation infrastructure, electricity is mainly produced at large generation facilities with individual nameplate ratings in the hundreds of MW, and transmitted though the national grid to end consumers.

Today, all but one of Singapore's power plants are located in the western region of Singapore. Notwithstanding a high demand from the industrial estates and petrochemical complexes, the power transmission grid in the west faces constraints on the maximum amount of power it can deliver to the rest of Singapore.

Optimal land utilisation has always been a cornerstone of urban planning in Singapore, hence the recent efforts to locate new industrial estates to the other parts of Singapore, such as the aerospace hub in Seletar and silicon wafer park in Tampines. With increasing power demand from commercial buildings and industrial hubs (these account for more than 80% of demand), the challenge is to supply power as efficiently as possible to demand centres.

Singapore needs to generate greener power to shrink its carbon footprint, to consume energy less wastefully, generate cost-effective power in the east, and ensure energy security by diversifying its energy mix. Renewable energy and energy efficiency technologies are obvious solutions.

Today, Singapore has a vibrant and growing sustainable energy industry ecosystem covering clusters such as carbon management, clean/renewable energy, energy efficiency and finance. More than 200 companies provide technologies (proven allied technologies and R&D), engineering services, consultancy, energy audit and efficiency services, and environmental services to retail and finance services. Many of these companies use Singapore as their regional head office to do R&D (e.g. to tropicalise their technologies or to optimise the design and cost of their technologies for the very competitive Asian market). Singapore also provides technical support, engineering, procurement, spare parts support, project financing, and marketing and sales support. Most of these companies are members of the Sustainable Energy Association of Singapore (SEAS).

Within Clean Energy, there is a strong focus on solar energy given Singapore's strategic location in the tropical sunbelt and its complementary semiconductor capabilities, and biomass energy, given Singapore's extensive greenery throughout the island. There is growing emphasis on energy management technologies covering smart grids, energy storage, electric vehicles, demand response, and home and building energy management systems.

Development of Renewable Energy (RE) in Singapore

The environmental industry landscape in the early 1990s comprised companies in pollution control and environmental treatment systems. These companies typically traded in water and waste water solutions as well as air purification systems, from US, Europe and Australia, and also supplied them to markets in the region. This did not add value to Singapore's economy nor did it grow new and innovative technologies in this space. The government then promoted solutions for this part of the world by investing in research and development. This led to homegrown companies such as Hyflux, now a global leader in water purification technology. Singapore also established the Singapore Association for Environment Companies (SAFECo). This association was started by the private sector and supported by the Singapore government to encourage the private sector to graduate from buying and selling systems to setting up homegrown cleantech companies. This then led to the development of specialist environment associations which started branching out from SAFECo. These associations included the Singapore Water Association (SWA), the Waste Management and Recycling Association of Singapore (WMRAS) and the Sustainable Energy Association of Singapore (SEAS). SEAS was founded after Singapore signed the Kyoto Protocol in February 2006. During this period much interest was generated in carbon trading, energy efficiency and renewable energy.

To support companies in the various associations in their areas of specialisations, the institutes of higher learning (IHLs) — polytechnics and universities — started research institutes (RIs) to focus on R&D in water and wastewater treatment, waste to energy/resource technologies, and renewables. Some examples of key RIs include the Solar Energy Research Institute of Singapore (SERIS), the Energy Research Institute at NTU (ERI@N), the Nanyang Environment and Water Research

Institute (NEWRI) and the NUS Environment Research Institute (NERI). Much of their research has achieved international recognition especially in water and waste-water treatment. Many of the largest companies in the world have developed part-nerships with Singapore's RIs, e.g. General Electric, Siemens, Rolls Royce, and BMW, to name a few. Singapore is a great place to do R&D — its size makes it a convenient living laboratory where pilot plants and prototypes can be tested in market conditions to ensure proof of concept and also to prove the value of the technologies. Many companies from temperate climates in Europe or the US seek to tropicalise their existing systems, so they can apply and adapt their technologies to the hot and humid conditions in Singapore and Asia.

As a financial hub, Singapore offers technology companies a wide array of fund-ing options for further R&D, project financing, or even venture capital to grow their company and markets in Asia. With Asia's large Renewable Energy (RE) markets and Singapore's potential to deploy RE on a large scale, we will now look at the potential, benefits, and viability of RE in Singapore. As a natural extension, we will also examine the export of these technologies to the region, which is projected to be the largest growing RE market in the world in the next 20–30 years.

Companies across the spectrum of manufacturing, project development, and consulting have based their headquarters in Singapore to access thriving regional clean energy markets. Some of these companies are not only market leaders in tech-nology and innovation, but also use Singapore's strength as a financial centre to develop innovative financial engineering solutions and business models. They attract private capital looking for bankable clean energy projects in the region.

Singapore is also developing as a viable market for solar photovoltaics (PV) is leading with, and aims for with strong policies, relatively high electricity tariffs and minimum political risk. The government programmes like SolarNova 350 MW of solar power to be installed on government buildings by 2020. Combined with com-petitive prices for solar PV and adequate funding, the stage is set for solarising Singapore.

Deployment of Renewable Energy in Singapore

In Singapore, the most viable sources of RE are currently solar PV, biomass and biogas. The deployment of RE will bring extensive economic, environmental and social benefits to Singapore and are discussed below.

i. *Commercial viability*

Renewable Energy is cost effective against conventional energy in Singapore without government subsidies. The relatively high market tariff of electricity in Singapore and the falling price of renewable technology (in particular solar PV) and the accumulated system installation experience have made RE economically viable. This chapter will specifically address the financial viability of solar PV, biogas and biomass in Singapore.

ii. *Reducing CO₂ emissions*

Global demand for electricity will rise by 80% by 2040, and 90% of that will originate from countries with fast developing economies like Singapore, a country currently largely dependent on imported fossil fuels. Many countries envisage a gradual shift from traditional fossil fuels to cleaner and sustainable energy alternatives to secure their growing energy demand. Singapore cannot afford to ignore or deviate from the low carbon path.

Displacing more conventional energy with renewable energy will enable Singapore to cut greenhouse emissions. 3,635 GWh/year of clean electricity from RE sources will mitigate 1.74 million metric tonnes of CO_2 per year. This is based on Singapore's Electricity Grid Emission Factor[1] of approximately 0.5 tonnes of CO_2 per MWh generated by our fossil fuel power plants.

According to the National Climate Change Secretariat (NCCS), Singapore has pledged to reduce its emissions to 16% below the 2020 business-as-usual (BAU) level if there is a legally binding global agreement in which all countries implement their commitments in good faith. Singapore has also started to implement mitigation and energy efficiency measures, to unconditionally reduce its emissions by 7% to 11% below 2020 BAU level (NCCS, 2015). A focussed approach to increasing the deployment of RE will certainly reduce emissions in Singapore.

iii. *Security of energy supply*

For energy security it is essential to have a diversified mix of energy generation technologies rather than relying on imported natural gas which now provides more than 90% of our power generation. Displacing more conventional energy with RE will enable Singapore to depend less on imported fuel. Singapore should maximise the percentage of energy it can generate based on economically viable alternative energy solutions.

iv. *Singapore as a clean energy hub*

Creating a sustainable green economy means building up industrial capacity within the entire supply chain. This leads to research and innovation, enhancing labour skills and

---

[1] Grid Emission Factor (GEF) measures average CO_2 emission emitted per unit net electricity generated, and is calculated using the Average Operating Margin (OM) method. This is the generation-weighted average CO_2 emission per unit net electricity generation of all generating power plants serving the electricity grid.

education levels in the workforce. Designing, constructing, operating and maintaining RE power plants creates many direct local jobs throughout the value chain. The sector also creates high-level indirect jobs in R&D, consulting and financing.

Increases in RE will strengthen cleantech/renewable energy clusters in Singapore and attract domestic business and investment flows. Singapore is already a testing ground for the commercialisation of innovative renewable energy solutions adapted to the tropics. But Singapore is also the first natural (unsubsidised) market in the ASEAN region, giving the country a head start with exportable expertise to the wider ASEAN region, positioning Singapore as a hub for renewable energy.

RE can also be a means to strengthen economic ties between Singapore and its neighbouring countries through joint projects and by sharing technological know-how.

The Scale and Potential of RE in Singapore

With a multifaceted approach to accelerate the adoption of RE in Singapore, RE sources can generate about 3,635 GWh of electricity each year, or approximately 7.3% of Singapore's forecast 2025 demand, with no government subsidies (compared to <1% today). There is also scope for significant penetration of renewable energy beyond 10% after 2025.

In this conservative and realistic scenario, solar PV will generate 2,400 GWh/year or 4.8% of 2025 forecasted demand; biogas will cover 350 GWh or 0.7%, and biomass 785 GWh/year or 1.6% of the 2025 forecasted demand.

Higher levels subsequently (i.e. to 2050) are technically feasible. It is possible to decarbonise electricity generation by lowering technical, commercial and regulatory barriers, and by encouraging near-to-market and cost-effective technologies, such as solar photovoltaics and biomass tri-generation systems.

(i) *Solar photovoltaics (PV)*

Solar PV is a natural choice for Singapore. Thanks to its position very close to the equator, the country has high solar irradiation levels with minimal seasonal variation.

Despite the scarcity of land, Singapore has enough space to accommodate 6 GWp of solar PV, which can generate 7.2 TWh of electricity each year, or approximately 17% of Singapore's current electricity demand.

The capacity of 6 GWp is based on installing approximately 100 Wp/m^2 of PV on 60–65 km^2 of available space as shown in Table 1 above.[2] For various reasons, not all accessible space will be tapped. Even if it makes good commercial sense to install

---

[2] SERIS (NCCS-NRF Solar Energy Technology Primer Workshop, 14 Apr 2011): Net usable area on buildings, LRT tracks, islets and reservoirs = approximately 60–65 km^2.

Table 1.   Available space for PV installations in Singapore.

Space type	Area used	Total area [m²]	Area utilisation factor	Net-usable area [m²]	Estimated mid term usage	Estimated usage 2025–2030
Roof-top	HDB blocks	14,000,000	0.48	6,700,000	100%	100%
	Other buildings	42,000,000	0.65	27,300,000	100%	100%
Facades	Top-5 storeys	40,000,000	0.40	16,000,000	0%	100%
Infrastructure	MRT tracks	390,000	1	400,000	100%	100%
Islets	Ground-mounted	50,000,000	0.20	10,000,000	25%	100%
Inland waters	Floating PV (mainland only)	20,000,000	0.25	5,000,000	40%	100%
Total				65,400,000	40 km²	65 km²

PV on a rooftop, not every building owner will choose to do so. Facades might prove too expensive for practical installation. As land cost is at a premium in Singapore, large solar farms might not receive approval for installation, whether on the mainland or on islets. The Government is however exploring floating PV modules on inland reservoirs. We therefore **assume a conservative penetration rate of only 33%, or 2 GWp**.

Two Gigawatts peak of installed PV will generate **2.4 TWh per year, or 4.8% of 2025 forecasted electricity demand by 2025**, which is too substantial a figure to ignore when projecting Singapore's energy mix.

According to the EMA, the installed capacity of grid-connected solar PV systems was 33.1 MWp by the end of 2014. The non-household sector constituted about 93% (or 30.8 MWp) of total capacity, with the remaining capacity contributed by household installations. This meets less than 1% of Singapore's electricity demand.

Thanks to the attractive commercial and environmental returns of solar PV, there is a growing demand for bigger PV systems. Building and Construction Authority CEO John Keung mentioned during his speech at the Solar Pioneer Awards 2014 that Singapore looks set to install between 80–100 MWp islandwide within the next 18 months.

(ii) *Biomass*

Singapore currently depends on horticultural waste and wood waste to produce biomass fuel. According to 2012 statistics published by NEA, out of 591,960 tonnes/year (average of 1,622 tons/day) of biomass waste derived from horticultural and wood wastes, only 344,000 tonnes/year (average of 942 tonnes/day) are recycled as reused wood and biomass fuel. This represents a recycling rate of 58.1%.

Table 2. Biomass waste output, disposed and recycled in 2012 (Source: NEA, 2014).

Waste type	Total waste output (tonnes)	Total waste recycled (tonnes)	Waste disposed (tonnes)	Recycling rate (%)
Wood/timber	343,800	236,000	107,800	69
Horticultural waste	247,800	108,000	139,800	44
Total	**591,600**	**344,000**	**247,600**	**58.1**

Already in 2012, NEA statistics show that 110,300 tonnes of wood/timber and horticultural waste were used to fuel biomass power plants as shown in Table 2.

(iii) *Potential biomass energy from horticultural and wood waste*

With an enormous area under greenery (the government's "city in a garden" concept), Singapore produces a large amount of wood and horticultural waste (clippings). This sector is seeing significant investment and is expected to be fully exploited within the next few years.

The average annual increase for biomass waste from 2008 to 2012 was 4.5% per year. Much of the wood waste is driven by the construction sector, which looks set to continue for a few years before levelling off. Horticultural waste comprises mostly garden waste and tree pruning, and is less likely to grow. Assuming that the past rate of growth for total biomass waste is maintained for the next five years, then the total biomass waste from 2013 to 2018 shall increase at the same 4.5% rate and then stabilise from 2018 onwards at 770,400 tonnes/year (2,100 T/day).

In August 2012, NEA imposed restrictions to prohibit disposal of recyclable wood waste to the four public incinerators. As a result, it is anticipate that more and more such waste will be recycled as biomass fuel.

Figure 1 below shows the amount of biomass waste that will be recycled; assuming that the current recycling ratio of 58% will increase by 10.5% per annum to reach full recovery by 2016.

Figure 2 below shows the potential growth of biomass energy, under the following assumptions:

- Biomass feedstock = wood/timber and horticultural waste, which continues to grow at 4.5% annually until 2018, when it levels off.
- Recycling rates increase from 58% in 2012 to 100% by 2016.
- Average energy content of biomass in 2,300 kCal/kg, or 2.67 MWh/tonne.
- Conversion efficiency for simple biomass power plant is 31%, and for co-generation plant is 68%.

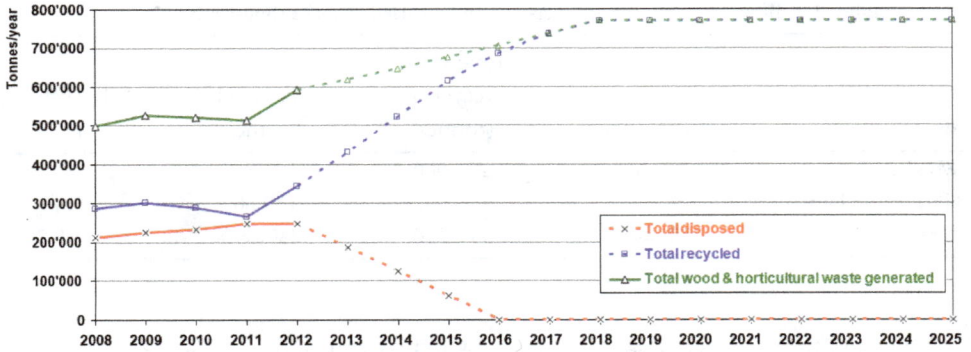

Figure 1.   Historical and projected growth of biomass waste (wood and horticultural) availability in Singapore (2008–2018).[3]

Notes:

1. *Horticultural and wood wastes quantity (2013–2025) estimated based on historical data from 2008 to 2012.*

2. *Availability of horticultural and wood waste is estimated to remain stable from 2018 onwards and achieve NEA target of recycling 100% of these wastes.*

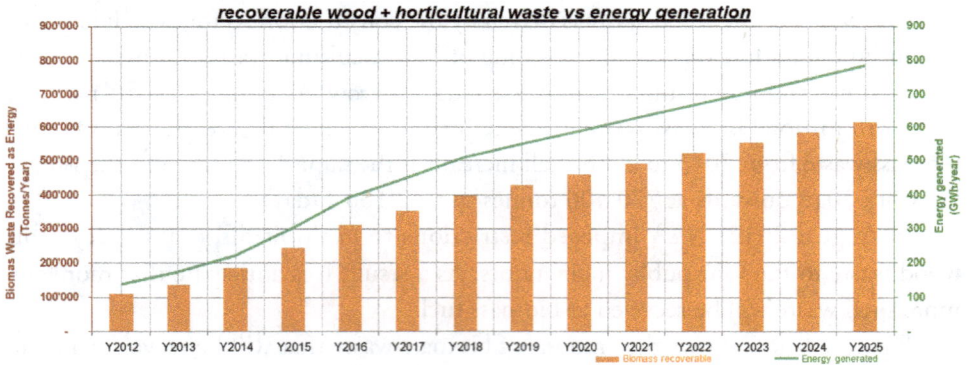

Figure 2.   Growth forecast for energy generated from recoverable wood and horticultural waste.

- Recovery of available wood/horticultural waste to make biomass power with conventional combustion and power systems grows linearly from 32% in 2013 to 80% in 2025.

---

[3]NEA Waste Statistics (2008–2012).

- CHP share of total biomass plants starts at 45% in 2012, dropping to 35% when CGNPC 9.9 MWe power plant (non-CHP) starts operation in 2014 and returning to 45% from 2016 as new CHP plants are constructed. This is a conservative assumption.

The above growth scenario leads to 785 GWh/year from biomass power plants by 2025. This is conservative and the figure can be much higher, if Singapore promotes CHP and tri-gen plants co-located with off-takers that can exploit the heat and chilled water production from such plants for their operations (such as biomedical park in Tuas and silicon water parks in Woodlands and Tampines).

(iv) *Biogas — food waste*

Figure 3 shows the potential to generate 264 GWh per year of energy from food waste by 2025.

This is based on a number of assumptions:

- Organic food waste will grow in direct proportion to Singapore's population, which will reach 6.3 m by 2025.[4] Thus food waste is forecast to grow from 703,200 tons in 2012 to 834,000 tons in 2025.
- Recovery of food waste improves from 12% in 2012 to 80% by 2025.

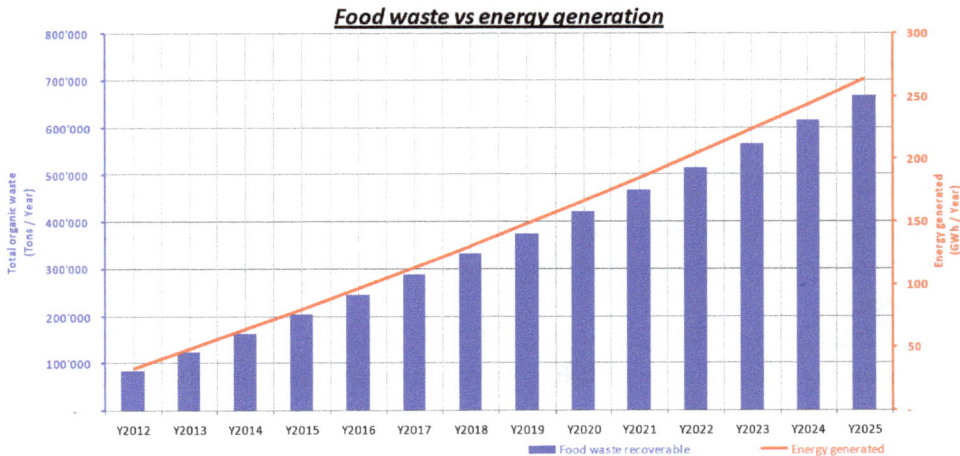

Figure 3.   Growth forecast for energy generated from food waste: 264 GWh in 2025.

---

[4] Please refer to SEAS (2014), p. 10, Figure 4.

- Anaerobic digesters produce 150 Nm^3 of gas per ton of recoverable food waste, with 60% CH_4 (methane) content. (Nm^3 is a cubic metre of gas under normal atmospheric pressure.)
- CH_4 has a density of $0.66kg/m^3$ and an energy value of 55.7 MJ/kg.
- Gas engines operate with an efficiency of 43%.

Thus each ton of recoverable food waste generates $150 \times 60\% \times 0.66 \times 55.7 \times 43\% = 1{,}423$ MJ = 395 kWh.

It makes sense to divert food waste from incineration to feed anaerobic digesters because food waste has a high moisture content, which reduces the net calorific value (NCV) of incinerated waste. If incinerators need to burn wet fuel, they lose significant energy to vaporise the water content.

The above case assumes all biogas plants operate as stand-alone, without harnessing the waste heat. However, Combined Heat and Power (CHP) or tri-gen plants will increase total operating efficiency to approximately 68% and 75% respectively. Where possible, biogas plants should be co-located with an operation that takes advantage of the heat by-product.

Conservatively, we assume a mix by 2025 of:

- 80% are stand-alone systems at 43% efficiency
- 10% combined heat and power (CHP) at 68% efficiency
- 10% tri-gen at 75% efficiency

This results in a potential energy production of 300 GWh from food waste by 2025.

(v) *Biogas — chicken waste*

Singapore currently has three chicken farms, all of which are scheduled to expand operations significantly as part of Singapore's efforts to decrease its dependence on imported eggs.

By 2025, each chicken farm will have 1.3 to 1.5 million chickens, each producing approximately 100 g of manure daily. This comes to approximately 50,000 tonnes per year for each farm.

Figure 4 below illustrates the conversion of manure feedstock to 60% methane gas in an anaerobic digester (AD). The gas then powers a gas engine to generate electricity. Some of the waste heat is recovered to maintain the AD at an optimum operating temperature of approximately 43–44°C for the microbes to do their work.

Between them, the three chicken farms can produce close to 50 GWh a year of electricity by 2025 from captive biogas power plants.

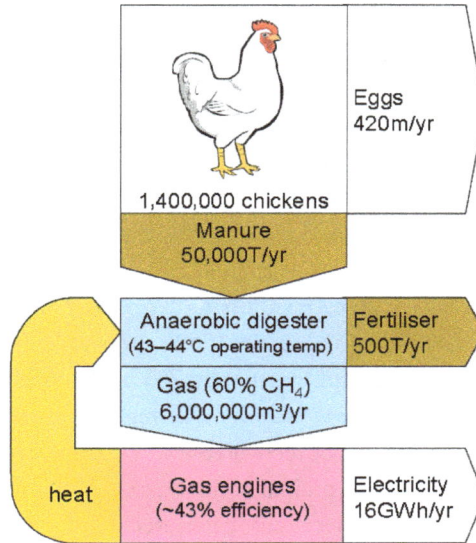

Figure 4.   Operating principles of biogas power plant using chicken manure as feedstock.

Providing Future RE Solutions to Singapore and the Region

From 2004 to 2014 electricity consumption per capita in Singapore was a steady 8 MWh/year. Assuming this continues, while Singapore's population grows to 7 million by the year 2050, we can project electricity consumption at about 56 TWh/year.[5]

The previous section considered quite conservative forecasts for RE deployment up to the year 2025. Beyond that year, we anticipate increasing global alignment on the need to reduce CO_2 emissions, and more compelling RE economics to satisfy the demand for climate change solutions. These trends will encourage more ambitious deployment of RE technology in the years to 2050. Many of those technologies are still in R&D or test-bedding phase today, but will be commercially ready well before 2050. This following pages examine RE's contribution to Singapore's energy needs in a scenario of proactive policies.

Extrapolating Existing Proven RE Technologies

Solar PV: Based on a scenario of high efficiency PV systems with average area factors of 200 Wp/m^2 and a maximum implementation of energy efficiency in industries and homes, solar PV if deployed in the 65 km^2 projected total effective area after

---

[5] For more statistics on consumption data, please see Department of Statistics, Singapore, http://www.singstat.gov.sg.

2030 (Solar PV Roadmap for Singapore—June 2014) can contribute approximately 13 TWh/year or approximately 23% of the electricity demand in 2050.

Onshore & offshore floating PV: Floating PV farms are being tested at our inland reservoirs. Extending these to shallow offshore water regions of Singapore not used for shipping, we could add another 2 GWp of floating PV, which can generate 2.4 TWh/year, or approximately 4% of 2050 demand.

Bio-gas from organics: Based on all food waste (approximately 2,500 tpd) and other organics (animal manure from chicken, horse, zoo animals, etc.) including sewage sludge, industrial sludge, fats, oil and grease (FOG) from grease traps (approximately another 1,000 tpd) bio-gas (65% methane/35% CO_2) can produce approximately 4.0 TWh/year or approximately 7% of demand.

Power from biomass (waste wood cuttings and municipal solid waste incinerators): Based on about 800,000 tons/year of recoverable wood and horticultural waste generated and about 8,000 tons of municipal solid waste generated per day that will be incinerated or gasified, the total electricity generated from these waste resources will be approximated 900 GWh/year plus 2.0 TWh/year from wood waste and MSW respectively. This gives approximately 3.0 TWh/year or 5% of demand.

Wind energy: There are 2 types of wind turbines — horizontal axis (HAWT) and vertical axis (VAWT). Singapore's low wind speeds (average of 2–4 m/sec measured at a height of 90 m) restrict the application of wind turbines to roofs of high rise buildings and to offshore locations off our southern coast, with water depths less than 20 metres (shallow water) and unused by maritime traffic. A potential of up to 370 MWp can be harnessed from offshore wind to support remote islands of Singapore and approximately 130 MWp for VAWT generation on buildings in Singapore providing a total of 500 MWp, which can generate about 4 TWh/year for wind, or approximately 7% of demand.

Biofuel from algae: Algae and bio-organisms grow more abundantly in Singapore's tropical conditions than they do in other parts of the world. We have complementary industries, such as petroleum and oleochemical refineries, including biomedical. Thus we could synthesise biofuel from algae and use it to generate power.

Developing New RE Technologies Currently in the Experimental Stage

Energy storage: Energy storage and distributed generation are technically viable solutions that are becoming more attractive as storage costs decline. Energy storage adds most value at the edge of the grid and like solar PV, it will have the biggest impact in microgrids, or co-located with commercial, industrial and residential loads. Hybrid systems like solar PV/storage are already considered attractive alternatives to rehabilitating or building new transmission infrastructure, especially in small and remote communities. Floating storage stations can serve as offshore facilities, providing electrical power to a ship at anchorage while its main and auxiliary engines are turned off. Emergency equipment, refrigeration, cooling, heating, lighting and other equipment will still be able receive continuous electrical power while the ship loads or unloads its cargo. Floating storage stations are quick to deploy as emergency back-up power during disasters, and can provide power to remote communities along the water side.

Power from marine energy: experiments to tap tidal in-stream energy show it might extract between 300–600 GWh/year without any significant environmental impact. There is also potential to tap wave energy up to 53 GWh/year. The combination leads to approximately 1% of 2050 demand. Pilot studies are currently in progress at the Tanah Merah Ferry Terminal with ERI@N's prototype design.

Reversed Electro Dialysis (RED) and Pressure Retarded Osmosis (PRO): these technologies exploit salinity gradients and osmotic pressure. They could recover up to 100 GWh/year, tapping waste brine from NEWater and other desalination plants.

Power from hydrogen: hydrogen can also play a role in peak shifting, which improves the capacity factor of power plants. They can produce hydrogen during off peak periods and store it for use in peak demand periods. An ERI@N project with two European companies is exploring power to gas (P2G) processes. The gravimetric energy density will be 2,000 Wh/kg, with a volumetric energy density of 1,570 Wh/l. Researchers are developing new catalyst technology to enable this. Similarly, seawater electrolysis can generate hydrogen. The challenge is to prevent chloride ions from poisoning the platinum catalyst in PEMFC (proton exchange membrane fuel cell) or

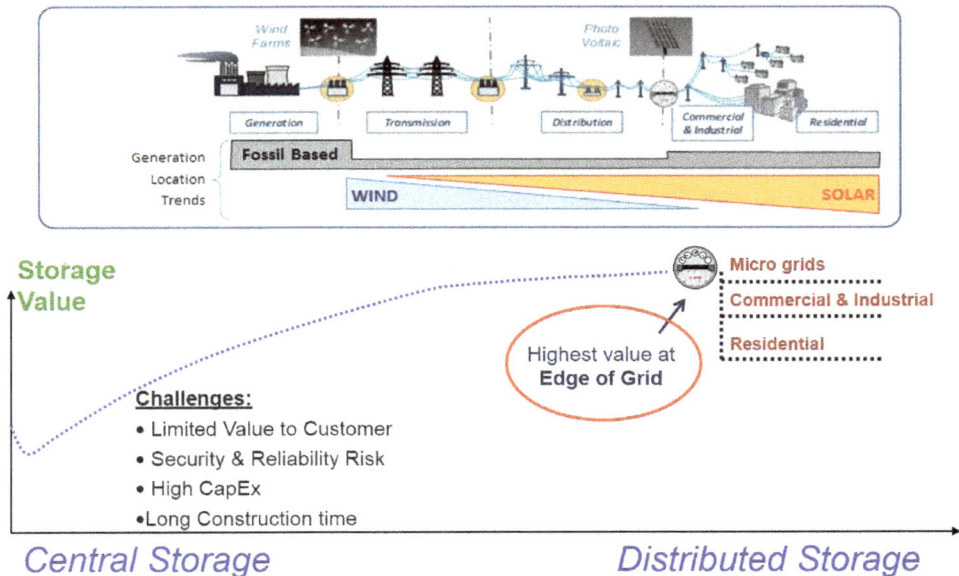

Figure 5.   The value of storage in energy grids.

AFC (Alkaline Fuel Cell). The key solution is a catalyst for low temperature fuel cells. The presently proposed EIRP (Energy Innovation Research Programme) will address this issue.

All these technologies can be commercially viable and operating in Singapore for commercial applications by 2050. The power generated by these technologies will be measured, monitored and controlled by a smart grid, with microgrids as subsidiary systems. Solar will generate the bulk of the clean energy (approximately 27%) injected into the grid and the other renewable energy components can contribute another 20–25% of the total requirement of the grid (56 TWh/year), thereby contributing a total of about approximately 50% of demand by 2050.

Twenty years from now we will have proven these new technologies and be using them in and around Singapore. In another 10–20 years these technologies will have become economically viable and Singapore can supply fully integrated RE systems to urban cities all over the world. This follows Singapore's success with water recycling and treatment, producing NEWater and applying the latest in membrane technologies to reduce the cost of recycling drinking water that exceeds WHO drinking water standards.

Singapore will become a green showcase, demonstrating how a tropical city can sustainably supply 40% or more of its energy needs from renewable sources. If we supplement this with hydro, geothermal, wind and even nuclear power from our neighbours (Indonesia and Malaysia) via subsea cables or the ASEAN grid, Singapore could effectively run on 100% clean and renewable energy, leaving a zero carbon footprint.

The supply of renewable energy from our neighbours is a distinct possibility as Indonesia and Malaysia have many large uninhabited (or only sparsely inhabited) islands which can be developed into integrated power islands to supply power via the ASEAN grid.

We can envision Singapore as a sustainable metropolis by 2050:

- Producing all its electricity from renewable clean sources (solar PV and thermal, marine tidal systems, wind, biomass, biogas, biofuels, co-gen, etc.);
- Still manufacturing and generating a quarter of its GDP from high tech manufacturing (petrochemical, pharmaceutical, silicon wafer, food products, etc.) but using clean renewable energy to do so;
- Having a total transport system that is electrically driven, with driverless and driven e-vehicles;
- Being the largest data centre in the world supplied by clean renewable energy;
- Having the lowest per capita carbon footprint globally;
- And being the cleanest, greenest, most sustainable city in the world, with the lowest PM2.5 reading in the world, the cleanest drinking water in the world, and a rich biodiversity. See the City Biodiversity Index developed by the National Parks

Board and adopted at the Nagoya meeting of the Conference of the Parties to the Convention on Biological Diversity.

Economically, this will bring Singapore billions of dollars of contracts to provide renewable energy infrastructure throughout the world, using its engineering and project management competence, operations and maintenance know-how, and financial capabilities.

A vigorous RE industry will also provide skilled employment for technicians, engineers and scientists who graduate from Singapore's ITEs, Polytechnics and Universities. Singapore will attract the very best researchers to stay at the cutting edge of these technologies. The world desperately needs these technologies, to mitigate climate change and ensure that we continue to enjoy life in an environment that can sustainably supply the clean water, energy and food that we all need.

Future Challenges and Opportunities Facing the Energy Industry

Urbanisation is arguably the most important global trend affecting energy infrastructure. The number of people living in cities is forecast to double from 3.5 billion (50% of world population) in 2008 to almost 7 billion (70% of world population) by 2050. Cities generate the majority of a country's GDP, and cities are also the source of 70% of the world's greenhouse gases. However, cities also allow for more efficient use of infrastructure and facilities, and can act as a great catalyst for upward social mobility. City councils are increasingly embracing the concept of the smart city with main interests in liveability (in general), IT and telecoms, and clean energy. But topics on their agenda also include water, sewage, waste treatment, transportation, health, resource efficiency, social infrastructure and sustainable economies. Sustainability, attractiveness and interconnectivity are regarded as important characteristics of a smart city.

A city can be labelled as "smart" when investments in human and social capital and traditional (transport) and modern (ICT) infrastructure fuel sustainable economic development and a high quality of life, with wise management of natural resources, through participatory action and engagement (Caragliu *et al.* 2009 as cited in the 4th China-Italy Innovation Forum). Recently the Singapore government introduced a slew of initiatives towards its goal of going beyond a Smart City, to become the world's first Smart Nation. The next 10 years will see Singapore developing smart communities driven by intelligence, integration, and innovation.

Singapore must recognise and understand the key global energy trends when planning for future city infrastructure. These include: the growing share of renewables; increasing complexity and interdependence of power systems; increasingly vocal and engaged consumers, conscious of new energy options; rising demand for reliability (less acceptance for outages and failures) due to larger dependence on energy, and the increasing threat of cyber security with increased automation of energy infrastructure. It must also consider the advent of more disruptive technologies, e.g. energy storage, solar PV, and electric vehicles that are possible game-changers as the cost of technology drops. It must manage "Big Data" with increased penetration of smart meters, sensors and M2M communication. And it must accommodate rising demand for transparency and progressive policies with more publicly available information.

These key global trends present several opportunities to further leverage our current experience in solar PPA schemes, biomass co-generation Private Public Partnership (PPP) Scheme, Intelligent Energy System pilot, Semakau Landfill and Pulau Ubin microgrids, and the Energy Efficiency grants and programmes.

Singapore is extremely vulnerable to the adverse effects of climate change, i.e. rising sea levels, increasing intensity of storms, heat waves, etc.; and therefore must seize this opportunity to influence the future design of cities, which will be the key consumers of the world's resources as well as the key sources of emissions.

Transition from Centralised to Distributed Generation

The drive to reduce greenhouse gas emissions means that Singapore must improve energy efficiency and decrease its dependence on its current centralised, fossil-fuel-based generation model. The best candidate to complement the existing electricity infrastructure is distributed generation, where electricity is produced close to its point of use. Co-location avoids costs of transmission and distribution.

Solar power plants on rooftops will supply the buildings beneath them, and any surplus power will supply the neighbouring buildings. This reduces the burden on the centralised transmission and distribution infrastructure.

Combined Heat and Power (CHP) or tri-generation facilities have conversion efficiencies in excess of 70%, or almost double that of conventional steam generation, by co-generating heating and/or cooling. Distributed generation, e.g. CHP or tri-generation is therefore a highly desirable solution. The current market structure allows for the installation of power generators smaller than 10 MW that are used solely for on-site demand, i.e. they do not export power to the grid. The market also includes embedded generation with much larger capacities, seen primarily in the petrochemical sector.

Distributed generation can therefore reduce the cost of electricity to end users and even supply cooling to residential and commercial buildings in a more efficient manner.

In reviewing opportunities to relocate other facilities underground, these energy systems can also be constructed below the demand centres to supply energy (electricity, heating and cooling) more efficiently, while keeping noise away, and also freeing up land for other uses.

The proliferation of distributed generation systems raises concerns about the reliability of the grid, which was not conceived to accommodate a plethora of generators connected to the distribution network. Smart grid solutions for grid management, and business models like "interruptible load" and other Demand Response schemes, can mitigate these concerns. They open more possibilities to reduce the impact of distributed generators on grid reliability, by easing the strain on the grid during unplanned events.

Variability of solar PV is a genuine concern for grid operators in maintaining grid reliability, but one that is easily solved with a combination of technology and market structure.

Singapore operates a wholesale electricity market. This market trades energy, reserves, and frequency response. Reserves are scheduled so that if the biggest operating generator trips, there will be sufficient spare spinning (fast response) capacity to fill the gap in supply and make sure consumers are not affected. But this mechanism is less relevant to widely dispersed, distributed generators, even if they are individually intermittent. Although a cloud can suddenly obscure the sun's rays from a solar PV array, the same cloud will not obscure a PV system further away until sometime later. Figure 6 shows how the aggregated average sunshine across Singapore varies far more smoothly than at any individual site.

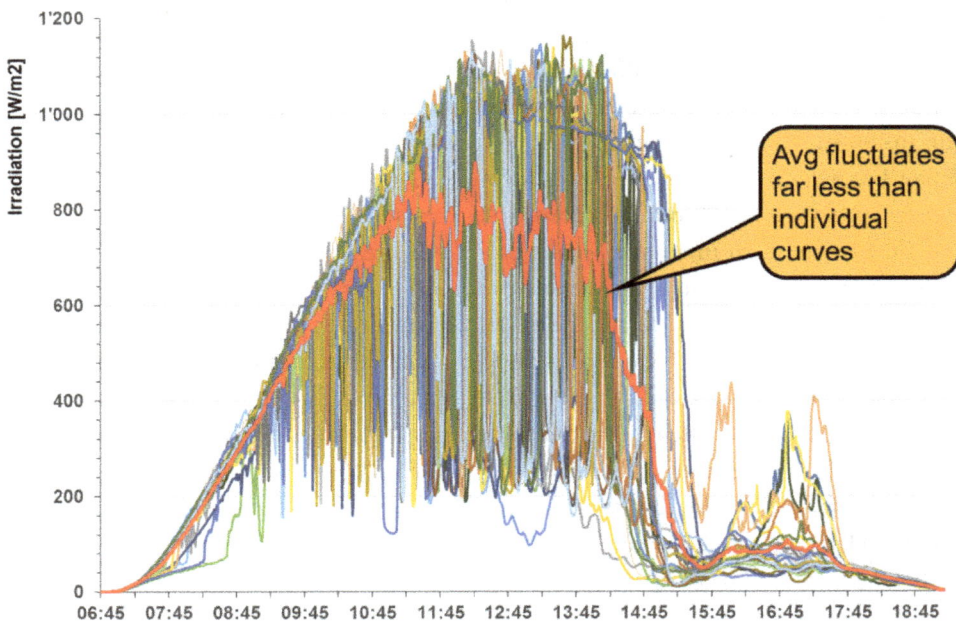

Figure 6.   Solar irradiance measured by 25 SERIS sensors across Singapore on a typical day.

Thus the nation-wide aggregate PV output is not intermittent, and the sudden failure of a single PV plant has too little impact to destabilise the grid. SERIS's island-wide network of irradiation sensors can track geographic variation in solar irradiation and use vector algorithms to forecast solar production for the grid operator.

Economic Benefits

Thanks to a significant decline in PV system costs, relatively high electricity tariffs and ample solar irradiation, PV power has become commercially viable in Singapore. The SEAS White Paper published in 2014 showed how massive increases in global PV module production capacity have driven costs low enough in recent years (2011–2013) for a rooftop PV system in Singapore to pay for itself in 7–10 years, depending on system size. This has resulted in an unlevered project IRR of 8–13%, making PV a very attractive investment, and one that needs no additional incentive schemes to justify its viability. Prices will continue to decline, although at a much slower pace than they did in the last 2–3 years.

Assuming average system prices that will gradually decline from a range of S$2.00–3.00/Wp in 2013, to perhaps S$1.20–1.60/Wp by 2025, two Gigawatts of PV will require S$3–4 billion in total investment. This investment will come from the private sector, and not from the government. The share of these investment flows that remain in the country will depend on the share generated from Singapore-based players, which also depends on policy and incentives in place. Assuming half of components/labour are sourced locally and not imported (Singapore hosts one international module manufacturer (REC), and several installation firms, investors and consultants) the in-country investment flow is approximately S$2 billion. As one of the main Asian financial hubs, Singapore can accommodate a growing number of cleantech investments funds, and more RE companies may feel encouraged to list on the SGX.

Furthermore, an increased uptake of PV will create cleantech/renewable clusters in Singapore that support a sustainable green economy and create more "green" jobs. 30% to 70% of value can be added locally, depending on where the PV modules are made. The PV industry creates jobs all along the value chain from the production phases to installation work. The European Photovoltaic Industry Association (EPIA) estimates that PV module manufacturing creates 3–7 direct jobs in production zones and about 12–20 related indirect jobs for each MWp of PV modules produced and installed (whole PV value-chain, incl. research centres, installers, producers of silicon, wafers, cells, modules and other components). This is highly relevant for regional and global exports, building capacities (in terms of skills and expertise) for local companies who can then expand into regional and global markets. As annual PV deployment in Singapore grows from 10 MWp in 2013 to a projected 200 MWp by 2017, employment could increase by a similar factor. Using EPIA's figures, with 30 FTE for solar EPC and O&M by end of 2012, this could increase to 600 FTE from 2017 onwards.

Singapore is therefore poised to grow with sustainable energy solutions to reduce carbon emissions in the face of climate change and to actively promote sustainable development, integrating policies with research and development and test-bedding new technologies. With the renewable energy opportunities, know-how and roll-out described above between now and 2050, Singapore needs to take full advantage of what renewable energy will bring. It can be a Renewable Energy Hub for the world, a living lab to hothouse and test-bed solutions. It can be a showcase for the various renewable energy technologies and their applications in a highly urbanised setting, and even in remote communities such as ERI@N's Renewable Energy Integration Demonstrator Singapore (REIDS) at Semakau Island. Following successful outcomes from these experiments and test-beds, companies can commercialise and bring these solutions to the region, which has projected annual growth rates of 43% from 2013–2020. The 2013 investment figures are already US$250 billion globally (International Energy Agency Mid-Term Report Renewable Energy Report 2014), and 70% of this growth is expected in the Asia Pacific region.

Positioning Singapore as the Global Centre for RE Technology

In the last five years, Singapore has positioned itself as a living lab, building on the back of 50 years of prudent economic policy and visionary leadership with bold ideas. It has grown its commitment to new energy technologies, investing both in research and in living platforms for demonstration projects. This has captured the imagination of entrepreneurs and researchers, resulting in new solutions and ideas both local and foreign in Singapore's energy arena. However, we are losing our first-mover advantage of using our island state as a "living lab", as the concept has caught on in many cities around the world.

To position Singapore as a model city of the future in urban sustainable energy management, it must re-design its power systems and electricity market to integrate technologies that capitalise on natural resources and exploit the increasing energy value of waste. It needs enabling policies and business models that empower consumers while rewarding entrepreneurs.

As a sustainable energy industry hub with an ecosystem of renewable energy and energy efficiency technologies, Singapore can bring fully integrated solutions to Asia and the world, exploiting the huge market in Asia and then leveraging on that to serve the world market. The right enabling policies and strategies will attract many MNCs and technology SMEs from all over the world to set up in Singapore when they see that we have all the critical ingredients to become the centre for renewable and sustainable energy.

References

Contact Singapore. (2014). Engineering (Including Aerospace, Cleantech and Engineering Services). Retrieved 25 February 2015 from http://www.contactsingapore.sg/key_industries/engineering.

Ministry of Trade and Industry, Singapore (MTI). (2011, December 13). A Changing Energy Landscape: The Energy Trilemma. Retrieved 25 November 2014 from http://www.mti.gov.sg/mtiinsights/pages/energy-.aspx.

National Climate Change Secretariat, Singapore (NCCS). (2015). International Actions. Retrieved 25 November 2014 from https://www.nccs.gov.sg/climate-change-and-singapore/international-actions.

National Environment Agency (NEA). (2014). Waste Statistics and Overall Recycling. Retrieved 25 November 2014 from http://app2.nea.gov.sg/energy-waste/waste-management/waste-statistics-and-overall-recycling.

Sustainable Energy Association of Singapore (SEAS). (2014). White Paper on Accelerating Renewable Energy in Singapore.

The 4th China-Italy Innovation Forum. (2013). Smart City. Retrieved 25 November 2014 from http://cittc.org.cn/forum/looknewsdo_en.php?id=67.

Glossary

Main power producers	Enterprises that produce electricity as their principal activity.
Autoproducers	Enterprises that produce electricity typically for their own use, but for whom this production is *not* their principal activity.
Contestable customers	Electricity consumers who are allowed to purchase electricity either from third-party retailers or the wholesale market.
Non-contestable customers	Consumers who can only buy electricity from the regulated service provider (SP Services). These are typically residential and small commercial consumers.
Grid Emission Factor (GEF), Average Operating Margin (OM)	GEF measures average CO_2 emissions per MWh of electricity. It is calculated using Average Operating Margin method, which is the generation-weighted average CO_2 emission per unit of net electricity generated by all power plants serving the grid.
Grid charges	What is paid to the utilities to recover the costs of transporting electricity through the grid.
Demand Response	Contractual arrangements that encourage consumers to curtail their electricity demand in response to pricing signals. Consumers shift some of their demand from peak to off-peak periods, thereby reducing peak electricity demand. See EMA's consultation paper: https://www.ema.gov.sg/media/com_consultations/attachments/508127e67a4c3-Demand_Response_Consultation_Paper_final.pdf.
Interruptible load (IL)	Loads whose supply can be interrupted, providing reserve services to the grid. (IL reserve is an alternative to holding reserve on spinning part-loaded generators).
Wp, kWp, MWp	Watt-peak, Kilowatt-peak and Megawatt-peak. The rated capacity of a PV panel or system under standard test conditions.
kWh	Kilowatt-hours. The basic billable unit of electricity 1 kWh = 3,412 BTUs (British Thermal Units)
MWh, GWh, TWh	Megawatt-hours = 1,000 kWh Gigawatt-hours = 1,000 MWh Terawatt-hours = 1,000 GWh
MWe, MWth	Megawatt of electrical power Megawatt of thermal power
toe	Tonne of oil equivalent = the energy released by burning 1 tonne of crude oil 1 toe = 41.868 GJ = 11.63 MWh[6]
ktoe, Mtoe	kilo-tonnes of oil equivalent Mega-tonnes of oil equivalent = 1,000 ktoe
Cost of abatement	The cost of treatment or reduction of waste

---

[6] IEA/0ECD definition. But the actual energy in 1 tonne of crude oil varies according to calorific value of the oil.

CHAPTER 9

Community Engagement to Promote Environmental Ownership and Secure Our Future

Chew Gek Khim

Chairman
National Environment Agency (NEA), Singapore

Abstract

This chapter illustrates the development of Singapore's strategy of engaging the community in caring for the environment. From the outset of the establishment of Singapore as an independent nation state, community engagement was recognised as being pivotal and integral to raising environmental standards and contributing to a sustainable urban environment. This chapter will provide more detail on how Singapore has adapted itself to meet the demands for greater community involvement and building a more inclusive society. There is greater emphasis placed in encouraging ground-up, community-led activities and movements, focussing on inculcating values and building positive social norms. The support for localised engagements and leveraging touch points, both through traditional and social media, is necessary to reach out to a more diverse populace. The emphasis on promoting considerate behaviour and environmental ownership will be illustrated through the initiatives implemented by the National Environment Agency.

Introduction

Singapore is a small city-state with limited physical and natural resources. In spite of its resource constraints, it is now an affluent society, with per capita GDP of SGD$71,318 as at 2014 (Department of Statistics, 2014b). Over the decades, as its economy grew, resources were allocated to fund environmental programmes, R&D, and develop key environmental infrastructures.[1] Notwithstanding Singapore's dense

---

[1] Singapore was ranked first globally, in terms of infrastructural development. See Department of Statistics (2014b).

population, it is consistently ranked highly in city liveability indices.[2] Regional and international benchmark studies such as the Mercer Quality of Living Index, Yale Environmental Performance Index (EPI) and Asian Green City Index recognise and rank Singapore highly in their respective studies, with Singapore's clean and green environment often cited as one of the key contributing factors.

This high environmental quality was achieved not by chance, but was largely due to Singapore placing a high priority on protecting the environment right from its inception as a nation. Effective law enforcement, strong political will and effective institutions are often cited as important attributes in sustaining a viable system, and this is no different when it comes to the environment.

Challenges of the Early Post-independence Era (circa 1960–80s)

Singapore achieved self-government in 1959. In 1963, it formally merged with Malaya, Sarawak and Sabah to form the Federation of Malaysia.

9 August 1965 marked its formal separation from Malaysia and the day it became an independent nation. The newly formed nation faced high unemployment and although there were public health services, many still lived in overcrowded conditions in the city. Lacking natural resources such as water, food, and energy, Singapore also had to establish itself in a new socio-political environment.

The first course of the day was to mitigate rising unemployment. Industrialisation by attracting local and foreign investments through various tax incentives and labour-intensive industries was promoted. However, with industrialisation came pollution. In 1972, the Ministry of Environment was set up to balance the conflicting demands of economic and industrial development with environmental protection.

Engaging the Populace to Change their Lifestyles and Habits to Achieve Higher Environmental Standards

Following the nation's independence in 1965, the first Singapore concept plan — the State and City Planning Project — was conceived in 1967 and completed in 1971. This was after a four-year long study under the United Nations Development Programme's special assistance scheme for urban renewal and development for emerging nations. Preceding this Concept Plan, Singapore had already enacted the landmark Land Acquisition Act in 1966, which granted the government greater control over land use and town planning. Both instruments were instrumental to Singapore's plan for urban renewal and national development.

---

[2] Singapore's population density as at 2013 is 7,540 persons/sq km. See Department of Statistics (2014a).

One of the overarching principles which guided this first concept plan was the need to enhance the existing infrastructural network, and implement a degree of wealth redistribution to drive the economy. This was judiciously balanced with the need to safeguard the environment and control the pollution inevitably caused by industrialisation and urbanisation. The key focus was to improve the living conditions of the majority of the people and enhance environmental standards, primarily in the areas of public health and pollution control. Concomitantly, legislation and fiscal measures were passed to serve multiple and broader societal goals in line with this impetus.

The Ministry of the Environment was formed as a regulator of environmental standards and the implementor of environmental infrastructure such as the sewerage system as well as the waste management and disposal system. One of the key challenges the Ministry was entrusted with during the 1970s was the decade-long Singapore River clean-up. Many Singaporeans who grew up during this era will recall the metamorphosis of the once dirty river. From squatter premises without proper sewage facilities, backyard and cottage industries and farms along its banks, the river was cleaned up and its banks redeveloped into modern residential areas, commercial and financial institutions.

While investments in infrastructure can help to transform the city, the benefits of infrastructural improvements and fiscal intervention will be short-lived and unsustainable if they are not supported by the populace in changing their lifestyles and habits. Hence, many community programmes were launched during this period. In other words, public education was deemed necessary to effect social and physical changes to support national development objectives.

Numerous campaigns were launched during the period to educate the people to change their lifestyles and adopt behaviour more befitting of citizens of a developed country. The campaign taglines in the 1970s, such as "Keep Singapore Clean", "Do Not Spit", "Keep Our Water Clean", "Flies are Dangerous to Health — Prevent Fly Breeding", "Use Plastic Bags for Your Refuse", were reflective of the nature of the environmental priorities during this period.

Education through Different Communication Platforms

The growth of mass media such as television and radio during this period facilitated the dissemination of campaign messages via radio and television interviews, films, talks and features for educational and teaching purposes. For instance, in 1973, the Ministry produced a film on "The Hawker Problem in Singapore" with the assistance of the then-Broadcasting Department (Ministry of the Environment, 1974). National campaigns on public issues such as vermin control, cholera, typhoid and anti-spitting or environmental pollution issues such as water pollution, anti-littering and proper disposal of refuse were communicated through film shows and talks. Within the Ministry, public education campaigns were undertaken by the Training and Education Department. This department also developed posters and pamphlets for distribution or display at the common amenities of Singapore heartlands, such as bus stops, hawker centres and community centres.

Following the inception of the Keep Singapore Clean and Tree Planting Campaign (see Box Story 1 and 2) in the 1970s, more public education campaigns

---

Box Story 1: Keep Singapore Clean Campaign: Educating the Population on Responsible Behaviour through Mass Media and Engagement

The origins of the first environmental campaign dates back to the 1960s, when thousands of hawkers sold food openly on the streets alongside busy traffic without consideration of hygiene. The food waste and litter generated created an unpleasant stench and cluttered many parts of the road, including the Singapore River and Kallang Basin, turning many areas into slums. If Singapore was serious in transforming itself, a massive clean-up needed to be done first. Hence, the Keep Singapore Clean Campaign was launched on 1 October 1968.

The Keep Singapore Clean (KSC) Campaign was the first environmental campaign to be launched on such a massive scale in the modern history of Singapore. The objective was simple: to get all Singaporeans to always keep this country clean. The extent of outreach, however, proved to be a complex and intensive endeavour. There was extensive national coverage over mass media such as radio and TV, as well as community outreach via posters and banners. In local communities, the campaign was raised to a higher profile through the involvement of MPs and community leaders in organised "broomstick brigades". These public actions by community leaders were significant symbolic gestures and set a good example for residents and volunteers to follow suit.

Apart from educating the public, the government also adopted the "carrot and stick" approach to sustain the effort in the long term. Contests pitching the cleanest heartland areas against each other were organised, and these helped to inculcate a drive within the communities to keep the local spaces clean. Communities which kept their areas clean were recognised. Punishments, however, were meted for the litterbugs. Those who grew up during this period will recall that offenders were firmly disciplined by their school principals and made to sweep their classrooms or school compounds. Adult offenders were not spared either and fines were used to enforce social behaviour. Hefty fines of up to $500 (at a time when the per capita GDP was $708[1]) were meted out to the offenders under the Environmental Public Health Act (EPHA) established in 1968. Recalcitrant adult offenders were prosecuted and their names were published in the local press, sending a strong message of deterrence to the public. These measures were effective in raising public awareness on the need to keep Singapore clean and that littering, as a socially unacceptable act, should not be tolerated.

Box Story 2: Tree-Planting Day

In 1971, the first Tree Planting Day was conceptualised, heralding the start of Singapore's community-based green movement. Dr. Goh Keng Swee launched the event on 7 November 1971, Sunday, by planting a rain tree in the morning at the summit of Mount Faber. On that day, a total of 8,400 trees and 21,677 shrubs and creepers were planted around the island. Schools also got into the act, with over 60 schools planting 600 fruit trees. Subsequently, all Tree Planting Days were held on the first Sunday every November, which is the beginning of the monsoon season, to minimise watering requirements and thus conserve precious water resources.

This strong mandate was borne out of former PM Lee Kuan Yew's vision to make Singapore a tropical garden city. It was believed that the greenery raised morale and gave people a sense of national pride and identity. There was no differential treatment between middle-class and working-class areas — thousands of trees were diligently planted all over the island with no special emphasis given over any one area. It also showcased the effort and discipline put into maintenance, which gave everyone, including foreign visitors a sense that the country was well run.

However, the planting of beautiful trees and shrubs needed to be matched with appropriate public behaviour. The beauty of the plants attracted pilferage — people removed the pots and saplings for their own gardens. Others caused destruction by trampling over newly planted grass and parked their bicycles or motorcycles against larger plants. There was a need to teach people how to take care of plants. Schools got the children to plant trees and tend to gardens, and the children returned home with the message to relay to their parents. Today, greenery blending seamlessly with towering skyscrapers, road shoulders bearing neat rows of flowering shrubs and mature trees are a common sight. The world took notice, and Singapore became well known as a tropical garden city.

were developed throughout the 1980s. Public toilet cleanliness gave rise to "Let's Keep Public Toilets Clean" in 1985. The "Clean Rivers Education Programme" in 1987 was created to continue educating the public and industry on water pollution. There was also strong collaboration with grassroots organisations, the Singapore Armed Forces, schools and the Housing Development Board. Although largely instructive and didactic in nature, these efforts over the past 20 years have proven to be successful and laid the foundation for more sophisticated forms of outreach in the new millennium.

Creating Platforms to Galvanise Greater Community Participation (circa 1990–mid-2000s)

Cities are constantly changing. Urban landscapes usually undergo stages of transformation in line with the city's economic and sociopolitical progress. Singapore is no exception. In fact, Singapore's landscape in the first two decades after independence underwent dramatic transformation. The nation cleaned up its rivers and streets, added greenery, phased out or re-sited pollutive industries, put in place appropriate legislative and institutional measures, invested in environmental infrastructure and embarked on a series of educational efforts nation-wide to change behaviour towards the environment.

The Ministry of the Environment was the main government agency responsible for formulating environmental policies. It also worked closely with other authorities such as the Urban Redevelopment Authority, the Economic Development Board and Jurong Town Corporation to implement these policies and monitor their impact. Although Singapore experienced recessions in 1985, 1998 and 2001, the impetus to ensure sustainable growth remained steadfast. Ultimately, it was economic growth that enabled the government to dedicate more resources to environmental programmes and policies. By the 1990s, Singapore had become one of the cleanest and greenest city-states in this region.

Singapore, however, was unique in more ways than one. The entire island was a city-state, which meant that the lack of a hinterland and natural resources, as well as a burgeoning population would exert severe pressure on the environment if it was not carefully managed. It was not tenable for the country to support economic growth without constantly reviewing its strategy to meet the evolving social and developmental needs. This was evident in the Singapore Master Plan, which underwent five revisions from 1965 to 2000. Consistent with the city-state's focus on sustainable urbanisation, it published the first Singapore Green Plan (SGP) in 1992 which set out its long-term vision of a model Green City. One key area in the Plan was the focus on engaging the population. The SGP was, in fact, amongst the first public planning documents that established an extensive public engagement process, where public feedback and aspirations were solicited to develop a more inclusive, holistic plan. The SGP 1992 stated:

> In the Plan, new areas for action have been identified and the action programmes formulated to implement the Plan in these new areas are discussed. One key area is environmental education, to build an environmentally aware and proactive population so that all would be involved in the protection and improvement of the environment.

This statement was consistent with the recommendations put forth in the Agenda 21 agreement signed during the United Nations Conference on Environment and

Development in Rio de Janeiro in 1992 of which Singapore is a signatory. The agreement called upon governments to adopt national strategies for development in a sustainable manner. Policies should be holistic and mutually reinforcing, where communities and businesses must be informed to help them make choices which are compatible with the principles of sustainable development. For the review of SGP 1992 in 2001, this approach was taken a step further when stakeholders from various sectors of society such as business organisations, academics and civil groups were invited to either lead or be a member of the three focus groups to review and update the plan (see Box Story 3).

The SGP was an example of how the community could be involved in urban planning of the city-state. Building on this momentum, the Ministry of the Environment continued with its public education efforts to encourage greater community action.

Box Story 3: Consulting Singaporeans through the Singapore Environmental Master Plans

The Singapore Green Plan (SGP) was a master plan which guided and articulated the sustainability goals of Singapore. The first document was published in 1992, and in 1999, the Ministry of the Environment undertook a review of the SGP to account for the new ideas, technologies and concerns that had emerged since its original publication. The SGP 2012 was launched and presented at the World Summit on Sustainable Development in Johannesburg in September 2002. A subsequent review of the SGP 2012 in 2005 was an opportunity for individuals, businesses and NGOs to be consulted on a range of issues that would affect them. More than 17,000 people participated in the review, resulting in a document which was more robust and inclusive (MEWR, 2006). The public consultation process did not end with the publication of SGP 2012. The plan was made available online to gather public comments and a closing public forum was held, where members of the public were invited to meet the review panel to address public feedback. Subsequently, the Sustainable Singapore Blueprint was developed in 2009 to chart Singapore's sustainable growth up till 2030, superseding the SGP 2012 as most of the targets had been met. By that time, a consultative mode of engagement had entrenched itself as the norm. It was only through involving the community, NGOs as well as the business stakeholders that everyone could come together as a collective entity to understand the challenges and co-develop and co-own the solutions for a more sustainable future.

1990s: Towards More Consultative Governance

1990 marked a period of transition for Singapore, the year in which the nation's second Prime Minister, Mr. Goh Chok Tong took office. Public participation in environmental campaigns and engagement of the key stakeholders had been gaining momentum over the last 25 years. This was given a boost when Mr. Goh articulated a more consultative governance on 28 November, 1990:

> The style of the next Government will have these three components: participation, accommodation, consensus, whereby, "participation" would mean having as many Singaporeans involved in the political process as is practical; "accommodation" would mean that alternative viewpoints to the Government will be heard with an open mind and changes made to accommodate valid views; and efforts will be made to achieve "consensus" between the government and the people on the major issues that affect (the citizens') lives. (Goh, 1990)

The environmental scene had grown increasingly complex over the years. The views and concerns of the public were also getting increasingly diverse, as people became more aware and conscious of the environmental impact of development. A consultative mode of engagement was recognised as the best strategy for both the government and people as it helped to increase the public's awareness of environmental issues and inculcate greater ownership of national policies.

The 1990s saw increased participation by civil societies on environmental issues. One example was a local non-governmental organisation (NGO) that was a branch of the Malayan Nature Society. In 1991, it became formally recognised as the Nature Society (Singapore). The Nature Society has since established itself as the entity promoting the awareness and appreciation of nature, and has made significant contributions to the preservation of several natural heritage sites. In 1995, the National Environment Council was formed to educate and inspire individuals, business and various interest groups to collectively care for and protect the environment. It was subsequently renamed the Singapore Environment Council. Three years later, in 1998, the Restroom Association (Singapore) was formed to promote better personal hygiene and public toilet user etiquette.

With the emergence of more environmental NGO groups, the government's relationship with the people evolved to one which was more consultative, with NGOs empowered to take on co-leading roles in various issues and participate actively in aiding policy formulation and master planning.

Charting a New Period in Environmental Governance

By the late 1990s, the Ministry of the Environment recognised that implementation of policies and provision of services would be more effective if the responsibility for delivery was devolved to locally accountable bodies. In 2001, PUB was transferred from the Ministry of Trade and Industry to the Ministry of the Environment, and together with the sewerage and drainage departments from the Ministry of the Environment, reconstituted to become Singapore's national water authority, overseeing the entire water loop. The following year in July 2002, a new statutory board — the National Environment Agency (NEA) — was formed (see Box Story 4 and 5) mainly from divisions in the Ministry of the Environment to take over the role of the regulator and implementor for a clean environment. At the same time, the regional offices under NEA aligned the areas under their respective purview with the geographical boundaries of the five Community Development Councils (CDCs) to better meet the local needs and challenges within each district. Both PUB and NEA remains Statutory Boards under the Ministry of the Environment which in September 2004 was renamed to what it is today — the Ministry of the Environment and Water Resources (MEWR).

The new consultative mode of engagement and the importance of establishing networks with the local community and stakeholders was set to become a permanent feature in Singapore's environmental planning process. Developing a partnership between the People, Public and Private (3P) sectors became a key approach towards achieving sustainability goals.

Engaging the People, Promoting Greater Environmental Ownership (mid-2000s–Present)

As Singapore moved into the new century, public interest and awareness of environmental issues continued to grow. Fuelled by an increasingly connected world, global environmental issues such as climate change and resource conservation began to gain prominence in local discussions and programmes.

In line with this increased awareness, NEA formalised the 3P partnership approach, to involve the People, Private and Public sectors in addressing environmental challenges and promoting environmental ownership. NEA was amongst the first government agencies to institute this approach, committing manpower and resources to educate, engage and empower the community to care and act for the environment. The shift in NEA's engagement strategy underscored the importance of joint responsibility of the community in shaping our future towards sustainable development.

However, it was soon recognised that Singapore needed to do more to continue developing in a sustainable way. To bring development to the next level, an attitudinal shift was required at the individual and institutional-level, focussing on longer term solutions and developing a stronger sense of personal responsibility for the environment and consideration for the community. This became the next milestone in NEA's approach towards 3P partnership engagement — inculcating personal values and building social norms for an engaged citizenry to care for the environment.

Box Story 4: Formation of NEA

The Ministry of the Environment recognised that a new statutory board with greater administrative autonomy and flexibility was deemed necessary to ensure that Singapore's air, land and water remain clean in order to maintain a high standard of public health. The objective was to achieve a Ministry focussed on policy in tandem with a statutory board focussed on operations. The National Environment Agency (NEA) was thus formally established on 1 July 2002. The restructuring led to an integration of the Environmental Public Health Division and the Environmental Policy and Management Division of the Ministry of the Environment, and the Meteorological Service Department of the Ministry of Transport, under the aegis of NEA.

Environment management had long relied on laws implemented via surveillance and enforcement. However, to ensure the sustainability of environmental ownership, it was important for NEA to forge a synergistic relationship with the community and stakeholders. Mr. Lim Swee Say, then Minster for the Environment, remarked, "If we want people to litter less, we can fine them more. If we want people to consume less water, we can charge them more. (So) we can use a pricing mechanism to produce short-term results. But if you think about long-term sustainability, (I think) nothing is better than adopting a 3P (People-Private-Public) approach." As a new agency, NEA was in the position to chart a new trajectory to stay relevant and be responsive to the needs of the Singapore and its people.

The 3P partnership approach was widely regarded as a significant paradigm shift. Externally, the challenge was to encourage the public to take greater ownership of the environment. The strategy was to foster a collaborative partnership between NEA and the community, creating shared ownership of initiatives. Internally, NEA recognised that regulation and enforcement were still necessary to ensure compliance with strict environmental standards. NEA would need to balance its twin roles of an enforcer and promoter for the environment.

In 2003, NEA's five regional offices were aligned with the boundaries of the Community Development Councils (CDC) which in turn were in charge of community bonding and building social cohesiveness on the ground. This strategic move paved the way for NEA's ground operations to be integrated with grassroots initiatives. Within each regional office, there was a dedicated 3P unit that planned and implemented outreach campaigns with, and for the community. In the same year, NEA launched a new 3P Partnership Fund to empower the 3P sector to champion an environmental movement in the community.

Box Story 5: Singapore's OK Campaign

The resilience of a newly-formed NEA was put to the test when Singapore was affected by the SARS outbreak in 2003. NEA staff members were swiftly deployed to help in the crisis. Their role involved cleaning affected areas, disposing contaminated items, contact tracing and promoting good personal hygiene to reduce the spread of the virus.

NEA launched the "Singapore's OK" campaign to heighten awareness of the importance of good hygiene practices. The campaign was rolled out progressively to eateries, markets, public toilets, schools, hostels, workers' dormitories and construction sites. At each location, NEA staff worked with businesses and the public to ensure that adequate hygiene practices were in place before endorsing the site with the "Singapore's OK" label. It was a massive 3P partnership exercise on a nation-wide scale. Beyond the threat of the virus, the SARS outbreak was an opportunity to test NEA's partnership networks. NEA's role in maintaining public hygiene standards helped to instil confidence and encourage the public to continue visiting public areas and amenities.

The nation was finally declared SARS-free by the World Health Organisation in May 2003. The SARS episode was a sobering reminder to the nation of the impact of a public health crisis. It also showed NEA the importance of close community partnerships in managing environmental and public health concerns.

With an active public engagement framework and process in place, coupled with its extensive network of 3P partners cultivated over the years, NEA was able to engage different stakeholders in pursuing this next milestone. It launched a S$1.5 million a year 3P Partnership Fund to encourage greater ground-up action by the 3P partners. Awards such as the President's Award for the Environment and the EcoFriend Awards were presented from 2006 and 2007 respectively, to recognise the sustained efforts of environmental advocates and proactive organisations, spurring others to emulate their achievements.

While the provision of resources and platforms for recognition was effective in incentivising partners to co-develop localised ground-up initiatives, the main challenge continues to lie in encouraging greater environmental responsibility in every individual, household and corporation. A new approach was needed to establish in the citizenry a better understanding of environmentally appropriate behaviour and to encourage community ownership for the environment.

Promoting an Environmentally Responsible Behaviour

In 2010, NEA completed a sociological study on littering to develop better behavioural insights into the psyche of the litterbug. The study concluded that cultural and personal value systems were significant factors in influencing littering behaviour. While enforcement was a deterrence to would-be offenders, a strong social support system was needed to bring about behavioural changes for those who occasionally litter. There was a need to establish a social norm that littering was an anti-social act and should not be tolerated.

The study recommended areas for improving community outreach and communication strategies, such as the need for customised messaging for different target groups and engaging mothers and peers as key influencers who would make a positive impact on an individual's personal values.

This was a landmark study in developing customised intervention measures to promote desired behaviour for topical issues. Subsequent studies on promoting energy efficiency and recycling were commissioned by MEWR with similar objectives. While the studies were useful in developing insights to guide topic-specific intervention, there was also a need to prioritise measures which would contribute to a paradigm shift in behaviour of the population at large. It was clear that behavioural changes had to be underpinned by the right set of social values, starting with the young.

Inculcating Right Values from Young

Education plays a pivotal role in inculcating personal values. Singapore's education system has always played a critical role in supporting social and economic development. It stems from the need to prepare Singaporeans for an increasingly complex and competitive society. While the curriculum has evolved in tandem with each changing era, schools continue to develop the skills, character and values in our young to enable them to contribute to our progress.

Recognising the importance of values-based education, the Ministry of Education (MOE) launched a new Character and Citizenship Education (CCE) syllabus in November 2012 to inculcate a set of core values in students, focussing on self, family, school, community and nation. This new CCE syllabus ties in well with NEA's steadfast focus on inculcating a sense of personal responsibility for the environment, as it gave added impetus to start the young off on the right foot, so they may internalise this sense of environmental ownership throughout their lives.

NEA aligned existing programmes to place more emphasis on inculcating values in the young. Working in tandem, NEA and MOE also co-developed programmes to integrate environmental protection and conservation under the core values of Care, Respect and Responsibility. Experiential learning journeys were conducted for students to build a stronger identity with their school and neighbourhood, and to establish a better emotional connection between the student and the environment. The Keep Singapore Clean Movement for Schools was launched in MOE schools in July 2014 as a student-driven, school-supported effort for students to take ownership of the cleanliness of their school and the environment. In line with MOE's Values-in-Action framework, NEA and Marsiling Primary School launched the Project Buddy Clean Resource Kit in November 2014 (see Box Story 6) to share best practices in

---

Box Story 6: Project Buddy Clean in Marsiling Primary School

Good infrastructure and public cleaning services can help to keep the environment clean. However, these are resource-intensive endeavours which will require significant public funding to sustain. More importantly, to ensure a clean environment, it is essential to promote good behaviour, and it starts with imbuing a sense of strong civic and social values in our young.

A sociological study published by NEA in 2010 revealed that only 30% of students said they would never litter. Clearly, this shows more needs to be done. Motivated by the need to inculcate and reinforce positive social values in their students, Marsiling Primary School started a pilot project, Project Buddy Clean in partnership with NEA. What made Project Buddy Clean significant was the move to leverage off peer influence to cultivate a sense of community in the school and ownership for common spaces. The Primary 5 students took charge and led their Primary 3 juniors to participate in the fortnightly cleaning of their school. In addition, school-wide activities were undertaken to recognise the efforts of and to learn from the school cleaners. The responsibility of keeping the school clean was transferred from the cleaners to the students. After this exercise, students demonstrated a greater ownership of their school environment, as seen from a marked 40% reduction in litter count.

This project also helped develop the students' social and emotional skills through interaction with their peers and school cleaners. 86% of students (up from 75%) agreed that it was the shared responsibility of the community, including themselves, to keep the school clean. More importantly, two-thirds of the Primary 5 students (up from one-third) strongly agreed that through cleaning activities, they appreciated the cleaners better.

This project ties in well with the Ministry of Education's focus on the holistic development of our students; the goal is not just about educating students on the importance of keeping the environment clean, but engaging in subtle persuasion of our young, imbuing them with a sense of community spirit, guiding them to always take the right actions to improve our living environment.

establishing a new school-wide norm of cleaning, and to foster shared responsibility for the cleanliness of common spaces.

Promoting values and new school-wide norms, however, should not be regarded as an end in itself. The values acquired early in life tend to have the greatest influence, as every new social norm is built upon pre-existing ones. If the objective is to foster a stronger sense of responsibility for the environment throughout a person's life, community stakeholders need to play a key role in reinforcing this value system.

Facilitating Ground-up Movement

The establishment of the 3P partnership approach in NEA has facilitated closer collaboration with the grassroots and NGO sectors. The formation of more environmental NGOs such as the Singapore Environment Council and Restroom Association (Singapore) in the 1990s played an important role facilitating greater presence and action by civil society.

In Singapore, the NGOs complement government efforts, providing an alternative platform to raise environmental awareness and promote environmentally friendly habits. Beyond playing the role of influencer, NGOs contribute views that help shape Singapore's urban planning and development process. For example, various established green groups have canvassed for the preservation of green spaces such as Pulau Ubin, which has the last remaining "kampong" in Singapore.

In 2008, the Restroom Association (Singapore) co-chaired the Inter-Agency Working Committee on Public Restrooms with the World Toilet Organisation, to gather feedback from the public and industry stakeholders on what constitutes a good public restroom design. The resulting guidelines were subsequently integrated into the Code of Practice on Environmental Public Health as standards for better public restroom design with NEA.

While previous public consultation exercises in developing Singapore's national green plans were undertaken by the government, the Singapore Environment Council initiated a three-month long national conversation in 2014 to understand the values of Singaporeans and re-define the vision for our environmental future. Held in conjunction with the review of the Sustainable Singapore Blueprint, the suggestions and ideas from the consultations were then formulated into an ENVision statement and presented to MEWR for consideration.

In recent years, the members of various environmental and non-environmental NGOs have also championed environmental conservation as part of their social mandate. The National Youth Achievement Award Council promotes the values of environmental responsibility in their youth leadership programmes, while members of NGOs and community groups have been trained and granted limited statutory powers to record the particulars of people who litter for enforcement purposes.

Today, NGOs contribute to Singapore's environment, helping to resolve the diverse environmental challenges and ensuring a sustainable, clean and green living environment for the community. The public engagement process has become less government-driven, as personal responsibility cannot be mandated from the top, but has to be developed from ground up and come from the people.

Besides NGOs, many ground-up organisations have also stepped forward to promote pro-environmental values. The Keep Singapore Beautiful Movement (KSBM) was initiated by a coalition of civil and youth groups, corporations and individuals to foster a stronger sense of social and environmental responsibility in every Singaporean. Various youth-led programmes were organised to encourage individuals to go the extra mile to keep Singapore clean and beautiful.

The Public Hygiene Council (PHC) collaborates with corporate and grassroots partners to galvanise the community and industry to raise cleanliness and hygiene standards in Singapore. They partnered the Singapore Kindness Movement to organise the Keep Singapore Clean Movement (KSCM) (see Box Story 7), championing the message that small, gracious actions by every individual can create a collective and significant impact on Singapore's public cleanliness. Community litter-picking activities were regularly organised to encourage Singaporeans from all walks of life to participate.

Recognising that the community is taking a greater interest in the environment, various government agencies are also intensifying their efforts to sustain this environmental movement. Programmes have been developed to maximise the opportunity for various target groups to acquire the relevant knowledge and skills, and to inculcate the right attitudes to solve localised environmental challenges.

The National Parks Board (NParks) works with interest groups to promote social bonding and appreciation of the greenery through community gardening projects. PUB promotes the adoption of waterways with corporate organisations and schools, as a way to inculcate the values of keeping Singapore clean and conserving water. The Community Development Councils have become an integral part of the environmental movement where each district develops its own eco-plan. These eco-plans set the strategy and outline the programmes for achieving the district environmental goals in support of the Sustainable Singapore Blueprint.

Individuals and community stakeholders are not the only ones that have joined in the environmental cause; corporations are also integrating environmental Corporate Social Responsibility (CSR) into their core business. Businesses are focussing not just

---

Box Story 7: Keep Singapore Clean Movement

Recognising that a collective effort is required to change people's attitudes and move towards a social norm of zero tolerance for littering, the Public Hygiene Council (PHC), together with Singapore Kindness Movement (SKM), Keep Singapore Beautiful Movement (KSBM) and NEA launched the Keep Singapore Clean (KSC) movement in September 2012. The KSC Movement is a concerted effort by individuals, NGOs and community groups to take the lead in championing various ground-up programmes to exert social pressure on those who litter, to improve public cleanliness.

An example of such a ground-up effort was the "Bright Spots" Programme. PHC embarked on this initiative to identify littering "Hot Spots" around Singapore. Multi-stakeholder partnerships were established amongst individuals, schools, businesses and community organisations to improve the cleanliness and hygiene standards of these areas, turning them into litter-free "Bright Spots". Collectively, the adoption of more Bright Spots would help to establish greater ownership and establish a social norm of keeping our common spaces clean.

Grassroots organisations, in particular, were strong supporters of the KSC Movement. One good example is Nee Soon South Grassroots Organisations which embarked on HABIT @ Nee Soon South (Hold on And Bin IT), with a series of programmes to achieve the vision of a Clean and Beautiful Nee Soon South. These include monthly educational outreach activities such as litter-picking, creation of publicity materials and working with schools in the constituency to promote anti-littering messages.

To facilitate more partners to come on board the Bright Spots Programme, PHC developed a Bright Spot Starter Kit for these partners to implement their own litter-picking activities. As of October 2014, there were already more than 300 Bright Spots in various local neighbourhoods.

---

on corporate sustainability practices to improve on their environmental performance, but are also initiating community programmes to enhance their engagement with stakeholders and growing a stronger corporate brand in the process. The Sustainable Singapore Blueprint (SSB) has defined the approach and articulated the measures and frameworks in place to guide the development of corporate sustainability and CSR practices.

Promoting the Development of Corporate Sustainability Practices

The SSB published by the Inter-Ministerial Committee on Sustainable Development (IMCSD) in 2009 outlined the need for Singapore to be more efficient in its use of resources in tandem with its aspiration to build a vibrant economy. Resource efficiency was actively promoted to enhance the competitiveness of industries and at the same time, contribute to mitigating climate change. The government had also identified environmental and water technologies, including clean energy as strategic areas where Singapore has a competitive edge that could help generate future growth (NRF, 2015).

Government-funded training schemes were put in place to enhance the capabilities of the workforce. An example is the collaboration between the Singapore Environment Institute and the industry to conduct training courses on topics such as energy and waste management, sustainable reporting, disease vector management and radiation safety (SEI, n.d.). Various funding and support schemes were also made available to the industry to promote energy efficiency, clean energy, green buildings, water and clean environmental technologies, green transport and shipping, waste management and energy and greenhouse gas management (Tay, 2012).

Businesses looking for ways to enhance their business competitiveness or sustainability performance were provided with various voluntary platforms to support their business transformation. For example, the Singapore Packaging Agreement (SPA) launched in 2007 was a collaborative platform between NEA and industries to reduce packaging waste. SPA promotes the reduction of consumer packaging throughout the product lifecycle. Consultation and discussion of issues affecting the recovery, utilisation and disposal of consumer packaging were regularly organised for the industry to share best practices. The 3R Awards were launched to recognise and spur corporations to develop their long-term environmental sustainability measures.

The Energy Efficient National Partnership (EENP) programme launched in 2010 is a voluntary scheme for corporations to implement energy management practices to reduce their energy consumption and carbon footprint, and enhance their long-term business competitiveness in the process. By joining the EENP programme, corporations can expect support through the sharing of best practices, resources related to energy efficiency as well as incentives and recognition for their energy management achievements.

The Building and Construction Authority (BCA) works with developers to ensure that all new buildings achieve the BCA Green Mark Certification, setting the standard for environmental performance in areas such as energy efficiency, water efficiency and indoor environmental quality of a building development (BCA, 2010). The certification was extended to existing buildings in 2009 and a new S$50 million Green Mark Incentive Scheme for Existing Building and Premises was introduced in September 2014 to drive green building retrofits and practices to existing buildings (BCA, 2014).

Caring for the Community:
Corporate Social Responsibility (CSR) Practices

To support this CSR movement, NEA developed capacity building programmes, such as the Corporate Environment Champions Programme, to educate participants in systems thinking and design thinking. These individuals will then go on to initiate corporation-wide initiatives within their companies or collaborate with community stakeholders to promote environmental ownership.

One such example was the Panasonic Environment Champion Industry Module. This was a joint partnership between Panasonic and NEA to showcase the application of environmental sustainability measures on an industrial scale to schools in Singapore. Various telcos, consumer electronic developers and recycling companies, recognising the environmental impact of e-waste, have worked together with support from NEA to set up e-waste recycling initiatives across the island. City Developments Limited, a leading developer and building owner in Singapore, leveraged SEC's network to promote Project Eco-Office, which helps companies adopt environmentally-friendly practices in the workplace.

Setting the Next Milestone

Community engagement on the environment has come a long way, moving from educating the public through banners and multiple small campaigns in the 1960s, to engaging community participation in various large-scale, nation-wide campaigns in the 1980s. Today in the 2000s, we have moved to empowering the community by co-developing solutions, in partnership with NGOs and other local groups.

The evolving strategy of community engagement over the years shows a clear trend of moving away from broad-based engagement to one which celebrates the role of the informed individual, active community and responsible stakeholders co-leading environmental movements and crowd-sourcing for ideas, leading to better joint ownership of solutions.

In order for the public engagement process to remain relevant, public institutions need to understand the ever changing sentiment on the ground and adapt to the evolving needs of the people and changing socio-political climate. A longer term plan is a good starting point to identifying the requisite timeframe and resources required to achieve its target.

Cognisant of this need, NEA developed a 3P engagement plan in 2014, articulating the desired outcomes for 2020, strategies and approaches in engaging students, youth, working adults, families and seniors. It has identified the following three strategies to guide the Agency in achieving its outcome of cultivating individuals with pro-environmental behaviour and building cohesive communities with an active interest in contributing to local environmental solutions:

(1) Promoting environmental ownership through the values of responsibility, respect and care from young where our actions reflect the positive values and norms of our Singaporean identity;
(2) Growing the ground-up movement: Creating and empowering circles of influence to reinforce positive values and social norms in society; and
(3) Heightening and sustaining public awareness and consciousness.

Today, the community engagement process is more than just developing environmental programmes as a platform to facilitate community participation. The process of facilitating and enabling 3P partners, influencing the right behaviour and establishing the acceptable social norms will become increasing relevant and critical in promoting environmental ownership. The increasing need to engage the public with a more personal approach, crowd-source for solutions, as well as enable various platforms for social networking and feedback will be essential for effective community engagement.

Meeting Changing Societal Needs, Safeguarding the Future

The confluence of factors in the 50 years of post-independence Singapore has brought about unprecedented change to its economic, social and environmental landscape. Even as the country continues its pursuit of economic growth and urban development, the challenge of meeting social and environmental objectives remains. This challenge has fuelled the momentum for stronger community engagement — an underlying foundation for strengthening the urban governance process — to meet the changing needs of Singapore's evolving society.

While community engagement efforts are not new to Singapore, it has become increasingly challenging to cater to the diverse voices and public needs that demand a more personable mode of engagement. Moreover, given the multi-disciplinary nature of environmental issues, the government needs to re-examine its engagement strategies to ensure that its efforts move towards a more qualitative approach — one that accounts for both the complex sociopolitical and personal behavioural contexts. This will provide the necessary perspective to shape the role of community engagement in the next leg of Singapore's environmental protection work.

Evidence-Based Community Engagement Process

The rapid changes in Singapore's demographic profile have given rise to a rich tapestry of ethnic and social groups, bringing with it specific challenges when trying to adequately engage each segment. Inherently, adopting a more targeted, evidence-based behavioural science engagement process becomes increasingly important, as it provides a conceptual base for understanding and influencing attitudes in caring for the environment.

Leveraging behavioural science for community engagement serves multiple purposes. Primarily, it helps to focus on the personal behavioural motivators for each segment. With better insights, the appropriate localised intervention measures at the institutional or social level can be developed, for improved behavioural outcomes. Ultimately, the aim is to instil a greater sense that caring for the environment is a shared responsibility in every individual and that environmentally friendly behaviour is sustained by social norms.

The anti-littering outreach approach undertaken by NEA was a good case study that bears scrutiny. The 2010 sociological study on littering, as highlighted earlier, represented a positive collaboration between public agencies and academics, leveraging on social theory to lend rigour to the practical implementation of its outreach. Its intervention-based engagement process was illustrated by, firstly, defining what constitutes littering, followed by identifying key influencers of the anti-littering habit and subsequently developing messages targeting specific segments to encourage and reinforce the anti-littering habits.

Outreach at such a broad-based level needs to be complemented with localised outreach, in order to sustain the effort. Hence, at the local level, NEA leveraged upon ground-up volunteer groups, such as the Waterways Watch Society (WWS) (see Box Story 8), building up their capacity to complement NEA's effort. WWS volunteers walk the ground, reporting localised cleaning lapses or offering friendly reminders to keep our public spaces clean.

Other interest groups also participated in localised litter-picking activities, which fulfilled two primary objectives. Firstly, it highlighted the consequences of inconsiderate littering to participants, instilling a sense of pride and personal ownership to have made a positive social impact by keeping their neighbourhood clean. Secondly, at a passive level, the presence of volunteers helped to entrench a positive social norm that keeping the neighbourhood clean is a shared responsibility.

The approach of leveraging local community groups to establish a social norm was also evident in NEA's strategy towards dengue prevention. Local community

Box Story 8: Waterways Watch Society

The Waterways Watch Society (WWS) is a voluntary organisation formed in 1998 with just 30-odd members, to inculcate awareness on the importance of restoring and protecting the aesthetics of Singapore's waterways. They are also one of the longstanding partners of the Clean and Green Singapore Campaign, International Coastal Clean-up and World Water Day.

In partnership with schools, public agencies and corporations, they conduct numerous outreach programmes along the Singapore River and Kallang Basin in their boats and bicycles over weekends. They also provide regular feedback on littering trends to the authorities, to help curb pollution at its source.

When NEA started the Community Volunteer Scheme to deter littering in 2013, they sent key members for training as community volunteers. Fifty-one WWS volunteers have undergone this training as of September 2014 and they are now empowered to request for the particulars of littering offenders for NEA to follow up with enforcement action.

Over the years, WWS has grown to about 350 members, enhancing their capacity to initiate more programmes for the community. This has spurred the opening of their first branch at My Waterway@Punggol in March 2014. At Punggol, the focus is to spread the message of keeping waterways clean to more residents in the heartlands and conduct patrols along the waterway.

WWS' environmental programmes have been supported by NEA, PUB and NParks over the past decade, and it was awarded the President's Award for the Environment (2006) and PUB Watermark Honorary Award (2007).

groups conduct surveillance in the affected neighbourhoods, based on reports on the latest dengue trends. Community vigilance and a strong community presence is the key to sustaining the prevention of mosquito breeding in the neighbourhood (see Box Story 9).

Apart from localised engagement, there were also efforts to target behavioural change at an individual level. This was most evident in Singapore's push for every household to adopt more energy efficient practices to reduce their carbon footprint.

Our consumption behaviour is mainly swayed by rational decision-making processes, with our purchasing decision based on the potential enhancement of our personal welfare. If every individual will, at some point in time, have to make purchasing decisions on household electronic products to meet their own needs, then developing

Box Story 9: Do the Mozzie Wipeout Campaign

Over the years, nation-wide dengue campaigns have been successful in instilling a sense of heightened awareness for dengue prevention. The challenge, however, remains in getting people to translate this awareness into action, to keep their premises mosquito-free on a sustained basis. To accomplish this, NEA developed and implemented the "Do The Mozzie Wipeout" Campaign to promote the steps to prevent mosquito breeding. The threat and danger of contracting the dengue virus was also highlighted in the campaign messaging, to create the sense of protecting family members and loved ones as the key motivator to get the public to adopt dengue preventive measures.

Sustaining General Public Awareness

A comprehensive use of the local media has helped to sustain people's awareness on the dangers of dengue. Posters at bus shelters and MRT stations, advertisements in newspapers and dengue messaging on radio and TV were used extensively to sustain awareness and maintain community vigilance.

Dedicated online media and mobile platforms such as an NEA dengue Facebook page, website and the myENV app complement the traditional media, by reminding the public on dengue preventive measures and the dengue situation in a timely fashion.

Target-specific and Localised Outreach Programmes

Publicity on its own, however, is not sufficient in urging the community to take action against mosquito breeding. Therefore, NEA has forged partnerships with various stakeholders to mobilise the whole community to combat dengue together.

NEA employs a target group-specific approach and engages retail outlets, business associations and other public agencies to educate the community and foreign workers on dengue prevention. Dengue prevention collateral in various languages was developed to reach out to specific target groups.

In addition, NEA worked closely with grassroots organisations to train volunteers under the Dengue Prevention Volunteer (DPV) programme. DPVs were equipped with the necessary knowledge and skills to educate fellow residents on dengue prevention and to check their estates for potential breeding sites. These DPVs help NEA and grassroots organisations to carry out house visits, neighbourhood dengue prevention activities and ground surveillance to eliminate

(Continued)

Box Story 9: (*Continued*)

potential breeding sites. An example of a close collaboration with a grassroots organisation on dengue volunteer training is with the People's Association (PA) Community Emergency Response Teams (CERT). It employs a neighbour-to-neighbour approach that is considered most effective due to the familiarity factor. With PA's help, NEA convenes training sessions for new groups of grassroots leaders and members of the community. As of September 2014, NEA has trained over 3,200 DPVs.

a market of energy-efficient products will help guide consumers to make an informed decision to consume responsibly.

The MEWR research on Singaporeans' attitude and behaviour towards energy efficiency indicated that 3 out of 4 consumers look for the Mandatory Energy Labelling Scheme (MELS) label when purchasing electrical appliances, as the rising energy cost was a main concern influencing their purchasing decision. This implies that the MELS label has fulfilled its intended objective of providing information on energy savings to guide consumer behaviour.

The behavioural study has underscored the fact that although individual welfare is an important consideration, consumer choices can be influenced through rational persuasion. In fact, rational persuasion plays an important role in community engagement to influence the behaviour of our increasingly educated citizenry.

Enhancing Government-to-People Dynamics through Social Media

The exponential growth of social media usage over the last few years has broadened the sphere of engagement beyond traditional avenues of engagement and communication. While traditional media avenues are still relevant (as they facilitate the dissemination of information in a timely manner across a diverse populace), key information can be crowded out by other communication platforms that are competing for greater public mindshare in a media-saturated Singapore.

Unprecedented connectivity has increased the level of networking and communication on the internet. At present, more than 70% of Singaporeans visit social networking sites regularly (Infographics.sg, 2013). If the public is recognised as the main driver of online interaction and people are demanding a quicker and more personalised level of communication, then public institutions should enhance their online presence and provide alternative channels for people to express their opinions and share ideas.

The NEA, like many public institutions, has already caught on to the trend of social media and established its presence on online platforms such as Facebook, Twitter or mobile applications. These platforms are used in many ways — to consult on new policy proposals, to share information or provide an avenue for feedback on service lapses.

In 2013 and 2014, when we faced another cycle of dengue cases, the NEA dengue platform on Facebook was used to disseminate the latest dengue hotspot information, serving as a timely reminder to all users to remain vigilant or participate as volunteers to combat dengue. Such platforms are generally welcomed, as they serve to reduce the communication barrier, changing the dynamics of government-to-people engagement in the process.

Co-creating Solutions with Civil Society and the Community

An increasingly vocal and prominent civil society has been progressively claiming a larger stake in Singapore's social space. Working with civil society and various interest groups, we are able to leverage each other's resources (see Box Story 10), generating new values and co-creating solutions.

This process inspires greater social innovation, to develop new solutions to environmental challenges. In addition, through such a collaborative engagement, the public will also better understand how complex the community engagement process can be. Polarising opinions, competing interests and expectations from the different stakeholders are practical concerns, while at the same time, there is a need to ensure that the views and interests of minorities are not compromised.

While a collaborative and consultative approach may need a protracted period to achieve outcomes — counter-intuitive to Singapore's emphasis on efficiency, consistency and results — it helps to foster greater understanding and consensus for policies. At the same time, citizens who are actively engaged in the process also gained a stronger sense of ownership of the process, increasing the potential for consensus and positive outcomes.

The Singapore Environment Council (SEC)'s ENVision exercise in 2014 was one such example. SEC organised 19 dialogue sessions over a three-month period, involving 440 participants to gather feedback from the ground on Singapore's environmental future. The process demonstrated the active involvement of our civil society, by lending a balanced and neutral voice to articulate people's aspirations and hopes for the environmental development of Singapore. The Singapore Compact for CSR worked with various corporate stakeholders and NEA to develop an online resource portal, helping practitioners and corporations to develop their CSR programmes and operate in a socially responsible manner. Another example was the Clean and Green Hackathon (see Box Story 11) organised by NEA, to get interested individuals to leverage software applications to solve environmental challenges and work on new

Box Story 10: Call for Ideas Fund

The Call for Ideas Fund by NEA was launched in November 2012 as an outcome-based grant to encourage innovative projects from the community to address environmental challenges. The Fund was created to support the shift towards a more proactive, open mode of community engagement and encourage greater co-creation of solutions with the community. Co-funded projects must fulfil the objectives of strengthening environmental ownership in the community, or enhancing NEA's operational service delivery. Some of the projects supported by the Fund include the following:

Save That Pen

Save That Pen is a project by a group of students from the National University of Singapore. The project collects donated pens and refills and redistributes them to underprivileged students locally and in the region. Collection bins were placed around various tertiary institutions and the NTUC Centre for people to make pen donations. The group has since collected more than 32,000 pens, of which 4,000 pens have already been distributed to needy students.

The founders have expanded the project to various schools, benefitting more needy students and conserving resources at the same time.

Ms. Kah Jie Hui, the Project Co-Director remarked: "The Call for Ideas Fund is a great platform that helps interest groups like Save That Pen to realise our ideas and contribute to the cause that we believe in. We are thankful for this opportunity, and look forward to more youth environment projects."

Panasonic E-Waste Recycling Project

The Heartland E-Waste Recycling is an initiative by Panasonic Asia Pacific to inculcate greater awareness on recycling electronic waste. In exchange for the recyclables collected, Panasonic donated energy efficient light bulbs to needy households to promote more efficient use of energy.

In collaboration with public waste collectors — Cimelia and SembWaste — they set up an additional 10 recycling points in schools and locations across Mountbatten and Marine Parade constituencies to make it more convenient for residents to recycle their electronic waste. The town councils also helped to collect and store bulky electronic waste items before collection by the waste companies.

Within 6 months of the project, a total of 10,204 kg of e-waste was collected and 2,719 energy-efficient light bulbs were donated to the needy households in the South East district.

Box Story 11: Clean and Green Hackathon

The Clean and Green Hackathon is the first-ever public agency-led hackathon organised by the NEA. It provides a platform for the 3P (People, Public and Private) sectors to come together to collaborate and co-create solutions for the environment. Through this initiative, NEA is able to tap on the strengths of each of the 3P sectors to generate solutions.

The community and civil society contribute through their creativity and participation; the government plays the role of facilitating the ideation process and supplying the relevant information and necessary datasets; and the corporate sector provides the technology and technical expertise. Such active involvement across the different segments of society in generating solutions will help to ensure that the municipal services provided by the government correspond with the needs and expectations of the community. This, in turn would lead to a deepening of understanding between citizens and the government.

Other than enabling the community to work with different stakeholder groups on solutions to address environmental issues, the Clean and Green Hackathon also serves as a channel for the community to surface their ideas and suggestions to the government. Through the process of active community participation in co-creating solutions, we are able to forge better mutual understanding and bring the engagement between citizens and the government to a much deeper level.

The Clean and Green Hackathon was also well-received by the participants. As Mr. Niko Tan, a participant of the 2nd Clean & Green Hackathon, in his interview with Challenge Magazine (May/June 2014) summed up: "The government is not as distant as before. After the hackathon, we managed to reach many public officers and developed our idea further. I now see the government more as a partner that offers citizens the opportunity to make a difference and create something for the community through hackathons."

---

collaborative ideas. These Hackathons are also useful for NEA to partner other public agencies and reach out to the information and communication technologies community for more innovative solutions.

Conclusion

Environmental issues are multidisciplinary in nature, and the government is not the sole stakeholder in ensuring a good living environment for all; it is an issue where all Singaporeans must do their part. The primary objective of encouraging the community to develop a personal stake in the environment has remained steadfast, even with each changing era. But as society evolves, there is a need to recalibrate the approach at which community engagement is implemented, leveraging available resources and identifying ways to collaborate with active community groups and civil society.

Community engagement extends beyond passive education or creating platforms which encourages greater public participation; it is also about building relationships and trust with the people. The process may be challenging and it could be protracted at times, but public agencies have to persevere and take conscious steps at fostering a culture of inclusiveness and enabling better mutual understanding between the community and government.

In this regard, the NEA will continue to harness local knowledge of the community and interest groups to co-create solutions, as well as support advocates and volunteers to galvanise Singaporeans to protect our clean and green environment. The values we embody will always guide us in doing the right thing. Ultimately, it is about the vision we have set for ourselves and for our future generations.

Acknowledgements

I would wish to acknowledge the contribution by the following officers from the National Environment Agency: Mr. Khoo Seow Poh, Deputy CEO, Mr. Tan Wee Hock, Divisional Director (3P Network Division), Ms. Paula Kesavan, Deputy Director (3P Network Division), Mr. Ng Chee Yong, Assistant Director (3P Network Division) and Ms. Jasmine Chen, Senior Executive (3P Network Division).

References

Building and Construction Authority (BCA). (2014, September 1), New BCA Incentive to Drive Green Building Retrofits and Practices under 3rd Green Building Masterplan. Retrieved 10 February 2015 from http://www.bca.gov.sg/Newsroom/pr01092014_3GBM.html.

Building and Construction Authority, Singapore (BCA). (2010). *BCA Green Mark: Certification Standard for New Buildings*, GM Version 3.0. Retrieved 10 February 2015 from http://bca.gov.sg/EnvSusLegislation/others/GM_Certification_Std.pdf.

Department of Statistics, Singapore (2014a), Singapore: Population trends. Retrieved 17 February 2015 from http://www.singstat.gov.sg/docs/default-source/default-document-library/publications/publications_and_papers/reference/sif2014.pdf.

Department of Statistics, Singapore (2014b), Time Series on Per Capita GDP at Current Market Prices. Retrieved 17 February 2015 from http://www.singstat.gov.sg/statistics/browse-by-theme/national-accounts.

Goh, C. T. (1990). *Speech by Mr Goh Chok Tong. First Deputy Prime, Minister And Minister For Defence, at the City East District Awards Presentation Ceremony, At NTUC Pasir Ris Resort, 1 Pasir Ris, Monday, 7 May 1990 At 7.30 pm: Participatory Democracy.* Available from the

National Archives of Singapore. Retrieved 17 February 2015 from http://www.nas.gov. sg/archivesonline/data/pdfdoc/gct19900507.pdf.

Infographics.sg. (2013, June 7). Social Media Usage Statistics in Singapore, Digital Static Infographic. Retrieved 9 February 2014 from http://infographics.sg/?portfolio=social-media-usage-statistics-for-singapore-static-infographic.

Ministry of the Environment, Singapore. (1974). *The Ministry of the Environment Annual Report 1973*. Singapore: Author.

Ministry of the Environment and Water Resources, Singapore (MEWR). (2006), *The Singapore Green Plan 2012: 2006 Edition*. Singapore: Author. Retrieved 9 February 2015 from https://www.cbd.int/doc/world/sg/sg-nbsap-v2-en.pdf.

National Research Foundation, Singapore (NRF). (2015), Environmental and Water Technologies: Call for Proposals. Retrieved 10 February 2015 from https://rita.nrf.gov. sg/ewi/default.aspx.

Singapore Environment Institute (SEI), National Environment Agency. (n.d.), Complete List of All SEI Professional Programmes. Retrieved 10 February 2015 from http://sei.nea.gov. sg/Courses_all.html.

Tay, E. (2012). 2012 Guide to Singapore Government Funding and Incentives for the Environment, Green Future Solutions. Retrieved 10 February 2015 from http://www. greenfuture.sg/2012/05/30/2012-guide-to-singapore-government-funding-and-incentives-for-the-environment.

CHAPTER 10

Island in the World: Singapore's Environment and the International Dimensions

Simon Tay and Cheong Poh Kwan
Chairman, and Assistant Director
Singapore Institute of International Affairs

Introduction: Island in the World

By many measures, Singapore enjoys a good environmental record. From the Republic's very start, it aimed to be a "clean and green" city and the government gave attention to environmental protection. The first pollution control unit reported directly to the Prime Minister's office and the Ministry for the Environment was established back in 1972, when few other governments in the world thought the issue was worthy of a full ministry. Even as the economy boomed and the city grew, Singapore has managed its urban environment and pollution control credibly. We can and should hope that the next 50 years match and even surpass this achievement.

One critical area for Singapore is, however, the external environment. What happens regionally and globally matters greatly to Singapore and yet there is only so much that this small country can do to influence the outcomes. This is true for the economy and in matters of politics and society. In these past decades, money, people and ideas have flowed across borders more easily and in greater volume with globalisation. So it is with environmental concerns.

Singapore is an island in the world, but not isolated from global events. We are living on an island but cannot and must not be insular people.

In this essay, we wish to explore three issues that relate to the regional and international dimensions of Singapore's environment. They are (1) the regional haze from fires in Indonesia; (2) global climate change; and (3) our global ecological footprint in consumption, trade and finance. While each is a distinct issue, these three topics also interlink and this essay will explore the linkages that could be made between them, in both positive and negative ways.

In discussing the above topics, we shall limit descriptions of the present situation in the interests of length, but try to suggest the emerging trends and how Singapore might respond in the medium and longer term future. We will then conclude with some observations and suggestions about Singapore's role in the region and the international community on environmental issues and sustainability.

In summary, our main points in this essay are as follows:

1. **Transboundary Haze**: This is a major and indeed key problem that confronts not only Singapore but also for the region and the world. Yet, after almost two decades since we experienced one of the worst haze episodes in 1997–1998, the noxious fumes continue to billow — largely from Sumatra and Kalimantan of Indonesia. But, efforts have been made and progress can be discerned. The possibilities for a solution have increased recently. In large part, this is because the initial approach of blame assignment among neighbouring governments and societies has shifted towards policies of engagement and cooperation (Tay, 2008). To progress further, Singapore will need to deepen that engagement not only with the new Indonesian government of President Joko Widodo, but also with the private sector and non-governmental organisations (NGOs). Steps in this direction should be firmly pursued.

2. **Climate Change**: While initially reluctant to engage in this global issue, Singapore has increasingly come to recognise the heavy and perhaps existential costs of inaction. It has therefore taken a more active role, not only in international negotiations for a 2015 accord on climate change, but also in preparing and rallying different sectors of the economy and society to respond to climate change. Given the global and interdependent nature of the challenge, more ambitious steps must await an agreement among the world's major countries. Still, Singapore has pledged to reduce its Emissions Intensity (amount of greenhouse gases emitted per dollar GDP) by 36% from 2005 levels by 2030. It also aims to stabilise its emissions by around 2030 (NCCS, 2015).

3. **Ecological Footprint and Green Global Cities**: Although Singapore has been successful in greening itself, and in driving its economic growth, criticisms have arisen about Singapore's ecological footprint (WWF, 2014). Given our high Gross Domestic Product (GDP) and other factors, this is consistent with patterns of industrial development, urbanisation and increased consumption observed in other countries and, especially, cities. However, through trade and finance, Singapore can also be a positive regional and global influence on patterns and systems of production and consumption. With this, together with a better management of our own consumption, Singapore can up its sustainability bar. This closely ties to another opportunity for Singapore in a regional and global context. With rapid urbanisation across Asia, many in the region have looked up to Singapore as one example of a well-managed city, in terms of economy, infrastructure, housing and other dimensions. Singapore can further serve as an example of how a global city can be greened.

In total, what we describe can be seen as a newly emerging approach for Singapore in dealing with the regional and international dimensions of environmental problems. In the early decades of its independence, Singapore focussed on its domestic environment. But moving ahead in the 21st century, the city-island-state is ever more vividly aware of its interdependence with the region and the world — in economic, environmental and moral dimensions.

Recognising this interdependence, there has been a sea change in its approach from a relatively self-focussed one to a more outward looking one. Singapore has been more proactive in engaging other countries over environmental concerns, but it has to go beyond foreign policies and diplomacy. There is also room and need for the engagement of the private sector in the economic activities of trade, investment and finance, as well as citizens and environmental NGOs in relation to their consumption habits and advocacy work, respectively.

The emerging policy environment will be considerably more complicated. It requires more cooperation between sovereign states. The Singapore government also has to engage more deeply with non-state actors. But these are the necessary approaches needed to deal with the current and emerging global and regional environmental challenges, and we believe such engagement across sectors and governments will only bode well for Singapore's future.

The Haze: From Blame to Engagement to Cooperation

The haze is a recurring environmental and public health disaster not only for Indonesia, where the major fires burn, but also for Singapore, Malaysia, Brunei and other neighbouring states in Southeast Asia. Its impact also transcends our region: the release of vast amount of climate-warming greenhouse gases and the loss of forests, peatlands and biodiversity make this a truly global concern (Wibowo, 2013).

The issue first gained international attention during the fires of 1997–1998, when the United Nations Environment Programme (UNEP) declared it a "global disaster" (Choong and Kwok, 1998). Our region was then shrouded in haze for half a year, when El Nino wreaked havoc and prolonged the fires in Sumatra and Kalimantan. There was anger at the time, and there continue to be grumbles whenever the haze recurs. This is expressed perhaps most strongly by Singapore, but is equally felt by others in Malaysia and Brunei who have to brave the haze over the years.

The proximate causes are clear: the haze stems from the use of fire to clear land for plantations, mainly in the Indonesian provinces of Riau, Jambi and West Kalimantan, by large companies as well as small-scale farmers. Modern satellite technology has helped zoom in on the sources of the fires (Sizer, 2013).

Considerable efforts have been made or planned, but the haze is a complex problem and its solutions remain elusive. In Indonesia, the issue of capacity gap is evident: too many permits covering too vast an area of land have been issued that the local firefighting and enforcement capacities could barely keep pace. Furthermore, many plantations also manage to stay off the radar. Take Riau for example. It is estimated that half of the four million ha of oil palm estates in the province are being run without official permits (Anggoro, 2014).

There is also the problem of ambiguous property rights. It is not uncommon for forest conversion permits to be granted within the boundaries of existing concessions or customary forests (Gill and Tan, 2013), creating multiple owners for the same plot of land and making it possible for them to deflect responsibility when fires break out in their concessions. Above all, plantation owners are emboldened by lax enforcement, rare conviction and lenient sentences, although more arrests have been made since the 2013 severe haze spell, leading to the jailing of one plantation manager so far (Widhiarto, 2014).

Given that Indonesian provinces have been the primary location of the fires and the haze, national and local actions are essential. Absent these, there was considerable finger-pointing at Indonesia not only for its policies and lack of capacity, but also on questions of corruption and complicity.

Understandably, among some sections of the Indonesian political elite came the reverse: the assertion of nationalism and the country's rights to develop its natural resources. There was also finger-pointing in the other direction with the recurring accusation that Malaysian and Singapore-based companies and investors were complicit in the fires. One Indonesian government spokesperson even suggested that rather than "making noise" over "one week of smoke", Singapore and the region should be grateful for the oxygen supply from Indonesian forests (Au Yong, 2010).[1]

While such statements and back-and-forth accusations attracted headlines, this approach of "blame" did not augur well for progress on the issue. We therefore note the efforts within the framework of the regional bloc ASEAN (Association of Southeast Asian Nations) that has tried to move from "blame" to "engagement". Although some of those sentiments of blame among the various countries and governments do resurface when the haze occurs, the ASEAN effort has been to make "engagement" the primary approach in addressing the haze.

For more than a decade, ASEAN has taken a step-by-step approach to foster engagement among the countries most affected by the haze. This proceeded from the Regional Haze Action Plan to regular meetings among ASEAN's environment ministers, as a group of 10 and more frequently, as a group of five involving the most

---

[1] More recently, Indonesian Vice-President Jusuf Kalla also chided Malaysia for overreacting about the haze (Tay and Cheong, 2015).

affected countries — Indonesia, Brunei, Malaysia, Singapore and Thailand.[2] A Haze Task Force has been set up and there have also been open forums to discuss the haze issue candidly. More bilateral and ground-up efforts have resulted. Malaysia helped with air quality monitoring and peatland restoration in the Indonesian province of Riau (ASEAN Secretariat, 2014), while Singapore helped run a wide-ranging fire prevention programme in the province of Jambi, including the introduction of fish farming as a form of alternative livelihood for local farmers (Gill and Tan, 2013). All these were carried out with the approval of the central authorities in Jakarta.

These efforts are notable as they have demonstrated a regularity and candour that go beyond most ASEAN diplomacy, whether on environmental or other issues. Regular meetings and negotiations among officials also subsequently yielded the ASEAN Agreement on Transboundary Haze, a formal and legally binding treaty ("Haze Treaty"). Such treaties are rare in ASEAN, where (as often among neighbours) informal declarations and plans of action have been the norm.

But engagement has its limits. Even after the Haze Treaty was inked in 2002, new doubts emerged of Indonesia's will and intention to abide by its terms and increase efforts to stop the haze. This was because Indonesia until 2014 had declined to ratify the treaty, thereby accepting the legal obligations contained. The Indonesian Parliament objected as some of its members felt that the Haze Treaty imposed considerable obligations on the country to address the haze issue, but without a reciprocal recognition of Indonesia's own transboundary environmental concerns, such as illegal logging, fishing and the movement of potentially hazardous materials (Loh, 2008).

For almost a decade, the Indonesian President at that time, Susilo Bambang Yudhoyono, did not muster the Parliamentary support to overcome this opposition to the Haze Treaty. His administration did however take a number of steps that assisted the fight against the haze. These included: (1) a moratorium on granting new plantation and logging concessions in primary forests and peatlands; and (2) moving forward to help create and participate in the climate change-related regime for the Reducing Emissions from Deforestation and Forest Degradation (REDD) (Bland, 2013). President SBY (as he is known) pledged to reduce the haze even if he cannot stop it entirely, and for a number of years — largely up to 2009, this was the case.

In this period, the haze that affected Singapore often took place just over a few days or perhaps a week, usually in the dry season, culminating in September and October. The concentration of pollutants was relatively low. In many years, Singapore experienced only moderate levels of haze. The Pollutant Standards Index (PSI)

---

[2] Southern Thailand is occasionally affected by the haze from Indonesia and Thai government officials have been present at the meetings, although not as consistently or as deeply involved as other countries. Of late, Thailand has also reported a similar but separate phenomena of "Northern" haze, from fires in its own territory as well as its Indo-Chinese neighbours.

breached the unhealthy 100 mark several times in 2006, but the scale of the pollution did not reach anything like the 1997–1998 episode.

This changed however in 2013, when Singapore suffered the most intense episode of haze: passing the hazardous mark of 300 and reaching 401 on June 21 ("PSI hits new all-time high", 2013). On top of this extreme incident, the overall duration and severity of the haze in 2013 and 2014 went far beyond the bounds of the preceding years. For instance, in 2014, thermal hotspot counts in Sumatra, Borneo and West Malaysia surged even in January, which is usually outside of the season (Meteorological Service Singapore, 2014). In 2013 and especially 2014, the consensus is that the haze in Singapore could have been worst if not for the onset of wetter conditions and rain. This is humbling, given the many years of engagement efforts between the neighbouring states.

This has served as a wake-up call. The 2013–2014 episodes of haze changed the mindset that the problem was contained and limited. They awakened Singapore and the region to the recognition about their underlying causes: the ongoing practice of slash-and-burn, the problem with Indonesia's land use policy, weak enforcement and others. With plans in Indonesia and also East Malaysia for continued expansion of their plantation and forestry concessions, many of which involve the conversion of fire-prone peatlands (Davidson, 2014), there is every risk that the transboundary pollution would not abate but rather intensify in the years to come.

This period has of course witnessed statements of recrimination and blame, as must be expected given the severity of the haze episodes. But on the whole, building on the past decades of engagement, there have been steps forward. This was helped considerably by the fact that the 2013–2014 fires have very clearly impacted the Indonesian provinces themselves, with airports and schools shut at the worst of the haze. A state of emergency was declared by then Indonesian president SBY (Hussain, 2014). Military troops were tasked to assist in fire suppression — even if these efforts came a little too late.

There is, within Indonesia, a growing recognition that the haze is first and foremost a problem that inflicts its worst impacts on Indonesians. From this, we believe that a new commitment to work alongside other countries can emerge, so that from the "engagement" efforts can emerge a new era where "cooperation" can become the dominant mode between countries.

Several developments in 2014 also gave us reasons to be optimistic.

First, Singapore has passed the Transboundary Haze Pollution Act ("Haze Law"), designed to punish agriculture and forestry players that contribute to haze in Singapore as a result of them practising or condoning slash-and-burn (AGC, 2014). Under the new law, errant parties can be hauled into a Singapore court even if the offence is committed outside our borders. Many hailed Singapore for taking a "bold" step forward (Shen, 2014), given the long-established pro-business climate and deep-seated respect for non-interference among ASEAN members.

The Haze Law has yet to be tested since it came into effect on September 25, 2014. There have since been a few episodes in which the 3-hour PSI slipped into the unhealthy range (101–200), but it did not stay above 100 for a continuous 24 hours or longer — the threshold required to apply the law (NEA, n.d.). This criterion, coupled with the foreseeable challenge in gathering evidence and assembling witnesses in a foreign country, have raised doubts over the Haze Law's enforceability.

But its deterrent effect is clear. This has less to do with the monetary fine, which can amount to S$2 million if an entity causes haze for a continuous period of 20 days or more (AGC, 2014). The sum may appear punitive, but it in fact represents less than 1% of the average net profits for seven key agroforestry firms in 2013 (Chua and Cheong, 2014). However, companies are not taking the law lightly, for any legal charges against them could inflict reputational harm and hurt their stock prices and access to bank loans. Banks and major investors here have also sat up and taken notice. At the Second Singapore Dialogue on Sustainable World Resources, a multi-stakeholder forum organised by the Singapore Institute of International Affairs (SIIA), Minister for the Environment and Water Resources Dr. Vivian Balakrishnan made an appeal to banks and investors, which have significant influence on the corporate behaviours, "to do a hygiene check" and "be responsible and ethical in their investments or loans" (MEWR, 2015). Moving forward, we can expect more financial institutions to be assessing the environmental and social impact of the businesses they plan to finance much more carefully. They would not want to risk bad press and public backlash (Chong and Chen, 2014).

A second reason for optimism is Indonesia's ratification of the ASEAN Agreement on Transboundary Haze. Twelve years after the agreement was first signed, the last batch of Indonesian lawmakers moved to ratify it in September before parliament was dissolved (Siswo, 2014). This came on the heels of firmer actions against slash-and-burn culprits, whose conduct has been described as a "crime against humanity" by former president Susilo Bambang Yudhoyono (Soeriaatmadja, 2014).

The ratification would likely pave way for closer cooperation among ASEAN member states in the years ahead. Joint action programmes such as the 2007 Singapore–Jambi collaboration is one example. This programme could be reviewed and revived in haze-afflicted areas in Indonesia. Singapore had previously offered to introduce the S$1 million project to more provinces in Indonesia, but its suggestion was turned down (Au Yong, 2010). However, there are reasons to believe that Indonesia is likely to be more receptive towards such partnerships following the ratification.

This is predicated on our third and perhaps most reassuring point: the clear priority and resolve that Indonesian President, Joko Widodo (or "Jokowi") has shown on the issue.

Early in his term, President Jokowi went to Riau for "blusukan asap" soon after a resident there filed an online petition against a controversial concession holder.[3] During his visit, President Jokowi made clear his position on several points of concern, including the management of peatlands and peat fires, the source of up to 90% of transboundary haze (Global Environment Center, 2010). He endorsed that peatlands, regardless of depth, should be protected as they constitute a special ecosystem. The President also warned companies that have converted peatlands to monoculture plantations that their licences might be revoked if they are found to have caused damage to the ecosystem. Finally, he also prioritised the allocation of arable land to small-scale farmers, instead of big corporations (Laia, 2014).

These are encouraging signs that point to the new president's readiness to prioritise environmental protection for the sake of people's welfare. He also told the Singapore press soon after inauguration that holding the errant parties accountable is a matter of political will (Ibrahim and Hussain, 2014), hinting that he will not tolerate excuses for weak enforcement. The President's efforts in this area are moreover, first and foremost motivated by his pledge to do what is best for the benefit of his own people. There were some anxieties after President Jokowi announced the merger of the Environment and Forestry ministries under his term (Murdiyarso, 2014). Observers feared that environmental protection would play second fiddle to resource development, as the environment team was far outnumbered by the forestry team. But the concerns should have largely been eased following his visit to Riau. The new Minister of Environment and Forestry, Dr. Siti Nurbaya, has also won praise for her frequent consultations with both the private sector and civil society. She is closely monitoring lawsuits brought against forest-burning suspects, and has personally challenged the verdict when a court dismissed charges against a firm in Riau's Meranti Islands regency (Jong, 2015).

A fourth reason to believe that progress on the haze is possible going forward is the advancement of satellite technologies. It is now possible to show what is happening on the ground at near-real time basis. The availability of online monitoring platforms such as the Global Forest Watch-Fires, developed by US-headquartered think tank World Resources Institute (WRI) (WRI, 2014b), would make it much harder for unsustainable land clearing practices to go unnoticed and unpunished. Such methods have had success elsewhere; Brazil, for example.[4] Increasingly, camera-equipped

---

[3] "Blusukan", or an impromptu visit, was Jokowi's trademark activity during his term as the governor of Jakarta and throughout his presidential campaign in 2014. "Asap" refers to the haze or smoke in Bahasa Indonesia. See Laia (2014).

[4] Brazil managed to cut deforestation by 70% in the last decade after the introduction of DETER, a forest cover loss monitoring platform developed and launched by the Brazilian Space Agency in 2005. The authorities have been able to better enforce forest laws with the near real-time feeds on where illegal clearing activities are taking place. See Butler (2014). See also, Busch and Ferretti-Gallon (2014).

drones, or unmanned aerial vehicles, are also used in the private sector for plantation mapping and fire monitoring.

In ASEAN, the Singapore government has for many years been using similar satellite technology to help monitor the situation. This has since 1998 been shared with the Indonesian government. However, the information has not been widely distributed among the different ministries and officials, let alone with the public.

Since the 2013 haze spell, there have since been increasing calls from the Singapore government as well as regional and international NGOs for the release of official concession maps to show which plots of land have been allocated to which corporations. Indonesia and Malaysia, however, have yet to agree. This is one reason why the ASEAN joint haze monitoring system (HMS) has failed to take off, although ASEAN leaders have in principle endorsed it in late 2013.

Satellite data and concession maps, when reliably available and accurately over-laid in a digital platform, could help flush out fire starters at the corporate level. Such effort should therefore be collectively pursued in ASEAN, both at the governmental and non-governmental levels; although we should always take pains to verify the information against ground observation and eyewitness accounts.

The data used in existing fire monitoring platforms are not perfect. Thermal hotspots are not always accurate indicators of ground fires. On the other hand, peat-land fires, which lead to many haze episodes, may not be detected by satellites at all if they smoulder underground. Official concession maps from Indonesia and Malaysia remain out of reach, as both countries cited sovereignty and legal concerns. Even official maps can be subjected to dispute, especially in the case of Indonesia, where governments at the federal, provincial and regency levels are known to have different interpretations of concession boundaries.

Concession maps currently used on WRI's Global Forest Watch-Fires plat-form come mainly from the Indonesian Ministry of Forestry, when such data were still publicly downloadable before the severe haze spell of 2013. Some industry players have said that these maps, dated 2010, are outdated. WRI is also reviewing a new set of maps submitted to the Roundtable on Sustainable Palm Oil (RSPO) (WRI, 2014a), a multi-stakeholder certification body. RSPO has made it manda-tory for its grower members to submit concession maps for their plantations by September 2014 (Roundtable on Sustainable Palm Oil, 2014). This rule, however, does not apply to non-members and members which are registered as processors and traders. Hence, when published, this set of new maps is still likely to be far from complete, although they should still go a long way in keeping companies on their toes.

This brings us to the fifth reason for optimism: major agribusiness players are showing more sustainability commitment than ever before. In the span of less than a year, major palm oil producers and traders such as Wilmar, Golden-Agri Resources,

Cargill and Bunge have sworn off unsustainable practices in their plantations or their suppliers' (Chain Reaction Research, 2014). More consumer goods companies have also pledged to remove unsustainably-harvested products from their supply chains, largely due to NGO campaigns and mounting public pressure (Aubrey, 2014).

Singapore is well placed to ride the momentum and make more companies adopt greener practices. It is home to over 700 financial institutions (MAS, 2014). It has a 20% share of global agri-commodities trade, and is the world's largest rubber trading hub (IE Singapore, 2014a). Much of the region's supply of palm oil and pulp and paper are traded through Singapore. A number of major resource companies are headquartered here and listed on the Singapore Exchange. These companies often avail themselves to the financial services and loans from Singapore-based banks. A number of them have also raised capital through bond issuance in the Singapore market. As such, much can be done in Singapore to stop the haze even if the fires are started elsewhere. For this, it must slowly and surely move towards integrating environmental concerns into its policies and regulations for trade, investment and finance.

The Transboundary Haze Pollution Act mentioned earlier, is a key step. This legislates sanctions not only against those directly involved in slash-and-burn but also entities that "condone" such actions. The term, while not precisely defined in the Act, could be interpreted as those who trade with, invest in or lend to entities that cause the haze. This can therefore pressure banks, traders and buyers to take steps to ensure that those they deal with have a fire and haze-free policy. Besides, the government could also consider setting the bar higher for new applicants to the Global Trader Programme, an IE Singapore's initiative aimed at drawing global trading houses here with tax incentives. "Green conditionalities" and sustainability achievements should be factored in.

These are therefore five reasons to look forward with some degree of optimism that, after more than a decade of blame and engagement, it will be possible to foster a deeper cooperation that can finally bring an end to the haze.

Yet, although we have reasons for a positive outlook, there is contrary evidence. Take for example, a recent study by the Centre for International Forestry Research (CIFOR). The non-profit research group predicted that our region will experience severe bouts of haze more frequently due to continuing deforestation and extensive drainage of peatlands for agriculture (Neo, 2014). In Riau, for example, fires in 2013 were mostly short-lived. But in the span of a week, they generated an amount of greenhouses gases that is equivalent to the emissions from 50 million cars in a year. The disproportionately huge amount largely came from fires that rage on newly deforested peatlands.

The Malaysian state of Sarawak can potentially be another hotbed of peat fires. The state government is pursuing an ambitious roadmap to turn much of the state's peatlands into commercial plantations, as part of its poverty eradication programme and revenue generating model. Sarawak has cleared a third of its peatlands between 2005 and 2010 (Chain Reaction Research, 2014), and is aiming to double its oil palm estates to two million ha by 2020 (Teoh, 2011). While the state government is concurrently running a Tropical Peat Research Laboratory to find ways to improve peatland management, some academics and activists in the field remain doubtful about its environmental commitment.

We should note that peatlands are difficult to manage, and peat fires difficult to suppress. After peatlands are drained, the dry and carbon rich soil will become extremely fire prone. In the absence of rain, fires that spread on peatlands can smoulder underground for a long time, releasing a huge amount of acrid smoke due to incomplete combustion. Even if there is no burning, the vast tracts of drained and abandoned peatlands in ASEAN are already a significant source of carbon emission. The loss of water from the upper layers of peatlands will result in oxidation, which then leads to an increase in the emission of carbon dioxide, adding to the threat of climate change (Lo and Parish, 2013).

This understanding is important as it creates an opportunity for us to find synergy between regional efforts to combat haze and the global drive to slow climate change. Once forested peatland is cleared and its hydrology altered, it releases more carbon dioxide than it absorbs, and even more so if there is fire that leads to dense smoke. Leaving as much of the natural ecosystem intact is the best way to safeguard citizens in the region from transboundary haze and other potential impacts of climate change.

Climate change negotiations within the United Nations have outlined a programme called Reducing Emissions from Deforestation and Land Degradation (REDD) that may be able to address this issue. Under the scheme, developed countries can pay developing countries to preserve their forested lands and thereby their carbon stock (UN-REDD Programme, 2009). This will hopefully help reduce the overall carbon emission and slow down the rate of climate change.

Indonesia was an early advocate for this programme and has received in principle approval of up to US$1 billion from Norway. While REDD remains to be developed, and Indonesia has yet to fulfil the criteria for effective implementation and verification, this approach holds promise for future cooperation. It could also help spur a review of Indonesia's land and forest policies, and encourage it to move towards increasing conservation and better management.

Linking the haze to climate change can therefore help both efforts to end the haze and to curb climate change emissions. This is an approach that Singapore should encourage and support.

Climate Change: From Caution to Growing Commitment

In the last years, the international consensus has gained considerable momentum in the global community. While naysayers remain, the Intergovernmental Panel on Climate Change (IPCC) has helped generate recognition among governments and many more citizens around the world that human activity is causing changes to the global climate, especially through the emissions of greenhouse gases. Concentrations of carbon dioxide, methane and nitrous oxide are now at their highest in at least the last 800,000 years, according to the IPCC in its 2014 Synthesis Report (IPCC Secretariat, 2014).

Latest figures from the United Nations World Meteorological Organisation (WMO) show that, since the 21st century began, we have witnessed 14 of the 15 warmest years on record (Shukman, 2014). The continued warming of our planet could lead to catastrophic events from extreme droughts to severe floods, water stress, food scarcity and many others. These and are other possible impacts of climate change would be global, and Singapore will not be immune to the consequences.

Already, there is evidence that Singapore is experiencing the effects. Our annual mean surface temperature has increased by about 0.8°C since 1948, according to the National Climate Change Secretariat (NCCS). The mean sea level in the Straits of Singapore has risen by about 3 mm per year over the past 15 years (NCCS, 2014). This is of utmost concern to Singapore given that one-third of our island lies less than 5 m above the mean sea level.

Singapore also experienced its longest dry spell on record in January and February 2014 (Ee, 2014b). This brought climate change into everyday experience for everyday Singaporeans through the brown, brittle grass in tropical Singapore, the hundreds of fish found dead in the river flowing through Bishan-Ang Mo Kio Park (Ee, 2014a). A further 160 tonnes of fish at several offshore farms also could not survive the unusually low levels of dissolved oxygen as a result of the dry spell (Lee, 2014).

As some states in nearby Malaysia declared states of emergency, the dry conditions brought home the possible impacts on water and food security.[5] Since Singapore imports more than 90% of our food, we are particularly vulnerable to fluctuations in global food supply and therefore, food prices. Further, a warmer Singapore could also lead to the faster spread of vector-borne diseases, such as dengue (NCCS, 2014).

Yet, as awareness and concerns grow about the impacts of climate change, the question for Singapore has always been what we can do about it. Our country

---

[5] Negeri Sembilan of Malaysia declared a state of crisis while Selangor started water rationing. Singapore's Public Utilities Board (PUB) had to increase the supply of recycled and desalinated water as water levels in reservoirs plunged. See Reuters (2014).

accounts for less than 0.2% of global emissions (NCCS, 2013). As such, even if Singapore was to take the strongest measures to reduce our emissions, this would not have any impact. Only action taken in concert with the rest of the international community would be sufficient. However, the world's largest economies and emitters such as China and the United States have for a long time not moved on the issue. Indeed, for the US, the previous Bush administration was a noted climate sceptic.

Given the mixed international attitudes to climate change, Singapore was initially cautious about climate change, rather than being an active champion for carbon emission cuts (Hamilton-Hart, 2006). The government signed the United Nations Framework Convention on Climate Change (UNFCCC) in 1992 and ratified it in 1997 to support the overarching goal of stabilising atmospheric concentrations of greenhouses gases. As the UNFCCC developed the Kyoto Protocol, Singapore's caution against committing ourselves to carbon emission cuts continued.

Not without sound reason. Under the UNFCCC, the international community recognised the principle of "common but differentiated responsibilities" (UNFCCC, n.). This was taken to mean that developed countries should take the lead in preventing climate change by committing themselves to emission caps whereas developing countries were not obliged to observe emission goals. This continued and was entrenched as a fundamental element in the Kyoto Protocol of 1997, with only the 37 developed countries named in Annex 1 having to cut their emissions.

As Singapore was not classified as a developed country, it followed that the country assumed no obligation to set emission targets. The caution of Singapore showed also in that, despite this, the country did not accede to the Kyoto Protocol of the UNFCCC until 2006. This has attracted some criticisms. But, Singapore is not the only high-income country to have shied away from Kyoto Protocol. The US under President George W. Bush declined to ratify the Kyoto Protocol (Sanger, 2001). South Korea, a G20 (Group of 20) and OECD (Organisation for Economic Co-operation and Development) economy, was also not included in Annex 1.

Some governments, like Bush's America, expressed doubts about climate change and denied the growing scientific evidence. This was not Singapore's position. Rather, Singapore's caution was measured in terms of what it could do about reducing its emissions while continuing to generate sufficient energy and continue growth given our export-driven economy.

Ahead of the 15th United Nations Climate Change Conference (COP15) in 2009, the then Senior Minister for the government Professor S. Jayakumar explained Singapore's position and the constraints faced. He described Singapore as an "alternative energy-disadvantaged country" (NCCS, 2009), with low wind speed and little hydro, tidal and geothermal power to exploit. Nuclear energy remains a risky venture. Consequently, Singapore needs to rely on oil and gas for most of its energy needs, making emission cuts a difficult goal.

Even then, the government recognised solar energy as the most viable option for Singapore, and committed to a cluster of research facilities in this sector. Moreover, Singapore also pledged to reduce emissions by 16% below the business-as-usual (BAU) levels by 2020 if COP15 results in a legally-binding deal for all countries. That deal did not eventuate but the Singaporean pledge remains: the country will take action provided it is part of a global commitment.

Given this, the initial caution that Singapore showed on the issue of climate change has given way to concerted efforts to study and prepare for steps in the event of a global agreement post-2015. Others in Asia have taken similar steps.

South Korea, another highly urbanised and industrialised "developing country" under the UNFCCC and a non-Annex 1 country in the Kyoto Protocol, is one example. The Koreans have voluntarily set a 2020 emissions reduction target in an effort to help roll back climate change (Meeyoung, 2009). China, the world's biggest carbon polluter since 2006, also surprised many when it announced a joint commitment to curb emissions with the US in late 2014. Under the deal, China is to cap its carbon emissions and increase the share of non-fossil fuels to 20% of its energy mix — both by 2030. The US will in turn lower its emissions by 26–28% compared to the 2005 levels by 2025 (Nakamura and Mufson, 2014). As more countries, both developing and developed, recognise the need for absolute cuts in emission levels, Singapore should and will move in concert with global norms.

Without leadership from the largest countries, international action has not been possible, despite the ongoing attempts to negotiate a new climate change agreement under the auspices of the UN. But, with the newfound bilateral understanding between the US and China, and the 2015 deadline to reach an agreement, climate change negotiations are entering a new phase of urgency.

The Singapore government has been responding to these developments. At the Conference of Parties in Lima, Peru, in December 2014, Minister for Environment and Water Resources Vivian Balakrishnan outlined an approach that balances the principles of the international framework and the new initiative to accept Intended Nationally Determined Contributions (INDCs). He called on countries to recognise each other's respective and unique national circumstances provided that "we will all put forward, in good faith, our best effort". He further emphasised, "we are all in this together and there will not be any free-riders in Paris" (MEWR, 2014), which in 2015 will host the conference that aims to conclude an international agreement.

Singapore has, in this sense, shifted from caution to a conditioned participation and indeed advocate for consensus and progress on the issue. It ratified the Doha Amendment to the Kyoto Protocol, and has in July 2015 submitted its INDC to the UNFCCC — five months before COP21. Singapore is committed to reducing its Emissions Intensity (amount of greenhouse gases emitted per dollar GDP) by 36% from 2005 levels by 2030. It also aims to stabilise its greenhouse gases emissions by around 2030 — even if the economy continues to grow beyond that year (NCCS, 2015).

Domestically, Singapore has also launched the Sustainable Singapore Blueprint, which builds on earlier and quite significant steps to reduce the country's carbon footprints — some of which were taken long before climate change became a hot-button issue on the global stage. For example, vehicle growth was first capped at 3% and reduced to 1.5% since 2009; energy efficiency labelling was introduced for electronic appliances, IT equipment and buildings. Since 2001, Singapore also switched to natural gas, the cleanest form of fossil fuel, which now generates over 90% of the electricity in place of fuel oil. This has helped reduce emissions from the power sector by 25% (MEWR, 2012).

Another significant step taken by the government came in 2010 when the National Climate Change Secretariat (NCCS) was formed directly under the Prime Minister's Office. Headed by a Permanent Secretary who reports directly to the Deputy Prime Minister, this new institution is tasked to coordinate climate policy among different ministries — which is critical as climate change relates to not just environmental policies but also what a country does for investments, infrastructure and industry developments, among others.

There have also been more concerted efforts to study the impact of climate change on Singapore and the possible mitigation plans. The National Environment Agency (NEA) in 2007 commissioned the first National Climate Change Study. In 2014, a new national study on the impact of climate change on Singapore's roads, drainage systems and other infrastructure was launched. The study involves the participation of all ministries and statutory boards, and its findings will feed into Singapore's "Resilience Framework", a blueprint developed in 2012 to protect the country from climate change consequences over the next 50 to 100 years (Shah, 2014).

Various research bodies here, including the Earth Observatory of Singapore (EOS), the Institute for Catastrophe Risk Management (ICRM), and the NUS Centre for Hazards Research are also conducting their own studies on climate change (NTU, 2010). These efforts underscore the preparations that Singapore has been making to be ready for an eventual commitment to the global effort to curb climate change emissions.

But, even if the government is ready to embrace its climate obligation, the citizens will have to be better prepared for the impacts that will ripple into their everyday lives. A 2014 survey by the NCCS found that most respondents — 70% of them — are concerned about climate change, but this was down from 74% when a similar poll was done in 2011. Further, only 39% (down from 56% in 2011) think individual action matters, while 40% (up from 26% in 2011) feel the responsibility should lie with the government (Fang, 2014).

Given that energy use and carbon emissions relate to everyday activities in the household, transport and other private domains of activity, public awareness and commitment will need to be increased if Singapore is to effectively commit to limiting our carbon footprint. This ties to a broader question for Singapore in engaging on international environmental issues: our ecological footprint.

Ecological Footprint: A Greener Record Needed

Our ecological footprint per head in 2014 was ranked the 7th largest out of 152 countries, up from 12th in 2012. This ranking, compiled by the World Wide Fund for Nature (WWF) and published in its biennial Living Planet Report, also placed us on the top spot in Asia Pacific consistently (WWF Global, 2014). The environmental NGO, as it is wont to do, has painted the issue starkly: If every person in the world lives like Singaporeans, we need 4.1 planets to sustain our needs. Imported food and services, as well as our energy-intensive industries are among the key contributors to our high footprint (Philomin, 2014a).

The Singapore government has questioned WWF's methodology which, unlike the globally-accepted version endorsed by the UNFCCC, attributes the emissions embodied in imported goods to importing countries, and not exporting countries. The Ministry of Environment and Water Resources (MEWR) does not agree with this carbon accounting methodology as importing countries have "no control over the upstream manufacturing and processing of imports — hence their footprint" (Philomin, 2014b).

This methodology also allocated the emissions from bunker fuel that the Singapore port and airport supply to transiting vessels based on its share of international trade volume. This, MEWR points out, unfairly puts Singapore at a disadvantage as it "sits on a vital global shipping route and has one of the busiest transhipment ports in the world" (Philomin, 2014b). Singapore's per capita carbon footprints are therefore over-estimated, as much of them came from international travel and trade.

It has also been pointed out that the WWF ranking, based on data compiled by the Global Footprint Network (GFN),[6] would unfairly "penalise" Singapore and most other built-up cities (Cheam, 2012). In order to do well in this ranking, countries would have to "live within their means" by consuming no more than their land can produce. Using this methodology, big, sparsely populated countries which are agriculturally endowed would almost always do better than small, densely-populated city-states with little or no natural resources.

Singapore has performed better in other indexes. For instance, the International Energy Agency (IEA) puts Singapore at 113th place out of 140 countries in terms of

---

[6] Global Footprint Network (GFN) is a global think tank that provides Ecological Footprint accounting tools. It measures a country's consumption, or ecological impact, by adding imports to and subtracting exports from its national production. See more of its methodology here: http://www.footprintnetwork.org/en/index.php/GFN/page/methodology.

carbon intensity, or carbon dioxide emissions per dollar GDP (Siau, 2014). This is a reflection of an economy that is able to use its polluting energy such as coal, oil and gas rather efficiently. While Singapore's GDP grew by 76% between 2000 and 2010, its greenhouse gas emissions increased by a relatively modest 21%.

Still, this does not change the fact that Singapore's emission level is going up steadily. The issue deserves our attention as it does impinge on Singapore's record as a "green" city. After all, another international dimension of Singapore's environmental record is the degree to which it can set an example for other cities in the region. This is a vital question as Asia rises economically and, in parallel, urbanises rapidly.

Singapore's role in this in fact goes beyond simply serving as one possible role model. Singaporean companies are increasingly participating in the development, construction and provision of infrastructure, utilities and services for other cities in the region. This can be seen in the high profile Tianjin Eco-City, a pilot project endorsed by the Chinese government, and in which they have visibly sought to involve the government and government-linked companies in Singapore (IE Singapore, 2014b). There are many other instances in which Singaporean's expertise in diverse areas of urbanisation such as city planning, public housing, city "greening", water utilities and infrastructural development have been tapped.

If Singapore's record is sound, this can help other cities move towards a greener and more sustainable path. On the other hand, if the Singapore example is negative — as the WWF ranking appears to suggest, other cities that tap the Singapore experience may also be taking a less-than-ideal path.

In any case, Singapore should always aim for a better record even in the absence of any international appraisals. Reducing consumption and improving operational efficiency should be pursued for the health of our global climate. This has been recognised by the government as different agencies roll out additional efforts and ratchet upwards to higher-standards. Policies for government procurement have also increasingly focussed on this aspect. Different labelling schemes are now in place, such as the Energy Star and Green Platinum Mark (NCCS, 2012).

At the consumer level, eco-labels and other efforts have also been made to promote awareness so that market demands can respond to environmental and energy issues and not simply react to lower prices and cooler brand image. Like any consumer society, the questions remain over whether our consumers are willing to pay more for green products, or even better, buy only what they need.

Concluding Remarks

Singapore as a small island could be tempted to be insular. This is especially as its history and development have been quite different, perhaps even unique, in the region and among developing countries that came to independence in a similar period.

Singapore as part of Asia has experienced a boom in economic growth and indeed, when compared to global moderation, is still growing rapidly.

With such growth, and the attendant rise in consumption, it would be too easy to focus on the economy alone, and neglect questions of societal and ecological health. Singapore as one of the most developed cities today in Asia and the world, and a hub for trade, finance and other services, could also look more at the benefits and rights of its status as a hub city.

But these same factors — of limited size, economic development, and its hub status — have at the same time raised a different consciousness. More and more, the Singapore government, its companies and people are coming to recognise their interdependencies with the much larger world. Singapore cannot prosper alone and by itself secure its own environment against threats like haze pollution and climate change on which this chapter has focussed.

While not assuming a role as a green champion, Singapore has been shifting its policies towards wider engagement and deeper cooperation with both the regional and global communities. For the protection of its own environment, Singapore has come to recognise itself as an island that cannot be isolated, but one that must more actively engage in the global stage: an island in the world.

References

Anggoro, F. (2014, August 6). Riau's two million hectares of oil palm plantation illegal: Minister. *Antara News*. Retrieved 30 November 2014 from http://www.antaranews.com/en/news/95203/riaus-two-million-hectares-of-oil-palm-plantation-illegal-minister.

ASEAN Secretariat. (2014). *Haze Action Online: Indonesia-Malaysia Collaboration*. Retrieved 10 November 2014 from http://haze.asean.org/?page_id=238.

Attorney-General's Chambers, Singapore (AGC). (2014, September 26). *Transboundary Haze Pollution Act 2014*. Retrieved 26 September 2014 from http://statutes.agc.gov.sg/aol/search/display/view.w3p;page=0;query=CompId%3A113ccc86-73fd-48c9-8570-650a8d1b7288;rec=0.

Aubrey, A. (2014, September 18). Sweet: Dunkin' Donuts and Krispy Kreme Pump Up Pledge On Palm Oil. *NPR*. Retrieved 1 November 2014 from http://www.npr.org/blogs/thesalt/2014/09/18/349562067/sweet-dunkin-donuts-and-krispy-kreme-pump-up-pledge-on-palm-oil.

Au Yong, J. (2010, October 22). PSI Crosses 100; Govt Urges Jakarta to Act. *The Straits Times*.

Bland, B. (2013). Indonesia Extends Logging Moratorium to Protect Rainforests. *Financial Times*. Retrieved November 30, 2014, from http://www.ft.com/intl/cms/s/0/ae495afc-bd37-11e2-890a-00144feab7de.html.

Butler, R. A. (2014, June 5). *In Cutting Deforestation, Brazil Leads World in Reducing Emissions*. Retrieved November 30, 2014, from Mongabay: http://news.mongabay.com/2014/0605-brazil-emissions-reductions-amazon.html.

Busch, J., and Ferretti-Gallon, K. (2014). *Stopping Deforestation: What Works and What Doesn't.* Washington, D.C.: Centre for Global Development.

Chain Reaction Research: Sustainability Risk Analysis. (2014, October 28). *Bunge Announces Forest Conservation Policy.* Retrieved 30 November 2014 from http://chainreactionresearch. com/2014/10/28/the-chain-bunge-sarawak-and-reducing-peat-risk-in-borneo.

Cheam, J. (2012, April 5). How green is this little red dot? *Eco-Business.* Retrieved 15 December 2014 from: http://www.eco-business.com/opinion/how-green-is-this-little-red-dot.

Chong, Z. Y., and Chen, J. (2014, April 8). *Corporate Responsibility Moving up Asian Governments' Agenda: Singapore's Transboundary Haze Pollution Bill.* Retrieved November 30, 2014, from CSR Asia: http://www.csr-asia.com/weekly_news_detail.php?id=12364.

Choong, T. S., and Kwok, Y. (18 March, 1998). The Fires are Back. *Asiaweek,* p. 46.

Chua, C. W., and Cheong, P. K. (2014, July 11). *Making Haze Crimes Pay.* Retrieved 12 July 2014 from *TODAYonline* http://www.todayonline.com/singapore/making-haze-crimes-pay.

Davidson, D. (2014, September 25). Sarawak Not Bowing to New Threat on its oil Palm Policy, Says Masing. *The Malaysian Insider.* Retrieved 1 November 2014 from http:// www.themalaysianinsider.com/malaysia/article/sarawak-not-bowing-to-new-threat-on-its-oil-palm-policy-says-masing.

Ee, D. (2014a, February 5). Hundreds of Dead Fish Found in Bishan-Ang Mo Kio Park River. *The Straits Times.* Retrieved 5 February 2014 from http://www.straitstimes.com/ breaking-news/singapore/story/hundreds-dead-fish-found-bishan-ang-mo-kio-park-river-20140205.

Ee, D. (2014b, February 25). Singapore Experiencing Record Dry Spell — And It Could Get Worse: NEA. *The Straits Times.* Retrieved 25 February 2014 from http://www.straitstimes. com/breaking-news/singapore/story/singapore-experiencing-record-dry-spell-20140225.

Fang, J. (2014, March 24). Survey Shows Fewer S'poreans Worried About Climate Change. *TODAYonline.* Retrieved 30 November 2014 from http://m.todayonline.com/singapore/ survey-shows-fewer-sporeans-worried-about-climate-change.

Gill, A., and Tan, S. (2013). *Transboundary Haze: How Might the Singapore Government Minimise its Occurrence?* Singapore: Lee Kuan Yew School of Public Policy, National University of Singapore.

Global Environment Center. (2010). *Technical Workshop on the Development of the ASEAN Peatland Fire Prediction and Warning System.* Kuala Lumpur: ASEAN Peatlands.

Hamilton-Hart, N. (2006). Singapore's Climate Change Policy: The Limits of Learning. *Contemporary Southeast Asia,* 363–384.

Hussain, Z. (2014). Riau Declares Province-Wide State of Emergency. *The Straits Times.* Retrieved 1 November 2014 from http://www.straitstimes.com/breaking-news/se-asia/ story/indonesia-haze-riau-declares-province-wide-state-emergency-20140226.

Ibrahim, Z., and Hussain, Z. (2014, August 22). Jokowi Vows to Get Tough with Haze Offenders. *The Straits Times.* Retrieved 22 August 2014 from http://www.straitstimes. com/the-big-story/joko-widodo/story/jokowi-vows-get-tough-haze-offenders-20140822.

IE Singapore. (2014a). Key Commodity Clusters. Retrieved 30 November 2014 from http:// www.iesingapore.gov.sg/trade-from-singapore/commodities-trading.

IE Singapore. (2014b). Overview of the Sino-Singapore Tianjin Eco-city project. (2014). Retrieved 30 November 2014 from http://www.iesingapore.gov.sg/Content-Store/Industrial-Parks-and-Projects/Overview-of-the-Sino-Singapore-Tianjin-Eco-City-project.

IPCC Secretariat. (2014). *Climate Change Synthesis Report*. Retrieved 30 November 2014 from http://www.ipcc.ch/news_and_events/docs/ar5/ar5_syr_headlines_en.pdf.

Jong, H. N. (2015, February 21). Govt Ramps Up Efforts to Prosecute Agroforestry Firms. Retrieved 15 April 2015 from http://www.thejakartapost.com/news/2015/02/21/govt-ramps-efforts-prosecute-agroforestry-firms.html.

Laia, K. C. (2014, November 27). Jokowi Pledges to Act Against Forest Fires. *Jakarta Globe*. Retrieved 27 November 2014 from http://thejakartaglobe.beritasatu.com/news/jokowi-pledges-to-act-against-forest-fires.

Lee, A. (2014, February 12). 160 Tonnes of Dead Fish Found in Farms Along Johor Straits. *TODAYonline*. Retrieved 30 November 2014 from http://www.todayonline.com/singapore/160-tonnes-dead-fish-found-farms-along-johor-straits.

Lo, J., and Parish, F. (2013). *Peatlands and Climate Change in Southeast Asia*. Petaling Jaya: ASEAN Secretariat and Global Environment Centre.

Loh, C. K. (2008, March 15). Haze Efforts at a Standstill. *TODAY*.

Meeyoung, C. (2009, August 4). South Korea Unveils CO2 Target Plan. *Reuters*. Retrieved 30 November 2014 from http://www.reuters.com/article/2009/08/04/us-korea-climate-target-idUSTRE5734VW20090804.

Meteorological Service Singapore. (2014). *Update of Regional Weather and Smoke Haze*. Retrieved 30 November 2014 from http://www.weather.gov.sg/wip/pp/ssops/reparch/feb14.pdf.

Ministry of the Environment and Water Resources (MEWR). (2012). *Singapore's National Climate Change Strategy*. Retrieved 30 November 2014 from http://app.mewr.gov.sg/data/ImgUpd/NCCS_Chapter_3:_Mitigation.pdf.

MEWR. (2014, December 9). *National Statement of Singapore Delivered by Dr Vivian Balakrishnan*. Retrieved 9 December 2014 from http://app.mewr.gov.sg/web/Contents/Contents.aspx?Yr=2014&ContId=2058.

MEWR. (2015, May 13). *Fostering Sustainability: What Consumer Countries Can Do?* Retrieved 1 July 2015 from https://www.hazetracker.org/article/fostering-sustainability-what-consumer-countries-can-do-2015-05-12.

Monetary Authority of Singapore (MAS). (2014). *Types of Institutions*. Retrieved 30 November 2014 from http://www.mas.gov.sg/singapore-financial-centre/types-of-institutions.aspx.

Murdiyarso, D. (2014, November 7). Insight: Merging Environment and Forestry Ministries: Quo Vadis? *The Jakarta Post*. Retrieved 30 November 2014 from http://www.thejakartapost.com/news/2014/11/07/insight-merging-environment-and-forestry-ministries-quo-vadis.html.

Nakamura, D., and Mufson, S. (2014, November 12). China, US Agree to Limit Greenhouse Gases. *Washington Post*. Retrieved 12 November 2014 from http://www.washingtonpost.com/business/economy/china-us-agree-to-limit-greenhouse-gases/2014/11/11/9c768504-69e6-11e4-9fb4-a622dae742a2_story.html.

Nanyang Technological University (NTU). (2010, January 21). NTU Launches the First Multi-Disciplinary Catastrophe Risk Management Research Institute of Its Kind in Asia [Press Release]. Retrieved 30 November 2014 from http://news.ntu.edu.sg/pages/ newsdetail.aspx?URL=http://news.ntu.edu.sg/news/2010/Pages/NR2010_Jan21. aspx&Guid=04c1421e-9732-4735-b992-5e8a5fec393d&Category=News%20 Releases.

National Climate Change Secretariat (NCCS). (2009, December 2). Points Made by Senior Minister S. Jayakumar at the Climate Change Media Interview. Retrieved 16 February 2014 from https://www.nccs.gov.sg/news/points-made-senior-minister-s-jayakumar-climate-change-media-interview-2-december-2009-10am.

NCCS. (2012). The Fight Against Climate Change Begins With You. (2012). Retrieved 1 November 2014 from http://app.nccs.gov.sg/data/resources/docs/Documents/NCCS-2012_brochure_eng.pdf?AspxAutoDetectCookieSupport=1.

NCCS. (2013, June 28). *Singapore's Emissions Profile.* Retrieved 30 November 2014 from http://app.nccs.gov.sg/page.aspx?pageid=158&secid=157.

NCCS. (2014, October 28). *Impact of Climate Change on Singapore.* Retrieved 30 November 2014 from http://app.nccs.gov.sg/page.aspx?pageid=160&secid=157.

NCCS. (2015, July 3). *Singapore's Submission to the United Nations Framework Convention on Climate Change (UNFCCC).* Retrieved 3 July 2015 from https://www.nccs.gov.sg/news/ singapore%E2%80%99s-submission-united-nations-framework-convention-climate-change-unfccc.

National Environment Agency, Singapore (NEA). (n.d.). *Historical PSI Readings.* (n.d.). Retrieved 30 November 2014 from http://www.haze.gov.sg/haze-updates/ historical-psi-readings.

Neo, C. (2014, November 7). Major Haze Episodes in Region 'Likely to Be More Frequent'. *TODAYonline.* Retrieved 7 November 2014 from http://www.todayonline.com/singapore/ major-haze-episodes-region-likely-be-more-frequent.

Philomin, L. E. (2014a, October 7). Lion City's Green Ranking Worsens. *TODAYonline.* Retrieved 30 November 2014 from http://m.todayonline.com/singapore/lion-citys-green-ranking-worsens.

Philomin, L. E. (2014b, October 24). WWF Report 'Does Not Reflect S'pore's Environmental Constraints'. *TODAYonline.* Retrieved 30 October 2014 from http://m.todayonline.com/ singapore/wwf-report-does-not-reflect-spores-environmental-constraints.

PSI hits new all-time high of 401 on Friday. (2013, June 21). *Channel NewsAsia.* Retrieved 30 November 2014 from http://www.channelnewsasia.com/news/specialreports/mh370/ news/psi-hits-new-all-time/719496.html.

Roundtable on Sustainable Palm Oil. (2014, July 8). *Transparency in Plantation Concession Boundaries.* Retrieved 30 November 2014 from http://www.rspo.org/news-and-events/ announcements/transparency-in-plantation-concession-boundaries.

Sanger, D. (2001, June 12). Bush Will Continue to Oppose Kyoto Pact on Global Warming. *The New York Times.* Retrieved 30 November 2014 from http://www.nytimes.com/ 2001/06/12/world/bush-will-continue-to-oppose-kyoto-pact-on-global-warming.html.

Shah, V. (2014, July 9). Singapore Steps Up Efforts to Weather Future Climate Change. *Eco-Business*. Retrieved 30 November 2014 from http://www.eco-business.com/news/singapore-steps-efforts-weather-future-climate-change.

Shen, R. (2014, August 6). Singapore's Groundbreaking Haze Law Faces Uphill Challenge. *Reuters*. Retrieved 7 August 2014 from http://www.reuters.com/article/2014/08/06/us-singapore-haze-idUSKBN0G611P20140806.

Shukman, D. (2014, December 4). World on Course for Warmest Year. *BBC News*. Retrieved 4 December 2014 from http://www.bbc.com/news/science-environment-30311816.

Siau, M. E. (2014, December 11). Singapore Cut Carbon Intensity by 30 Per Cent. *TODAYonline*. Retrieved 11 December 2014 from http://www.todayonline.com/singapore/singapore-cut-carbon-intensity-30-cent.

Siswo, S. (2014, September 16). Indonesia ratifies regional haze pact after 12-year wait. *Channel NewsAsia*. Retrieved 16 September 2014 from http://www.channelnewsasia.com/news/singapore/indonesia-ratifies/1365294.html.

Sizer, N. (2013, June 21). Peering through the Haze: What Data Can Tell Us About the Fires in Indonesia. *World Resources Institute*. Retrieved 1 November 2014 from http://insights.wri.org/news/2013/06/peering-through-haze-what-data-can-tell-us-about-fires-indonesia.

Soeriaatmadja, W. (2014, March 16). Clearing Land by Burning 'A Crime Against Humanity': Indonesia President. *The Straits Times Asia Report*. Retrieved 10 September 2014 from http://www.stasiareport.com/the-big-story/asia-report/indonesia/story/clearing-land-burning-crime-against-humanity-indonesia-pre.

Tay, S. (2008). Blowing smoke: Regional cooperation, Indonesian democracy, and the haze. In D. K. Emmerson (Ed.), *Hard Choices: Security, Democracy, and Regionalism in Southeast Asia* (p. 219). Stanford: Walter H. Shorenstein Asia-Pacific Research Center Books.

Tay. S. and Cheong. P. K. (2015, March 11). Tackling Haze: Look Beyond Words to Action Taken. *TODAYonline*. Retrieved 15 April 2015 from https://www.todayonline.com/commentary/tackling-haze-look-beyond-words-action-taken.

Teoh, S. (2011, February 4). Palm Oil Risks All Sarawak Peat Forests by 2020, Says Study. *The Malaysian Insider*. Retrieved 30 November 2014 from http://www.themalaysianinsider.com/malaysia/article/palm-oil-risks-all-sarawak-peat-forests-by-2020-says-study.

United Nations Framework Convention on Climate Change (UNFCCC). (n.d.). *Full text of the convention*. Retrieved 30 November 2014 from http://unfccc.int/essential_background/convention/background/items/1355.php.

UN-REDD Programme. (2009). *About REDD+*. Retrieved 30 November 2014 from http://www.un-redd.org/aboutredd/tabid/102614/default.aspx.

World Resources Institute (WRI). (2014a, June 4). *Release: First detailed public maps of RSPO certified palm oil concessions released*. Retrieved 30 November 2014 from http://www.wri.org/news/2014/06/release-first-detailed-public-maps-rspo-certified-palm-oil-concessions-released.

WRI. (2014b, July 22). *Release: Indonesia's government and Global Forest Watch join forces to launch powerful new system to combat fires and haze*. Retrieved 30 July 2014 from http://www.wri.org/news/2014/07/release-indonesia%E2%80%99s-government-and-global-forest-watch-join-forces-launch-powerful-new.

World Wide Fund for Nature (WWF). (2014). *Living Planet Index*. Retrieved 30 November 2014 from http://wwf.panda.org/about_our_earth/all_publications/living_planet_report/living_planet_index2.

WWF Global (2014). *Living Planet Index*. Retrieved 30 November 2014 from http://wwf.panda.org/about_our_earth/all_publications/living_planet_report/living_planet_index2/.

Wibowo, A. (2013, November). *Greenhouse gases assessment from forest fires: Indonesia case study — Preliminary assessment report*. Retrieved 1 November 2014 from REDD-Indonesia: http://redd-indonesia.org/images/events/20131119/CIFOR/3_Greenhouse_Gases_from_Forest_and_Land_Fires/GHG_Assessment_From_Forest_Fires_--_Indonesia_Case_Study.pdf.

Widhiarto, H. (2014, September 11). Malaysian Firm Fined, Executives Get Prison for Role in Forest Fires. *The Jakarta Post*. Retrieved 25 November 2014 from http://www.thejakartapost.com/news/2014/09/11/malaysian-firm-fined-executives-get-prison-role-forest-fires.html.

PART 3

Moving into the Future

CHAPTER 11

Environmental Sustainability and Sustainable Development

Tan Yong Soon

Former Permanent Secretary
Ministry of the Environment and Water Resources (MEWR)

and

Kwek Leng Joo

Deputy Chairman, City Developments Limited (CDL);
President, Singapore Compact for Corporate Social Responsiblility;
Chairman of the Board of Trustees, National Youth Achievement Award Council

Over the past 50 years, Singapore has transformed from a third world country to one of the world's most advanced economies. According to World Bank data, Singapore is ranked fourth in the world in terms of GDP per capita based on purchasing power parity per capita (World Bank, 2015). The rapid expansion, fast population growth and rising affluence have led to greater demands for energy, water and other resources as well as increased greenhouse gas emissions.

Singapore has been able to achieve a good balance between economic growth and environmental sustainability. The choice is never either solely the environment or the economy; instead, it is both. A clean and green environment offers a high quality of life for its residents as well as enhances economic growth. Achieving a good balance between the two requires continuous attention and effort.

Nevertheless, the challenge going forward will be greater, not less. Singapore needs to ensure that it has the resources it needs to fuel its growth while alleviating the negative impacts to the environment. In continuing to achieve environmental sustainability and sustainable development, Singapore will also act as a model for cities in the world to achieve a sustainable pathway. This is critical as the challenge is global and all of us have to do our part.

Today, 54% of the world's population lives in the city, up from 34% in 1960. This proportion is expected to increase to 66% by 2050, when the urban population could increase by another 2.5 billion people, with close to 90% of the increase concentrated in Asia and Africa (UN, 2014a). The surge in population and the proportion of city dwellers will result in the increase of resource consumption and greenhouse emissions. At the 2014 United Nations Climate Summit, it was reported that cities are responsible for about 70% of greenhouse emissions. The challenges for sustainable development will thus be increasingly concentrated in cities.

Consequently, we must not only understand how we got here: our critical success factors, our challenges, and our constraints. We must also realise that to flourish while going forward, we must be bold and be willing to test our limits and forge new pathways. In achieving successful sustainable development, Singapore would not only offer its people a better quality of life, but also act as a model for other cities and thus make an invaluable contribution to the world.

Political Leadership

Political leadership is key to achieving a good balance between economic growth and environmental sustainability. The very top must have a clear vision that a clean and good quality living environment is important, a strong commitment to implement such a vision, as well as the ability to communicate that vision so that it can be shared and supported by everyone.

Singapore has achieved so much in such a short span of time because of former Prime Minister Lee Kuan Yew's political leadership in Singapore's early years. He recalled in 2008: "We are a small island, densely populated. So when I faced the prospect of becoming an independent nation in 1965, making a viable economy and a society out of this little piece of land with then two million people, I had to envision the kind of ways we could move forward.... So, to distinguish ourselves from other cities in the neighbourhood, my intention was to create a First World oasis in a Third World region and I coined the slogan 'Clean and Green Singapore'" (SG Press Centre, 2008).

He and his fellow leaders in Singapore's early years had the foresight, the commitment and the ability to communicate their vision and win the support of the people. They were able to conceptualise the kind of city they and their people would want to live in: that people should be able to enjoy clean air, safe drinking water and food, and they had the idea that economic growth should not be at the expense of the environment; in fact, they recognised that a good environment would enhance economic development. They had the commitment to dedicate resources to improve the environment in the face of competing immediate needs and also the willingness to legislate, the wisdom to educate and the toughness to enforce the rule of law when necessary. And they had the ability to communicate such a vision to the people to help them understand the long-term benefits of those policies and to be willing to defer their gratification such that scarce resources could be set aside for improving the environment instead of bringing about more immediate gratification.

The key role of the government cannot be over-emphasised. Professor Richard Vietor, who has been teaching a course on Business, Government, and International Economy at Harvard Business School for the last 30 years, began his book, *How Countries Compete: Strategy, Structure and Government in the Global Economy* with: "Countries compete to develop. This is one result of globalisation. They compete for markets, for technology, for skills and investment. They compete to grow and raise their standards of living. In this competitive environment, it is government, invariably, that provides distinctive advantages to firms" (Vietor, 2007, p. 1).

From its early years of development, Singapore has had the good fortune of having a government that understands the benefits of a good environment. Leaders must have the vision, commitment, dedication and sacrifice to bring about environmental sustainability and sustainable development, and the ability to communicate and bring along the people to support and commit to such a vision. We will do well if we continue to have such leaders to lead Singapore into the future.

Government-ware

In turning vision to reality, organisation and people in the public service are key to ensuring good policy and good administration. Singapore has had the benefits of a good public service. The Anti-Pollution Unit (APU) reported directly to the Prime Minister. And the Head of APU, Mr. Lee Ek Tieng, would prove himself more than capable of the task, subsequently rising to become the Permanent Secretary of the Ministry of the Environment and then Head of the Civil Service. The dedicated Ministry of the Environment formed in 1972 would oversee public health as well as sanitation and cleanliness. Sewerage and water production would be brought together in a restructured Public Utilities Board (PUB), the national water agency, thus facilitating reclamation of sewage and turning it to NEWater. In 2010, the National Climate Change Secretariat was established within the Prime Minister's Office, headed by a Permanent Secretary, to coordinate the national effort to address climate change challenges.

The ability of public servants to work as an integrated government with vision and long-term thinking is critical. Proper land use zoning and critical environmental infrastructure are needed as well as good rules, legislation, enforcement, education and assistance wherever necessary.

Sound economic principles are applied to environmental policy and decision-making. Externalities are taken into account and polluters are required to pay for the negative externalities that they cause. Environmental goods are priced correctly, while assistance is provided to low-income households so that no one will be deprived of drinking water or clean air. Water production facilities may be privatised but the water policy making, price determination and supply remain as government agency functions. Production is privatised where higher productivity and quality can be achieved and people's standards of living can be improved. But there must always be a clear understanding that markets have their limits and we cannot and must not rely exclusively or predominantly on commercial terms alone.

As we move towards the future, government-ware must continuously evolve. Environmental standards must be raised as our understanding of public health risks improves. Take for instance, air quality and particulate matter. For years, it has been readily understood that there is a close proportionate relationship between exposure to high concentrations of small particulates and increased mortality or morbidity, both daily and over time. But the choice of indicators for particulate matter has not always been clearly understood. Initially, the majority of epidemiological studies used PM10 (particles smaller than 10 μm in diameter) as the exposure indicator. Thus the US EPA used PM10 as an indicator only until 1997 when it introduced PM2.5 as an indicator, together with PM10. Even then, the 24-hour level in 1997 in the US was 65 μg per cu metres. It dropped to 35 in 2006. Primary annual mean level introduced in 1997 was 15 $\mu g/m^3$, dropping to 12 in 2012. In fact, WHO Air Quality Guidelines 2005 Global Update recommended even lower levels, 25 and 10 $\mu g/m^3$ for 24-hour and annual mean respectively, as the final guidelines, accepting that many countries would need quite a few years to achieve these standards. The same WHO 2005 Update also highlighted ultrafine (UF) particles, i.e. particles smaller than 0.1 μm in diameter, as having recently attracted significant scientific and medical attention. However, as the existing body of epidemiological evidence at the time was insufficient for the WHO to reach a conclusion on the exposure–response relationship of UF particles, it did not provide any recommendation on guideline concentrations of UF particles. The WHO is still seeking better understanding of UF particles. A crucial point to note is that we must constantly familiarise ourselves with possible new dangers and higher standards that we must strive to uphold, whether it is air quality, water quality, noise or smell pollution. Achieving better environment and public health standards will incur higher cost, but not meeting these higher standards will be far more costly.

The government must put in place the necessary pollution control requirements and regulations to ensure a high standard of a clean living environment. While standards must be set taking into consideration the availability and cost of measures to improve the environment, the government must constantly be on the lookout for and develop effective and cost-efficient solutions to improve our environment. Improving public health and environmental quality will improve the quality of life of the people and is thus of absolute importance. The government must continue to be bold in putting in place the necessary standards and enforce the regulations, even if additional cost may be a concern for some companies or industries. Where necessary, the government will have to help affected companies and industries to transit to the new standards. It is necessary to strike the right balance between economic growth and environmental protection and sustainability.

And the government must continue to envision and plan ahead for the future, as sustainability is a long-term challenge. Singapore has produced long-term water, green and sustainable development blueprints. The water demand forecast for 2060, and the long-term plans to meet the increased demand in an economical and efficient manner can be found on the PUB's website. The Singapore Green Plan, Singapore's environmental blueprint for the future, was first formulated in 1992. The Singapore Sustainable Blueprint 2009 was launched by the Inter-Ministerial Committee on Sustainable Development (IMCSD), which was set up in January 2008 to "formulate a national strategy for Singapore's sustainable development in the context of emerging domestic and global challenges". It encompasses key strategies for Singapore's sustainable development including boosting resource efficiency, enhancing the urban environment, fostering community action and building capacities and addressing what the government, businesses and individuals can do for sustainability. It also highlighted the importance of joint action by the people, the private and public sectors or what is commonly referred to as the 3P Model. All long-term plans are reviewed regularly.[1] It is important to ensure that the plans are robust and that all of us do our best to achieve sustainable development targets which test our limits, and not simply go for safe targets.

Private Sector's Role and Partnership

Environmental sustainability is not the sole responsibility of the government. "Everyone shares responsibility for the present and future well-being of the human family and the larger living world," as stated in the Earth Charter which went on to affirm a set of principles: "for a sustainable way of life as a common standard by which the conduct of all individuals, organisations, businesses, governments, and transnational institutions is to be guided and assessed". The private sector is certainly in the position to contribute to sustainable development, as businesses are often good at innovating and searching for opportunities. In fact, there are ample business opportunities in the green economy. Global trade in environmental goods is already estimated to be around US$1 trillion annually, and is growing quickly (USTR, 2014).

Consumers and investors increasingly want to know that the companies they deal with are socially responsible. Globally, it has been shown that companies that have integrated responsible practices into their business are more successful. For instance, the Global Compact 100 (GC 100) is composed of a representative group of

---

[1] An updated Sustainable Singapore Blueprint was released in late 2014 (MEWR and MND, 2014).

companies committed to the United Nations Global Compact's 10 Corporate Social Responsiblility principles. How these companies are chosen is contingent on their ability to implement the Global Compact's CSR principles, their executive leadership's demonstration of their commitment to CSR and also showing steady baseline profitability. This stock index that was announced in September 2013 showed a total investment return of 26.4% in 2014, surpassing the general global stock market of 22.1%.

To help throw the spotlight on businesses that have excelled in corporate sustainability and to spur others to re-examine their positions, regional broadcaster Channel NewsAsia, in partnership with CSR Asia and Sustainalytics, launched the *Channel NewsAsia Sustainability Ranking* for Asia's top businesses at the CSR Asia Summit in September 2014. The ranking identifies leading firms in corporate sustainability across ten key Asian economies.

India's Tata Consultancy Services (TCS) emerged at the top of the ranking for its focus on water conservation. Across TCS-owned buildings, rainwater-harvesting systems are installed, allowing for rapid replenishment of the surrounding groundwater supply. By 2020, TCS aims to be 100% groundwater neutral. Indeed, the Tata Group is a good example of riding on the environment and CSR to achieve business success. Approximately 66% of the equity of Tata Sons, the promoter of the major operating companies of the Tata Group, is held by philanthropic trusts, therefore giving back to society (Tata, n.d.).

Second in the ranking is Singapore's developer, City Developments Limited (CDL). It has a well-integrated approach to "green construction". To demonstrate its commitment to the principle of sustainability, CDL sets aside up to 5% of construction costs for green design elements such as recycled or sustainable building materials for all its new developments (Channel NewsAsia, 2014). CSR is the bedrock of CDL's business strategy and operations. The company has been championing sustainable development through green buildings and best practices as early as 1995, and has been reaping benefits. In recent years, there has been a growing demand for green space by commercial lessees, especially from MNCs that have to report their carbon footprint. Even residential customers have shown greater appreciation of the green features in the developments.

Third is Unilever Indonesia, which has set an ambitious goal to sustainably source 100% of its agricultural raw materials by 2020.

Although the global CSR community is growing, companies that truly practise the full spectrum of CSR and sustainability are still in the minority. According to the GRI database, only 32 Singapore organisations produced CSR or Sustainability Reports in 2013, of which 27 are listed on the SGX. However, on a positive note, there have been more small and medium-sized enterprises (SMEs) disclosing sustainability indicators in the past year.

SMEs and their potential role in environmental sustainability is often not addressed in policy or business discourse on sustainability. However, their possible impact is undeniable. There are 182,700 SMEs in Singapore, providing 66% of employment and accounting for 49% of nominal value added of enterprises here (Department of Statistics, 2014). Despite their business enormity, SMEs have not been aggressively engaged in the discourse of environmental sustainability. It is often assumed that most are disinterested as they lack resources or are too caught up in dealing with daily operational issues to survive. But SMEs are critical to sustainable development and the government must do more to engage them, including considering green financing and grants focussing on smaller businesses or additional tax incentives for green businesses — either to make their business processes more environmentally-friendly or to develop sustainable products. SMEs too can see business opportunities in sustainability or creative green ideas and should be encouraged and nurtured to do so.

One good example of businesses working effectively with government to achieve environmental sustainability is the Singapore's Building and Construction Authority (BCA)'s Green Building Masterplan. Buildings account for 40% of global energy consumption and 25% of global water resources and produce approximately 30% of greenhouse gas emissions (UNEP, n.d.). With an emphasis on "Public" and "Private", the first masterplan focussed on new buildings and the second masterplan on existing buildings. Using a synergistic combination of regulatory control, incentives (policies and initiatives) and working closely with the building industry, Singapore has enjoyed an astounding greening rate of its space. The number of green buildings has grown from 17 in 2005 to 2,100 today — equivalent to a quarter of Singapore's total gross built up area. BCA recently unveiled its third Green Building Masterplan that would guide the country's green building strategy for the next 5 to 10 years. This time, recognising the vital role played by the "People", the third plan has more focussed policies and measures to foster greater awareness amongst tenants and occupants.

Overall, businesses still have a long way to go. While many are beginning to see business opportunities in the green economy, not enough corporations are accounting for environmental externalities or mitigating environmental risks. The industrial sector, for instance, has to do more on energy efficiency, which not only contributes to the environment but also improves economic competitiveness in the medium to long term. Nevertheless, there is an inexorable march towards a demand for greater CSR and the need to minimise our ecological footprints to achieve environmental sustainability. The SGX has announced that it will be enforcing a "comply or explain approach" to sustainability reporting for all listed companies in the near future.[2] Singapore businesses must be prepared for this trend and be able to reduce

---

[2] SGX announced this at the annual International Singapore Compact CSR Summit in October 2014 (Shah and Cheam, 2014).

their footprints in a cost-efficient manner and offer green products and services. Business leaders can lead by example while the government creates a conducive regulatory framework for environmentally responsible businesses to thrive. Environmental sustainability is the collective responsibility of the government, businesses and the people.

People and Environmental Responsibility

We need to build a community in Singapore where everyone adopts a more environmentally responsible lifestyle. Environmental responsibility must be part of our people and business culture.

Public cooperation and participation are critical to a better environment. It took many years of public education to enable the public to develop a sense of civic consciousness, social responsibility and discipline. The first national public education effort was a month-long "Keep Singapore Clean" campaign in 1968. Such government-led platforms were followed by mass participation, sharing of long-term plans and bottom-up initiatives by a healthy civil society.

The Singapore public is generally responsible, cooperative and collaborative on achieving a clean and green environment. Yet, more than 40 years later, environmental responsibility has not been fully ingrained. Take littering as an example. There is the feeling among some Singaporeans that Singapore has gotten dirtier. This is reinforced by the photographs of various dirty places sent to the Waterways Watch Society, an anti-littering volunteer group in Singapore. The formula that has helped to make Singapore known for being one of the cleanest cities in the world has four components — providing good and reliable public cleaning services and collecting refuse daily; educating the public on the need to keep the environment clean; strict law enforcement; and investing in infrastructural improvements. We must continue with such a multi-pronged approach. Singapore cannot afford to reach the tipping point where littering behaviour is generally condoned and littering becomes a common occurrence, a place kept clean only by an army of cleaners. Achieving the desired state of environmental ownership is a long process, and will take time.

Engaging people is key. But people must want a better environment for themselves. *The Economist* mentioned, "All industrial nations one day hit an environmental turning point, an event that dramatises to the population the ecological consequences of growth" ("China and the Environment", 2013). The article cites the incidents where the Cuyahoga River in Ohio, US, was so polluted that it caught fire in 1969 and the Minamata mercury poisoning that forced a clean-up in Japan as examples of such events that prompt governments into action. Both countries learned from their experiences to improve their environment. In the US, the Cuyahoga incident led to the formation of the EPA in 1970. Today, Japan still hosts regular workshops on the impact of environmental contamination of the Minamata Bay and the lessons learnt to exhort developing countries to take care of their environment.

It is fortunate that Singapore did not have to experience ecological disasters in the same vein for its people to desire a good quality living environment. Political leadership guided people towards a good environment. Initially people may be more attuned to their immediate needs and have to be persuaded of the benefits of a good and clean environment. But once people have reaped the benefits of a sound environment, they would be inclined to desire it and may even be a few steps ahead of the government, if the government is slow in delivering a good environment.

People must organise and educate themselves, and act responsibly. There is a fine balance between the need to protect and sustain the environment and economic development. The needs of the former should not stand in the path of the latter.

Mr. Lee Kuan Yew said at the launch of the inaugural Keep Singapore Clean campaign in 1968:

> We have built, we have progressed. But no other hallmark of success will be more distinctive than that of achieving our position as the cleanest and greenest city in South Asia. For only a people with high social and educational standards can maintain a clean and green city. It requires organisation to keep the community cleaned and trimmed particularly when the population has a density of 8,500 persons per square mile. And it requires a people conscious of their responsibilities, not just to their own families, but also to their neighbours and all others in a community who will be affected by their thoughtless anti-social behaviour. Only a people proud of their community performance, feeling for the well-being of their fellow citizens, can keep up high personal and public standards of hygiene. (Lee, 1968)

It is imperative for all of us living in Singapore to continue striving to achieve these standards as envisaged by Mr. Lee, to view it as our responsibility to keep Singapore clean and green, and to take greater ownership of the environment.

Our people can do more to adopt a Green Lifestyle. While businesses are starting to be convinced to produce greener products, consumers are still not buying into the green economy, either due to lack of knowledge or higher prices. Singapore can gear up and promote greater environmental education in schools as well as consumer education on the importance of supporting a green economy. It would be beneficial to promote a "greener life" that is a departure from the traditional notion that "more is good" which encourages rampant materialism to one that places emphasis on consuming responsibly and to "buy right". Richard Robbins, Professor of Anthropology and author of *Global Problem and the Culture of Capitalism* writes that:

> Yet of the three factors environmentalists often point to as responsible for environmental pollution — population, technology, and consumption — consumption

seems to get the least attention. One reason, no doubt, is that it may be the most difficult to change; our consumption patterns are so much a part of our lives that to change them would require a massive cultural overhaul, not to mention severe economic dislocation. (Robbins, 1999, pp. 209–210)

These three variables are inextricably linked and it is vital that sufficient attention is paid to all of them and their interrelationship in order to bring about positive change to the environment.

An active and responsible civil society can help to work towards a better environment. NGOs such as the Nature Society, Waterways Watch Society, Singapore Environment Council, Singapore Compact for CSR and the National Youth Achievement Award Council have done much to educate the public, create interest and organise the local community to protect the environment. The media in Singapore, too, has a vital national role to play in stepping up coverage on CSR and other environmental topics to raise awareness of the issues that affect the environment.

We must continue to forge a community of people who care for one another and take pride in their performance as a part of the community.

Resource Conservation

As the global population increases, the demand for and the cost of energy, food and other resources will rise. Resource conservation is thus of the utmost importance.

Singapore has a good system of integrated solid waste management that is much lauded and emulated by others in the world. From waste collection to incineration to offshore landfills, the system is efficient and cost effective. Partly due to this, the 3Rs of the environment — reduce, reuse and recycle — have not taken off despite having a recycling corner in almost every educational institution, starting from primary schools, and in neighbourhoods. Perhaps Singaporeans do not see much practical benefit in recycling, paradoxically because of the country's successes in resource conservation and waste management.

It is important to discover better ways of boosting our resource efficiency. This means encouraging the more widespread adoption and practice of the 3Rs. We need to reduce the energy and water consumption per person, as well as the amount of water and energy required to produce per capita GDP. Suitable policies, appropriate pricing and incentives, as well as targeting major sources of waste are all vital.

Waste minimisation must start at the very beginning. It is important to move upstream to target waste generation at the source and to push for product stewardship, meaning that all the stakeholders along the supply chain, such as manufacturers, distributors, retailers, consumers, waste collectors, and recycling companies should be responsible for the afterlife management of the products and their packaging.

In Singapore, as much as one-third of household waste is packaging waste, of which a major part comes from the food and beverage sector. Waste minimisation can be promoted through either mandatory or voluntary means. The National Environment Agency has set up a voluntary programme with industry players to reduce packaging waste in Singapore. This arrangement (the first Agreement was signed in 2007) has yielded results, but at some point the voluntary agreement must be complemented by mandatory measures. Waste minimisation should be the main strategy to curb waste growth.

Singapore must also improve its efforts in recycling. While certain waste streams such as construction and demolition waste and copper slags are almost completely recycled (due to the high economic value of the recycled materials), the recycling rates of waste streams like food, plastics and e-products are very low. In Japan, food waste recycling is mandatory for businesses that generate more than 100 tonnes of food waste annually. Singapore has been studying options to promote the recycling of food waste for many years and will have to move faster to encourage stakeholders to carry out waste recycling.

Indeed, if we recognise that Singapore is a small island city state with no natural resources other than its people, we will better appreciate the wider picture of resource sustainability. In addition to the importance of recycling, Singapore will also need to develop new capabilities for renewable energy as well as increase our supply of renewable resources such as water, so as to ensure that there will be a sufficient supply for future generations.

Water is the key to Singapore's sustainability. Singapore is able to meet its long-term water needs through its "Four National Taps" strategy of local catchment sources, imported water, NEWater and desalinated water. However, there is the challenge of energy sustainability in generating NEWater and desalinated water. PUB is partnering the industry and universities in the research and development (R&D) of solutions that will significantly reduce the amount of energy used in water treatment processes.

At the broader area, Singapore has taken steps to conserve energy, but more needs to be done. The intention to mandate energy management requirements and to consolidate all energy efficient related legislation into an Energy Conservation Act was announced in early 2010, and came into effect in early 2013. As of early 2014, 166 of the most energy-intensive companies were registered with NEA under the Act. This must be only the beginning. As the authorities and companies understand the problem better and as more efficient solutions become readily available, standards must be tightened. The public sector must lead by example, making transparent the energy efficiency standards achieved at government buildings and facilities.

It is not solely about reducing the amount of resources we produce but developing ways to become sustainable in the future. As defined in the *Report of the World*

Commission on Environment and Development: Our Common Future, sustainable development is about "meet[ing] the needs of the present without compromising the ability of future generations to meet their own needs" (WCED, 1987).

Research and Innovation

The benefits of energy efficiency and sustainable energy and water systems are clear: protection of the environment, enhanced security of the energy and water supply, minimising the potential impact of climate change and the promotion of future compliant industries and jobs. But research requires financing, and in addition, application-oriented research requires strong links with the industry, and deployment involves policy and regulatory issues. In order to facilitate academic research and industry development, sustained government support is necessary.

In Singapore, the National Research Foundation (NRF) is one such initiative by the state to develop the nation's R&D capabilities. The NRF was set up in 2006 as a department within the Prime Minister's Office and it set the national direction for R&D, funds strategic initiatives and seeks to cultivate scientific talent. The essential aim of the foundation is to make Singapore an energetic hub for R&D, to be a part of a modern, pioneering and knowledge-intensive economy so as to attract even greater excellence in ground-breaking scientific research.

One of its first focusses was on Environment and Water Technologies. The Environment and Water Industry (EWI) Programme Office led by MEWR and PUB has helped build up the R&D and technology base for the Clean Water Industry sector and at the same time, developed the necessary talent and manpower to meet the needs of this growing and innovative sector. Water technology roadmaps and targeted disbursement of R&D grants ensure that market-relevant expertise is being nurtured in selected water domains. There is now a vibrant water research and industrial ecosystem, comprising both homegrown and international players. This has helped Singapore-based water companies to internationalise and grow their business overseas.

In 2011, the NRF launched the Energy National Innovation Challenge (ENIC) to develop cost-competitive energy solutions that can be deployed within 20 years to improve Singapore's energy efficiency, reduce its carbon emissions and broaden its energy options to sustain economic growth.

In support of the ENIC, the National Climate Change Secretariat and the NRF commissioned a series of Technology Primers to explore the potential and relevance of various technologies that can help Singapore improve its energy efficiency and security, and reduce its carbon emissions. These primers covering technology areas such as solar energy, air-conditioning system and carbon capture and utilisation were produced in 2011. Building on these efforts, the primers were developed into a series of technology roadmaps to chart the development and deployment pathways of technologies like solar photovoltaic systems green data centres, building energy efficiency and industry energy efficiency. Building energy efficiency is important in Singapore as buildings including households consume about 50% of the country's electricity. Industries emit over 50% of the nation's carbon emissions. As part of the follow-up to the technology road-mapping exercise, the government is providing funding totalling S$100 million to two major energy R&D initiatives. These are the Building Energy Efficiency R&D Hub that will be implemented and managed by BCA and the Green Data Centre Research Hub Programme to be managed by the Infocomm Development Authority of Singapore (IDA). These initiatives aim to improve the overall building energy efficiency and conduct more in-depth research into green data centres in Singapore.

Another important area is the chemical industry, which is a significant source of carbon emissions. As Singapore is one of the world's leading chemical industry hubs, it is important to work at the forefront to reduce emissions in this industry. NRF has partnered the University of Cambridge to establish the Cambridge Centre for Energy Efficiency in Singapore. The centre oversees research programmes to assess and reduce the carbon emissions of integrated petrochemical plants and the electrical network on Jurong Island in Singapore. The research is focussed on materials designs, energy efficiency of processes, waste heat utilisation and better systems integration. The resulting emission reduction will benefit the industry in Singapore and globally.

The cost of technological solutions will reduce in the future, most likely faster than we can imagine. We must continue to work to bring about such technological advancements to be ready for the future. Singapore must continue to focus on research and innovation. Academia, industry and NGOs must be involved in R&D together with the public sector. At the same time, research money must be spent wisely to bring about solutions which are not only innovative, but cost efficient. Both NUS (NUS Environmental Research Institute [NERI]) and NTU (Energy Research Institute at NTU [ERI@N] and Nanyang Environment & Water Research Institute [NEWRI]) have benefitted from such a push and are simultaneously conducting world-class research and working with the private sector to help them commercialise as well as to play a more international role in environmental sustainability.

But technology alone is not the answer. Governments must help to enable the deployment of viable technology. This involves not just industrial activities, but also smart financing and government regulations to be in place.

Constant innovation in policy and social research is important. Take the example of electro mobility (e-mobility). Singapore is small enough to implement electric cars on a massive scale. Hence the NRF has partnered with the Technical University of Munich (TUM) and NTU to set up a centre to carry out research relating to e-mobility in megacities, in areas such as energy storage, communication and computation, electric vehicles and infrastructure. A technology roadmap on e-mobility is in the pipeline. The research is expected to reap benefits for the industry when e-mobility takes off. But e-mobility will only succeed if it makes transportation more efficient and cost effective, thus benefitting the people and improving their quality of life. Research in social and policy areas are thus important, so that an appropriate land transport policy to facilitate the introduction of e-vehicles can be introduced. Technology exists not just to benefit the economy and industry; it is to be deployed in a way that benefits people as well. Singapore is ideally suited to test-bed and introduce new ideas on a practical scale.

NEWater is a unique Singapore success story. We are able to achieve water self-sufficiency because we have forged ahead and aligned our policy with technology and social research, and industry development. This success will have to be replicated in many other areas to bring about sustainable development in the country.

Global Partnership

A single country alone often cannot solve major environmental challenges. Countries must come together as we are all in the same boat, sharing the earth and depending on it for our well-being.

The defining challenge is that of climate change. The science of climate change is clear. The Intergovernmental Panel on Climate Change's (IPCC) Fifth Assessment Report (AR5) was released in four parts in 2013 and 2014. Working Group 1 on Physical Science Basis "considers new evidence of climate change based on many independent scientific analyses from observations of the climate system, paleoclimate archives, theoretical studies of climate processes and simulations using climate models", released its report in 2013 (IPCC, 2013). Its conclusion: "Warming of the climate system is unequivocal, and since the 1950s, many of the observed changes are unprecedented over decades to millennia. The atmosphere and ocean have warmed, the amounts of snow and ice have diminished, sea level has risen, and the concentrations of greenhouse gases have increased" (UN, 2014b). It went on to say that human influence on the climate system is clear.

The long-term effects will be devastating if there are no attempts to reduce carbon emissions. The solution to reduce carbon emissions is through generating electricity with lower carbon emissions and the more efficient use of energy (other than all of us making an effort to reduce our carbon footprint).

Singapore is investing in and experimenting with new and effective energy efficiency solutions and alternative energy generation methods. Besides being a responsible member of the global community that does its part in reducing carbon emissions, Singapore as a city can help by sharing its lessons and successes in carbon reduction and environmental sustainability with the majority of the global population living in cities. The Sino-Singapore Tianjin Eco-city is such an example, where the Singapore and China governments and private sectors work together to share expertise and experience in areas like urban planning, environmental protection, resource conservation, water and waste management and sustainable development, as well as policies and programmes so as to achieve "a thriving city which is socially harmonious, environmentally-friendly and resource-efficient — a model for sustainable development" ("Tianjin Eco-City", 2014).

Singapore as a living lab to test and implement practical green solutions can serve as a leading example and hub, and it has the responsibility of doing so. Furthermore, it can also work with the many global partnerships and initiatives that promote CSR and sustainability best practices, ranging from the C40 Climate Leadership Group to various UN bodies and international NGOs.

Conclusion

A good environment is possible only if the preconditions of security, economic well-being and social harmony are met. We must always be mindful that a country's security and even survival is not always guaranteed, even in today's peaceful modern world. Economic development is necessary because we need jobs and growth. And this does occur not easily. Countries compete to develop. And internal harmony is paramount. People must feel that they are fairly treated and can attain a better future if they work hard. Widening income gaps will be disruptive.

The introductory chapter of the 1991 book *Singapore: The Next Lap* stated that,

> We live in a world that is ever changing. External events can shake us, as they have in the past. Nothing is certain. We have to try to stay ahead in the race of nations. We must never forget the basics: we have to stay united, work hard, save, look after each other, be quick to seize opportunities and be vigilant to internal and external threats to our national security. No one owes us a living — we have to earn it. (p. 15)

This remains true today and will continue to be so in future.

Singapore's journey towards environmental sustainability in the first 50 years is a success story. Its economy grew rapidly while achieving a clean and green environment, providing its people a high standard of living.

But in our pursuit of economic development, we must not forget that as important as it is, it is not an end in itself but only a means to sustainable development.

Sustainable development, as mentioned earlier, is development that meets the needs of the present without compromising the ability of future generations to meet their needs. Sustainable development is important in that it brings together the three important aspects of development, namely economic, environmental, and social. It is the intersection of all these different aspects of development.

Sustainable development also informs us that the environment is not the only concern. The standard of environment will differ in each country, depending on its preconditions and the maturity of its people. Each country will also differ in terms of its environmental development, and even within a country, there will be different environmental standards at various points in its development. A society should aim and demand for high environmental standards, but should not be too impatient such as to want to attain those lofty standards overnight. We must ensure that we embark on the journey to bring about improvements in the environment and move in the right direction.

In the first 50 years, Singapore had leaders who had, and continue to have, the clear vision to see beyond economic development — that preserving the environment and growing the economy are not mutually exclusive but complementary. Its leaders had the mettle and foresight to build capabilities, and also the skills to communicate that long-term vision and persuade its people and businesses to suspend some of their immediate needs that the temporarily foregone economic development could have met.

Speaking at a tree-planting event in November 2014, Prime Minister Lee Hsien Loong recalled the beginning of the tree-planting campaign: "That was 1963. Fifty years later, we have planted millions of trees all over Singapore. But we also have to do more than just plant trees: we also have to make the whole of the environment sustainable, friendly to people, and also for Singaporeans to be friendly to the environment" (Lim, 2014).[3]

What will Singapore be like 50 years from now? We must continue to be prepared to see the long term and the big picture, and have the capacity to recognise the limitations of the environment's ability to meet both present and future needs, and that the needs of the present does not compromise the ability of future generations to meet their own needs. Singapore must also play its part as a responsible global citizen as its future is intrinsically tied to the future of the world. Singapore prospers if the world prospers, and vice versa.

As Singapore forges itself into the future in a sustainable manner — economically, environmentally and socially — we will create a home that we can all be proud of and our children and their children can all hope to have a good future.

Acknowledgements

The authors wish to thank Esther An, Chief Sustainability Officer of City Developments Limited, and Executive Assistant to Mr. Kwek Leng Joo, for her assistance and suggestions.

---

[3] Prime Minister Lee Kuan Yew started the tree-planting campaign by planting a mempat tree in Farrer Circus in June 1963. The first Tree Planting Day was held in November 1971, launched by Acting PM Dr. Goh Keng Swee.

References

Abu Baker, J. (2014, November 3). Tree Planting Day in Singapore: 5 Things About the 51-year-old Tradition. Retrieved 25 June 2015 from http://www.straitstimes.com/news/singapore/more-singapore-stories/story/tree-planting-day-singapore-5-things-about-the-51-year-o#sthash.jbUAfG4K.dpuf.

Channel NewsAsia. (2014). Sustainability Ranking: Celebrate the Success of the Top 20 Companies in Asia. Retrieved 24 November 2014 from http://sustainability-ranking.channelnewsasia.com/top20.html.

China and the Environment: The East is Grey (2013, August 10). *The Economist*. Retrieved 21 November 2014 from http://www.economist.com/news/briefing/21583245-china-worlds-worst-polluter-largest-investor-green-energy-its-rise-will-have.

Department of Statistics, Singapore. (2014). Infographics: Singapore Economy. Retrieved 21 February 2014 from http://www.singstat.gov.sg/docs/default-source/default-document-library/statistics/visualising_data/singapore-economy17022015.pdf.

Government of Singapore. (1991). *Singapore: The Next Lap*. Singapore: Times Editions: Government of Singapore.

Intergovernmental Panel on Climate Change (IPCC). (2013). Workshop on IPCC Fifth Assessment Report (IPCC-AR5). Retrieved 21 November 2014 from http://www.ipcc.ch/report/ar5/docs/ar5_outreach_malaysia.pdf.

Lee, K. Y. (1968). Speech by the Prime Minister Inaugurating the "Keep Singapore Clean" Campaign on Tuesday, 1st October, 1968, archived by the National Archives of Singapore. Retrieved 21 November 2014 from http://www.nas.gov.sg/archivesonline/data/pdfdoc/lky19681001.pdf.

Lim, Y. L. (2014, November 2). Recycling, Energy-saving to Figure in Green Plan. *The Straits Times*. Retrieved 21 February 2015 from https://www.nccs.gov.sg/news/straits-times-recycling-energy-saving-figure-green-plan.

Ministry of the Environment and Water Resources, Singapore (MEWR). (2014). About the Sustainable Blueprint. Retrieved 24 November 2014 from http://app.mewr.gov.sg/web/contents/ContentsSSS2.aspx?ContId=1293.

MEWR and Ministry of National Development, Singapore (MND). (2014). Our Home, Our Environment, Our Future: Sustainable Singapore Blueprint 2015. Retrieved 24 November 2014 from http://app.mewr.gov.sg/web/ssb/files/ssb2015.pdf.

Office of the United States Trade Representative (USTR). (2014). WTO Environmental Goods Agreement: Promoting Made-in-America Clean Technology Exports, Green Growth and Jobs. Fact sheet, July 2014. Retrieved 13 March 2015 from https://ustr.gov/about-us/policy-offices/press-office/fact-sheets/2014/July/WTO-EGA-Promoting-Made-in-America-Clean-Technology-Exports-Green-Growth-Jobs.

Robbins, R. (1999). *Global Problem and the Culture of Capitalism*. Boston, MA: Allyn and Bacon.

SG Press Centre. (2008). Minister Mentor Lee Kuan Yew's Dialogue at the Singapore Energy Conference, 4 November 2008. Retrieved 24 November 2014 from http://www.news.gov.sg/public/sgpc/en/media_releases/agencies/mica/transcript/T-20081105-1.

Shah, V., and Cheam, J. (2014, October 17). SGX to Make Sustainability Reporting Mandatory. *Eco-Business*. Retrieved 24 November 2014 from http://www.eco-business. com/news/sgx-make-sustainability-reporting-mandatory/.

Tata. (n.d.). Leadership with Trust. Retrieved 24 November 2014 from http://www.tata.com/ aboutus/sub_index/Leadership-with-trust?.

Tianjin Eco-City: A Model for Sustainable Development (2014). Retrieved 24 November 2014 from http://www.tianjinecocity.gov.sg.

United Nations (UN). (2014a). *United Nations World Urbanization Prospects (The 2014 Revision)*. New York: United Nations. Retrieved 24 November 2014 from http://esa. un.org/unpd/wup/Highlights/WUP2014-Highlights.pdf.

UN (2014b). Working Group I: Climate Change 2013: The Physical Science Basis — Major Findings. Retrieved 21 February 2015 from http://www.un.org/climatechange/ the-science/.

UN Environment Programme (UNEP). (n.d.). Why Buildings. Retrieved 24 November 2014 from http://www.unep.org/sbci/AboutSBCI/Background.asp.

UN World Commission on Environment and Development (WCED). (1987). Chapter 2: Towards Sustainable Development, in *Our Common Future: Report of the World Commission on Environment and Development*. Switzerland: WCED. Retrieved 8 December 2014 from http://www.un-documents.net/ocf-02.htm.

Vietor, R. H. K. (2007). *How Countries Compete: Strategy, Structure and Government in the Global Economy*. Boston: Harvard Business School Press.

World Bank (2015). Data by Indicators. Retrieved 12 February 2015 from http://data. worldbank.org/indicator/NY.GDP.PCAP.PP.CD.

www.ingramcontent.com/pod-product-compliance
Lightning Source LLC
Chambersburg PA
CBHW080550270326
41929CB00019B/3252